Language, Ideology and Sociopolitical Change in the Arabic-speaking World

For *Lexun*
A pearl of joy and hope

Language, Ideology and Sociopolitical Change in the Arabic-speaking World

A Study of the Discourse of Arabic Language Academies

Chaoqun Lian

EDINBURGH
University Press

Edinburgh University Press is one of the leading university presses in the UK. We publish academic books and journals in our selected subject areas across the humanities and social sciences, combining cutting-edge scholarship with high editorial and production values to produce academic works of lasting importance. For more information visit our website: edinburghuniversitypress.com

Edinburgh University Press Ltd
The Tun – Holyrood Road
12(2f) Jackson's Entry
Edinburgh EH8 8PJ

First published in hardback by Edinburgh University Press 2020

Typeset in Times New Roman by
Servis Filmsetting Ltd, Stockport, Cheshire

A CIP record for this book is available from the British Library

ISBN 978 1 4744 4994 6 (hardback)
ISBN 978 1 4744 4995 3 (paperback)
ISBN 978 1 4744 4996 0 (webready PDF)
ISBN 978 1 4744 4997 7 (epub)

Contents

List of Figures and Tables vii
Acknowledgements viii

1 Introduction 1

2 The Arabic Language Academy Phenomenon 17
The Arabic Language Academy Phenomenon Is Pan-Arab 18
The Arabic Language Academy Phenomenon Is a Form of Language Planning and Language Policy 34
The Arabic Language Academy Phenomenon Is Symbolic 38
The Arabic Language Academy Phenomenon Is Discursive 42

3 Arabic Diglossia and Arab Nationalisms 48
Diglossia as a Sociolinguistic Problem in Western Academia 49
Diglossia as a Problem in the Arabic Language Academy Discourse 52
Fuṣḥā and *ʿĀmmiyya* as Organisms 55
Fuṣḥā and *ʿĀmmiyya* as Instruments and Resources 66
Fuṣḥā and *ʿĀmmiyya* as National Symbols 77
Eliminating Arabic Diglossia 85
Arabic Diglossia, Pan-Arab Nationalism and Territorial-State Nationalisms 89

4 Arabi(ci)sation and Counter-peripheralisation 105
Introduction: Arabi(ci)sation and Peripherality 105
Inter-language Relations and Arabi(ci)sation 108

Conceptualising Arabi(ci)sation in the Discourse of Arabic Language Academies 111
Corpus and Status Arabicisation in the Discourse of Arabic Language Academies 126
Conclusion: Arabi(ci)sation as Symbolic Resistance and Symbolic Compensation 136

5 Language Modernisation between Self and the Other 144
Modernity and Modernisation between Self and the Other 144
'Catching up with Modern Requirements' versus 'Revival and Reform' 148
Modernising the Arabic Language: A History of Conceptual Formation 151
Conclusion: Reviving the Arab Nation and Counterbalancing the West 192

6 Conclusion: The Ideologisation of Language via Language Symbolism 197
Characteristics of the Ideologisation of Language via Language Symbolism 198
Effects of the Ideologisation of Language via Language Symbolism 201
Causes of the Ideologisation of Language via Language Symbolism 203
Prevalence of the Ideologisation of Language via Language Symbolism 213

Glossary 217
Bibliography 227
Index 247

Figures and Tables

Figures

Figure 2.1 Causality of LPLP: language is instrumental in inducing sociopolitical change 37
Figure 2.2 Language symbolism: language is symbolic in projecting and alleviating sociopolitical concerns 40

Tables

Table 2.1 A list of Arabic Language Academies and equivalent institutions 20
Table 3.1 Views on linguistic and functional features of *fuṣḥā and ʿāmmiyya* in the ALA discourse 68
Table 4.1 Examples of translating English medical terms into Arabic via compounding 128
Table 4.2 Two types of *naḥt* in Arabic 129

Acknowledgements

This book is a revised and updated version of the PhD dissertation I completed at the University of Cambridge in 2015, entitled 'Language Planning and Language Policy of Arabic Language Academies in the Twentieth Century: A Study of Discourse'. The book is a result of my decade-long exploration of the Arabic language in the social world. This exploration began with my dissatisfaction with a decontextualised paradigm of Arabic linguistics, in which I received my early academic training. In fact, language is not merely an instrument of communication. It is also a construct of ideology. It is deeply embedded in our sociopolitical life, mediating our relations with both ourselves and others. This is the general position I take in this book.

Writing this book has been a painful pleasure. While the pain lies in the many barriers of skills and knowledge I have been faced with during the process of research and writing, overcoming them with the valuable help and support from my mentors, colleagues, friends and family gives me a great sense of happiness and fulfilment. To these people I owe a huge debt of gratitude.

My supervisor at Cambridge, Prof. Yasir Suleiman, will always have my deepest gratitude and respect. I have benefited enormously from his challenging and thought-provoking supervisions, his meticulous and sharp comments on my writing, and his constant support and encouragement. I would also like to thank him for inviting me to present my research at the international conferences he organised in Beijing, Sharjah and Doha. Doing so has increased my exposure to a wider academic community beyond my libraries and fields.

I am grateful to Dr Paul Anderson, who not only read some of my draft chapters, but also asked me to present my work in progress to the Modern Middle East Research Group at Cambridge. I wish to thank Prof. Said Faiq and Prof. Reem Bassiouney for their meticulous criticism and constructive suggestions for revision. I also wish to thank Prof. James Montgomery, Dr Rachael Harris, Dr Amal Morogy, Dr Alice Wilson, Prof. Sue Wright and Dr Peter Crosthwaite for their comments on my work and suggestions for improvement.

I am indebted to Dr Emad Abdul-Latif, who arranged my interviews with four members of the Cairo Academy and introduced me to two Egyptian scholars in the field of language policy. My thanks also go to the staff at the Cairo Academy and the Arabisation Bureau in Rabat, who helped in securing some of the documents and publications of these institutes. Without their help, I would not have been able to carry out my fieldwork in Cairo and Rabat.

My heartfelt thanks go to Laura Williamson and Richard Strachan, my editors at Edinburgh University Press, whose warm and professional support has been indispensable to the completion of this monograph project – the first in my academic career.

In Cambridge, I have enjoyed the company and friendship of Shivan Mahendrarajah, Arshad Hadjirin, Yonatan Mendel, James Weaver, Drew Mecham, Manar Makhoul, Ignacio Sánchez, Bruno De Nicola, Chen Li, Zhiguang Yin, Yijie Zhuang, Jingting Zhang and Samar Samir Mezghanni. They have been good friends and reliable sources of support. In Peking University, I have received encouragement and support from my colleagues in the School of Foreign Languages and inspiration from the excellent students on my Arabic and linguistic courses. Finally, I can never fully acknowledge the contribution of my family to this book project. My wife, Siyuan, has sacrificed her leisure time in order to read my drafts and has created a cosy family environment in order to support my writing. I owe her much gratitude for this selfless, loving support. I am also indebted to my parents' long-term, fully committed support for my pursuit of knowledge in often far-off locations; I hope they will be satisfied with the completion of this book.

Yanyuan, Peking University
August 2019

1

Introduction

On the morning of 4 April 2018, the opening ceremony of the 84th Annual Convention of the Arabic Language Academy in Cairo was held in the headquarters of the Academy. Located on the banks of the River Nile, in Cairo's prestigious Zamalek Area, the building was receiving researchers, university professors and students, lovers of Arabic and diplomats from the Arabic-speaking world[1] and beyond, together with the members of the Academy – 'the eternals' (*al-khālidūn*) as they are always called, dressed in black gowns with ivory and maroon hoods to mark their special status at this ceremonial occasion.

Ḥasan al-Shāfiʿī, the octogenarian president of the Academy among whose predecessors are some big names of the Egyptian intelligentsia in the twentieth century – ʾAḥmad Luṭfī al-Sayyid (d. 1963), Ṭāhā Ḥusayn (d. 1973), ʾIbrāhīm Madkūr (d. 1996) and Shawqī Ḍayf (d. 2005), was addressing the assembly. He reminded the audience that the Arabic language is 'the foundation of our physical and cultural existence, the basis of our national identity and the anchor of our desired renaissance' (al-Shāfiʿī 2018: 6). This language, he claimed, is now facing both internal and external challenges, especially those calls for 'unilateral globalisation'. He announced that the theme of the 2018 convention was therefore 'Protecting the Arabic Language: Challenges, Means and Objectives', and invited the assembly to ponder and contribute. In a following speech, ʿAbd al-Ḥamīd Madkūr, Secretory of the Academy, detailed the challenges as coming from

> foreign schools, colloquial dialects, cultural globalisation, the alienation and exclusion of the [Arabic] language from many social fields, the

> overall severance (with few exceptions) of its link with the studies of sciences in universities and research centres, views depicting Arabic as an obsolete, Bedouin language improper to be a language of science, civilisation and modernity, the inaccessibility of the job market to Arabic learners, the absence of intimacy and pride with Arabic [in the general public], and the challenges of technological development, in that technicians have not yet figured out how to make [sufficient] use of technology to serve Arabic and facilitate its use. (2018: 9)

The scene was solemn and imposing, and the words were intense and alarming, all heralding a determined phase of policy-making which would rid Arabic of many of its challenges. Yet the Arabic language academies (henceforth ALAs), of which the Cairo Academy is one, have been tackling these 'internal and external challenges' for more than a century, but the challenges still persist. The language situation in the Arabic-speaking world at the turn of the twentieth century was qualitatively similar to what al-Shāfiʿī and Madkūr depicted: the confinement of Standard Arabic to religious, formal and written communication, the prevalence of colloquial varieties of Arabic in daily communication and calls for granting them official status, the spread of English and French in both public and private education, the imposition of Turkish in the Arab provinces of the Ottoman Empire, the crisis of rendering neologisms and terminologies from European languages to Arabic, and the costly adaptation of technology to print in Arabic script. It was in this context that ALAs were called for.

Ideally, there would be only one ALA, reifying a unified, pan-Arab language authority that tackles language issues in the Arabic-speaking world by force and with determination. In reality, however, the authority is divided and curtailed. Beginning with a few short-lived civil societies at the turn of the twentieth century and later absorbed into the apparatus of modern Arab states with the inauguration of the Arab Academy (now the Arabic Language Academy in Damascus) in 1919, ALAs burgeoned for a time in the Arabic-speaking world, reaching around a dozen by the end of the last century. Syria, Egypt, Iraq, Morocco, Jordan, Tunisia, Algeria, Sudan, Libya, Palestine and Israel – each has its own ALA(s) or some equivalent. These ALAs are entrusted with a common mission: 'preserving the integrity of Arabic and making it compatible with modern civilisation'. This pan-Arab mission, however, is caught up in inevitable tension with the interest of the territorial states in which the ALAs are situated. Competition and lack of coordination among the ALAs are common, leading to parallel projects of neologism coinage and dictionary making. In addition, the ALAs have power of neither legislation nor implementation. Some of them are not functional but symbolic. It is, therefore, not surprising to see that the neologisms and terminologies they coin are largely fading into oblivion, and the advice and rulings they issue seldom develop into implementable language policies. The ALAs have not been able to change the language reality. The internal and external challenges posed to Arabic as the ALAs envision persist.

But ALAs still matter, as makers of an enduring, vibrant genre of intellectual discourse in the Arabic-speaking world. The genre is meta-linguistic, as it uses language to talk about language. However, it differs from (but is surely related to or overlaps with) the scholarly meta-linguistic discourse known as *linguistics proper*. Unlike the latter, the former does not set the philosophical and empirical studies of the structure, grammar, meaning and use of language as its only agenda, but tends to engage language into a wider and more complex network of sociopolitical concerns and agendas, involving, first and foremost, negotiation of identities and power relations in situations that are conflictual and turbulent, as well as in those that are ordinary and peaceful. Accordingly, this genre of discourse loads language with values and meanings of sociopolitical significance and 'burdens' it with missions and responsibilities beyond its communicative instrumentality. I name this genre *linguistics sociopolitical*. The scene of 4 April 2018 was but one of the mundane occasions recurring yearly in the arena of ALAs to perform linguistics sociopolitical.

The endurance and vibrancy of linguistics sociopolitical is testimony to the ideologisation of language in the Arabic-speaking world, a phenomenon that has come under increasing academic scrutiny in the last decade (e.g. Suleiman 2013a; Bassiouney 2014; Bawardi 2016). In the Arab(ic) setting, language is not value-neutral but is always a target of meaning making, production, reproduction and reiteration, in accordance with attitudes, positions, views and ideologies. Language can be a source of dignity and humiliation, a fermenter of solidarity and fragmentation, and a marker of being and identity. It can be a site of conflict and reconciliation, a cause of war and peace, and a projector of power and hierarchy. It can also be a residue of history and memory, an outlet of exhilaration and pain, and a symbol of hope and despair. These conceptions of language cannot withstand rigid scientific, empirical tests. They are value-laden and ideological. Yet they constitute a precious body of insider, indigenous views about the Arabs, their languages and the worlds they are in. They are a window onto what actually happens on the ground and what actually matters to the Arabs. They are means to enrich our understanding of the interface of language and ideology in Arab society. They deserve systematic description and analysis.

This book explores linguistics sociopolitical as is represented in the discussions and debates of five leading and functional ALAs (the Damascus, Cairo, Iraqi and Jordanian Academies, and the Arabisation Bureau in Rabat). They run regular seminars and conferences and publish periodicals and collections of research papers. Some of them hold public lectures. By doing so, they become platforms of meta-linguistic discussions and debates on the situation and future of Arabic and its entanglements with the political and social lives of the Arabs. These discussions and debates are defined in this book as the Arabic Language Academy discourse (henceforth ALA discourse). Publications of the five academies and minutes of the Cairo Academy, which record a large and representative portion of the ALA discourse, are the texts the book draws on. More coverage is given to the discourse of the academies in Damascus and Cairo due to their overall weight in the history of the ALAs.

The ALA discourse is one among many interconnected strands of linguistics sociopolitical in Arabic. However, this does not reduce its value as representative data of the genre in question to explore the interface of language and ideology in the Arabic-speaking world. In fact, the ALA discourse can be regarded as the mainstream of the genre for the following reasons. First, Arabic language academies are part of the apparatus of modern Arab states, modelled on the Académie française to incorporate intellectuals of cultural and political influence under state patronage. Being a member of or having affiliation to the academies is seen as a public acknowledgement of one's intellectual status and achievement. This is naturally attractive, making the academies important sites for leading intellectual voices to mingle, exchange and converge.

Second, under state patronage, views articulated at the platforms of the academies are inevitably framed by the agendas and ideologies of their hosting states concerning language and its role in politics and society. Since the majority of these agendas and ideologies are, generally speaking, not coercive (i.e. relying on state machinery to enforce them in society), they tend to reflect those mundane, 'politically correct' views on language by public consent. In this sense, the ALA discourse reflects collective rather than parochial perceptions of language in the communities of their hosting state.

Third, for the integrity of Arabic as a common asset of all Arabs to be a shared concern of the academies, their orientations tend to be pan-Arab, notwithstanding the different agendas of their hosting states. The platforms they set up are open to the whole Arabic-speaking world. Scholars who are citizens of different Arab and non-Arab states are invited to join or affiliate to the academies, to speak at their conferences and to publish in their journals. Accordingly, the ALA discourse often expresses concerns and attitudes of a pan-Arab character.

Lastly, this discourse has exhibited a long-term stability in terms of its themes and arguments. This is due partly to the unchanged objectives of the academies and partly to certain enduring sociopolitical circumstances in the Arabic-speaking world that continuously frame perceptions of language, as I will explain below. The diachronic stability of the discourse makes it a key source to uncover the most enduring and resilient language ideologies in Arab society.

Focusing on the ALA discourse, this book sets out to answer the following question: how and why does the genre of linguistics sociopolitical continuously ideologise language in the Arab(ic) setting? By answering this question, the book aims to reveal a mechanism of language-ideology interface in the Arabic-speaking world.

Three features of the ALA discourse are the key to revealing this mechanism. The first is incompatibility between discourse and implementation in language planning and language policy (LPLP) of Arabic language academies. The discourse they produce is vibrantly replete with diagnosis of language problems in the Arabic-speaking world, criticism of language misuse and deviation, well-thought-out language policy advice, narration of the glorious past of Arabic and envisioning of the should-be language situation. In contrast, the academies have not so far managed to turn their discourse into concrete language policies that could be implemented in order to change the language situation and match it to the statements and perceptions made in the discourse. Weakness in policy-making and implementation only works to detach the ALA discourse from actual language practice on the ground, while fostering its ideological function as a distortion of reality (in the Marxist sense) and a compensation for what the academies cannot achieve.

The second feature is language symbolism, which ideologises language further to drive it out of the seemingly value-neutral linguistic world and into the bog of sociopolitical complications. Symbolism can be roughly understood as a 'stand-for' type of projection. Language symbolism projects what happens in the social world onto language, so languages and language varieties become symbols that stand for social agents, groups and institutions, and intra- and inter-language relations become symbols that stand for power relations between agents, groups and institutions. Synthesising two theories of the social meaning of language – indexicality (Silverstein 2003; Eckert 2008; Johnstone 2010) and language symbolism (Suleiman 2011a; 2013a) – this book understands the symbolism of the ALA discourse as consisting of two processes: indexication and proxification.

I use indexication to refer to the construction and reconstruction of indexical meanings of language. 'A sign is indexical if it is related to its meaning by virtue of co-occurring with the thing it is taken to mean' (Johnstone 2010: 30–1). Language variation at various levels, including accents, vocabularies, phrases, grammatical patterns, patterns of discourse, language varieties and languages *per se*, can index identities, social categories, power relations and sociopolitical realities. A language form or variety can have multiple indexical meanings, constituting what Eckert (2008) calls an 'indexical field'. Moreover, an indexical meaning of a given language form or variety, once constructed, is liable to endless ideological reiteration and reconstruction, thus producing multiple orders of indexicality (Silverstein 2003). For example, a feature of the speech of a given community can be noticed and then used to index a character shared by members of the community. It can then be used to index membership of the community and demarcate boundaries with other communities. In conflictual situations, it can be further used to index common history and pride of the community to boost morale and solidarity, and it can also be used by adversaries as a stereotype to express contempt and enmity. The process goes on.

The male code-switching from [ʔ] and [k] to [g] – three dialectal allophones of the Arabic phoneme [q] in Jordan in the 1970s – can be illustrative (Suleiman 2004: 96–136). In Jordan [ʔ] was by 1970 associated with the urban communities of 'Palestinians and Syrians who came to Jordan in the 1920s and early 1930s' (ibid.: 102), [k] was associated with the rural Palestinians who were forced en masse into Jordan as a result of the 1948 and 1967 wars with Israel, and [g] was associated with indigenous Jordanians who were linked by the collective memory of a largely obsolete Bedouin lifestyle. [ʔ] and [k], due to their Palestinian association, were seen by the Jordanians as 'alien', in contrast to the 'indigenous' [g]. After the confrontation between the Jordanian army and the Palestinian guerrilla fighters in September 1970, male Palestinians began to switch from [ʔ] and [k] to [g] when speaking with Jordanians in order to be identified in public with Jordan rather than Palestine. The allophonic difference became a de facto boundary setter between nationals and non-nationals. In the language of Silverstein, the allophone-community association is an n-th order indexicality, the allophone-indigeneity association is an n+1st order indexicality and the allophone-nation association is an n+2nd order indexicality. Higher-order indexicalities are built upon and developed from lower-order ones. The theory of 'orders of indexicality' explains how the allophonic variation of [q] participated in Jordanian national politics and the struggle over Jordanian national identity.[2]

Indexication in the ALA discourse mainly works on named languages and language varieties used in the Arabic-speaking world, such as *fuṣḥā* (Standard Arabic), *ʿāmmiyya/dārija/lahja* (Colloquial Arabic), Turkish, French, English and so on. It juxtaposes what happens among these linguistic entities with what happens among peoples, states, nations and civilisations, as if the linguistic and the sociopolitical were naturally correlated. This constructed, naturalised correlation justifies the former being an index of the latter. As will be detailed in this book, some recurrent strands of the ALA discourse (1) correlate the widening gap between *fuṣḥā* and *ʿāmmiyya* as polarised levels of Arabic (a phenomenon known as diglossia) with social division and political fragmentation in the Arabic-speaking world; (2) correlate the spread of foreign languages, especially English and French, with the perceived continuation of Western colonial/imperial hegemony over the Arabs; and (3) correlate the impotence of Arabic as an instrument of modern communication, notably in science and education, with the internal decline of Arab-Islamic civilisation and the external threats from Western colonialism and imperialism. These are not conclusions of scientific, empirical research, but products of ideology. Indexication constructs an inalienable link between the linguistic and the sociopolitical and makes the link seem as real and natural as facts. Those who are living in the same ideological environment are ready to accept the link on factual bases and to reproduce and develop it further.

Indexication naturalises correlation and co-occurrence of the linguistic and the sociopolitical, so the former can 'stand for' the latter. Yet language symbolism does not stop at indexication. It involves a second move that exploits indexical meanings of language to use it as a proxy 'to do politics through language, in the sense that talk about language becomes talk about the extra-linguistic world' (Suleiman 2013a: 5). In the case of the ALA discourse, the above strands suggest that, first, intra-language integration towards *fuṣḥā* is necessary to foster intra-state cohesion and inter-state solidarity in the Arabic-speaking world; second, recovering the historical status of Arabic and curbing foreignness in the corpus of the language are necessary to reverse asymmetrical power relations between the Arabs and the West; and, lastly, modernising Arabic is both catching up with Western modernity and reviving the Arab-Islamic tradition to counter Western hegemony. It is clear that, for those who produce these strands of the ALA discourse, their final target is not language *per se* but the sociopolitical world that language 'stands for'. They call for an ideal type of intra- and inter-language relations that 'stands for' the ideal world-system and sociopolitical order in their mind. By doing so, they hope either to change the world via language change or to compensate symbolically for what they cannot change in reality. In both cases, language serves as a proxy.

Both indexication and proxification are symbolic because, empirically speaking, language is not responsible for sociopolitical wrongs, nor does language change necessarily lead to the betterment of politics and society. It is through this symbolism that language starts to assume 'burdens' and responsibilities beyond being merely an instrument of communication.

The third feature of the ALA discourse is its routinisation evident in the repetition, reproduction and reiteration of certain statements in the above strands of discourse on the situation of Arabic and its sociopolitical significance and correlations. It is further evident in that these statements are constantly made in similar ways. The issue of *fuṣḥā* and *ʿāmmiyya* is often discussed within a tripartite framework that sees the Arabic language as an organism that co-evolves with the Arab nation, an instrument that contributes to the political and social cohesion and progress of the Arabs, and a national symbol that signposts and constitutes Arab national identities. Opinions on foreign language influence and restoring the status of Arabic are often articulated in line with the notion of inalienability between Arabic and the Arab people, on the one hand, and that of equilibrium in inter-language relations as a cover for de facto Arabic/Arab centrism, on the other. The issue of the impotence of Arabic and its maintenance and development is often located in a dyad of endogenous and exogenous narrative of modernisation.

These stable ways of discourse-making indicate the existence of a set of 'discursive habiti' in the ALA discourse. Habitus is a notion the French sociologist Pierre Bourdieu proposes to account for the reproduction of social actions in similar contexts. According to him

> as an acquired system of generative schemes [or dispositions, tendencies, etc.] objectively adjusted to the particular conditions in which it is constituted, the habitus engenders all the thoughts, all the perceptions, and all the actions consistent with those conditions, and no others. (Bourdieu 1977: 95)

Following Bourdieu and seeing discourse as a type of social action, I define 'discursive habitus' as socially embodied dispositions to habitually perform discursive acts in particular ways under particular circumstances.

Habitus captures the complicated relations of social agents, actions and circumstances that underneath the routinisation of the ALA discourse. Habitus is a property of social agents (including both individuals and institutions), and this property is a 'structured and structuring structure' (Bourdieu 1994: 170). According to Maton,

> It is 'structured' by one's past and present circumstances . . . It is 'structuring' in that one's habitus helps to shape one's present and future practices. It is a 'structure' in that it is systematically ordered rather than random or unpatterned. This 'structure' comprises a system of dispositions which generate perceptions, appreciations, and practices. (2008: 51)

In the case of the ALA discourse, the agents that produce this discourse comprise both individual members of ALAs and the academies *per se* as institutions. They together reify a common role as language authority in the modern Arabic-speaking world, giving authoritative assessment of the language situation and issuing prudent guidance on language maintenance, revival and modernisation. As will be detailed in Chapter 2, this role is framed by two sociopolitical circumstances that have endured in the Arabic-speaking world from the early twentieth century onwards. One is the rise of modern Arab states that vertically reshape Arab society and horizontally instil a duality of pan-Arab and territorial-state nationalisms, and the other is the peripherality of the Arabs in the modern world-system. As a key property of this role, the above-mentioned set of discursive habiti is also structured by these two *longue dureé* circumstances. In the meantime, these habiti structuralise the ALA discourse, producing those recurrent strands of discourse that, through indexication and proxification of language, respond to the *longue dureé* circumstances. Without a profound change of these circumstances in real terms, this response would reinforce the ways of perceiving and receiving these circumstances among members of the academies, which would strengthen the discursive habiti further. It follows that the recurrence of the strands of the ALA discourse would continue until the discourse goes into the state of routinisation.

The above three features of the ALA discourse together reveal a mechanism of language-ideology interface embedded in the genre of linguistics sociopolitical in the Arabic-speaking world. This mechanism consists of three intertwined dimensions of ideologisation. The first is the divorce of meta-linguistic discourse from actual language practice. Since no compatibility can be attained between the envisioned and the real language situations, the discourse becomes an autonomous site where an alternative language reality is constructed, in words not in deeds. The second dimension is the association of this alternative reality with the sociopolitical world through two processes of language symbolism: (1) indexication – projecting the sociopolitical onto the linguistic through naturalisation of the correlation and co-occurrence of the two; and (2) proxification – using the linguistic as proxy to negotiate identities and power relations in the sociopolitical world. The third dimension is habitual repetition, reproduction and reiteration of such processes of indexication and proxification over a long period of time to make them a routine of discourse that responds to the *longue dureé* sociopolitical circumstances engulfing the Arabic-speaking world.

By highlighting the role of the *longue dureé* sociopolitical circumstances in the working of the above mechanism that culminates in discursive routinisation, this book aims to show that the ideologisation of language in the Arab(ic) setting is an accumulative effect of continuous stimulation from similar sociopolitical stimuli over a long period of time. This, however, does not suggest that the Arabic-speaking world is stagnant and has witnessed little sociopolitical change over the past century until now. Nor does it suggest that short-term, epochal events, such as regime changes, orientation turns, policy adjustments, wars and conflicts, uprisings and movements, and revolutions and restorations, exert little influence on the ideologisation of language. Quite the contrary, the modern Arabic-speaking world has been volatile if not turbulent, and its modern history is replete with all kinds of the above-mentioned epochal events. Yet these events have not so far changed but only reinforced the two *longue dureé* circumstances. These events, accordingly, become those stimuli that continuously drive the ideologisation in similar directions.

Temporally, this book sets the twentieth century as the main span of its investigation. This is because ALAs, together with the ideologisation of language unfolding in their meta-linguistic discourse, are mainly a twentieth-century phenomenon continuing into the present. The last century witnessed the rise, spread, development and routinisation of this phenomenon, largely determining its essence and contour. Any serious study of this phenomenon should begin with this formative period, before delving into its contemporary development.

Geographically, the book studies the discourse of five ALAs together in order to address the common themes of linguistics sociopolitical that concern both the eastern (Mashriq) and western (Maghrib) parts of the Arabic-speaking world. In other words, the book aims to explore language ideologies of a pan-Arab relevance. This is because only on this pan-Arab scale can we approach the full complexity of the interface of language and ideology in the ALA discourse, especially concerning the linguistic projection of the duality of pan-Arab and state-territorial nationalisms and of the common experience of Arabs in a changing world order not in their favour.

Methodologically, the book adopts the general perspectives of critical discourse analysis (CDA). These focus on making transparent the link between discourse making and its sociopolitical and ideological surroundings. CDA is a label for a plethora of research agendas and approaches that are bound by such notions as discourse, critique, ideology and power (Wodak and Meyer 2009: 4–10). The overall purpose of CDA is to make transparent the overt and covert semiotic, meaning-construing activities (discourse) and their interaction with the circulation of ideology and the distribution of power in a given social environment. It is this purpose of 'making transparent' that endows CDA with the sense of 'critical' and distinguishes it from other approaches of discourse analysis. I also adopt this sense of 'critical' in this book. Unlike some CDA scholars, I use CDA for the purpose of analysis rather than that of uncovering social inequalities, correcting social wrongs and improving the human condition.

Although CDA is a powerful analytical tool, it lacks fixed approaches, models and agendas (Fairclough et al. 2011: 357). Among the three leading approaches of CDA, van Dijk's (2009) sociocognitive approach focuses on the triangle of discourse, collective/social cognition (or socially shaped perceptions in the forms of knowledge, attitudes and ideologies) and social structure in CDA; Wodak's (2006; 2009 with Reisigl) discourse-historical approach (DHA) 'attempts to integrate a large quantity of available knowledge about the historical sources and the background of the social and political fields in which discursive "events" are embedded' and 'analyzes the historical dimension of discursive actions by exploring the ways in which particular genres of discourse are subject to diachronic change' (2006: 175); Fairclough's (2009) dialectical-relational approach investigates (1) dialectical relations between different semiotic practices (Fairclough considers that every social practice, including the use of language, has a semiotic element) and between semiotic and non-semiotic elements of social practices and (2) how these relations form 'the semiotic aspect of social order' (Wodak and Meyer 2009: 27). My use of CDA in this book exhibits a synthesis of all three approaches. As will become clear in the following chapters, I explore the diachronic continuity of the ALA discourse within the long-term contexts of duality of nationalisms, counter-peripherality and modernisation in the Arabic-speaking world (discourse-historical). I also establish habitual, repetitive patterns of discourse-making that reflect the operation of a set of language ideologies in modern Arab society (sociocognitive) and reveal parallels between the ALA discourse on the one hand, and the semiotic aspect of the institutionalisation of ALAs (see Chapter 2) and other genres of Arab discourse (e.g. the discourse of Arab nationalism in Chapter 3) on the other (dialectical-relational). My synthesis confirms a common observation about CDA, which suggests that it is a multifaceted and 'multimethodical' framework and should thus be tailored to different research questions and agendas (Wodak 2006: 171; Fairclough 2009: 167).

Since the current study is designed to explain the *longue durée* reproduction, reiteration and routinisation of the ALA discourse throughout the twentieth century (see Chapter 2), CDA is modified to serve this research design in the following ways. First, the ALA discourse will be examined in line with the sociopolitical and ideological changes in the Arabic-speaking world. Since diachronically the ALA discourse exhibited more continuity and overlap than difference, it would be wrong to apply a rigid periodisation to this discourse. In order to reflect how the sociopolitical and ideological changes have affected the ALA discourse without subjecting the latter to uncritical historicism, I adopt a flexible strategy when examining the interaction between the ALA discourse on different language issues and its relevant sociopolitical contexts. For example, in Chapter 3 on Arabic diglossia, when less diachronic turns can be identified from the ALA discourse on this issue, I analyse three habiti of this discourse without 'periodisation' and then link the uneven diachronic vibrancy of these tendencies to three periods of Arab nationalisms. In contrast, in Chapter 4 on Arabi(ci)sation (*taʿrīb*) and Chapter 5 on language modernisation, when the ALA discourse on these two issues exhibited clearer diachronic features, I examine this discourse in line with several historical 'sites'. As will be shown in these two chapters, my division of the 'sites' considers both the continuance of the ALA discourse and the chronic sociopolitical and ideological changes in the Arabic-speaking world to avoid rigid periodisation.

Second, my use of CDA in the book combines content analysis – identifying statements explicitly made – and semantic analysis – excavating agendas, intentions and attitudes hidden behind these statements by analysing the use of semantic devices such as vocabulary, metaphorics and, to a lesser extent, semantically salient morphosyntactic elements. By doing so, I choose to pay less attention to other linguistic and discursive devices such as pronouns, demonstratives, deixis, negation, quantification, tense, aspect, modality and phonological and syntactic variations. Analyses of these devices, together with content and semantic analyses, are useful for thoroughly and rigorously examining the production of a limited number of discourses within their local contexts, but are difficult and uneconomic to carry out if the object of analysis is discursive reproduction and reiteration across a number of institutions and over a large time span, as in the case of the current study of the ALA discourse. In the latter case, it is better to focus on the circulation and reiteration, both synchronically and diachronically, of key concepts in the ALA discourse. For that reason, content and semantic analyses are prioritised in this book.

Third, since CDA has offered few satisfying approaches to explaining discursive reproduction, reiteration and routinisation, I bring in the notion of 'discursive habitus'. The discursive habiti identified from the ALA discourse are key to understanding the reproduction and routinisation of this discourse, because they have often reflected the dominant but taken for granted beliefs and ideologies – what Bourdieu (1977: 164) calls 'doxa' – that have led to ALA members continuing to openly describe Arabic and its situation in modern society in certain ways. It follows that the major aim of my use of CDA is to extract from the analyses of the content and the semantic devices of the ALA discourse its enduring discursive habiti.

Finally, I will link these discursive habiti to the sociopolitical contexts of the twentieth-century Arabic-speaking world to see what aspects of these contexts were temporal-spatially persistent that might contribute to the persistence of these discursive habiti.

Three clarifications need to be made concerning the use of CDA in this book. First, I use CDA to excavate ideological connections between conceptions of Arabic and their sociopolitical contexts in the ALA discourse. However, because of the ubiquity and banality of language ideologies, these connections are often covert. In many cases, I have to set them out by carefully analysing the choice of vocabulary and rhetorical devices in selected discourse and linking them to the sociopolitical contexts of their production. This mode of exploration does not mean that the connections I establish in this book are in any way fabrications of fertile imagination, for the following reasons: (1) LPLP scholars have conducted a large number of case studies revealing the ideological and sociopolitical nature of intervention into language situation across different language communities (e.g. nation-building and decolonisation as motivational and structuring factors in 'classical language planning'; see Chapter 2). The Arabic-speaking world is not exceptional. (2) ALAs are clearly shaped in the sociopolitical environment of the Arabic-speaking world. As will be discussed in the next chapter, ALAs are part of state structure in a number of Arab states. Like the banal existence of national flags, anthems, airlines, stamps, national holidays and so on, in these states ALAs carry a similar degree of banality, marking state authority over the representation of Arabic in public discourses. As a constituent of the state system, an ALA, especially its ideological orientation and membership composition, is naturally open to political and ideological considerations that respond to the political imperatives of the state. These external factors by extension also affect the conceptualisation of Arabic in the ALA discourse. (3) Some events in modern Arab history, such as the Arab defeat in the 1967 war with Israel, had a wide-ranging impact on the social life of the Arabs, which catapulted the Arabic-speaking world into long-term sociocultural malaise and trauma (Abu-Rabiʿ 2004; Ṭarābīshī 2005: 15–35, quoted in Suleiman 2011a: 130–1; Kassab 2010: 48–115). It would be counter-intuitive to dissociate the ALA discourse from the impacts of these events.

Second, as will be seen in the following chapters, my use of CDA attends to metaphors or metaphorical use of language in the ALA discourse. This is justifiable not only because metaphors are commonly used in the ALA discourse but also because they are devices of symbolic construction and ideological persuasion. 'Metaphor' is used here not merely as a collective term for figurative expressions but more broadly as 'a pattern of conceptual association' which Lakoff and Johnson (1980: 5) describe as 'understanding and experiencing one kind of thing in terms of another'. Following this view, Fauconnier and Turner (1994) develop a theoretical model depicting metaphor as 'blending' of 'selected conceptual material from two or more distinct sources' (Grady 2007: 198), a process involving at least four cognitive 'spaces'. For example, ʿAbd al-Qādir al-Maghribī (d. 1956), a member of the Damascus Academy, describes borrowings in Arabic as the offspring of Arab fathers and non-Arab 'concubines' (see also Chapter 3). In making this metaphor, al-Maghribī blends two 'input spaces' – one is lexical borrowing in Arabic and the other is ethnic interbreeding – into a 'blend space': borrowings are hybrids.[3] This 'blend space' is rationalised by an abstract 'generic space' – language is ethnicity, which reveals al-Maghribī's hidden intention: constructing an inalienable link between Arabic and Arab people, and conveying this link to his audience and readers. As will be discussed in Chapter 3, this link is ideological by nature because it is connected with considerations of Arab nationalism.[4]

The above example shows that the making of metaphors can be ideological. Metaphors are more than figurative expressions at the literal level and more than conceptual blends at the cognitive level. They are used to express new realities out of the familiar, or new relations between existing entities to concretise, support or propagate specific ideologies. This view of metaphor conforms to what Charteris-Black (2004: 21) calls the 'pragmatic criteria' of metaphor, which he describes as follows: 'A metaphor is an incongruous linguistic representation that has the underlying purpose of influencing opinions and judgements by persuasion; this purpose is often covert and reflects speaker intentions within particular contexts of use'. It follows that metaphors are windows onto the embodied sociopolitical concerns and ideological intentions behind discourse-making, and are thus valued in this book.

Finally, CDA is essentially a method of qualitative analysis and will be used accordingly in this book. I use qualitative analysis here because the ideological elements (for example, values, attitudes, sociopolitical agendas and so on) in the symbolism of Arabic in the ALA discourse are too elusive and subjective to quantify in line with the so-called 'objective' and 'scientific' principles. I believe qualitative analysis, if properly applied, can reveal subtle but nonetheless deep links between Arabic and its sociopolitical surroundings, and the prevalence of language ideologies in Arab society. However, I am also aware of the subjective nature of qualitative analysis. It should, therefore, be noted that my analysis of the symbolism of Arabic in the ALA discourse is just one way of approaching this phenomenon and cannot be the only way.

A synopsis of the contents of the following chapters is in order here. Chapter 2 gives a historical introduction and a sociological analysis of ALAs as institutional sites where the ALA discourse is produced. It explains how the rise and maturation of modern Arab states and the endurance of Arab peripherality have shaped and routinised a role of ALAs as not only language planners but also purveyors of language symbolism. This paves the way for the analysis of the ALA discourse. Chapter 3 investigates how Arabic diglossia is conceptualised in the ALA discourse from organic, instrumental and symbolic perspectives, and how the duality of pan-Arab and state-territorial nationalisms is projected onto the complex relationship between *fuṣḥā* and *ʿāmmiyya*, ranging from polarisation to re-integration. Chapter 4 discusses how Arabi(ci)sation is formulated in the ALA discourse as a symbolic resistance to and compensation for the spread and dominance of foreign languages in sections of Arab society as a symptom of the overall Arab peripherality in the modern world-system. It identifies two discursive habiti: one highlights the inalienability between Arabic and the Arab people, and the other argues for equilibrium in language contact and exchange. Chapter 5 examines how the modernisation of Arabic was discussed in the ALA discourse in accordance with a persistent dyad of exogenous and endogenous understandings of modernisation. A number of important themes, including language maintenance and reform, language and imperialism, and Arabic as a transnational world language, are addressed in this chapter. The conclusion gives a systematic description of language symbolism as a mechanism of language-ideology interface in and beyond the ALAs and the Arabic setting. It includes a comparison of the script Romanisation movements in China and the Arabic-speaking world to place the ideologisation of language in a global context of the evolvement of the hierarchical modern world-system and to dialogue with Orientalism from the perspective of language as part of the signage of global power relations. In the appendix, a glossary of the key terms and phrases of the ALA discourse discussed in this book is provided for reference.

A final note about the translation and transliteration of Arabic: all Arabic quotations are rendered into English; but in cases where the English translation cannot deliver nuances in Arabic, transliterations are provided as complements. My transliterations follow the standard of the *International Journal of Middle East Studies* (IJMES); all pronounced consonants, including the initial strong *hamza* (*hamzat al-qṭ*ʿ), and vowels are represented, but not the case endings. Proper nouns are transliterated in the same way unless they have conventional English spellings. Some Arabic terminologies, such as *fuṣḥā* and *ʿāmmiyya,* are kept in their original form because no proper English equivalents can be found. Individual explanations will be given whenever I choose to keep the original terminologies.

Notes

1. I use 'Arabic-speaking world' rather than the commonly used 'Arab world' to emphasise the language-centred definition and demarcation of Arab collective identity and locality. The former term has two advantages: (1) it fits the extra-linguistic, identity-related symbolic functions of Arabic that are studied in this book; and (2) it includes both the Arabic-speaking communities living in the Arab world and those in diaspora, who share similar ideological thinking on the role of Arabic in the social world.
2. Gender also constitutes the indexical difference between [k] and [g] and is interwoven with national politics in Jordan. See Suleiman (2004: 96–136) for a detailed analysis.
3. It should be noted that the metaphor 'borrowings are hybrids' is not an invention of al-Maghrībī but a well-established conventional metaphor in the Arabic linguistic tradition (see the discussion of *muwallada* in Chapter 3). However, its conventionality cannot deny its creativeness when it was first made nor its ideological saliency when it was reiterated in new sociopolitical contexts, as will be seen in the case of al-Maghrībī (Chapter 3).
4. This link has its root in the 'wisdom of the Arabs' principle long observed in the Arabic grammatical tradition, which served as a backbone for the symbolic link between Arabic and Arab nationalisms in the nineteenth and twentieth centuries (see Suleiman 2003).

2

The Arabic Language Academy Phenomenon

The diffusion of Arabic language academies (ALAs) in the twentieth-century Arabic-speaking world is a linguistic-cum-sociopolitical phenomenon.[1] 'Arabic language academy' (*majma' al-lugha al-'arabiyya*) is used here as a generic term for all official consultative bodies specialising, exclusively or partially, in preserving, regulating, promoting and modernising the Arabic language in individual Arab states or the Arabic-speaking world. These duties are often considered as state-led language planning and language policy-making, of which the evaluation concerns whether ALAs succeed in affecting the actual status and use of language to serve intra-state (e.g. state building and nation formation) and inter-state (e.g. decolonisation and regional competition) agendas. This understanding suggests a direct, unmediated, to some extent mechanical causality, premising that top-down language change will induce anticipated sociopolitical change. The actual situation is more complicated. The causality, for the most part as in the case of ALAs, is mediated. It is mediated through ideology-driven and discursively realised language symbolism that projects sociopolitical concerns onto language and uses the latter as a proxy to tackle the former. It follows that ALAs are not just authoritative language planners but also purveyors of language symbolism. This symbolism is framed by a role lodged in the mission and orientation of ALAs. The formation, evolvement and routinisation of the role is conditioned by the sociopolitical circumstances of the Arabic-speaking world. This chapter adopts four perspectives – pan-Arab, LPLP, symbolic and discursive – to reveal and explain this complicated entanglement between the linguistic and sociopolitical dimensions of the ALA phenomenon.

The Arabic Language Academy Phenomenon Is Pan-Arab

The ALA phenomenon is pan-Arab because it involves and affects the whole Arabic-speaking world. The foundation of ALAs could be seen as the diffusion of an institutional model in the Arabic-speaking world. Towards the end of the nineteenth century, there were sporadic calls for and experiments in ALAs modelled on the Académie française, mainly in Egypt (Chejne 1969: 104; Ḍayf 1984: 19–20; al-Ḥamzāwī 1988: 36–41; Fāyid 2002: 91–2; Sawaie 2007: 634).[2] Although all the precursors of ALAs failed to persist, the ALA as an institutional model became well known. The first ALA, the Arabic Language Academy in Damascus (*Majmaʿ al-Lugha al-ʿArabiyya bi-Dimashq*),[3] was established in 1919. Since then, a number of ALAs have been founded on both state and cross-state levels, as shown in Table 2.1.[4]

These ALAs are institutionally related in three further ways. First, they learn from each other in the matter of institutional organisation. For example, Iraq followed Syria by creating a department within the Ministry of Education to manage language affairs before developing it into an academy (al-ʾĀlūsī 1997: 13–53). The Jordanian government sent delegations to the ALAs in Syria, Egypt and Iraq to seek advice on the organisational structure and working methods of the Jordanian Academy before its establishment (Khalīfa 1987: 88). Similarly, the Cairo Academy made its administrative archive and database available to the Libyan Academy for its reference (al-Ahrām 2002). Second, these ALAs co-opt their members throughout the Arabic-speaking world. Some Arab intellectuals are members of two or more ALAs. Third, these ALAs organise pan-Arab conferences and seminars and disseminate their reports and periodicals to sister institutes and interested readers across the Arabic-speaking world. These institutional commonalities have turned these ALAs into a de facto pan-Arab communion of intellectuals who care about the Arabic language.

The diffusion of ALAs is due to the consolidation and routinisation of a role in Arab society. Role theory understands a role as a set of expected rights and duties, associated with a social position (Turner 2001: 233). The role of ALAs is a modern language authority called on to tackle concerns over the state of the Arabic language. For the Arabs, the Arabic language, or Arabic, or *al-ʿarabiyya*, is 'a cover term which refers to Arabic in its various forms, both synchronically and diachronically' (Suleiman 2006: 173). Synchronically, Arabic designates both *fuṣḥā* (the standard variety of Arabic used across Arabic-speaking communities) and *ʿāmmiyya/dārija/lahja*[5] (regional colloquial varieties of Arabic). *Fuṣḥā* enjoys a high status in Arab society, because it is the variety of Arabic in which the Qur'an was revealed verbatim, it has a long literary tradition, it is regarded as the most elegant and eloquent variety of Arabic, and it is considered to be a symbol of the Arab nation (whether it is primordial, constructed or both) and national identity (Suleiman 2003). Owing to this high status, the Arabs tend to equate Arabic with *fuṣḥā*. On most occasions when they speak of Arabic, they are referring to *fuṣḥā*. They distinguish between *fuṣḥā* and *ʿāmmiyya* only in discussions about internal differences in Arabic. This usage of 'Arabic', '*fuṣḥā*' and '*ʿāmmiyya*' will be followed in this book.

From the mid-nineteenth century onwards, concerns over Arabic arose across Arabic-speaking communities, focusing on three language situations. The first was Arabic diglossia, or the linguistic and functional disparity between *fuṣḥā* and *ʿāmmiyya*. The second was the spread of foreign languages, such as Turkish (before the collapse of the Ottoman Empire), French and English, in Arabic-speaking communities as well as foreign influences on the vocabulary, syntax and style of Arabic. These two language situations were often correlated and perceived as a deterioration in the status and standard of *fuṣḥā*. The third was the perceived archaic complexity of *fuṣḥā* and its unsuitability for expressing modern concepts and ideas. ALAs were called on for a collective response and a coordinated remedy. They were entrusted with the expected duties of the integration of *fuṣḥā* and *ʿāmmiyya* (to the advantage of the former) to develop a unified modern standard available to all social strata and applicable to all domains of public communication, as well as Arabi(ci)sation and the modernisation of Arabic. Nowadays, concerns over Arabic are still widely attested in public discourses, within ALAs and beyond, and these concerns still revolve around the language situations perceived as those above. The three duties, accordingly, are continuously demanded as such. They have crystallised into the long-articulated, unmodified agenda of ALAs: 'preserving the integrity of Arabic and making it compatible with modern civilisation'. The role of ALAs, therefore, is now well established in Arab society and has become a routine component of Arab modernity.

The diffusion of ALAs is also due to certain recurring and enduring sociopolitical circumstances across the Arabic-speaking world that drive the institutionalisation of ALAs along similar lines. It is admitted that epochal and country-specific circumstances, such as financial difficulties, partisan conflicts, regime changes, wars, reforms and protests, do affect the institution of the ALA, as they might prevent ALAs from performing their duties or impact on their stances towards Arabic in the short term. However, they did not usually massively recast the institution of ALAs. For example, administrative and financial difficulties forced the Damascus Academy to suspend its work for nearly a year between 1919 and 1920

Table 2.1 A list of Arabic Language Academies and equivalent institutions

Year of foundation	Name	English rendering	Location
1919	*Majma' al-Lugha al-'Arabiyya bi-Dimashq*	The Arabic Language Academy in Damascus	Damascus
1932	*Majma' al-Lugha al-'Arabiyya bi-l-Qāhira*[a]	The Arabic Language Academy in Cairo	Cairo
1947	*al-Majma' al-'Ilmī al-'Irāqī*	The Iraqi Academy	Baghdad
1961	*al-Maktab al-Dā'im li-Tansīq al-Ta'rīb fī al-Waṭan al-'Arabī bi-l-Rabāṭ*[b]	The Permanent Bureau for the Coordination of Arabisation in the Arab World in Rabat	Rabat
1976	*Majma' al-Lugha al-'Arabiyya al-'Urdunnī*	The Jordanian Arabic Language Academy	Amman
1983	*al-Majma' al-Tūnisī li-l-'Ulūm wa-l-'Ādāb wa-l-Funūn – Bayt al-Ḥikma*	The Tunisian Academy of Sciences, Letters and Arts – Beit al-Hikma	Tunis
1986	*Majma' al-Lugha al-'Arabiyya al-Jazā'irī*	The Algerian Arabic Language Academy	Algiers
1993	*Majma' al-Lugha al-'Arabiyya bi-l-Kharṭūm*	The Arabic Language Academy in Khartoum	Khartoum
1994	*Majma' al-Lugha al-'Arabiyya al-Lībī*[c]	The Libyan Arabic Language Academy	Tripoli
1994	*Majma' al-Lugha al-'Arabiyya al-Filasṭīnī – Bayt al-Muqaddas*[d]	The Palestinian Arabic Language Academy in Jerusalem	Ramallah
2007	*Majma' al-Lugha al-'Arabiyya fī Ḥayfā*[e]	The Arabic Language Academy in Haifa	Haifa
2008	*Majma' al-Qāsimī li-l-Lugha al-'Arabiyya*	Al-Qāsimī Academy for the Arabic Language	Baqa al-Gharbiyye
2013	*Majma' al-Lugha al-'Arabiyya al-Filasṭīnī – Ghazza*	The Palestinian Arabic Language Academy in Gaza	Gaza
2017	*Majma' al-Lugha al-'Arabiyya bi-l-Shāriqa*[f]	The Arabic Language Academy in Sharjah	Sharjah

a The Cairo Academy changed its name several times. It began as *Majma' al-Lugha al-'Arabiyya al-Malakī* 'Royal Arabic Language Academy' in 1932. It changed its name to *Majma' Fu'ād al-'Awwal li-l-Lugha al-'Arabiyya* 'Fu'ād I Academy for the Arabic Language' in 1938 in memory of the late king of Egypt. After the 1952 Revolution, the Academy gained a new name in 1954: *Majma' al-Lugha al-'Arabiyya* 'the Arabic Language Academy'. In 1960, following the 1958 union of Egypt and Syria, the name changed to *Majma' al-Lugha al-'Arabiyya bi-l-Qāhira* 'the Arabic Language Academy in Cairo' which has been used since then.

b The founding of the Bureau was initially a Moroccan initiative. It is now attached to the Arab League's Educational, Cultural and Scientific Organization (ALECSO). The Moroccan government established the Kingdom of Morocco Academy (*'Akādīmiyyat al-Mamlaka al-Maghribiyya*) in 1977. According to its charter, this Academy does not specialise in language affairs (AMM 2013), although it has been a member of the Union of Arabic Language and Science Academies since 1996 (MLAU 2008). A government decree (no. 10.02) was issued in 2003, announcing the establishment of the Mohammed VI Academy for the Arabic Language (*ʾAkādīmiyyat Muḥammad al-Sādis li-l-Lugha al-ʿArabiyya*) in Morocco (al-Fāsī al-Fihrī 2010: 21). There is no evidence that this Academy is currently functional.

c The Libyan government issued a decree announcing the establishment of the Libyan Academy in 1994 (MMU 46: 244). For unknown reasons, this Academy was not opened until 2002 (al-ʾAhrām 2002; Fāyid 2002: 97).

d A preparation committee was organised in Jerusalem in September 1987 to discuss the foundation of the Palestinian Language Academy, but soon stopped working due to a lack of funding and difficulties committee members had in travelling to Jerusalem (ʿAmrū 1999: 184–5). The committee resumed its work in 1994 and the founding decree of the Academy was passed on 24 June 1994 (ibid.: 186). It is worth mentioning that the Palestinian National Authority was officially formed in the same year, indicating a close link between ALAs and state-building in the Arabic-speaking world. This Academy is now temporarily based in Ramallah (ibid.: 193). In 2013, the foundation of another Palestinian Arabic language academy was announced in the Hamas-controlled Gaza Strip (Ṣawt al-ʾAqṣā 2013). This Academy also claimed Jerusalem as its permanent location. The two Palestinian language academies mirror the division of political authority between Fatah and Hamas in Palestine.

e There are two ALAs in Israel: the Haifa Academy, established in 2007 under the aegis of the Israeli government, and Al-Qasemi Arabic Language Academy (*Majmaʿ al-Qāsimī li-l-Lugha al-ʿArabiyya*), established within Al-Qasemi Academic College of Education in 2008 (Muṣṭafā 2013).

f The Arabic Language Academy in Sharjah is the first of its kind in the Arab Gulf states. Yet it differs from other, major ALAs in two respects. First, it was established by the Emirate of Sharjah rather than the State of UAE. Second, its charter does not stipulate that its working members need to hold UAE citizenship or residency. These two differences indicate that this Academy is not yet a state institute, as many others are. It is most probably an initiative of the al-Qāsimī ruling family of Sharjah to patronise and collaborate with other ALAs on some grand language and cultural projects such as the Arabic historical dictionary (al-Kharīj al-Jadīd 2017). The fact that Qatar, the regional adversary of UAE, announced its own Arabic historical dictionary project in 2013 and launched the first part of the dictionary online (www.dohadictionary.org) in 2018 has made the Sharjah Academy initiative more urgent. Once again (as I will show in the history of ALAs), the ALA seems to have become a proxy of competition for regional ascendency.

(Sawaie 2007: 635). A tight budget and a shortage of supplies during and after World War II caused the Cairo Academy to suspend its journal for eleven years (ibid.: 635). Power struggles between political parties in Egypt in the 1930s prevented prominent reformist Arab intellectuals, such as Ṭāhā Ḥusayn (d. 1973) and ʾAḥmad Lutfī al-Sayyid (d. 1963), who at that time belonged to the opposition block, from acquiring membership of the Cairo Academy in its early years (al-Ḥamzāwī 1988: 62). Difficulties of international travel (Ḍayf 1984: 154; Fāyd 2004: 27) and the reluctant but eventual collaboration of the Egyptian government with the British during World War II (Marsot 2007: 119–20) kept August Fischer (d. 1949), the German member of the Cairo Academy, from travelling to Cairo to complete his *Historical Dictionary of Arabic* project. These are neither major nor decisive factors in understanding the ALA phenomenon, but they show that ALAs can be affected by immediate sociopolitical concerns.

By contrast, enduring and pan-Arab sociopolitical circumstances tend to exert deeper and more profound influences on the institution of the ALA. Two of these circumstances are most relevant here. One is the emergence and consolidation of modern Arab states; the other is the continuing peripheralisation of the Arabs as a whole in the modern world-system. The former posits the 'state' as the new centre of gravity in the political, social and cultural life of the Arabs on the one hand, and perpetuates the duality of pan-Arab and territorial-state nationalisms on the other. The latter causes the spread of a feeling of coloniality in Arab society beyond the colonial period, making the relation between Arab Self and the hegemonic Other (mainly the West) a constant problem. A brief survey of the history of the ALA phenomenon shows how the institution of the ALA was shaped and conditioned along the above lines.

Arabic Language Academies between Pan-Arab and Territorial-State Nationalisms

Throughout the history of ALAs, tension has always existed between establishing a unified ALA as the only language authority in the Arabic-speaking world in line with the expected political unification of the Arabs and multiple ALAs in accordance with territorial Arab nationalisms. This tension was already manifest in the precursors of ALAs in Egypt in the late nineteenth and early twentieth centuries. These early 'ALAs' were pan-Arab oriented because they were expected to assume language authority in the Arabic-speaking world mainly with regard to correct usage and lexical coinages. They appeared in Egypt not because the Egyptian ruling elites ardently support their activities, but because, at that time, Egypt was a major hub of Arab intellectual life. Noticeably, these ALA precursors often defined themselves as civil and cultural rather than as official and political institutions, in order to eschew interventions of the Egyptian state in their activities. However, lacking financial and administrative support from the Egyptian government, these early 'ALAs' only existed for a short period (al-Ḥamzāwī 1988: 36–41; Sawaie 2007: 634).

The failure of the early ALAs shows that government support is vital for an ALA's survival. The connection between ALAs and territorial Arab states became inevitable, starting from the Damascus Academy. In 1918, Prince Fayṣal (d. 1933), son of Ḥuṣayn ibn ʿAlī al-Hāshimī (the Grand Sharif of Mecca who led the Arab Revolt (1916–18) against the Ottomans), captured Damascus and formed an Arab government in Syria (Cleveland and Bunton 2009: 161). This government created the Department of Translation and Compilation (*shuʿbat al-tarjama wa-l-taʾlīf*) to support its Arabicisation campaign of replacing Turkish with Arabic in administration and education. This department became the Damascus Academy in 1919 (Futayyiḥ 1956: 3; Subḥ 1970: 9; al-Faḥḥām 1996: 23; Murād 1996: 50–1; Marwān 2009: 1152–3; al-Mubārak 2009: 1165). The Academy was entrusted with cultivating a national language based on *fuṣḥā* and creating a national museum and a national library in Syria (Kurd ʿAlī 1921: 2; Subḥ 1970: 10; Murād 1996: 52–3). In doing so, it was, in fact, charged with constructing national symbols – language, history and literary tradition – for the young Syrian state and national community. The Academy relied on government funds, and its founding members were exclusively Damascus-based – two further pieces of proof of its association with the territorial Syrian state. However, the Academy was also pan-Arab oriented. It used the name 'the Arab Academy' (*al-Majmaʿ al-ʿIlmī al-ʿArabī*)[6] until 1960, showing that it was not restricted to Syria but belonged to the Arabic-speaking world as a whole. In other words, this territorially based academy had a pan-Arab ambition, seeing its work as having an effect extending beyond Syria. This pan-Arab ambition was in accordance with Syria's consistent endorsement of pan-Arabism under Fayṣal's Arab Kingdom of Syria and the following regimes.

The foundation of the Damascus Academy ushered in an era of state-sponsored ALAs. Territorial Arab states appearing after World War I competed to establish ALAs to vie to control the linguistic and cultural authority in the Arabic-speaking world. Lebanon, Iraq and Transjordan all tried in the 1920s to create ALAs similar to the Damascus Academy in their territories, but failed due to limited financial and intellectual resources (Fāyid 2002: 92–3; Khalīfa 1987: 87–8; al-ʾĀlūsī 1997: 13–33; al-Rāwī 2002: 7; Maṭlūb 2008: 5). Only Egypt was able to counterbalance

Syria in this matter. King Fu'ād of Egypt (d. 1936), who wrestled with the Hāshimite family to claim pan-Arab leadership and reintroduce the Caliphate demolished by the Turks, founded a number of cultural and educational institutes in the 1920s and 1930s to extend the cultural influence of the Egyptian royal family over the Arabic-speaking world (al-Ḥamzāwī 1988: 43–6). Among them was the Cairo Academy, then named the Royal Arabic Language Academy (*Majma' al-Lugha al-'Arabiyya al-Malakī*). This Academy was designed to be pan-Arab and cosmopolitan. Its membership was not confined to Egyptian citizens and Muslims; among the first academicians, Christian, Jewish and non-Egyptian Arab intellectuals and European Orientalists were included (al-Ḥamzāwī 1988: 73–99; Fāyid 2002: 94). Nonetheless, this Academy was still closely tied to the Egyptian state. It was founded by a royal decree (Madkūr 1964; 1978: 7) and included in its name a reference to the Egyptian monarchy until 1954 (see note 4). Appointment of its members was influenced by political disagreements among the king, the parliament and opposition groups (al-Ḥamzāwī 1988: 58–63). The proportion of non-Egyptian members might serve as a barometer showing how the Academy swayed between territorial and pan-Arab orientations. Half the total members were non-Egyptian in the 1930s; this figure dwindled to one-third in the 1940s, due partly to the travelling difficulties caused by World War II and partly to the popularisation of 'supra-Egyptian nationalism'[7] that entailed expansive representation of Egypt's various professional and intellectual strata among members of the Academy. The proportion rose again slightly in the 1950s to match, most probably, the pan-Arab agenda of the Egyptian regime led by Gamal Abdel Nasser (d. 1970).[8]

Syria and Egypt were ahead with regard to establishing ALAs. The original names of the two ALAs there – the Arab Academy and the Arabic Language Academy – clearly indicated that they were meant to represent the whole Arabic-speaking world. This discouraged other Arab states from creating their own ALAs. After all, the Arabic-speaking world ideally needed one unified ALA rather than several territorial ALAs. This situation changed in the late 1940s, and was foreshadowed by the foundation of the League of Arab States in 1945. As a loose confederation of Arab states rather than a reification of the expected political unification of the Arabs, its foundation indicated the acknowledgement of the multi-state system in the Arabic-speaking world. In line with this political development, more territorial ALAs began to appear. In 1947, the Iraqi Academy (*al-Majma' al-'Ilmī al-'Irāqī*) was founded (al-Rāwī 2002: 7; Maṭlūb 2008: 6). Including in its name a reference to its host state – which was not the case with the ALAs in Damascus and Cairo – the Iraqi

Academy identified itself openly with the orientations and interests of the Iraqi state.

The three ALAs in Syria, Egypt and Iraq began to seek collaboration with each other from the 1950s onwards. In 1956, the Arab League organised the first conference of ALAs in Damascus, which ended with a proposal to establish a union (*ittiḥād*) of territorial ALAs to coordinate their work (Chejne 1969: 122; Ḍayf 1984: 17; al-Rāwī 2002: 9). This initiative was temporarily abandoned after the merger of the Cairo and Damascus Academies into *Majmaʿ al-Lugha al-ʿArabiyya* 'the Arabic Language Academy' in 1960 as a result of the unification of Egypt and Syria in 1958 (al-Rāwī 2002: 9). The two ALAs became two branches of this unified Academy, renamed as the Arabic Language Academy in Cairo (*Majmaʿ al-Lugha al-ʿArabiyya bi-l-Qāhira*) and the Arabic Language Academy in Damascus (*Majmaʿ al-Lugha al-ʿArabiyya bi Dimashq*) respectively. With this institutional merger, the ideal of the unified ALA seemed realised and thus no union of ALAs was needed. However, this unified ALA soon broke up when the political unification of Egypt and Syria ended in 1961. The Cairo and Damascus Academies became once again independent from each other, but they retained their new names as though symbolically they were still branches of the same ALA.

With the failure of the unified ALA, the idea of the union of territorial ALAs regained its momentum (Chejne 1969: 123–4). In this regard, the Arab League made another attempt to coordinate the work of ALAs and similar language-related work carried out in Arab states. In 1961, the League organised the First Arabi(ci)sation Conference (*al-Muʾtamar al-Awwal li-l-Taʿrīb*) in Rabat (ʾAfsaḥī 1990: 194; ʾAḥmad 1999: 207), acknowledging the importance of North African Arab countries to the Arabi(ci)sation campaign commonly pursued across the Arabic-speaking world. This Conference called for establishing an Arabi(ci)sation committee[9] in every member state of the Arab League and creating, in Rabat, the Permanent Bureau for the Coordination of Arabisation in the Arab World to coordinate the work of these committees and the ALAs (Khalīfa 1987: 88; ʾAḥmad 1999: 207). The Bureau was formed in 1961 under the patronage of the late King Muhammad V (d. 1961) of Morocco but was collectively funded by a number of Arab states (ʾAfsaḥī 1990: 194). It was officially attached to the Arab League in 1969 and then to the Arab League Educational, Cultural and Scientific Organization (ALECSO) in 1972 (ʾAḥmad 1999: 204). The creation of the Bureau marked the consolidation of the multi-ALA system in the Arabic-speaking world. This system was further confirmed by the foundation of the Union of Arabic Language and Science Academies (*Ittiḥād al-Majāmiʿ al-Lughawiyya al-ʿIlimiyya al-ʿArabiyya*) in Cairo in 1971 (Ḍayf 1984: 17; al-Rāwī 2002: 9).[10] This Union was dominated by the Cairo Academy. The consolidation of the multi-ALA system led to a growth of territorial ALAs from the 1970s onwards. Jordan, Tunisia, Algeria, Sudan, Libya, Palestine and Israel established their own ALAs in various forms. Most of these ALAs incorporated in their names a reference to their host states. The single, unified ALA now seemed like a distant dream.

Arabic Language Academies, Territoriality and Sovereignty

The multiple ALAs founded in line with the demarcation of states in the Arabic-speaking world show a close congruity between ALAs and territorial states. This indicates that, in the states previously mentioned, the ALA seems to be an indispensable constituent of state infrastructure and a representation of state sovereignty over language use. Indeed, as will be shown below, the formation of the institution of the ALA is tied to the penetration of the 'state' as a central, regulative ideology into society – another effect of the rise of modern states in the Arabic-speaking world, in addition to the duality of pan-Arab and territorial nationalisms discussed before.

It should be noted that the 'state' is understood here as more than a bounded institutional ensemble acquiring and maintaining its inviolable territoriality and sovereignty through mechanisms of violence, coercion and regulation. The 'state' is also more than what Sharma and Gupta (2006: 5) call 'a cultural artefact' that is 'culturally embedded and discursively constructed, [i.e.] produced through everyday practices and encounters and through public cultural representations and performances' (ibid.: 27). These institutional, performative and discursive 'artefacts' are all manifestations of the 'state' rather than the 'state' per se, which is, essentially, an ideological reality deeply rooted in our minds, rationalising and regulating the organisation and (self-)identification of political subjects and communities along the lines of territoriality and sovereignty. This ideological reality manifests itself in various 'artefacts', mentioned above, but is also shaped, reinforced and reproduced through the making of these 'artefacts'. The rise of modern Arab states is an institutional manifestation of the coming and penetration of this ideological reality into the minds of the Arabs. This reality is so deeply rooted that it is often unfelt, especially when state-oriented nationalism retreats from overt articulation (see the discussion of banal nationalism later in this chapter). It is so overwhelming that it signposts and regulates almost every aspect of the modern Arab social life. Even though the institutions of Arab states may be weak and their overarching role in Arab society may be overstated (Ayubi 1995), the 'state' as an ideological reality is not.

In line with the above, ALAs can be seen as manifestations of the 'state' in the spheres of language and culture in Arab society, for the following reasons. First of all, ALAs act as brokers of language attitudes and language ideologies of different interest groups in Arab society. To explain this role of ALAs, let us start with Blommaert (1999: 9) who understands language ideology brokers as those who can 'claim authority in the field of debate [and contestation]' over the conception of language-society relations. According to this understanding, ALAs are no doubt language ideology brokers because they have already been revered as language authorities in the Arabic-speaking world. But this is only the tip of the iceberg. Digging deeper, we find out that the authoritative status of ALAs is determined by their three features of 'in-betweenness'. First, ALAs stand in the middle of a variety of intellectual perspectives on Arabic and its role in society because each ALA in its work brings together intellectuals from different parts of the Arabic-speaking world and from various religious and professional backgrounds as either academicians or advisors on specific language issues. Second, ALAs are capable of influencing language views of both the (ruling, literary, etc.) elites and the common people, because, as state-sponsored institutions, they act as 'middlemen', mediating between state and society. Third, ALAs posit themselves between the past and present and between tradition and modernity. ALAs as a social-cum-linguistic phenomenon have been a feature of the modern transition of the Arabic-speaking world from the late nineteenth century until now. The various sociopolitical changes (such as colonisation, decolonisation, nation-building, the rise and fall of regimes, wars and so on) during this transition have left marks on ALAs and their language ideologies, posing a challenge to ALAs of creating a coherent historical narrative for themselves, including considering themselves as both heirs to the Arab-Islamic intellectual tradition *vis-à-vis* the Arabic language and trendsetters in moulding this tradition to the demands of modernity. The above three features of 'in-betweenness' indicate that how Arabic is conceptualised in the ALA discourse is very likely a negotiated compromise of different nationalist, social, political and intellectual interests and historical contingencies that are projected onto this language. Indeed, this negotiation, as will be shown in the following chapters, is conducted by ALAs, who attempt to 'broker' a common ground that is (1) historically coherent and (2) ideologically acceptable to as many interest groups as possible. It is this act of negotiating and 'brokering' rather than the claim to authority that makes ALAs language ideology brokers. The authoritative status of ALAs is an auxiliary (or possibly a product) of rather than the determinant of their 'brokering' role.

This 'brokering' role is institutionalised by the territoriality and sovereignty inherent in the 'state'. Institutionalisation lies in the fact that ALAs follow a patterned framework that absorbs, negotiates and filters different language ideologies via granting membership, recruiting advisors, organising conferences and festivals, arranging publications and issuing rulings. The territoriality behind this institutionalisation is revealed through the following: (1) ALAs allocate their membership along citizenship lines, making sure that citizens of their host countries occupy the majority of the 'working members', while awarding membership of 'correspondents' to citizens of other Arab and non-Arab countries;[11] and (2) ALAs are based in the capitals of their host countries[12] and hold their seminars and conferences therein. Such arrangements guarantee that the results of ideological brokering by an ALA always lean towards the communal interest of its host territorial state.

If territoriality affects the role of ALAs horizontally along state boundaries in the Arabic-speaking world, sovereignty shapes this role vertically among interest groups in individual state-communities. By embracing language attitudes and ideologies (whether they are mutually supportive or antagonistic) in a state-community, and the contestation and negotiation in a single institutional framework authorised by the state, an ALA serves a function similar to that of parliament, where state-wide concerns are debated among representatives of interest groups and common ground is sought. Although in practice the ALA barely has any legislative power, as a parliament does, symbolically both are apparatuses and representations of state sovereignty over the control and regulation of the state community, albeit in different spheres.

Below I will discuss two enduring tensions in ALAs to show that ideological conflicts and contestations are commonplace therein. The fact that ALAs have managed to contain and sustain these conflicts and contestations demonstrates the backing of state sovereignty.

The rise of ALAs indicates a change and reshuffle of the components of the intellectual authority concerning language and knowledge in the Arabic-speaking world. In the past, it was the religious *ʿulamāʾ* who monopolised the interpretation and transmission of knowledge. From the mid-nineteenth century onwards, Arab intellectuals acquainted with modern European rational science and social institutions and imbued with passion for reforming the Arab-Islamic tradition began to challenge the monopoly of the traditional *ʿulamāʾ*. This reshuffle of authority is revealed in the tension between traditionalists and modernists on the one hand, and that between literati and scientists on the other, among members of ALAs.

With respect to the first tension, the change in the composition of the membership of the Cairo Academy serves as an example. When appointing the founding members of the Cairo Academy in 1932, the Egyptian government made a balanced combination of both religious scholars from *al-ʾAzhar* and modernists educated in the West (al-Ḥamzāwī 1988: 58–63). By making this balanced choice, the government was cautious not to weaken the representation of either camp in this newly formed language authority. In doing so, the Egyptian government in fact institutionalised the tension between traditionalists and modernists. The membership of the Cairo Academy was increased in 1940, with many renowned modernists such as Luṭfī al-Sayyid and Ṭāhā Ḥusayn becoming members of the Academy. This aggravated the tension between the two camps within the Academy. The traditionalist and modernists often took opposite positions in linguistic discussions concerning, for example, expanding Arabic morphology, accepting colloquial expressions and foreign neologisms, and defining the source and structure of modern Arabic dictionaries. These linguistic disputes marked a deep difference between the two camps regarding the duties of the Cairo Academy. The traditionalists wanted the Academy to be the guardian of the Arabic language and its linguistic tradition, while the modernists wanted the Academy to supervise the reform and modernisation of Arabic to meet modern communicative needs.

With respect to the tension between literati and scientists within ALAs, it is necessary to start with the different choices of naming among ALAs. There are two nomenclatural systems used by ALAs. The first is *al-majmaʿ al-ʿilmī*, literally 'the science academy'. However, *ʿilm* is not the equivalent of 'science' here. In traditional use, *ʿilm* simply means knowledge, including both religious scholarship and applied sciences. According to ʿAlī (1959: 318), *al-majmaʿ al-ʿilmī* is merely an imperfect translation of 'academy'; it does not refer to an academy specialising in scientific research. In fact, the focus of *al-majmaʿ al-ʿilmī* is the Arabic language as a medium of expressing and transmitting all sorts of knowledge. The other nomenclatural system uses *majmaʿ al-lugha*, literally 'the language academy'. This term specifies that the target of ALAs is language.

It is clear that ALAs adopting different nomenclatural systems do not differ in their specialities. Why, then, do they use different names? The answer lies in the relationship between language and knowledge (*ʿilm*) in the Arab-Islamic tradition, in which language served as a foundation for almost all religious and applied sciences (Carter 2007: 183). Sufficient knowledge of Arabic grammar, for example, was a necessary requirement for any scholar regardless of his or her area of speciality. This foundational role of language continued into the modern era, when modern sciences were introduced from Europe. These modern sciences posed a challenge to Arab intellectuals in terms of new knowledge of both the physical and social worlds, and of rational, positivist methodologies of research.

However, for many Arab intellectuals, this challenge was not perceived as relating to knowledge and methodology, but to language. In their view, modernising the Arabic language is the primary way to tackle the challenge of modernising knowledge; as long as Arabic can be used to express modern scientific ideas, Arabs can easily acquire modern sciences to pursue the revival of the Arab nation and make original contributions to the progress of science and technology (e.g. Khalīfa 1987: 39–40). Here, Arabic was used as a proxy to alleviate a deep crisis of knowledge. In this regard, *al-majmaʿ al-ʿilmī* and *majmaʿ al-lugha* are the same. What makes them different in their nomenclature choices is that the former points to the final target of their work – knowledge – while the latter accentuates the proxy/medium of their work – language. Perceiving the language-knowledge relationship in this manner reveals that, in the Arabic-speaking world, the introduction of new knowledge needs to be grounded in tradition.

However, not all members of ALAs perceived the language-knowledge relationship in the traditional way. Some Western-educated scientists insisted that the modern sciences should be studied on their own terms and not be tailored to match the established linguistic principles and conventions of Arabic. This belief led them to be in conflict with members of the literati, who believed in the foundational role of Arabic in all disciplines.[13] This conflict was another reflection of the tension between tradition and modernity within ALAs.

Two examples suffice here to illustrate the conflict between the literati and the scientists. The first concerns the choice between *ishtiqāq* 'word-making via derivation from Arabic roots' and *taʿrīb* 'word-making via transliteration of foreign words' as the primary method of lexical coinage in sciences. In this regard, the majority of the literati members of ALAs insisted on using *ishtiqāq* rather than *taʿrīb* to ensure the expression of modern scientific concepts and ideas in correct Arabic. In order to ensure *ishtiqāq* was able to meet the growing needs of coinage in the sciences, they discussed and authorised the expansion of existing derivational patterns of Arabic morphology. By contrast, scientists in their actual language practice preferred *taʿrīb* to create neologisms consistent with the original scientific terminologies in European languages. Those members of ALAs who were scientists themselves or sympathetic to the language habits of the scientists called for permitting the use of *taʿrīb*. In response, the Cairo Academy issued a ruling in 1934 permitting the use of *taʿrīb* under certain conditions, that is, as a last resort (MJMJ 1: 309, 348; MMQ 1: 33). This was a brokered compromise between the literati who tended to reject linguistic innovations deviating from the established grammatical principles of Arabic and the scientists who wanted to break the unnecessary 'linguistic shackles' placed on the development of scientific vocabulary in Arabic. Nonetheless, the issue of permitting *taʿrīb* has remained controversial throughout the history of ALAs, reflecting a prolonged tension between the literati and the scientists.

The second example concerns recruiting 'experts' to work for ALAs. 'Experts' are specialists in different disciplines, who are the actual users of Arabic in their own fields of speciality. ALAs increasingly rely on these experts to help with lexical coinage in their fields. Introducing the 'expert' system is an organic development of ALAs, because ALA members cannot cope with the vast demands for new vocabularies in an increasingly differentiated academic world. These experts are not members of ALAs, but their participation alters the balance between the literati and the scientists in ALAs. Like the scientists, the experts tend to put the demands of their own fields over the need to maintain the integrity of the traditional linguistic system of Arabic. This tendency aggravates the existing tension between the literati and the scientists in ALAs.

Arabic Language Academies, Coloniality and Peripherality

The rise of modern Arab states is certainly not the only enduring circumstance that shapes the institution of ALAs. The peripheralisation of Arabs that perpetuates the feeling of coloniality in Arab society is another. This is evident in the narrative of the origins of ALAs. In this narrative, the concept of ALA became a proxy through which these members responded to the peripheral position of Arabs in the modern world-system.

On narrating the origins of ALAs, members treated the connection between their academies and the Académie française in ambiguous ways. ALAs were more or less modelled on the Académie française. This was attractive to Arab statespeople because it offered a path for cultivating a state-sponsored intellectual authority, for constructing a national language and for formulating a unified, patriotic national public. It was attractive to Arab intellectuals because it provided an example for (1) adapting a national language to the communicative and educational needs of the modern age while protecting the integrity and purity of this language from colloquial and foreign encroachment, and (2) achieving an intellectual consensus institutionally among individuals or schools of thought concerning the use and development of Arabic in modern Arab society. The merits of the French model were first revealed to the Arabs when Napoleon Bonaparte established the Institut d'Égypte in Alexandria to study the history, culture and society of Egypt during his Egyptian Campaign

(1798–1801) (al-Ḥamzāwī 1988: 36–7). The first two ALAs in Damascus and Cairo emulated the Académie française in many respects, such as its organisation, its definition of academicianship and its orientations, missions and methodologies. When reflecting on the history of ALAs, their members often referred to the Académie française as their predecessor and model; the international reputation of the Académie française became a source of legitimation for their own language academies.

However, adopting the French model was disputed in the context of European colonialism and imperialism in the Arabic-speaking world. Consequently, any ALA should also justify itself by claiming to continue the work of its 'predecessors' within the Arab intellectual tradition. Only in that way can the ALA avoid being an alien body or colonial imposition and become an authentic institution developed by and for Arabs. In two early narratives of the Cairo Academy, Fahmī (1934) and al-Maghribī (1935b) locate this Academy in a historical and global continuum of (language) academies, from the Platonic Academy in Ancient Greece to the learning institutions in Medieval Europe and the Orient, especially the Arab-Islamic world. In this narrative, the learning circle patronised by the Umayyad Prince Khālid ibn Yazīd al-ʾUmawī (d. 85/704 or 90/709), the *Bayt al-Ḥikma* 'House of Wisdom' established by the Abbasid Caliph al-Maʾmūn (d. 218/833) and the Kūfan and Baṣran Schools of Arabic grammar all became the Arab-Islamic predecessors of language academies. The idea behind these narratives was to claim that both Europeans and Arabs contributed to the development of the language academy as a type of intellectual institution now spreading across the world. This continuum of academies was adjusted in favour of the Arab side from the mid-twentieth century onwards, driven by the increasing need for independent Arab states to justify themselves in nationalist and anti-colonialist terms. Fahmī (1962 [1957]) claimed that ALAs should first and foremost respond to the vital needs of Arab society of the time, defined as 'overall development and progress', 'liberal nationalism' and 'linguistic vitality'. Madkūr (1967) followed Fahmī by seeing the French model as unfit for the mission and responsibility of the Cairo Academy. He argued that, as a language academy of the twentieth century, the Cairo Academy should be more innovative and perform broader functions to serve the interests of Arabs than those stipulated by the Académie française, which was a product of the seventeenth century. In the late twentieth century, when Arab intellectuals were still anxious about the cultural imperialism of the West, they further emphasised the contributions of the Arabs and Muslims to the global development of language academies. For example, Khalīfa (1987: 48) proposed that the emergence of academies in Renaissance

Europe was inspired by the academy-like institutions that thrived in the past in Abbasid Baghdad, Muslim Spain, Sicily and North Africa.

Apart from the ambivalent attitude towards the Académie française, the self-narrative of ALAs often highlighted their role in the persistence and revival of the Arab nation under colonial and imperial threats. ALAs were perceived as strongholds (*maʿāqil*) that defended the Arabic language and nation, and their members as battalions serving the interests of this language and nation. In line with such perceptions, even the choice of the exact locations of the ALAs became meaningful. On explaining why the Damascus Academy, when it was founded, chose the *ʿĀdiliyya* Madrasa to be its location, al-Mubārak (2009: 1167–8) provides three theories. First, the *ʿĀdiliyya* Madrasa is one of the biggest madrasas in Damascus and used to be the gathering place for religious scholars and the residence of the Grand Judges. Second, this madrasa is inside the *Barīd* 'post' Gate of old Damascus, which in the past was the place where official correspondence was sent and received. The first two theories show that the Damascus Academy is treated in al-Mubārak's narrative as a continuation of the old Damascene intellectual and bureaucratic tradition, and is thus a symbol of national sovereignty. Third, al-Mubārak reports the *ʿĀdiliyya* Madrasa is surrounded by the tombs of Ṣalaḥ al-Ḍīn al-ʾAyyūbī (d. 1193) and Nūr al-Dīn Maḥmūd Zankī (d. 1174), two great Muslim leaders who defeated the Crusades, and al-Ẓāhir Baybars (d. 1277), who won a victory against the Mongol army. In al-Mubārak's view, these tombs symbolically make the Damascus Academy a defender and guardian of the Arabic language and the Arab nation against foreign invasions in various forms.

The above narratives of the origins of ALAs reflect how the institution of ALAs was legitimised in a social environment where psychological decolonisation was ongoing.

In sum, focusing on the diffusion of ALAs, the pan-Arab perspective shows that the ALA phenomenon bifurcates into two realms. Both are of a pan-Arab relevance. One is linguistic: a long-lasting concern over Arabic entailed the formation and routinisation of a role that ALAs take on to improve the state of the language. The other is sociopolitical: the institution of ALAs is shaped and continuously reinforced by the prevalence of the modern state, the duality of pan-Arab and territorial-state nationalisms and the peripheralisation of the Arabs in the modern world-system – those *longue durée* sociopolitical circumstances in the Arabic-speaking world. The cause for the diffusion of ALAs is traceable to both realms, indicating some connection between the two.

A most obvious connector is the role of ALAs. The role is routinised. Role theorists differ on the reason for role routinisation. Structuralists see roles as pre-existing and shaping individual behaviour, while interactionalists argue that roles are routinised in repetitive interactions of people (Franks 2007; Hindin 2007). In line with both views, the role of ALAs can be seen as pre-defined by their language-oriented duties and reinforced in the efforts ALAs continuously make to fulfil these duties. This explanation confines the cause for the routinisation of the role of ALAs in the linguistic realm.

Yet there is also a sociopolitical explanation: the role has gone through a process of institutionalisation with ALAs as its bearers in line with those enduring sociopolitical circumstances that demarcate the contour and orientation of the institution of ALAs. Role theory focuses on roles taken by individuals and pays little heed to institutional roles. It explains the dynamism between roles and individuals, no matter whether the roles are pre-existing or emerging in interaction. The theory does discuss collective role, but this notion does not mean that the role itself is collective, rather that it is assumed or made by a group of individuals. Institutional roles like the role of ALAs are different. It is assumed by the institution of ALAs as a whole and is in accordance with the ideological orientation of this institution. At the platform of ALAs, individual academicians have to tailor their stances to the ideological consensus brokered by ALAs, as the discussion of ALAs as ideological brokers shows.

This dual explanation for the routinisation of the role of ALAs indicates a conformity between the linguistic and the sociopolitical dimensions of the ALA phenomenon. Yet the connection between the two is more than conformity, as will be shown in the following perspectives.

The Arabic Language Academy Phenomenon Is a Form of Language Planning and Language Policy

Our second perspective is that the ALA phenomenon is an instance of language planning and language policy (LPLP). Language planning refers to 'efforts to deliberately affect the status, structure, or acquisition of languages' (Tollefson 2011: 357). Language policy refers to 'guidelines or rules for language structure, use, and acquisition' established and implemented in language communities (ibid.: 357). Together, LPLP involves how language policies are embedded in actual language practice, articulated in language ideology and modified and evaluated in language planning (Spolsky 2004: 5; 2012: 5).[14] LPLP occurs at different levels of language communities, ranging from families to institutions, to states, to international organisations, and in various domains of social communication (Neustupný and Nekvapil 2003; Spolsky 2009). The pattern of LPLP also varies, involving both conscious planning and implementation of new language policies and unconscious compliance with existing language policies (Spolsky 2004).

The ALA phenomenon belongs to conscious language planning and language policy-making at or above the state level, understood as 'classical language planning' (CLP) in LPLP literature (Jernudd and Nekvapil 2012: 22). The central premise of CLP is that 'language planning takes place at the level of the nation-state and the plans project onto the development of the entire society' (ibid.: 26). A frequently mentioned prototype of CLP is the work of the Académie française, founded in 1635 by Cardinal de Richelieu (d. 1642) to 'strengthen the unity and order of the French state through bringing about the unity and order of the language' (ibid.: 18; see also Cooper 1989: 3–11). The work of the Académie française shows how language planning can contribute to nation-building and state-formation.

Accordingly, CLP was widely performed in newly independent nation-states in Europe in the nineteenth and early twentieth centuries (Wright 2004; 2012). CLP intensified between the 1950s and 1970s, when post-colonial nation-states in Asia and Africa demanded unified, modern and nationwide (but not necessarily national) languages to support political, economic and social development.

Why does CLP co-occur with nation-building and state-formation of newly independent nation-states? It is because CLP is always connected with the immediate sociopolitical demands of these nation-states. Fishman (1968: 493–4) identifies two of these demands: national integration and technology-based modernisation. Fulfilling them entails 'ethnic authenticity' and 'modern [communicative] efficiency' (ibid.: 494). Both rely on the languages used nationwide. If these languages are rooted in existing language and linguistic traditions and are qualified enough for modern communication, authenticity and efficiency will be easily achieved. If not, mismatches between language and national demands will appear, making existing nationwide languages problematic. In this situation, language planning will intervene to solve these language problems. In doing so, its ultimate goal is always sociopolitical.

The above description of CLP fits the ALA phenomenon well. Early experiments of ALAs occurred in Egypt in the late nineteenth century because its rulers, Muḥammad ʿAlī (d. 1849) and his heirs, had been reconstructing Egypt since the early nineteenth century towards a modern polity and society modelled on European nation-states. Similarly, throughout the twentieth century, the foundation and development of ALAs were often accompanied by nation-building and state-formation in the Arabic-speaking world. Below are some examples taken from my introduction to the history of ALAs before, which are in need of repeating here to illustrate the state-academy link in Arabic LPLP. The Damascus Academy was founded in 1919 after Fayṣal ibn Ḥusayn (d. 1933) established the first modern Arab government in Syria. The Cairo Academy was founded in 1932 along with a rapid bureaucratic and institutional development of the Egyptian state under the aegis of King Fu'ād of Egypt (d. 1936).[15] The Palestinian Academy was announced in 1994 (ʿAmrū 1999: 186) when the Palestinian National Authority was officially formed.

As I have mentioned earlier, ALAs were founded to respond to three language situations: diglossia, foreign language influence and the archaic complexity of *fuṣḥā*. In the framework of CLP, these situations can be seen as language problems, which are believed to be detrimental to the interests of newly established Arab states. Diglossia impedes national integration, the influence of foreign languages weakens ethnic authenticity and archaic complexity hinders communicative efficiency. Solving these three language problems was vital for the consolidation of the Arab states.

The ALA phenomenon conforms to CLP in terms of the link between nationwide language problem-solving and nation-building. However, this phenomenon also differs from CLP in that it remained active even after the heyday of nation-building and state-formation in the Arabic-speaking worlds had passed. The ALA phenomenon seems to have become a routinised, long-lasting practice of language planning.[16]

Such routinised language planning has recently become the focus of LPLP studies. It is argued that language planning is not only identified with nation-building and state-formation in newly established nation-states, but is also attested in all language communities, all domains of communication and different episodes of sociopolitical change. Similarly, ethnic authenticity and communicative efficiency are not the only goals of language planning; more covert goals are also included. In this regard, Cooper (1989: 182) states that:

> language planning is such a complex activity, influenced by numerous factors – economic, ideological, political, etc. – and not only because it is directed toward so many different status, corpus, and acquisition goals, but more fundamentally because it is a tool in the service of so many different latent goals such as economic modernization, national integration, national liberation, imperial hegemony, racial, sexual, and economic equality, the maintenance of elites, and their replacement by new elites. That language planning should serve so many covert goals is not surprising. Language is the fundamental institution of society, not only because it is the first institution experienced by the individual but also because all other institutions are built upon its regulatory patterns. To plan language is to plan society.

More importantly, language planning also tends to be routinised because it is 'a result of complex historical and structural forces that shape the social system within which individuals must act' (Tollefson 2011: 367). In line with this understanding, language planning is produced by 'the social system' and is subject to constant reproduction as long as this system remains stable.

How can the above viewpoints help explain the routinisation of the ALA phenomenon? One answer to this question is that the sociopolitical causes behind this phenomenon are diverse. Nation-building and state-formation is just one among the many causes that demand the ALA phenomenon as a response.[17] Others, like wars and conflicts, may also cause mismatches between language and social demands, thus necessitating language planning as a remedy. However, these sociopolitical causes are often temporary or country-specific; they are not convincing enough to explain the routinisation of ALAs as a pan-Arab phenomenon. This routinisation is more likely caused by the duality of pan-Arab and territorial-state nationalisms (sustained by the consolidation of the multi-state system) and the peripheralisation of the Arabs in the modern world-system – the two above-mentioned sociopolitical circumstances enduring in the Arabic-speaking world. They perpetuate, in often hidden and unnoticed ways, the perception of diglossia, foreign language influence and archaic complexity as language problems. As long as these language problems endure, the ALA phenomenon as a response and remedy will persist.

The perspective of LPLP establishes a causality from the linguistic to the sociopolitical. This causality is direct, unmediated and to some extent mechanical. LPLP is seen as instrumental in attaining the various extra-linguistic goals, both overt and latent. These goals entail a specific language situation as a necessity. Mismatch between this and the real language situations is regarded as a problem. LPLP is thus required to solve

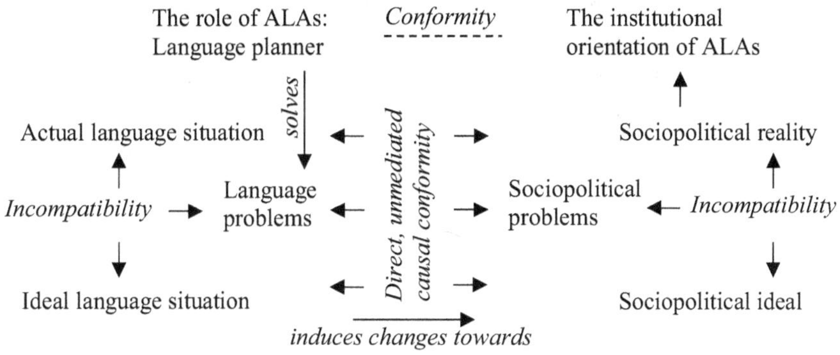

Figure 2.1 Causality of LPLP: language is instrumental in inducing sociopolitical change

this problem. It follows that LPLP can induce anticipated sociopolitical change. Indeed, 'to plan language is to plan society'.

The causality of LPLP offers an explanation for the connection between the linguistic and sociopolitical dimensions of the ALA phenomenon beyond mere conformity. The connection is a casual one. The three language situations – diglossia, foreign language influence and the archaic complexity of *fuṣḥā* – are incompatible with the linguistic ideal: a strong national standard of Arabic, devoid of diglossia and foreignness and used in all domains of public communication. This linguistic ideal is set to accord with the sociopolitical ideal – an empowered, unified Arab nation able to catch up with modernity and stand on a par with the West in the modern world-system. Incompatibility with this language ideal is seen as problematic, and attaining this ideal is believed to bring about the desired sociopolitical scenario. Accordingly, the role that ALAs assumes is as a language planner and language problem solver. When language problems endure, the role of ALAs becomes routine.

Yet the above explanation is still not satisfactory, and the causality of LPLP raises new questions. Since the language situation was problematised against the language and sociopolitical ideals, how were the ideals set in the first place? Does this problematisation go in certain directions rather than others? If so, why? Do language problems truly impede progress towards the sociopolitical ideal, and does solving these problems actually induce desired sociopolitical change? Two further perspectives that accentuate the symbolic and discursive sides of the ALA phenomenon are called on to answer these questions.

The Arabic Language Academy Phenomenon Is Symbolic

Our third perspective is that the ALA phenomenon is more symbolic than instrumental. These are the two roles language planning plays in promoting social change. The unmediated causality tells us that language planning is instrumental because it seeks to modify the status and structure of language as an instrument of communication to serve various sociopolitical causes, such as national integration and societal modernisation. Yet language planning is also symbolic, because it constructs indexical parallelism between language as 'the fundamental institution of society' (Cooper 1989: 182) and other social institutions to make the former stand for the latter (indexication) and uses language as a proxy to address sociopolitical concerns and attain extra-linguistic goals (proxification).

Symbolism is so evident in language planning that even the instrumental side of planning is often symbolic. It is generally accepted that there are two basic types of language planning: corpus planning, referring to 'efforts to affect the structure of language'; and status planning, referring to 'efforts to affect the social position of language varieties' (Tollefson 2011: 359; see also Kloss 1968; Cooper 1989). Commenting on corpus planning, Suleiman suggests that 'the instrumentality of language is most directly relevant to corpus-planning, wherein the prime concern is providing the language with the resources that it needs to discharge its communicative role in society'; however, 'with time, some corpus-planning resources start to assume ideological meanings (at least more than others), making them subject to contestation in cultural politics' (2013a: 15). Status planning, by contrast, tends to be symbolic because 'the choice of a language for communication carries with its narratives of group identity that are historically, culturally and politically significant' (ibid.: 15).

With regard to the ALA phenomenon, its instrumental side is relatively weak, in that it fails to change the corpus and status of Arabic according to the plans it proposes.[18] ALAs have coined large numbers of neologisms and scientific terminologies and compiled hundreds of terminological glossaries and dictionaries. These coinages often suffer from internal disparities among ALAs and indifference from Arabic users. ALAs aim to compile historical and modern dictionaries to reflect diachronic developments and current uses of the Arabic lexicon respectively; however, so far only *al-Muʿjam al-wasīṭ* 'the intermediate dictionary' and *al-Muʿjam al-wajīz* 'the concise dictionary' have been published by the Cairo Academy,[19] and they are faced with competition from other modern Arabic dictionaries, especially the *al-Mawrid* and *al-Munjid* series. ALAs sporadically discuss reforms of the Arabic script and orthography and Arabic pedagogic grammar and rhetoric in order to make the acquisition of Arabic reading and writing skills easier; however, no plans in this regard have been successfully implemented. ALAs also consistently criticise the deteriorating standard of *fuṣḥā* Arabic in media and education, but they lack the clout to improve the de facto situation of *fuṣḥā* in Arab society. Compared with the radical reform of Turkish in Turkey, the revival of Hebrew in Israel and the modernisation of Japanese, Chinese and Korean in East Asia, ALAs have been remarkably less successful in reshaping Arabic according to their design.

By contrast, the symbolic side of the ALA phenomenon is strong. This is revealed in two types of activities ALAs persevere with: intellectual discussions and public engagement. ALAs organise regular seminars, meetings and conferences of leading Arab linguists and scientists to identify and tackle the problems of the Arabic language. In doing so, ALAs construct a set of representations of Arabic in modern Arab society,

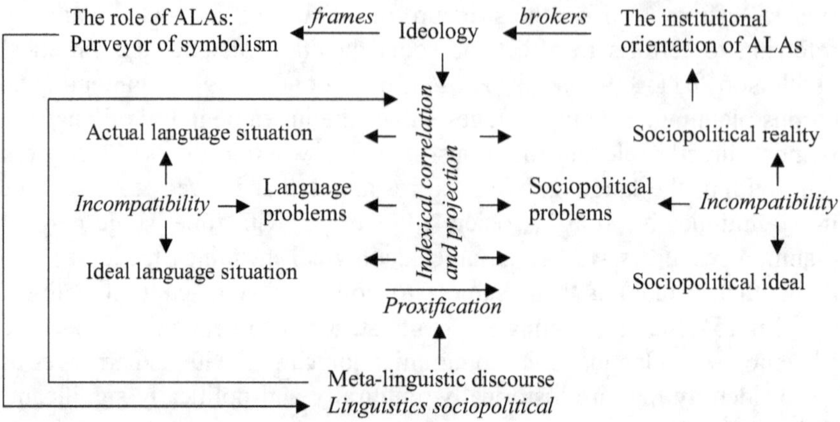

Figure 2.2 Language symbolism: language is symbolic in projecting and alleviating sociopolitical concerns

often emphasising continuity of the principles of language use with the Arabic linguistic tradition and the vitality of Arabic in changing social circumstances. These representations are then disseminated to the public via the linguistic rulings the ALAs issue, the public lectures, cultural ceremonies and literary awards they host and the journals and books they publish. These representations reflect the ideological positions of ALAs on the relationship between Arabic and Arab society, and are used by ALAs as proxies to sustain, improve, or transform extant sociopolitical circumstances and to advocate their visions for the Arab future and the place of Arabic in it.

ALAs, therefore, are more purveyors of language symbolism than language planners and language policy-makers. Their weakness in changing actual language use shows that they can neither realise nor prove direct causality from the linguistic to the sociopolitical. In the case of ALAs, the causality is largely mediated through ideology-driven language symbolism. The linguistic ideal is but an indexical projection of a remote sociopolitical ideal that is imagined to reverse unfavourable sociopolitical circumstances and to compensate for what cannot be changed in reality. Accordingly, the so-called language problems are but second-order projections of the disparity between the sociopolitical ideal and reality. The above projections are ideological, because they are the product of a specific ideological stance brokered by ALAs towards language and society. The projections will be different if they are allied with a different ideological stance. Some ardent supports of territorial nationalisms in Lebanon and Egypt, for example, do not problematise Arabic diglossia as lack of unity between *fuṣḥā* and *ʿāmmiyya* within Arabic but as the 'alien', 'Bedouin' *fuṣḥā* usurping the rights of the 'native' Lebanese and Egyptian languages (Lebanese *ʿāmmiyya* and Egyptian *ʿāmmiyya*) to be the true national language for the Lebanese and the Egyptians respectively. In line with this, they call for *fuṣḥā* to be replaced with *ʿāmmiyya*, rather than seeking integration between the two. Language problems, therefore, are not necessarily causal correlates of sociopolitical problems on a factual basis, and language problem-solving may not be able to correct socio-political wrongs. In cases of LPLP where the above causality proves to be mediated by symbolism and ideology, LPLP becomes no more than a gesture that uses language as a proxy to alleviate extra-linguistic concerns at the symbolic level.

The symbolic side of the ALA phenomenon is so manifest that it contributes to the routinisation of this phenomenon in the Arabic-speaking world. ALAs, due to their persistence in symbolic acts of construction, proxification and dissemination, have developed into an intellectual authority over Arabic and its role in modern Arab society. This is most evident in that, in the public sphere, ALAs are often called 'strongholds' (*maʿāqil*) of the Arabic language and culture, and their members are honoured as 'the immortals' (*al-khālidūn*).[20] Even though the public may not be aware of what ALAs do and who their members are, they are aware of the existence of these institutes as language authorities in the Arabic-speaking world and are familiar with, or able to surmise, their general positions on Arabic. For the public, ALAs are the source of linguistic and cultural security in a world where diglossic stratification, code-mixing, multilingualism and weakness in *fuṣḥā* tend to be the norm in language use and where peripherality and duality of nationalism tend to be routine in sociopolitical and cultural life. Accordingly, the ALAs are constantly needed even though they are not able to change the linguistic and socio-political reality instrumentally. The work of the ALAs is accepted as a regular and indispensable social practice in modern Arab society. In other words, the ALA phenomenon is routinised. It can be called 'banal language planning', a type of language planning that constantly produces and reproduces certain views about language and society in a routinised way that correspond to Billig's (1995) 'banal nationalism', referring to the unnoticed reproduction of nations and nationalisms in public spaces and mundane narratives.

The concept of banality further reveals the symbolism of the ALA phenomenon. The central tenet of 'banal nationalism', in the words of Billig, is that nationalism 'is not [just] a flag which is being consciously waved with fervent passion: it is the flag hanging unnoticed on the public building' (ibid.: 8). In other words, nationalism is not only associated with nationalist movements and nation-building, and disappearing when nation-states are firmly established. Instead, nationalism becomes banal; it penetrates into the mundane aspects of national life, into the everyday displays of the national existence in public and collective national unconsciousness. Banal nationalism does not need passionate propaganda or emotional expressions; it is sustained through a standard ensemble of national symbols. ALAs become national symbols in the above sense. It does not matter whether ALAs are instrumentally effective or not. Their mere existence symbolically marks the sovereignty of Arab states over language use and language conceptions in their state-communities and the legitimacy of Arabic as the national language in the Arabic-speaking world.[21]

The Arabic Language Academy Phenomenon Is Discursive

Language symbolism in the case of ALAs is mostly realised in words rather than deeds, so it is now necessary to bring up our final perspective: the ALA phenomenon is discursive. To understand this, we need to review briefly what discourse is, how it functions and how it relates to the ALA phenomenon. Discourse is 'a form of social practice' (Fairclough et al. 2011: 357) which exploits semiotic, meaning-making resources, such as 'words, pictures, symbols, design, colour, [and] gesture' (ibid.: 357), to constitute 'representations of the world, social relations between people, and people's social and personal identities' (ibid.: 370). The primary semiotic resource used in discourse is language. The above-mentioned symbolic activities of the ALAs – intellectual discussions and public engagement – are language/semiotic activities constructing particular representations of Arabic in society. It follows that the ALA phenomenon is discursive as well as symbolic. What makes the ALA discourse special is that it is a language discourse about language, making it a meta-linguistic discourse. Moreover, a large portion of the ALA discourse contributes to the ideologisation of language that stretches language into sociopolitical complexities, making the discourse a genre of linguistics sociopolitical.

Since discourse is a form of social practice, it naturally interacts with its sociopolitical context. On the one hand, discourse is shaped by context. On the other, discourse also sustains or transforms context. This sociopolitical context includes both synchronic and diachronic considerations. The former refers to the sociopolitical events co-occurring and the immediate sociopolitical situations co-existing with the discourse when it is produced, while the latter refers to the enduring sociopolitical circumstances, relations, structures and systems that accompany the production, reproduction and development of the discourse. Concerning the ALA discourse, it is framed by both immediate events and situations in modern Arab history and the enduring sociopolitical circumstances of the Arabic-speaking world. This discourse also aims to fulfil immediate sociopolitical demands and transform the enduring circumstances. However, the effect of the discourse is confined to the symbolic realm, having little impact on the sociopolitical reality. In fact, it often helps to maintain the status quo. The ALA discourse is, therefore, continuously needed to mediate the disparity between the ideal and the reality. This leads to the routinisation of this discourse, where the enduring circumstances exert a more profound influence.

This routinisation is evident in the repetition, reproduction and reiteration of similar statements on Arabic and its linguistic and social situations. These statements mainly concern the three language problems mentioned above (diglossia, foreign language influence and archaic complexity) and the means of tackling them (standard-dialect integration, Arabi(ci)sation and modernisation). The routinisation of the ALA discourse is further manifest in that these statements are constantly made in similar ways. The issue of diglossia and standard-dialect integration is often discussed within a tripartite framework that sees the Arabic language as an organism, a tool and a symbolic constituent of the Arabs' national identity (Chapter 3). Opinions on foreign language influence and Arabi(ci)sation are often articulated in line with inalienability between Arabic and Arab people on the one hand, and equilibrium in language contact on the other (Chapter 4). The issue of archaic complexity and language modernisation is often located in a dyad of endogenous and exogenous understandings of modernity (Chapter 5). These stable ways of discourse-making could be seen as a set of 'discursive habiti' in the ALA discourse.

As already mentioned in the Introduction, habitus was proposed by the French sociologist Pierre Bourdieu to explain the routinised reproduction of social practices (Jenkins 1992; Hanks 2005). Following Bourdieu, we can define 'discursive habitus' as socially embodied dispositions to habitually perform discursive acts in certain ways. This definition needs some clarification to show how discursive habitus functions vis-à-vis the routinisation of the ALA discourse. First, discursive habitus is both generative and restrictive: not only does it set in motion regular, habitual acts of discourse but it also determines the latitude of these acts. When performing these acts, discourse-makers are conscious of their language/semiotic performance but are not usually aware of the role of discursive habitus in their performance. Discursive habitus, therefore, is hegemonic in Gramsci's sense because it serves as a common-sense ideological system within which individuals consent to accept, reproduce and reiterate certain discourses without critical and conscious self-reflexivity.[22] In this way, discursive habitus, as explained in the introduction, becomes the reification of language ideologies.

Second, discursive habitus cannot be nonetheless equated to 'discursive formations' (Foucault 1972: 31–9; cf. Fairclough 1993: 40), i.e. rules of discourse-making, but to the inclinations of discourse-makers to consistently make certain (not other) statements in certain (not other) ways. This is because rules have a dehumanised side, making them external to discourse-makers,[23] while the concept of 'inclination' highlights their internal agency, which is a central element of discursive habitus, as will be explained in the next point.

Third, discursive habitus is centred on human agency, because this habitus embodies the role discourse-makers perform in their social field. In the case of the ALA discourse, the role refers to the rights and duties collectively and institutionally shared among members of the ALAs, and the field is Arabic language planning. How to behave like an ALA member is determined by the missions and orientations of Arabic language planning, and these missions and orientations are, in the long run, deeply embedded in the enduring sociopolitical circumstances of the twentieth-century Arabic-speaking world. On that account, embodying the role of ALAs is actually internalising the sociopolitical circumstances into discursive habitus (Jenkins 1992: 49).

Finally, the habitual performance of discursive acts tends to reinforce the discursive habitus, which in turn strengthens the role the habitus embodies and the sociopolitical circumstances it internalises. This cyclic connection among acts of discourse, discursive habitus, role and sociopolitical circumstances explains the routinisation of the ALA discourse and enriches our understanding of the relationship between this discourse and its wider sociopolitical context.

To sum up: although the ALA phenomenon in our common understanding is language-oriented, it is sociopolitical in nature. This phenomenon responds to immediate sociopolitical concerns involving the Arabic language; however, in the long run, it is perpetuated by the *longue durée* sociopolitical circumstances affecting the Arabic-speaking world as a whole. The latter is most evident in the routinisation and banalisation of ALAs not only as language planners but also as purveyors of language symbolism and brokers of language ideologies in Arab society. The banality of the symbolic, ideological side of the ALA phenomenon presents itself through the continual reproduction and reiteration of certain statements about the structure and state of Arabic in the ALA discourse. This reproduction and reiteration reflects the existence of a set of discursive habiti that is key to investigating the banality of the ALA phenomenon and its underlying ideological agendas and sociopolitical causes. I will begin this investigation in the next chapter.

Notes

1. I use the term 'phenomenon' here not because of its conceptual accuracy but because its openness allows me to show the multifaceted nature of ALAs and their work throughout the twentieth century. ALAs can be depicted as intellectual movements, institutions of language planning, linguistic-cultural authorities, ideology brokers and so on. The work of the ALAs can be understood as language planning, social planning, state-building, nation-building, institutionalisation and bureaucratisation of intellectuals, etc. If one term is needed to denote ALAs without sacrificing their multiple facets, it has to be one as broad as the term 'phenomenon' chosen here.
2. Some of these early ALAs in Egypt were: (1) *Majmaʿ al-Lugha al-ʿArabiyya* 'Arabic Language Academy' established in 1892 by Muḥammad Tawfīq al-Bakrī (d. 1933); (2) *Jamʿiyyat Tarqiyat al-Lugha al-ʿArabiyya* 'Association for the Promotion of Arabic' established in 1908 or shortly before; (3) *Nādī Dār al-ʿUlūm* 'Dār al-ʿUlūm Club' established in 1907/1908 by a group of Dār al-ʿUlūm graduates led by Ḥafnī Nāṣif (d. 1919); and (4) *al-Majmaʿ al-Lughawī al-ʾAwwal* 'First Arabic Language Academy' established in the Egyptian National Library (*Dār al-Kutub al-Miṣriyya*) in 1916/1917 by Luṭifī al-Sayyid (d. 1963) (Chejne 1969: 104; Ḍayf 1984: 19–20; al-Ḥamzāwī 1988: 36–41; Fāyid 2002: 91–2; Sawaie 2007: 634).
3. The Damascus Academy was originally called the Arab Academy (*al-Majmaʿ al-ʿIlmī al-ʿArabī*). It acquired its current name in 1960 following a short-lived merger with the Cairo Academy.
4. A related issue is why the ALA appeared so late in the Gulf. This is due to the following circumstances conducive to the rise of ALAs, which the Arab Gulf states are generally lacking: (1) the gradual consolidation of a new political order that reorganises all segments of society and all walks of social life based on the principle of sovereignty and territoriality and centred on the state as the ultimate, if not the only, authority; (2) an enlarging base of the literate middle class who have been at least partially educated in a modern-style, Europe-influenced education system in which the traditional, largely religious authority of knowledge has little say; (3) national experiences and moments that arouse nationalist awareness of a large segment of society, becoming a force for further nationalist mobilisation; (4) direct experience of colonialism and imperialism that manifest the hierarchical power relations in the world-system and justifies the struggle of the peripheral for the defence of its rights and authenticity against the domination of the powerful core on both political and cultural fronts. In the Arab Gulf states, the state form did not take shape, or the state apparatuses in the fashion of modern sovereign states remained embryonic, until the 1970s; the modern-educated social strata had been comparatively thin until recently (Kuwait is probably an exception); the traditional authority of knowledge and learning is still strong; social mobilisation is based more on rent distribution than on national moments and sentiments; colonial penetration was indirect and often unfelt; and formal,

legal decolonisation was gradual. See Hertog (2016) for a discussion of some common features of the Arab Gulf states.

5. All three terms refer to Colloquial Arabic. *ʿĀmmiyya* is more frequently used in the Mashriq, *dārija* is more often heard in the Maghrib, and *lahja* tends to be a more value-neutral term. To be concise, I will only use *ʿāmmiyya* in the rest of the book.
6. See the next section for why *al-Majmaʿ al-ʿIlmī al-ʿArabī* is rendered as 'the Arab Academy' rather than 'the Arab Science Academy'.
7. Gershoni and Jankowski argue that Egypt in the 1930s and 40s witnessed a rise of supra-Egyptian nationalism which 'drew its nourishment from the Islamic-Arab heritage which Egypt shared with peoples outside the Nile Valley, and viewed Egypt's proper external affiliations as being not with the West, which it defined as alien and aggressive, but with the peoples of the Arab, Muslim, and Eastern worlds' (1995: 213). They suggest that this supra-Egyptian nationalism was both outward- and inward-looking; it linked Egypt to the Arab and Muslim worlds and foreshadowed the rise of pan-Arabism in Egypt in the 1950s and 60s, but it also appealed to all strata of Egyptian society and contributed to the development of a popular, mass-based national collectivity in Egypt (ibid.: 213–19). It should be added that the competition between the Egyptian monarchy and the Hāshimite family over pan-Arab leadership, as mentioned earlier, was an important factor behind the outward-looking side of supra-Egyptian nationalism.
8. See Ḥāfiẓ and Shūsha (2010) for the changes of membership arrangements in the decrees of the Cairo Academy.
9. These Arabi(ci)sation committees were similar to ALAs in terms of some common missions (e.g. lexical coinage) they undertook. The Jordanian Academy was founded in 1973 from the Arabi(ci)sation committee of the Jordan Ministry of Education, which was established in 1961 as a response to the resolution of the First Arabi(ci)sation Conference (Khalīfa 1987: 88).
10. See Ḥusayn (2011) for an overview of the history of the Union.
11. Citizenship of ALA members is always noted in the lists of members published by the ALAs.
12. The two Palestinian ALAs claim Jerusalem as their permanent location even though they do not actually conduct their work there for practical reasons (see note d on p. 21). Their claims are symbolic gestures indicating that their territoriality is in accordance with the territoriality of the Palestinian state in whatever form.
13. In a personal interview, Ṣalāḥ Faḍl (2 July 2012), a member of the Cairo Academy, told me that the conflict between scientists and literati was a constant feature of life in the Academy.
14. Spolsky prefers to term this understanding of LPLP as 'language policy' (in a broad sense) and 'language planning' as 'language management'.
15. Although the development of the modern state system in Egypt started as early as 1805 (Marsot 2007: 64), this process received two new stimuli in the early twentieth century. One was the end of the British Protectorate over Egypt and the declaration of Egypt as an independent institutional monarchy in 1922 (ibid.: 96–7). The other was the wave of state-formation in the former Arab provinces of the Ottoman Empire following World War I, which

dragged Egypt into competition for authentic claims to pan-Arab leadership with newly established Arab states such as Syria and Iraq.

16. This is also the case with the Académie française, which has survived the French Revolution (1789) and multiple regime changes and is now a banal, routine component of state infrastructure and a symbol of state sovereignty over the French language.
17. It should be mentioned that nation-building and state-formation are still a work in progress in the Arabic-speaking world. Accordingly, they tend to exert a long-term influence on ALAs.
18. For example, commenting on the work of the Cairo Academy, Chejne says: 'the work of the academy was widely criticized both in Egypt and abroad, particularly with regard to the creation of new words' (1969: 106); 'its effectiveness was hindered by needless controversy about which word would be best suited for a particular need' (ibid.: 107).
19. The Cairo Academy also published *Muʿjam ʾalfāẓ al-qurʾān al-karīm*, a linguistic dictionary of Qur'anic words. Its ambitious *al-Muʿjam al-kabīr* 'the big dictionary' project is still ongoing.
20. The term *al-khālidūn* is an Arabic translation of the French phrase *les immortels* 'the immortals', which has been used to refer to the forty life members of the Académie française. However, *al-khālidūn* has its own cultural signification in the Arabic context. In the Qur'an, it is used to mean the eternity of abode in heaven or hell as a reward or punishment respectively by Allah. In modern usage, *al-khālidūn* is often associated with martyrs (*shuhadāʾ*) who sacrifice their lives in struggles, fights, or battles for national independence, social justice, and the defence of Islam and Islamic principles (who are thence awarded eternal places in heaven). Describing the members of the ALAs as *al-khālidūn* may imply that they will be awarded immortality in their afterlives due to their contribution to rescuing, defending, protecting and perfecting the Arabic language – long revered as the language of Islam and a symbol of the Arab nation.
21. When watching the live coverage of Mohamed Morsi's inaugural ceremony as President of Egypt on 30 June 2012, I noticed that Ḥasan al-Shāfiʿī was officially invited to witness the inauguration as President of the Cairo Academy among other VIPs such as the Grand Mufti of *al-ʾAzhar*. This clearly indicates that the Academy is needed as one of the symbols that display the existence and sovereignty of the Egyptian state in the public sphere, more evidently on ceremonial occasions.
22. Suleiman (2013a: 93–166) has dealt with the quotidian circulation and reiteration of certain language ideologies around tropes of crisis, fossilisation and war in Arabic paratexts and poetry to show that, while often the Arabic language 'is subject to ideological fashioning or manipulation at the deepest level' (ibid.: 145), this process remains invisible and these ideologies are 'givens' (ibid.: 95) for most people. Suleiman's findings support my argument that discursive habitus (as the reification of language ideologies) tends to be hegemonic and unfelt.
23. In Foucault's own words: 'In the analysis proposed here, the rules of formation operate not only in the mind or consciousness of individuals, but in discourse itself; they operate therefore, according to a sort of uniform anonymity, on all individuals who undertake to speak in this discursive field' (2002: 69–70).

3

Arabic Diglossia and Arab Nationalisms

Diglossia, referring to the strict functional specialisation of at least two varieties of one language, has been regarded as a defining feature of the sociolinguistic profile of the Arabic-speaking world since Ferguson's pioneering study on this phenomenon (1959). The rigid formality of *fuṣḥā* is put into sharp contrast with the colloquialism of *ʿāmmiyya*. Recent literature on Arabic diglossia is replete with models designed to depict as accurately as possible the complicated functional distribution, along the linguistic continuum, between the two poles of *fuṣḥā* and *ʿāmmiyya*. However, there are also studies addressing how Arabic diglossia is perceived by native Arabic speakers (Zughoul 1980; Mahmoud 1986; Suleiman 1986; Amara 1995; al-Kahtany 1997; Suleiman 2013b). This chapter follows the latter tradition and argues that the nativist dimension of diglossia is important, as it reveals how a seemingly linguistic issue is in fact deeply embedded in the sociopolitical and ideological environment of the native language community and is laden with extra-linguistic considerations, including how varieties of Arabic go beyond their communicative instrumentality to become political and ideological proxies.

This chapter examines the conception of Arabic diglossia as a linguistic-cum-sociopolitical problem in the ALA discourse and explores the reason behind the continuing reiteration of this conception therein. It identifies three discursive habiti viewing *fuṣḥā* and *ʿāmmiyya* as organisms, instruments and national symbols respectively. The first habitus sees *ʿāmmiyya* as a set of imperfect, hybrid lineages of *fuṣḥā* but nonetheless still affirms the role of *ʿāmmiyya* in keeping Arabic alive; the split and the anticipated reunification of Arabic are correlated with the fragmentation and reunification of the Arab nation. The second habitus understands *fuṣḥā* and *ʿāmmiyya* as tools of different qualities, values of utility and degrees of distribution in Arab society; the lack of integration between the two is believed to impede social cohesion and national solidarity. The third habitus considers *fuṣḥā* a key element in uniting the Arab nation but is ambivalent towards the various *ʿāmmiyya*s as symbols of both the political fragmentation and the geographical and cultural diversity of the Arab nation. To explain the reiteration of this 'diglossia as a problem' thesis in the ALA discourse, this chapter suggests that a major reason behind this is the persistent feeling of instability and insecurity concerning state-cum-national identities among Arab intellectuals against the background of politically unrealised pan-Arabism and the rise and consolidation of modern Arab states.

Diglossia as a Sociolinguistic Problem in Western Academia

Ferguson's article 'Diglossia' (1959), which Boussofara-Omar (2006) calls 'a rite of passage' in diglossia literature, makes two observations about this phenomenon. The first sees diglossia as 'a relatively stable language situation' (Ferguson 1959: 336) that consists of a high variety (H) used for formal, written purposes and a low variety (L) used for informal and often oral communications. Following this approach, scholars working on the Arabic language have continuously revised and refined Ferguson's H-L model in order to give a more precise and nuanced description of Arabic diglossia. They pay attention 'to the structure of the mixed kinds of Arabic produced in the "semiformal" and "cross-dialectal" situations that were excluded from [Ferguson's] model' (Holes 2004: 342).[1] They have identified various intermediate varieties or levels of Arabic between H and L (Blanc 1960; Badawī 1973; Meiseles 1980) and tried to discover regular patterns of the mixing or switching between these varieties or levels in different situations of language use (Parkinson 2003; Boussofara-Omar 2006). A recent study shows that it is more proper to understand Arabic diglossia as a linguistic continuum, with 'the semi-liquidity or viscosity of the Arabic language situation at its outer ends and its liquidity in the middle' (Suleiman 2013b: 265).

However, Ferguson's second observation, which addresses how diglossia tends to be perceived in diglossic communities as a linguistic-cum-sociopolitical problem, has received little attention in recent studies on Arabic diglossia. Ferguson argues that

> Diglossia seems to be accepted and not regarded as a 'problem' by the community in which it is in force, until certain trends appear in the community. These include trends toward (a) more widespread literacy

> (whether for economic, ideological or other reasons), (b) broader communication among different regional and social segments of the community (e.g. for economic, administrative, military, or ideological reasons), (c) desire for a full-fledged standard 'national' language as an attribute of autonomy or of sovereignty. (Ferguson 1959: 338)

These three trends demand a (national) community-wide standard language whose emergence is impeded by diglossia. To understand this perceived negative effect of diglossia on the standardisation of language use, we need to refer to the distinction Ferguson makes between diglossia and 'the familiar situation of a standard language with regional dialects' (ibid.: 336) as follows:

> diglossia differs from the more widespread standard-with-dialects in that no segment of the speech community in diglossia regularly uses H as a medium of ordinary conversation, and any attempt to do so is felt to be either pedantic and artificial (Arabic, Greek) or else in some sense disloyal to the community (Swiss German, Creole). In the more usual standard-with-dialects situation the standard is often similar to the variety of a certain region or social group which is used in ordinary conversation more or less naturally by members of the group and as a superposed variety by others. (Ibid.: 336–7)

In other words, what makes diglossia unique is that it characterises a language situation where no single autonomous language variety is able to cover all, or at least the major, domains of communication, including both formal and informal language uses. For example, the language situation in contemporary China cannot be described as one of diglossia but as standard-with-dialects, because although there are many dialects within the Chinese language, there is nowadays a standard variety called Putonghua 'the common tongue' in Mainland China, or Guoyu 'the national language' in Taiwan, which is widely used in formal and information, official and ordinary, and written and oral communications. Children learn this standard variety from both family osmosis and school education. Using Standard Chinese is instrumentally useful because it facilitates cross-dialectal communication. Using Standard Chinese is also ideologically positive because it is believed to foster social mobility, social equality and national solidarity.[2] The situation in the Arabic-speaking world is different. *Fuṣḥā* is almost excluded in everyday conversations due to the feeling of artificiality of such use, while the use of *ʿāmmiyya* or code-mixing between *fuṣḥā* and *ʿāmmiyya* in formal occasions tends to be considered, especially by some conservatives, as inappropriate or a sign of linguistic incompetence (nonetheless still common). With respect to language acquisition, *fuṣḥā* is mainly acquired through a long period of formal education, while *ʿāmmiyya* is often picked up naturally within the family. The contrast between Chinese and Arabic shows that a characteristic feature of a diglossic community is the lack of a fully functional standard language.[3]

At the time when Ferguson wrote his article, this standard 'deficit' was commonly perceived among LPLP scholars and language policymakers around the world as a negative feature of social communication, a sign of socioeconomic underdevelopment, or even a social problem. This problem was mostly associated with 'developing nations'. During the 1960s, many newly established nation-states in Asia and Africa were just beginning nation-building and social development. In spite of the fact that they were faced with different sociopolitical situations and affected by different ideological currents, these nation-states more or less followed similar objectives of development: a sovereign state that represents the popular will of the citizens and is responsible for their rights and welfare, an efficient bureaucracy that manages all state-citizen affairs, a literate and enlightened citizenry that sustains the national public sphere and so on. Achieving these objectives depends on smooth communication between the state and its citizens and among different social strata, which further relies on the formation of a state-wide standard language. A lack of this language was believed to impede necessary sociopolitical communication, thus delaying state-formation, nation-building and social development, and even causing the failure of the state.

For some Western scholars who were interested in analysing 'language problems of developing nations' during the 1960s and 1970s (Fishman et al (1968), the lack of efficient communication by means of standard languages is considered a problem peculiar to developing nations due to their overall underdevelopment. Neustupný (1968: 290), for instance, linked what he called 'dialectal stratification' (which can be seen as a core feature of diglossia in line with the standard 'deficit' motioned before) to 'the context of a highly segmented society with low social mobility' which was common to developing nations. He went on to argue that, just as there were socioeconomically 'developing nations', there were also 'developing languages' and 'developing features of communication'; the former and the latter were usually correlated (ibid.: 290). Elsewhere, Neustupný (1965) termed what he perceived to be 'developing languages' as 'Oriental languages'.

Establishing peculiar, often negative features of 'Oriental languages' and relating these features to social underdevelopment or to the backwardness of Oriental society in general belong to a pattern of perceiving the Orient spearheaded by Montesquieu's 'Oriental despotism', continued by Burke, James and John Stuart Mill, Alexis de Tocqueville, Karl Marx and Max Weber (Curtis 2009). According to this trend, the Orient has certain characteristic features of political structure, religious tradition and modes of production that have prevented the rise of capitalism, modernity and democracy. As will be discussed later in this chapter and the next, these theories of 'Oriental peculiarities' were received by Arab intellectuals as both causes for the underdevelopment of their society and colonial/imperial conspiracies against the Arab nation.

According to the 'language problems of developing nations' framework mentioned above, since 'Oriental languages' were 'developing languages', they contained problems and 'deficits' which needed to be overcome so that they could develop into 'developed languages'. In the Arabic setting, diglossia was perceived to be one of the biggest linguistic-cum-sociopolitical obstacles for education, economic development and nation-building (al-Zaghlūl 1980). The diglossic situation in the Arabic-speaking world needed to be changed. Ferguson (1959: 340) confirmed this by envisaging the situation of Arabic around 2150, when a number of regional standard Arabic languages, 'each based on an L variety with heavy admixture of H vocabulary', would take shape, and diglossia would gradually disappear.

Nowadays, few Western scholars perceive Arabic diglossia as a problem to be overcome. Rather, motivated by theories of 'linguistic ecology', 'sociolinguistic diversity' and 'linguistic rights', diglossia is seen as a natural phenomenon to be discovered and described. However, as shown by the ALA discourse, many Arab intellectuals still retain a negative attitude towards diglossia and struggle to alleviate and erase this phenomenon. The motivation behind this attitude, as I will show below, is far more complicated than that which guided diglossia studies in Western academia during the 1960s and 1970s.

Diglossia as a Problem in the Arabic Language Academy Discourse

The ALA discourse consistently treats Arabic diglossia as a problem rather than as a natural phenomenon. To begin with, this discourse tends to dismiss the descriptive approach adopted by many Western Arabists to classify Arabic synchronically into a number of relatively discrete varieties. A common typology of Arabic in the Western Arabist tradition can be summarised as follows. (1) Classical Arabic (CA): the Arabic variety that has been codified based mainly on the Qur'an, the pre- and early-Islamic poetry, and the speech samples of some Arabian tribes collected in early

Islamic periods. (2) Modern Standard Arabic (MSA) or Modern Literary Arabic (MLA): the Arabic variety that descended from CA with the rise of modern Arabic journalism, translation and prose writing in the nineteenth century. MSA keeps most of the phonetic and syntactic features of CA while bringing significant innovations in vocabulary and phraseology. (3) Arabic dialects: the colloquial varieties that differ from CA and MSA in phonetics, phonology, syntax and vocabulary. Arabic dialects can be classified into sub-groups in line with geographical, sectarian, or urban-rural divisions. Some regional dialects are regarded as having trans-regional impacts, such as Egyptian Colloquial Arabic (ECA), which has achieved wide popularity in the Arabic-speaking world due to the spread of modern Egyptian cinema and pop culture. (4) Intermediate, cross-bred varieties between CA/MSA and Arabic dialects. For example, among Badawī's (1973) 'five levels' of Arabic, which are heritage *fuṣḥā*, *fuṣḥā* of the age, dialect of the educated, dialect of the literate and dialect of the illiterate, the first two levels correspond to CA and MSA respectively, the last level roughly corresponds to Arabic dialects, and the third and fourth levels can be understood as the intermediate forms of Arabic.

In the ALA discourse, however, whether MSA and intermediate Arabic can be acknowledged as independent, discrete varieties is contentious. Conservatives stick to the integrity of *fuṣḥā*, arguing that it is not necessary to distinguish between classical and modern Arabic and that MSA being an independent variety is an illusion. According to them, the various theories identifying intermediate forms of Arabic are disguised appeals for promoting the use of *ʿāmmiyya* at the expense of *fuṣḥā* (al-Zaghlūl 1980; ʿAbd al-Laṭīf 19 June 2012 [personal interview]). Modernists acknowledge that there are different levels of Arabic, but they are distributed along two sets of varieties only: the *fuṣḥā* set and the *ʿāmmiyya* set (Faḍl 2 July 2012 [personal interview]). For them, MSA is a modern development and an integral part of *fuṣḥā*, rather than independent from it (Ḥasan 1962; Ḍayf 1978; al-Sāmrāʾī 1995, 2001).[4]

Secondly, it is very difficult to legitimise descriptive Arabic dialectology in the ALA discourse. Among the five language academies studied here, only the Cairo Academy has embraced 'studying modern Arabic dialects' into its official agenda and established a committee specialising in this matter; while other academies generally exclude dialect studies from their agendas. Even within the Cairo Academy, the position of dialectology was not always stable. Fāyid (2004: 286–7) reports a debate within the Cairo Academy about removing the article that stipulates dialectology to be part of the Academy's mission from its charter in 1937. The debate ended in a deadlock, and the president of the Academy had to bring two academicians for and against the removal respectively to the Egyptian Minister of Education to settle the debate. This article finally remained in the charter promulgated in 1940. According to Manṣūr Fahmī, members who supported the removal were not against dialect studies but were against the very act of institutionalising these studies in the official agenda of the Cairo Academy (MJMJ 4: 57). For these members, writing the dialectology article into the charter had a symbolic consequence: the official recognition of Arabic dialects as a subject of study that is equal to *fuṣḥā*, which was not acceptable. The belief that *fuṣḥā* and *ʿāmmiyya* cannot share equal status was very consistent, even among non-conservative academicians. For example, Faḍl (2 July 2012), who claimed himself to be among the more modern-minded members in the Cairo Academy, told me in a personal interview that *ʿammiyya* is not a 'language' like *fuṣḥā*. Moreover, dialectal studies conducted by the Cairo Academy were not purely descriptive. The main purpose of these studies was identifying and recovering the *fuṣḥā* origins of *ʿāmmiyya* vocabularies so that the gap between *fuṣḥā* and *ʿāmmiyya* could be narrowed (Fāyid 2004: 288). In other words, Arabic dialects were not studied for their own sake but for their 'elevation' and, finally, integration into *fuṣḥā*.

More often, the relationship between *fuṣḥā* and *ʿāmmiyya* was perceived to be conflictual in the ALA discourse. Some arguments in this regard commonly found in this discourse are: (1) *ʿāmmiyya* as a whole is a set of simplified, reduced and corrupted varieties of *fuṣḥā*; the spread of *ʿāmmiyya* will weaken the *fuṣḥā* competence of Arabic speakers and compromise the purity and integrity of *fuṣḥā*; (2) *ʿāmmiyya* is degenerate and ungrammatical, thus not as competent as *fuṣḥā* for use in administration, education, the press and media, and literature; besides, it should not be encouraged for use in the family and markets; the penetration of *ʿāmmiyya* into domains of public communication, which are supposed to be dominated by *fuṣḥā*, threatens the official status of *fuṣḥā*, increases illiteracy and impedes social cohesion and national integration in individual Arab states; (3) *fuṣḥā* is the language of Islam and Arabness; it links Muslims and Arabs to the Arab-Islamic heritage and retains cultural solidarity and unification among them; by contrast, *ʿāmmiyya* is a symbol of political fragmentation, civil strife (*fitna*) and territorial nationalisms (*ʾiqlīmiyya*) in the Arabic-speaking world as well as colonialist/imperialist conspiracy against Arab solidarity. More details of these arguments will come in the following sections.

The above arguments reflect the general attitude of the ALAs towards *fuṣḥā* and *ʿāmmiyya*. For them, *fuṣḥā* is ideally the only competent and legitimate variety of Arabic to become the standard language in all public domains of communication in the Arabic-speaking world. However, the diglossic reality and its persistence throughout the twentieth century (no matter how hard these academies have tried to change this reality) have made any commitment to this *fuṣḥā* ideal difficult to maintain. The dissociation between ideal and reality causes Arabic diglossia to be a prolonged problem and a 'chronic crisis' (*'azma muzmina*) in the ALA discourse (al-Ḥamzāwī 2000). This crisis of diglossia has propelled ALAs to make various public statements concerning Arabic diglossia in the last decade of the twentieth century and the first decade of the twenty-first century. The Cairo Academy set '*fuṣḥā* and *ʿāmmiyya*' and '*fuṣḥā* and *ʿāmmiyya* in the media' as the themes of its annual assemblies in 1999 and 2000 respectively. Choosing these two themes at the turn of the century symbolically made Arabic diglossia a 'millennium' issue. In the opening ceremony of the 1999 Assembly, Shawqī Ḍayf, the president of the Cairo Academy (1996–2005), appealed to Arab governments to defend the status of *fuṣḥā* in public domains via legislation and suggested that all government staff should speak *fuṣḥā* when talking to the common people (2000a: 6). The Jordanian Academy submitted a draft Arabic Language Law to the Jordanian prime minister in 1990, stipulating the use of 'the sound Arabic language' (*al-lugha al-ʿarabiyya al-salīma*) in the naming of and correspondence within and between government, public and private institutions (MMU 39: 349).[5] The Syrian government issued a new law in 2001 to regulate the work of the Damascus Academy, incorporating an article stating that the Academy should 'strive to prevent the exacerbation of [the use] of *ʿāmmiyya* in various sections' (MMD 78–1: 110).

These pro-*fuṣḥā* and counter-*ʿāmmiyya* statements with the involvement of state legislation were natural results of the development of a discourse on diglossia in the ALAs. Throughout the twentieth century, this discourse persistently problematised the co-existence of *fuṣḥā* and *ʿāmmiyya* in the Arabic-speaking world and considered the rapprochement between the two necessary. To understand the ideological underpinnings that sustained the development, reproduction and reiteration of this discourse, below I will explore three of its discursive habiti identified from the various seminar minutes, research papers, policy documents and statements the ALAs have produced so far vis-à-vis Arabic diglossia.

Fuṣḥā and *ʿĀmmiyya* as Organisms

The first discursive habitus along which the ALA discourse on diglossia was formed insists that *fuṣḥā* and *ʿāmmiyya* come from the same origin and are closely associated with each other. To support this argument, this discourse proposes two modes of organic connection between *fuṣḥā* and

ʿāmmiyya that are similar to the biological relations between organisms in the natural world. The first is 'family and hybridity', the second 'symbiosis in ecosystem'. Let us start with two examples of the first:

(1) It is clear that every eloquent (*faṣīḥa*) human language has on its part a language born (*mutawallida*) of it, which is the colloquial (*ʿāmmiyya*) language or the popular (*dārija*) language. This colloquial language is, in fact, the daughter of the eloquent. Some people claim that the former is an abridgement (*ikhtizāl*) of the latter. (al-Maghribī 1923: 236)

(2) Like in the families of the human being there are children of the concubines (*ʾabnāʾ al-ʿallāt*), or children born from one father but different mothers, in the Arabic language there are also 'children of the concubines'. Often we see a group of words containing the same [consonantal] letters and listed in the same [dictionary] entry, but some of these words come from pure Arabic roots while others are Arabicised [i.e. transliterated] borrowings from non-Arabic origins, e.g. Persian. These Arabic and Arabicised words join together to become half-brothers in one language family, having the same father but different mothers. (al-Maghribī 1955: 253)

In example (1), al-Maghribī understands the rise of *ʿāmmiyya* as a natural process of linguistic propagation in all language families. Here *fuṣḥā* is the 'parent' language while *ʿāmmiyya* varieties are its descendants. However, the blood lineage between *fuṣḥā* and *ʿāmmiyya* is not a pure one. The word '*mutawallida*' al-Maghribī uses here is reminiscent of *muwallad*, which has a negative connotation in traditional Islamic literature. As a term of Islamic history, *muwallad* refers to 'a cross-breed, half-caste or even, . . . one who, without being of Arab origin, has been born among the Arabs and received an Arabic education' (Ed. et al 1993: 807). As a linguistic term, *muwallad* refers to the words and expressions that are used by those 'cross-breed' Arabic speakers and are not found in the orthodox corpus of the Arabic language (the Qur'an and pre-Islamic poetry). This ethnic-cum-linguistic hybridity appeared following the Arab conquests of Mesopotamia, Great Syria and Egypt in the seventh and eighth centuries, due to intensive contact between Arab emigrants and the local people in the conquered land. From then on, until roughly the tenth century, only some Bedouin tribes remaining in Arabia who had minimal contact with non-Arabs were regarded as ethnically pure; their use of Arabic set the highest standard of *fuṣḥā*. The Arabic languages spoken in the conquered land, by contrast, were perceived to be corrupted, thus not trustworthy for the purpose of grammar-making. These metaphorical and allusive meanings of *muwallad* reveal al-Maghribī's attitude towards *ʿāmmiyya*, which is hidden behind his words: *ʿāmmiyya* is a hybrid language variety of *fuṣḥā* and foreign languages.[6]

In example (2), al-Maghribī deploys a similar 'family and hybridity' metaphor to describe the possible non-Arabic origins of some words that happen to contain the same root letters as other, pure Arabic words. Although here the issue he deals with is lexical borrowing and assimilation in Arabic, how he perceives the relation between Arabic and Arabicised words also reveals his attitudes towards the relation between *fuṣḥā* and *ʿāmmiyya*. This is because, in the ALA discourse, lexical borrowing and the rise of various Arabic dialects following the Arab conquests are perceived to be two products of the same process – contact with non-Arabic speaking people in the conquered land (see the discussion on *laḥn* below). Therefore, if Arabicised words are seen as 'descendants' of the Arabic 'father' and his non-Arabic 'concubines', *ʿāmmiyya* can also be understood as 'children of the concubines': the varieties whose origin is *fuṣḥā* but which are heavily influenced by the sounds, vocabularies, morphology, syntax and styles of non-Arabic languages.[7]

'Family and hybridity' is just one of the two ways to situate *fuṣḥā* and *ʿāmmiyya* in an organic world; 'symbiosis in the ecosystem' is the other. Let us consider the following example.

> Ever since *fuṣḥā* separated from *ʿāmmiyya*,[8] the integrity of its [*fuṣḥā*] grammar, vocabulary and derivational principles has been maintained for fifteen centuries and will continue to be preserved as God wishes. *Fuṣḥā* looks like a gorgeous garden (*ḥadīqa ghannāʾ*) where both fruitful and fruitless trees exhibit their dazzling beauty; the chief guardians of the garden are the Noble Qur'an and the literary legacy we have inherited, including the *Jāhiliyya* poetry, scholastic books and other materials adopted by Arabic dictionaries. *ʿĀmmiyya* is a big area of thickets (*ghiyāḍ*) that surrounds the garden, mixed with thorns and brambles, growing and multiplying in a disorderly way, and obtaining water and nutrition from the garden. This area of thickets prevents the thorns from penetrating into the garden and damaging the beautiful trees, but it also forbids the guardians to bring new, different plants from outside into the garden. (Qudsī 1923: 180–1)

In the above example, Qudsī depicts *fuṣḥā* as an efflorescent garden full of beautiful trees. Obviously, these 'trees' are linguistic components of *fuṣḥā*, some of which are 'fruitless' (referring to those data of *fuṣḥā* that are *samāʿī*, i.e. culled from actual language use of 'pure' Arabs in the first centuries of Islam, but not used to establish analogical patterns in Arabic grammar) while others are 'fruitful' (referring to those data of *fuṣḥā* that are *qiyāsī*, i.e. used to established analogical patterns based on which infinite *fuṣḥā* words and sentences can be made). This garden is not only natural, but also well attended by its 'guardians' – the codified database of *fuṣḥā* such as the Qur'an, pre-Islamic poetry and other classical literary writings. The guardians maintain the orderliness and beauty of the garden, and, if possible, develop and refine the garden by bringing new plants into it. *ʿĀmmiyya*, by contrast, is an unattended land of thickets, which may not be harmful, but are surely not as beautiful as the trees in the garden. This land of thickets is mixed with thorns and brambles, which are intruders (referring to non-Arabic languages or linguistic elements) potentially harmful to both the thickets and the garden. The thickets in this *ʿāmmiyya* land share water and nutrition with the trees in the garden; in return, these thickets block the penetration of the thorns and brambles into the garden. However, these thickets also block the importation of new trees into the garden.

Qudsī's metaphor illuminates certain features of *fuṣḥā*, *ʿāmmiyya* and their relations. First, *fuṣḥā* is the most refined variety of Arabic while *ʿāmmiyya* is unrefined, immature and mixed with non-Arabic elements. This is most evident in the contrast between 'trees' on the one hand and 'thickets' (*ghiyāḍ*), thorns and brambles on the other. The verbal form of *ghiyāḍ* is *ghāḍa*, meaning 'to decrease and diminish'. Its verbal noun *ghayḍ* means 'prematurely born foetus' and 'small amount'. It is clear that *ghiyāḍ* refers to those small plants that are not developed enough to be counted as 'trees'. As for thorns and brambles, they are intruders not belonging to the original ecosystem of *fuṣḥā* and *ʿāmmiyya*, i.e. linguistic elements of non-Arabic origins. It is no coincidence that the term *ikhtizāl* used by al-Maghribī in example (1) also carries similar perceptions of *ʿāmmiyya*. In modern usage, *ikhtizāl* means 'abridgement', so *ʿāmmiyya* is an abridged form of *fuṣḥā*. In old usage, *khazal*, the lexical root of *ikhtizāl*, means sluggishness and disruption in walking, as if there are 'thorns pricking the feet [of the walker]' (Ibn Manẓūr 1302 AH: 216). Due to this 'sluggishness' and 'disruption', the walker should frequently 'halt' his or her feet, 'terminate', or even 'cut short' his or her journey, and thence comes the meaning of 'abridgement'. Here, *ʿāmmiyya* contains 'thorns' that prevent the use of Arabic in its complete (*salīm*) and eloquent (*faṣīḥ*) manner. Second, *fuṣḥā* represents the pure version of Arabic while *ʿāmmiyya* varieties are mixtures of the 'abridged' version of Arabic and non-Arabic languages. This understanding reiterates the perception of *ʿāmmiyya* in the 'family and hybridity' metaphor before. Third, *fuṣḥā* and *ʿāmmiyya* belong to the same linguistic ecosystem and are mutually dependent on and restrained by each other. The *fuṣḥā* 'trees' supply the *ʿāmmiyya* 'thickets' with water and nutrition; the 'thickets' both protect the 'trees' and block any change to them. Again not coincidentally, Muḥammad Ḥamāsa ʿAbd al-Laṭīf, a late member of the Cairo Academy, told me in a personal interview (19 June 2012) that the Arabic language is always developing but the developments are mostly revealed in *ʿāmmiyya*. In sum, Qudsī's metaphor reflects a standpoint in the ALA discourse that *fuṣḥā* and *ʿāmmiyya* co-exist in symbiosis with unequal statuses and qualities.

The above perceptions of *fuṣḥā*, *ʿāmmiyya* and their relations were consistent in the three ways deployed in the ALA discourse to explain the derivation of *ʿāmmiyya* from *fuṣḥā*: abridgement (*ikhtizāl*), corruption (*fasād*) and deviation (*inḥirāf*). As will be shown in the following analyses, these three explanations were widely circulated and diachronically reiterated in the ALA discourse, demonstrating the existence of a discursive habitus that views *fuṣḥā* as *ʿāmmiyya* as in organic connections and that marks the routinisation of this discourse on Arabic diglossia.

'Abridgement' refers to the simplification of linguistic codes. Al-Maghribī (1923) has told us that abridgement is a universal phenomenon of human languages, evident in the fact that many languages have both eloquent and colloquial varieties. He alludes that the colloquial variety usually comes from abridgement of the eloquent variety, because people constantly simplify their linguistic codes to fit the changing circumstances of their life. Twenty years later, Marqaṣ (1943: 35–6) gives a similar explanation to al-Maghribī's – that people tend to use their language in a simpler, more hasty way to meet communicative needs in their daily lives, which leads to the formation of the relatively simpler colloquial varieties called *ʿāmmiyya*s. ʾAbū Ḥadīd (1953: 207–8) points out that many *fuṣḥā* words are distorted in *ʿāmmiyya*s because of reduction (*takhfīf*) and simplification (*taysīr*) in speech. Similarly, Mārdīnī (1970: 617) states that *ʿāmmiyya*s are derived from *fuṣḥā* because of convenience and speed in speech.

On the surface, the 'abridgement' view establishes a natural tendency of language change – languages develop from complexity to simplicity because of the increasing pace and rhythm of social life – to explain the appearance of *ʿāmmiyya* in the Arabic-speaking world. However, this explanation is shaky for the reasons below. First, the tendency towards simplicity cannot be treated as a natural law of language change. This tendency is understood as 'the principle of least effort' (Zipf 1949) or 'linguistic economy', which Martinet (1955) defines as 'the unstable balance between the needs of communication – which are always changing – and natural human inertia, two essential forces [or impulses] contributing to the optimization of the linguistic system' (quoted in Vicentini 2003: 39). The first impulse in the above definition, the needs of communication, requires using sufficient linguistic units to achieve clarity and precision, while the second impulse, natural human inertia, often reduces effort of speech by seeking fewer linguistic units to fulfil the purpose. However, the principle of 'least effort' or 'economy' is not the fundamental cause but, at best, a catalyst for language change that makes use of and accelerates any already existing potential for structural innovation in the language in question (Aitchison 2013: 156).

Second, it is contestable that *ʿāmmiyya*s are simpler than *fuṣḥā*. If 'simplicity' concerns linguistic structures, *ʿāmmiyya*s are simpler than *fuṣḥā* in some aspects (e.g. the disappearance of interdentals in non-Bedouin dialects, the dropping of case endings, the loss of dual number in inflection, etc.) while more complicated in others (e.g. elaborate vowel systems, a drift from a more rigid, patterned morphological structure, as in *fuṣḥā*, to more flexible and less predictable analytical structures and so on). If 'simplicity' concerns ease of language acquisition, *ʿāmmiyya*s are easier to learn than *fuṣḥā* as first/native languages, because they are the mother tongues of native Arabic speakers. However, *ʿāmmiyya*s are more difficult to learn as second/foreign languages, because *ʿāmmiyya*s do not have the same codified linguistic corpus and established grammatical tradition as found in *fuṣḥā*.

Despite these two obvious fallacious arguments, the 'abridgement' view was not challenged in the ALA discourse because it accorded with a deeply ingrained language ideology endorsed by the majority of ALA members: *ʿāmmiyya*s, regardless of their various linguistic and sociocultural merits, are deficient forms of Arabic, while *fuṣḥā* always represents the highest, golden standard of Arabic. Compared with the perceived perfect sophistication of *fuṣḥā*, the 'abridgement' and 'simplicity' revealed in *ʿāmmiyya* could not be considered as positive changes of Arabic in the minds of many ALA members. For them, simplicity is equivalent to weakness, neglect and imperfection. The 'abridgement' view merely adopted a seemingly objective, scientific explanation of language change (the principle of 'least effort' or 'linguistic economy') to support this deeply ingrained language ideology. Although this ideological underpinning seemed covert, it became more evident in the 'corruption' and 'deviation' views discussed below.

'Corruption' refers to the erroneous use of *fuṣḥā*, which has nonetheless been accepted as normal in *ʿāmmiyya*. The erroneous use is called *laḥn* (grammatical errors) in Arabic grammatical tradition. This tradition saw *laḥn* as linguistic corruption caused by the contact between pure Arabic and various foreign languages during and after the Arab conquests. Accents, vocabulary and the stylistic features of Greek, Persian, Syriac, Aramaic, Berber and, later, Turkic languages came into the Arabic language, causing deviations in the use of Arabic. Such deviations varied in different Arab regions, forming the basis of various regional *ʿāmmiyya*s. This traditional concept of *laḥn* was received by members of the ALAs as a 'taken-for-granted' feature of the language situation of Arabic when they talked about the development of *ʿāmmiyya*s (see Marqaṣ 1943; al-ʿAwda 1957; al-Shabībī 1960; al-Baṣīr 1978; Salmān 1988; al-Tarzī 1990; Muḥjāzī 2005).

Although traditionally *laḥn* mainly referred to the linguistic corruption occurring during and after the Arab conquests, some ALA members extended this concept to cover a longer historical spectrum. Marqaṣ (1943: 31) understands *ʿāmmiyya*s as the result of intensifying linguistic decay over centuries. According to this view, *laḥn* initially appeared to a very limited extent during the first two centuries of Islam. It started to swell from the early Abbasid period (from the late second/eighth century onwards) and became widespread in the fifth/eleventh century. It continued to proliferate in 'the age of decline' (*ʿahd al-inḥiṭāṭ*, from the ninth/fifteenth to thirteenth/nineteenth centuries, i.e. the Ottoman Empire) and, as a result of this, *ʿāmmiyya*s suffered from their 'most extreme weakness' (*muntahā rakākatihā*) in history. Al-Nakdī (1957: 191–2) holds the same opinion that the *laḥn* was limited before the weakening of Arab rule and the rise of non-Arab dynasties in the Islamic Empire. He speculates that the early *laḥn* was caused by contact and exchange between Arab conquerors and indigenous residents in the conquered lands, while the later, large-scale *laḥn* was caused by the political fragmentation of the Arabic-speaking world, which allowed for the infiltration of more foreign and regional linguistic elements into the Arabic language.

Why do Marqaṣ and al-Nakdī distinguish these two phases of the development of *laḥn* and identify the different causes behind each phase? What makes the two phases different? To answer these questions, we should consider the following historical narratives that were commonly shared among members of the ALAs. During the first phase of *laḥn* (from the first/seventh to the fourth/tenth centuries), the Arabs mounted the conquest and established a vast empire from Central Asia to North Africa. The Arabic language at that time was the conquerors' language and enjoyed unchallenged prestige over the languages of the conquered peoples. When the conquered peoples started to adopt Arabic, they brought their old linguistic elements and habits into Arabic, causing *laḥn* which, in al-Nakdī's eyes, only slightly contaminated the pure Arabic language. During the second phase of *laḥn* (from the fifth/eleventh to thirteenth/nineteenth centuries), the Abbasids lost their control over the empire, left their power to various non-Arab dynasties and were finally replaced by the Ottomans in the ninth/fifteenth century. The Arabs lost their prestige and became people ruled by others. This time , the Arabic language became the 'victim' and, according to al-Nakdī, was widely infiltrated by neighbouring foreign languages.

In essence, the two situations that Arabic met in these two historical phases were both phenomena of language contact, albeit happening in different political contexts. This political difference makes al-Nakdī perceive the two contacts in different ways. When the Arabs were in the dominant position, Arabic was also dominant, so the influence of neighbouring languages was limited; the Arabs were still able to use their language correctly, and it was mainly non-Arabs who committed the *laḥn.* When Arabs lost political prestige, Arabic was challenged, so foreign linguistic elements became prevalent, and, this time, the Arabs themselves were responsible for the *laḥn*. Therefore, in the first phase, Arabic was only contaminated, while in the second phase Arabic was in decline, giving more room to the growth of regional, hybrid varieties collectively called *ʿāmmiyya*s. As far as diglossia is concerned, al-Nakdī connects the destiny of Arabic with the destiny of the Arabs, their political status and their social position. I will elaborate on the relation between language and nation later when discussing the symbolic perspective on diglossia.

Apart from language contact during both political dominance and political fragmentation, al-Qulaybī (1978) gives a third cause to explain the gradual decline of the Arabic language. He quotes Ibn Khaldūn's view that the reason why Arabic was transmitted without error from one generation to another was that the Arabs had the *malaka* 'natural disposition' or 'innate faculty' that helped them acquire Arabic naturally at a very young age. Al-Qulaybī argues that the decline of Arabic was caused by the decay of this *malaka*, which prevented younger generations acquiring the language correctly. Here we see that al-Qulaybī follows the same rationale as al-Nakdī – the destiny of Arabic changed alongside that of the Arabs.

The 'corruption' view characterises the development of the Arabic language from the fifth/eleventh to thirteenth/nineteenth centuries as a process of decline, which brought about the many *ʿāmmiyya*s still in use today. (Arabic in the twentieth century was treated in a different way, which I will address later.) The decline seemed inevitable, governed by external factors such as the rise and fall of the Arab nation and the perceived change of fortune of the innate linguistic faculty of the Arabs.

However, not all ALA members treated diglossia as a product of linguistic decline. Al-Shabībī (1960) distinguishes two types of foreign influence exerted on the structure of the Arabic language. The first type is errors (*laḥn*) and anomalies (*shudhūdh*) on the morphological and syntactic level. These errors and anomalies can be corrected via the teaching of grammar and principles of *ʾiʿrāb* 'desinential inflection' (ibid.: 129). The second type is deviations (*taḥrīf* or *inḥirāf*) at the lexical level. Deviations are hard to correct because they have been moulded by environmental, geographical and cultural features of different regions and peoples in the Arabic-speaking world (ibid.: 129). Unlike proponents of the 'corruption' view, al-Shabībī does not perceive the development of *ʿāmmiyya*s and the accompanying diglossia as symptoms of linguistic decline. Instead, he regards *ʿāmmiyya*s and diglossia as the results of a range of language variations that inevitably occurred in environmentally and culturally heterogeneous areas. For the purpose of convenience, I call this idea the 'deviation' view.

But how did environmental and cultural factors shape the Arabic language and its dialects? Early in 1957, Munīr al-ʿAjlānī, member of the Damascene Academy, writes (1957: 41):

> In fact, the single beautiful, rich language was the result of a long period of mixture and coexistence, giving and taking, buying and selling, subordination and dominance, and exchange and selection. It was the result of the persistent intellectual, spiritual and material life that moulded different groups of people into one community and that converted different dialects into one language – the language that was refined and polished and was given to members of the nation as a common inheritance.

Al-ʿAjlānī's reasoning about diglossia provides a seemingly unbiased speculation about language contact. According to this speculation, when different languages mingled, some of their components were preserved, some were changed and others were weeded out. The remaining components were incorporated into a single prestigious language variety that was intelligible to peoples who previously came from different speech communities but who now belonged to the same community. Deviations from the original Arabic language were not seen as errors, but the reshuffling of available linguistic sources from which new language situations emerged. Every language variety, including both *fuṣḥā* and *ʿāmmiyya*, was subject to the force of reshuffling – the law of language change in al-ʿAjlānī's eyes.

ʿAbd al-Qādir (1960: 362–3) echoes al-ʿAjlānī by comparing language with a living creature (*kāʾin ḥāyy*). He contends that (1) like a living creature, every language goes through phases of strength and weakness, progress and backwardness, and youth and senility; (2) like a living creature, every language is influenced by both inheritance and environment; and (3) like a living creature, language splits into different groups and sub-groups.

This seemingly unbiased 'deviation' view situated *fuṣḥā* and *ʿāmmiyya* in a linguistic system where both of them exist in a mutually dependent way – constantly changing through the reshuffling of existing elements and the absorbing of new elements from each other and other languages, while at the same time maintaining a relatively stable diglossic structure. This image is reminiscent of a parallel trend in Western linguistics today that calls for preserving the diversity of languages. This trend views languages as part of an ecological system that is similar to the organic world. It emphasises that no one language is better than any other in terms of the ability to convey meanings; every language is equally unique, beautiful and precious; language diversity is a natural given and is not a hindrance to modernisation and social mobility. Therefore, language diversity should be protected, and every human language or variety has its position in the human world (see also Chapter 4 for a critique of this ecological view of language).

However, the 'deviation' view in the ALA discourse is not unbiased to the extent that it supports language diversity in the Arabic-speaking world. Indeed, it does not perceive *ʿāmmiyya*s as the decadence of *fuṣḥā*, but nor does it treat *ʿāmmiyya*s and *fuṣḥā* as equally important. Al-Shabībī's term *taḥrīf* still indicates a sense of 'irregularity' as if there were a regular and standard Arabic variety. Al-ʿAjlānī mentions 'subordination and dominance' in the process of language contact and emphasises that there is always a national language that carries all the merits of the language and varieties that are used in a nation-community.

Moreover, ALAs often express negative evaluations of *ʿāmmiyya*s, although not always in the strong sense of 'corruption'. For example, in a recent article addressing language deviation in the Arabic-speaking world published in the journal of the Damascus Academy, Muḥjāzī (2005) views language deviation as a kind of linguistic error caused by ignorance and illiteracy among speakers.

A common feature of the 'abridgement', 'corruption' and 'deviation' views, as can be seen from the discussion above, is that they all presuppose the perennial existence of a perfect, pure and unified Arabic language named *fuṣḥā* as either the origin of *ʿāmmiyya*s or a selected, refined version of them. According to this presupposition, *ʿāmmiyya*s are always perceived as anomalous (whether they are abridgements, corruptions, or deviations) rather than normal in the Arabic language system. Accordingly, it is natural that all three views, as will be explained below, suggest a common directionality of future language change in the Arabic-speaking world – a new, standard Arabic variety based on *fuṣḥā*, which will in the end unify language use in the Arabic-speaking world and eliminate, at least partially, the problem of diglossia.

Let us consider the 'abridgement' view first. Although al-Maghribī (1923) considers diglossia as a universal feature of human languages, he does not claim that diglossia should be left unattended, as it were. He believes the prevalence of *ʿāmmiyya*s in the Arabic-speaking world has jeopardised Arabic speakers' competence in *fuṣḥā*. He therefore calls for replacing trite (*mubtadhala*) words and expressions of *ʿāmmiyya*s with their *fuṣḥā* equivalents. By claiming that intervention in diglossia is necessary, al-Maghribī does not conceal his belief that language varieties in the Arabic-speaking world will eventually converge towards *fuṣḥā* through careful language cultivation and planning.

As for the 'corruption' view, although its proponents consider that the Arabic language went through a process of continuous decline down to the nineteenth century, they treat the development of Arabic in the twentieth century differently. In their eyes, linguistic corruption, manifest in Arabic diglossia, is being reversed in their time. For example, al-Nakdī (1957: 199) confidently claims that in the last thirty years *ʿāmmiyya*s have been elevated closer to *fuṣḥā*. He believes that this process of elevation will continue; and that the tendency that different Arabic varieties will be unified around *fuṣḥā* is unstoppable. For proponents of the 'corruption' view, the twentieth-century Arabic-speaking world witnessed unprecedented social progress, including the introduction of media and public education, which would reverse the decline of Arabic as had occurred in the past, promote the elevation of *ʿāmmiyya*s to *fuṣḥā* and, finally, realise linguistic unification in the near future.

Compared with the proponents of the 'corruption' view, those who advocate the 'deviation' view believe even more ardently in the directionality of language change in the Arabic-speaking world towards unification. The gist of their argument is that although deviations are caused by different environmental factors which are hard to correct via codification in grammar and lexicon, intensifying contact and exchange between peoples in the Arabic-speaking world will finally realise the unification of the Arab nation politically and, accordingly, the convergence of Arabic language varieties into a new, eloquent nation-wide language.

Generally speaking, the organic perspective on the origin and development of Arabic diglossia sets up a law of language change in a long historical period, with possibly a perfect, unified Arabic language in the remote past (as in the case of seeing *ʿāmmiyya*s as descendants of *fuṣḥā*) and another perfect, unified Arabic language in the near future. Between the two 'perfect' poles of this historical process, Arabic has gone through and is going through abridgement, deviation, corruption, split, decline, revival and reunification. Arabic is imagined as an evolving organism, and the laws of nature would ensure its constant progress towards a better future. The belief in the natural law and directionality of language change, as a thread of thought, runs through the development of the ALA discourse on diglossia and over time becomes as routine and banal as the discourse itself.

What makes this belief so durable? It is the ideological association between Arabic and the Arab nation that is similar to the nineteenth-century Romanticist idea of the inherent congruity between language and nation. The belief in the historical change of Arabic from perfection and unification to decay and fragmentation is reminiscent of, or may have been influenced by, a central tenet of nineteenth-century historical linguistics that modern languages are genealogies of a set of original protolanguages, which themselves may derive from a super protolanguage for all human beings. This tenet was often associated with the Romanticist myth about 'the original perfection and subsequent decay of language' and 'language as a reflection of the character [and strength] of a nation' (Fox 2006: 319). The belief in the future reunification of Arabic around *fuṣḥā* is, again, reminiscent of the Romanticist idea that speaking one common language testifies to the natural bond between members of a nation. It follows that people who belong to one nation should naturally speak one language. If this were not the case for the present, a rationalisation would be proposed arguing that the ancestors of these people used to speak the same language in the past as a common nation, and this linguistic uniformity will be recovered in the future with the awakening and revival of the nation. The above are, apparently, merely 'reminiscences'. The link between Arabic and the Arab nation as was perceived in the ALA discourse needs to be contextualised in line with the development of Arab nationalisms in the twentieth century. Such contextualisation will come after I explore the other two habiti of the ALA discourse on Arabic diglossia: language as an instrument and language as a symbolic entity.

Fuṣḥā and *ʿĀmmiyya* as Instruments and Resources

The second discursive habitus sees *fuṣḥā* and *ʿāmmiyya* as instruments of communication, whose qualities and functions can, therefore, be compared and evaluated, on the one hand, and changed and refined, on the other, according to communicative needs. The ALA discourse both qualifies and restates the common view of the Arabs that *fuṣḥā* and *ʿāmmiyya* are essentially different in terms of their linguistic qualities, communicative functions and speech communities. It should be recalled that, as mentioned in the last chapter, language instrumentalism is not devoid of language symbolism and ideologies. As will be seen in this section, the ALA discourse makes use of the instrumental dichotomy between *fuṣḥā* and *ʿāmmiyya* to demonstrate that Arabic diglossia is indexical of, and even responsible for, a series of sociocultural dichotomies which hinder social cohesion and political solidarity in Arabic-speaking countries and that, as a remedy, the difference between *fuṣḥā* and *ʿāmmiyya* should not be exaggerated, and efforts should be made to integrate these two instruments of communication into one. This correlation between diglossia and sociocultural dichotomies is no doubt symbolic in nature.

Among the many samples of the ALA discourse that exhibit a more or less instrumental view of language, al-Ḥabābī's *al-Lugha wa-l-wāqiʿ* 'Language and reality' (1978) is probably the most straightforward. In this paper, he compares language with the carpenter's toolkit:

> Language is an instrument (*ʾadā*) and an orderly cypress (*sarw manẓūma*). It is the entity that stimulates the mind and the medium where thoughts flow. [The relation between language and language users is similar to that between carpenters and their toolkit.] Carpenters cannot use the hammer for other than the purpose of knocking nails; they cannot use the hammer to saw apart timbers. However, since modern carpentry has entered its amazing golden age (its toolkit has been developed to meet current needs), carpenters have become more competent than before at innovation and renewal in their work. This also applies to [the Arabic language] and its users. . . . (1978: 49–50)

In the above paragraph, al-Ḥabābī clearly suggests that, like the carpenter's toolkit, the Arabic language embraces a number of linguistic 'tools' designed for different communicative purposes; and, like the development of the carpenter's toolkit, the Arabic languages should also be refined and reformed in order to serve Arabic speakers in various new domains of communication. Al-Ḥabābī's paper does not deal with the issue of *fuṣḥā* and *ʿāmmiyya*, but his instrumental view was overtly and covertly echoed in other texts addressing this issue directly.

The majority of these texts try to identify different linguistic and functional features of *fuṣḥā* and *ʿāmmiyya*, as well as evaluating these features against socio-communicative needs in the Arabic-speaking world. Common views in this regard are summarised in Table 3.1. These

Table 3.1 Views on linguistic and functional features of *fuṣḥā* and *ʿāmmiyya* in the ALA discourse

	Fuṣḥā	*ʿĀmmiyya*
(1) Integrity	*Fuṣḥā* has a sound phonological, morphological and syntactical system; grammatical properties of sentential components can be revealed when declensional endings are fully articulated.	*ʿĀmmiyya* has a fragmented and distorted phonological, morphological and syntactical system. Some characteristic features are: consonantal alternation, replacement, deletion and addition; vowel change; morphological simplification and integration; and abandoning declensional endings. (It is worth mentioning that these properties of *ʿāmmiyya* are cast against the *fuṣḥā* yardstick, but not vice versa.)
(2) Codification	*Fuṣḥā* has an established grammatical system and a number of dictionaries based on a codified body of linguistic databases, including the Qur'an, pre- and early Islamic poetry and a vast collection of classical literary writings.	*ʿĀmmiyya*, due to its ungrammatical nature, has few grammars and dictionaries. It changes constantly and freely and is thus hard to describe and regulate in a systematic manner. It has very few written records.
(3) Unity	*Fuṣḥā* is diachronically consistent and has few regional variations.	*ʿĀmmiyya* varies significantly throughout time and across different regional communities and social strata in the Arabic-speaking world.
(4) Intelligibility	*Fuṣḥā* is understood across all Arabic-speaking communities.	*ʿĀmmiyya* varieties spoken in different regional communities are barely mutually intelligible in most situations.
(5) Expressivity	Some argue that *fuṣḥā* is the most eloquent language; it has rich lexical, semantic and stylistic resources and is able to convey various meanings in a clear and precise manner. Others point out that *fuṣḥā* lacks lexical resources and derivational means to incorporate terminologies of modern science and technology.	Some hold that *ʿāmmiyya* can express nothing other than vulgar and trivial meanings in relation to basic needs in daily life. Others argue that *ʿāmmiyya* can more vividly and precisely describe the life and feelings of the common people than *fuṣḥā*.

(6) Vitality	The majority believe that *fuṣḥā* has the potential to become a modern language as long as new means are developed to enrich its lexicon and improve its expressivity. They reject the view that *fuṣḥā* is becoming a dead language. A minority contends that *fuṣḥā* carries too many pre-modern features and is in stagnation.	*ʿĀmmiyya* is constantly changing and adopting new vocabularies, morphological patterns and styles quickly and efficiently, albeit often in an unchecked manner. *Fuṣḥā* can benefit from the up-to-date lexical and stylistic resources of *ʿāmmiyya.*
(7) Pedagogy	The majority reject the view that *fuṣḥā* is difficult to learn but agree that the old methods and materials of pedagogy need to be reformed and simplified.	*ʿĀmmiyya* is acquired in the family. Its use in the school should be discouraged in order to provide a proper language environment for *fuṣḥā* acquisition.
(8) Applicability	*Fuṣḥā* is the language of the Qur'an; it has been and is still used for Islamic prayers and learning. With the Arabic *nahḍa* from the mid-nineteenth century, *fuṣḥā* has been widely used in modern education, science, journalism and media, literature and administration. *Fuṣḥā* is the only qualified variety of Arabic for writing; *fuṣḥā* has the potential to replace or integrate regional *ʿāmmiyya* varieties to become the common spoken language in the Arabic-speaking world.	*ʿĀmmiyya* is used mainly for daily oral communication between the common people and in folk literature and theatre. It is difficult to apply *ʿāmmiyya* to science and literature, because *ʿāmmiyya* lacks means and styles of formal writing. *ʿĀmmiyya* has increasingly penetrated into journalism and media. The calls for replacing *fuṣḥā* with *ʿāmmiyya* should be utterly rejected.

Sources: al-Maʿlūf (1923); Jabrī (1943); Marqaṣ (1943); al-Nakdī (1957; 1969); al-Shabībī (1957; 1962); al-Zayyāt (1957); Taymūr (1961); Fāḍil (1966); ʾAbāẓa (1966); Mārdīnī (1970); ʿAbd al-Malik (1971); ʿAbd al-Raḥīm (1972); Kunūn (1978); ʿAbd al-Mawlā (1979); al-Zaghlūl (1980); al-Sāmrāʾī (1990); al-Tarzī (1990); Ḍayf (1990; 2000a); al-Muʿallimī (2000)

views have been routinely circulated in the ALA discourse throughout its history, showing how instrumentalism-driven evaluations of Arabic diglossia constitute a discursive habitus that illustrates the routinisation of this discourse. However, two caveats need to be made here. First, these views only reflect a shared pool of evaluations of *fuṣḥā* and *ʿāmmiyya* in the ALA discourse. Individual academicians may agree with some of these views while disagreeing with others. Obviously, these views do not reflect the official positions of the ALAs and the consensus of their members vis-à-vis the issue of *fuṣḥā* and *ʿāmmiyya*. Second, these views are not expressed exclusively in the ALA discourse. Many of them may be frequently found in academic, journalistic, media and folk-linguistic discourses in the Arabic-speaking world. Quite often, members of the ALAs borrow these views from other sources and recast them in their own words to suit the agenda of these language academies.

It is clear from the above summary that the ALA discourse consistently evaluates *fuṣḥā* in a very positive way while *ʿāmmiyya* is often assessed negatively. Opinions diverge concerning whether this contrast reflects actual differences or conflicts between *fuṣḥā* and *ʿāmmiyya*, which shows that language instrumentalism is not free of ideological contestation. It suffices here to cite two examples from the ALA discourse, which perceive the relation between *fuṣḥā* and *ʿāmmiyya* in contradictory ways.

The first example, ʾAbāẓa (1966), proposes that *fuṣḥā* and *ʿāmmiyya* are fundamentally different because the former is a language while the latter is defective in the basic qualities of being a language. ʾAbāẓa claims that he intends to discuss the issue of *fuṣḥā* and *ʿāmmiyya* 'on purely objective grounds' (*ʿalā waṭīda mawḍūʿiyya maḥḍa*) (1966: 208), so he resorts to a theory popular among Western linguists which distinguishes between language and speech. ʾAbāẓa explains this theory by pointing out that language is the raw material (*māddat ghufl*) of which the product, speech (*kalām*), is made; speeches given by different speakers of the same language may be very different, just like different craftsmen make different products out of the same material. Notice that, by using the trope of crafting, ʾAbāẓa adopts an instrumental view of language. He continues to depict language as a store or repertoire of words and grammatical patterns, and speech as sentences made of certain elements drawn from this store for particular purposes (ibid.: 209).

By making this distinction, ʾAbāẓa mainly wants to illustrate two points in relation to his 'objective' understanding of language: (1) languages are repertoires of resources; and (2) the two primary components of these resources are words and grammar. He then applies these two criteria to the evaluation of *fuṣḥā* and *ʿāmmiyya*. According to ʾAbāẓa, *fuṣḥā* and *ʿāmmiyya* are two independent linguistic repertoires that operate at different levels of appropriateness (*ṣalāḥiyya*). This is because *fuṣḥā* has a codified lexicon and grammar which make it a well quantified and easily accessible repertoire, while *ʿāmmiyya* has no codified lexicon and grammar as such. This difference leads to a series of interconnected consequences that discredit the appropriateness of *ʿāmmiyya* as a language (ibid.: 211): (1) *fuṣḥā* can be learnt systematically while *ʿāmmiyya* can only be acquired by accessing its actual use (*samāʿ* lit. 'listening'). (2) Utterances in *fuṣḥā* can be judged as correct or incorrect; those deviating from the codified repertoire are incorrect, and the others are correct. Such judgements cannot be made of utterances in *ʿāmmiyya*, because the basis of judgement, the codified repertoire, is missing. (3) Similarly, one cannot assess and grade speakers' knowledge of and competence in *ʿāmmiyya* because there is no codified corpus against which such assessment and grading can be made. Every *ʿāmmiyya* speaker is equally competent or incompetent, and the only difference is the experience in using this 'language'. *Fuṣḥā* speakers, by contrast, can be graded into different levels, according to their knowledge of the codified repertoire of *fuṣḥā*. For ʾAbāẓa, consequence (3) reveals an important truism that people's horizons (*dunyā* lit. 'world') are decided by their knowledge of the language they use. This leads to consequence (4): the vision of *ʿāmmiyya* speakers is limited by its uncodified repertoire, so they never know how to upgrade their vision like *fuṣḥā* speakers; moreover, the corpus of *ʿāmmiyya* is so poor that its speakers have to frequently resort to *fuṣḥā* vocabularies when they need to discuss issues beyond the horizon defined by *ʿāmmiyya*. ʾAbāẓa then reaches his conclusion that, as a language, *ʿāmmiyya* is defective, because its repertoire is not and cannot be codified, it cannot be learnt formally, utterances in it cannot be judged, the competence of its speakers cannot be assessed and the horizon of its speakers is narrowly restrained. *Fuṣḥā*, therefore, is the only qualified and legitimate language variety of Arabic in ʾAbāẓa's view. Being or not being a language becomes the fundamental difference between *fuṣḥā* and *ʿāmmiyya*. At the end of his paper, ʾAbāẓa suggests that, considering the defective nature of *ʿāmmiyya*, ALAs should not accept *ʿāmmiyya* words and expressions into *fuṣḥā*.

ʾAbāẓa's paper has many hidden assumptions. To begin with, learning is formal, and it requires effort and commitment at various levels. One is not entitled to it without great effort. Owing to this, acquiring *fuṣḥā* via learning is a matter of accomplishment. This is not true of *ʿāmmiyya*. Also, in a culture of schooling where grading and progression can be checked and certified, it is possible to apply objective criteria to assess language competence. This applies to *fuṣḥā* but not to *ʿāmmiyya* as things stand at the moment. Third, since *fuṣḥā* is the language of instruction and is associated with schooling, and since education is linked to modernisation, *fuṣḥā* is linked to modernisation and the expansion of cultural horizons. Of course, these all follow from a sociopolitical decision to designate *fuṣḥā* as the language of formal education. A decision to designate *ʿāmmiyya* for the same purpose would turn it into the equivalent of *fuṣḥā*. However, such a decision could not be seriously entertained and would be fiercely opposed in the ALA discourse for ideological reasons linking *fuṣḥā* to the authenticity of Islamic beliefs and Arab nationalism in both pan-Arab and territorial forms, as will be discussed later in this chapter. ʾAbāẓa's arguments are therefore built on ideological considerations (which may be too ubiquitous and banal to be felt by himself and his audience) rather than factors of the objective world in its institutionally unmediated form.

In the second example, Taymūr (1961) takes a different position from that of ʾAbāẓa to demonstrate that *ʿāmmiyya* carries no less 'Arabness' (*ʿurūba*) than *fuṣḥā* and the claim that the two are fundamentally different is delusional (*mawhūm*). Taymūr starts his paper with an interesting observation: those who support *ʿāmmiyya* and intend to elevate it to the status of a fully fledged language write their ideas in *fuṣḥā*, and those who call for erasing *ʿāmmiyya* and defending *fuṣḥā* speak *ʿāmmiyya* in daily communication (ibid.: 126). The actual language practices of both camps ironically invalidate the stances of both. The disconnection between stances and practices shows that *fuṣḥā* and *ʿāmmiyya* are inseparable and complementary in language communication in the Arabic-speaking world and that neither of them can be disposed of.

Taymūr then lists three considerations showing that *ʿāmmiyya* varieties, like *fuṣḥā*, are indispensable parts of the Arabic language, or, in his words, the language of 'Arabness'. (1) *ʿĀmmiyya* varieties are older than *fuṣḥā*. According to Taymūr, before the rise of *fuṣḥā* as a lingua franca in Arabia, there were many *ʿāmmiyya* varieties of Arabic used by Arabian tribes and clans. After a long process of competition and natural selection, these varieties began to converge until a common linguistic 'mould' (*qālib*) appeared which contained selected features of different *ʿāmmiyya* varieties. This common 'mould' was later known as *fuṣḥā* in which the Qur'an was revealed (ibid.: 127). In other words, *fuṣḥā* and *ʿāmmiyya* share a common origin and the former was 'moulded' out of the latter. (2) The linguistic features and grammatical rules that differentiate *ʿāmmiyya* from *fuṣḥā* in the present age can also be attested in early records of *ʿāmmiyya* – the various dialects of Arab tribes in the pre- and early Islamic times. In Taymūr's view, this shows that *ʿāmmiyya* in the past had consistent grammatical rules. These rules, rather than exhibiting deviations of *ʿāmmiyya* from *fuṣḥā*, demonstrate that modern *ʿāmmiyya* developed from a pure Arabic lineage (*nasab*). Taymūr further argues that linguistic differences between *ʿāmmiyya* and *fuṣḥā* cannot be used to invalidate the 'Arabness' of *ʿāmmiyya*; in fact, these are merely different features of spoken and written varieties of the same Arabic language (ibid.: 130–1). (3) *ʿĀmmiyya* is characterised by a rich repertoire of words and phrases that clearly, precisely and vividly depict the experiences, perceptions, feelings and emotions of the common people. Although this repertoire is not free of foreign borrowings, the majority of it is in accordance with the morphological rules of the Arabic language. Besides, some *ʿāmmiyya* words and phrases are more expressive than their *fuṣḥā* counterparts. Contrary to ʾAbāẓa's arguments above, Taymūr believes that *ʿāmmiyya* has a richer lexicon than *fuṣḥā* and many Arabic neologisms used in *ʿāmmiyya* should be introduced into *fuṣḥā* to facilitate consolidating the latter in various domains of modern communication. Taymūr continues to claim that the repertoire of *ʿāmmiyya* includes priceless lexical treasures, which are 'live beehives' (*khalāya ḥayya*) of the Arab nation and 'the flowing blood in the vein' of Arabic speakers (ibid.: 132). Here, Taymūr resorts to the organic view of language, perceiving the Arabs, the Arab nation and the Arabic language as an organic whole, wherein *ʿāmmiyya* words and expressions are vital components.

Since *fuṣḥā* and *ʿāmmiyya* come from the same Arabic origin and possess similar linguistic traits, the claim that the two are linguistically different is said to be largely exaggerated. In fact, according to Taymūr, some Arabic speakers concoct gaps between *fuṣḥā* and *ʿāmmiyya* to show that the Arabic language they use is purely *fuṣḥā* and free of any *ʿāmmiyya* influence. For example, Taymūr reports that once he heard a radio anchorman using *suqāh* rather than *saqqāʾūn* as the plural of *saqqāʾ* 'water carrier'. Taymūr explains that, by using the broken plural pattern CuCaat rather than the sound masculine plural suffix *-ūn*, the anchorman thought he had chosen the correct *fuṣḥā* form instead of the popular *ʿāmmiyya* form of this plural. This is understandable because in Arabic *-ūn* is an unmarked plural pattern while CuCaat is a marked one; in the eyes of educated Arabic speakers, using the unmarked plural of a noun while there are one or more marked plurals of it is a sign of ignorance and lack of competence in *fuṣḥā*.[9] However, in this case, *saqqāʾ* has only the unmarked plural *saqqāʾūna* whilst *suqāh* is the plural of *sāqīn*, meaning 'cup-bearers in the banquet'. Artificial differentiation between *fuṣḥā* and *ʿāmmiyya* leads to linguistic errors and misunderstanding.

Taymūr concludes his paper by pointing out that, between *fuṣḥā* and *ʿāmmiyya*, there is an 'imagined curtain' (*sitār mawhūm*) causing widespread misunderstanding of and unnecessary enmity against *ʿāmmiyya*. He insists that this 'curtain' has to be removed; only then can *fuṣḥā* benefit from the rich resources of *ʿāmmiyya* and develop into a modern language able to meet the evolving needs of social communication. Taymūr's paper shows that, in the ALA discourse, the link between Arabic and the Arab nation is not constructed by reference to *fuṣḥā* only; *ʿāmmiyya* varieties have legitimate places in the expected unified Arabic language because they are believed to symbolise territorial, local and indispensable constituents of the Arab nation. I will return to this ideological ground later in this chapter.

No matter whether it is real or delusional that *fuṣḥā* and *ʿāmmiyya* represent two different linguistic instruments and repertoires in the Arabic-speaking world in terms of quality and function, neither ʾAbāẓa nor Taymūr supports diglossia. They both agree to develop a single standard Arabic language based on *fuṣḥā* which can serve both oral and written communications. What they disagree on is whether *ʿāmmiyya* should be incorporated into this process of standard language development. This negative attitude towards Arabic diglossia and this expectation for a linguistically refined and functionally sound standard Arabic language are echoed widely in the ALA discourse. From the instrumental point of view, this discourse proposes three reasons why Arabic diglossia is unfavourable and why sociolinguistic unity around a standard variety of Arabic is needed. I call these reasons instrumental because members of the ALAs base their reasoning on the premise that 'language is an instrument of communication'. However, as will be seen below, in actual reasoning, these members often stretch the instrumentality of Arabic beyond communication to make this language a symbolic proxy of extra-linguistic issues in Arab society.

Firstly, Arabic diglossia and illiteracy are perceived to correlate with each other. There is an underlying agreement in the ALA discourse that mass literacy is key to socioeconomic progress in Arabic-speaking countries (Mardīnī 1970; al-Ḥabābī 1978). However, some academicians suggest that the use of *ʿāmmiyya* has corrupted Arabic speakers' linguistic intuition, weakened their linguistic competence and alienated them from *fuṣḥā*, the native language of learning and literacy. This is because *ʿāmmiyya* comes from ignorance (*jahl*), and ignorance always kills knowledge (al-Nakdī 1957). Others mention a popular view in Arab society that the *fuṣḥā* taught in school contains too much archaic vocabulary and too many over-complicated grammatical rules, which do not suit modern communicative requirements; *fuṣḥā* pedagogy costs teachers and students too much time and energy; some young students even complain that learning *fuṣḥā* in school is like learning a foreign language (Kurd ʿAlī 1953; Taymūr 1961). It is then suggested that both *fuṣḥā* and its pedagogy need to be reformed so that mass literacy can be realised in a simplified and modernised version of Arabic (Ḥusayn 1966, quoted in ʾAbāẓa 1966: 223–4; al-Sayyid 1971).[10] On the other hand, illiteracy is considered to be the main cause of weakness in *fuṣḥā* and of the ascendancy of *ʿāmmiyya* in Arab society (al-Zaghlūl 1980: 145). In sum, the ALA discourse generally perceives illiteracy and the spread of *ʿāmmiyya* at the cost of *fuṣḥā* as two sides of the same coin, both indicating the backwardness of Arab society as a whole (Khalīfa 2001b).

Secondly, Arabic diglossia (in the sense that *fuṣḥā* is not accessible to the illiterate) is thought to perpetuate the gap between the literate elites (*al-khāṣṣa*) and the common people (*al-ʿāmma*), hampering social cohesion and national solidarity in individual Arab countries. The terms *al-khāṣṣa* and *al-ʿāmma* are old concepts instilled with new meanings. Generally speaking, *al-khāṣṣa* refers to the minority groups that hold power and authority over the control and distribution of economic and social resources in a community, while *al-ʿāmma* refers to all other groups lacking such power and authority. In traditional usage, *al-khāṣṣa* designates ruling families and court-patronised elites, including large landowners, religious scholars and legal experts; *al-ʿāmma* are the common people who constitute the middle or lower strata of society, having little access to political power and high culture. In modern usage, especially during the 1950s and 1960s when socialist ideas were popular in Arab political discourse, *al-khāṣṣa* and *al-ʿāmma* became labels of the high and low social classes respectively. Erasing class barriers and inviting *al-ʿāmma* into national politics were among the declared aims of various Arab socialist regimes in the second half of the twentieth century.

The ALA discourse links Arabic diglossia to the division between *al-khāṣṣa* and *al-ʿāmma* in Arab society as follows. (1) This discourse argues that *fuṣḥā* is the language used by the literate, but that *fuṣḥā* should also be used by the common people to guarantee progress and the equal sharing of public welfare in Arab society. This is because *fuṣḥā* is the medium of science, literature and knowledge; but if *fuṣḥā* is only used within the small group of literate elites without spreading to the common people, the latter's contribution to scientific progress and access to its benefits will be severely compromised. In a report submitted to the Annual Assembly of the Cairo Academy in 1948, it was declared that

> one nation (*ʾumma*) having two language [varieties] is not acceptable; the expanding gap between the language [variety] of living and that of

> thinking divides the nation into two: the literate minority and the illiterate majority; modern ideas, knowledge and literature will benefit the whole nation only if they are spread equally among *al-khāṣṣa* and *al-ʿāmma*; we [the Arabs] should remove the barrier between the insightful thinking minority (*al-qilla al-shāʿira al-mufakkira*) and the common manufacturing majority (a*l-kathra al-ʿāmma al-muntija*). (al-Zayyāt 1957: 184)

(2) The ALA discourse also incorporates the view that rejecting *ʿāmmiyya* elements as legitimate components and resources of the Arabic language and neglecting the linguistic creativity of the common people have prevented *fuṣḥā* from becoming a cross-strata language, thus exacerbating elite-closure in Arab society. This view argues that *ʿāmmiyya* is the language of the common people, who are part of the Arab nation and whose language is part of the Arabic linguistic repertoire. Accordingly, the living and rich coinages and styles used in *ʿāmmiyya* should be valued and incorporated into *fuṣḥā*. As the standard variety of Arabic, *fuṣḥā* should be developed for both the elites and the common people (Ḥusayn 1957; Jabrī 1968; Windfuhr 1973). It should be noted that, as an instrument of communication, *ʿāmmiyya* is not the language of the common people only but also the elites. Associating *ʿāmmiyya* with the former group in symbolic terms fits a populist reading of nationalism, which was common in the twentieth-century Arabic-speaking world, especially in the 1950s and 1960s. By making this symbolic association, incorporating *ʿāmmiyya* into *fuṣḥā* could be justified as a measure of integrating the common people into national/state communities in the Arabic-speaking world. It is clear that, in this case, Arabic has become a proxy of nationalist politics.

Lastly, the instrumental perspective of the ALA discourse suggests that Arabic diglossia leads to unintelligibility among territorial communities in the Arabic-speaking world, which undermines pan-Arab solidarity. General views in this regard in the ALA discourse include: (1) *fuṣḥā* is the only language variety of Arabic which can be understood across the Arabic-speaking world, thus becoming the natural linguistic link of the Arabic nation (Marqaṣ 1943; al-Maghribī 1948; al-Shabībī 1962; Ḥassān 1962, quoted in al-Shabībī 1962; Samʿān 1972; Windfuhr 1973; Maḥfūẓ 1978; Ḍayf 1997; 2000a; al-Muʿallimī 2000). (2) *ʿĀmmiyya* contains many mutually unintelligible regional varieties, impeding cultural exchange among the common, uneducated people in different *ʿāmmiyya*-speaking communities (al-Shabībī 1957; al-ʿAwda 1957; ʾAbāẓa 1966; Mardīnī 1970; al-Baṣīr 1978; al-Sāmrāʾī 1990). (3) The gap between regional *ʿāmmiyya* varieties, on the one hand, and between *fuṣḥā* and *ʿāmmiyya*, on the other, becomes a threat to the cultural solidarity of territorial Arabic-speaking communities (Khalīfa 2001b). The ALA discourse also positively evaluates the potential for the future integration of regional *ʿāmmiyya* varieties into *fuṣḥā*, due mainly to the rise of pan-Arab journalism and media, and increasing coordination between ALAs and educational institutions in the Arabic-speaking world (Fahmī 1962, quoted in al-Shabībī 1962; al-Bakrī 1976; Khalīfa 2001a).

On the surface, it seems that the instrumental perspective considers Arabic diglossia as a linguistic and communicative factor responsible for illiteracy, elite-closure and cross-dialectal unintelligibility in the Arabic-speaking world. However, none of these issues is purely linguistic and can be solved by merely optimising the instrumentality of Arabic. Rather, as I have mentioned above, these are in fact issues of state-formation and nation-building. Mass literacy and social mobility are necessary to the development of a sustainable political community in any modern sovereign state, and cross-dialectal communication is fundamental to pan-Arab solidarity. It follows that the instrumental considerations of Arabic diglossia in the ALA discourse are, on a deeper level, prompted by the relevance of this issue to the extra-linguistic national causes in the Arabic-speaking world. This relevance is largely symbolic, as will be shown in the section below on the symbolic perspective in the ALA discourse on diglossia.

Fuṣḥā and *ʿĀmmiyya* as National Symbols

The third discursive habitus running through the ALA discourse on diglossia symbolically links *fuṣḥā* and *ʿāmmiyya* to pan-Arab and territorial nationalisms in the Arabic-speaking world respectively, emphasising the mirroring effect between the Arabic language and Arab nation in their various forms. This habitus constructs a historical narrative wherein the consolidation and stagnation of *fuṣḥā* signify the strengthening and weakening of the Arab nation as a unified polity and civilisation, whilst the spread and promotion of *ʿāmmiyya* become symbols of the political weakness of the Arabs and the colonial/imperial conspiracy to divide, politically and culturally, the Arabic-speaking world further.

Before delving into the details of this discursive habitus vis-à-vis Arabic diglossia, I shall introduce the concept of 'construction' and 'construct'. 'Construction' literally means 'the action or process of building up'. 'Construct' is the result of construction. In sociology, construction refers to the process where various semiotic and discursive elements are employed to build a socially recognised entity or institution. And this 'constructed' social entity or intuition is a 'construct'. The construct has three characteristic features. First, it may not have an ontological existence, but it does exist in the epistemological space that is shared by members of a community. Second, its content – its reflection in the common epistemological space – is constantly changing, because the process of 'construction' that builds this construct never ends. Third, a construct is not an isolated entity. One construct is always co-constructed with other constructs or involved in the process of 'constructing' other constructs. New meanings may be brought into the content of the construct by means of continuing semiotic and discursive movements at the social level. Many familiar social entities or concepts can be seen as 'constructs', such as religion, law, nation, authoritarianism, liberal democracy and so on. Language could also be regarded as a social construct. Often, semiotic and discursive movements, in line with different sociopolitical agendas, endow language with meanings making it more than just an instrument of communication or a component of the human cognitive faculty. Since these additional meanings are usually manifest only in the epistemological space without real, or ontological, existence, language as a social construct is similar to a symbol, or a symbolic entity, which is manipulated by different agents to convey meanings serving various sociopolitical agendas and ideologies.

In the ALA discourse on diglossia, language is seen as a two-way social 'construct' in the sense that it both participates in and is subject to continuing semiotic and discursive construction. In one way, language is constantly 'constructed' in a historical process of sociopolitical transformation. In the other, language is regarded as actively engaged in 'constructing' or 'co-constructing with' other social constructs that carry considerable weight in the modern Arabic-speaking world, especially the constructs of 'nation' (*ʾumma*) and 'identity' (*huwiyya*).

Let us start with arguments about diglossia with respect to the premise that 'language is a construct'. The basis of these arguments in the ALA discourse is a shared historical narrative, which I have briefly touched upon before. In this narrative, the Arabic language and its inner divergence and convergence are treated as consequences of sociopolitical developments in the Arabic-speaking world in a long historical period, which could be roughly divided into the following phases (based on Marqaṣ 1943; al-Nakdī 1957; al-Shabībī 1957, 1960; al-ʿAbbādī 1957; al-ʿAjlānī 1957; Falīsh 1967; al-Muqaddasī 1971; Windfuhr 1973; Ibn al-Khūja 1978; ʿAbd al-Mawlā 1979; al-Zaghlūl 1980; al-Khūrī 1989; Ḥāfiẓ 1989; al-Sayyid 1990; al-Tarzī 1990; Ḍayf 2000a, 2000b; Ḥamāsa 2012). The reader should bear in mind that the following summary of this narrative is established from the writings of ALA members. This narrative may contradict our general knowledge about the historical development of Arabic, but nonetheless it reflects a common and routine way these members justified, historically, their attitudes towards diglossia in the modern Arabic-speaking world.

The first phase (roughly the seventh and eighth centuries), from the revelation of Islam to the completion of the Arab conquests, was the period when the Arabs conquered other peoples and civilisations and integrated them into a nascent Arab-Islamic empire. This vast expansion brought Arabic into contact with a wider world beyond the Arabian Peninsula and made it a lingua franca within the empire. According to Ḍayf (2000a: 3), this was a linguistic conquest, during which Arabic 'defeated' (*ẓafirat*) almost every language of the conquered peoples, including Persian, Aramaic, Nabatean, Syriac, Greek, Latin, and, later, Berber and Spanish. By contrast, al-ʿAjlānī (1957: 42) suggested that the spread of Arabic during the Arab conquests was not a linguistic imposition, but was due to the beauty of the language and its connection with Islamic revelation. Whatever the cause, the position of Arabic was believed to be consolidated in the Islamic empire, but at a cost nonetheless. The contact of Arabic with the languages of the conquered peoples increased its internal diversity. Regional Arabic varieties began to take shape, forming, as is often assumed, the typology of Arabic dialects still relevant today.

The second phase (roughly the ninth and tenth centuries) in the ALA narrative was the period when the Arab-Islamic empire reached its apogee. A remarkable degree of convergence and assimilation politically and culturally was thought to be achieved within the empire. Arabic, represented by its standard *fuṣḥā* variety, assumed dominant status in the empire and was significantly polished and enriched through a boom in learning, translation and literary production. Regional varieties during this phase were not considered to have spread to the extent that they could challenge the status of *fuṣḥā* and 'contaminate' its corpus severely. To prove this point, members of the ALAs tend to suggest that linguistic errors (*laḥn*) in the use of *fuṣḥā* during this phase were still moderate.

The third phase (roughly from the eleventh to the mid-nineteenth centuries) in the ALA narrative was a period witnessing the waning fortunes of the Arab-Islamic empire and the declining competence of native Arabic speakers in *fuṣḥā*. The Arabic-speaking world first witnessed centuries of political fragmentation with the rise and fall of territorial dynasties, the long war with the Crusaders and the devastating Mongol invasion. It was then reunified as part of the Ottoman Empire with a non-Arabic-speaking ruling dynasty. The colonial rule of European powers in the region from the mid-nineteenth to mid-twentieth centuries was the natural consequence of this centuries-long political weakness of the Arabs. The Arabic language gradually lost its old glory in the age of decline. *Fuṣḥā* was preserved thanks to Islam, the Qur'an and the pious religious scholars, but *ʿāmmiyya*, mixed with foreign tongues and vocabularies, flourished and spread to all middle and lower social strata in the region, overshadowing *fuṣḥā* in various domains of social communication. Moreover, from the mid-nineteenth century onwards, European colonisers and their Arab conspirators kept calling for *fuṣḥā* to be replaced with *ʿāmmiyya* varieties in individual Arab countries.

The fourth phase in the ALA narrative, starting from the mid-nineteenth century and continuing into the present day, was a period of awakening and revival. Modern political institutions were established, new ideas and values were spread, and the Arabic-speaking world witnessed continuous attempts made by the Arabs to regain their political initiative and cultural power. Considering the increasing contact, migration, cultural exchange, economic cooperation and political coordination between Arab countries from the mid-twentieth century onwards, many ALA members suggested that the Arabic language was now going through a new process of internal convergence: the gulf between *fuṣḥā* and *ʿāmmiyya* would be gradually reduced. They agreed that the ALAs should play a leading role in this process. However, according to Ḥāfiẓ (1989: 23) and ʿAbd al-ʿAzīz (11 July 2012 [personal interview]), this process has suffered from setbacks in recent decades (from the mid-1970s onwards), when *ʿāmmiyya* became popular in school, media and communications among young people at the expense of *fuṣḥā*.

The ALA discourse generally holds that the Arabic language has gone through the above historical phases, being shaped by sociopolitical shifts in the Arabic-speaking world (Muḥjāzī 2005). It is commonly agreed among ALA members that these shifts have left marks on Arabic, making it a 'container' (*wiʿāʾ*) in which a large number of historical traits of the academic, religious, economic, political and social life of the Arabs are encoded (*tastawʿib*) (Jabrī 1968; al-Baṣīr 1978; Ḥāfiẓ 1989, 2000; Ḍayf 1997). The term *wiʿāʾ* comes from the root verb *waʿā*, which means 'to memorise something' to the extent that the person who memorises the thing is always aware of its existence in his or her memory. So *wiʿāʾ* here indicates that the Arabic language does not only preserve the traits of the Arabs, but also has the potential to activate these 'preserved traits' in new historical situations. In this sense, Arabic is both 'constructed' by and 'constructing' the sociopolitical environment of the Arabic-speaking world. The term *tastawʿibu*, meaning 'to embrace or to enclose', implies that Arabic provides a thorough record of the sociopolitical life of the Arabs. Thus, the concept of 'container' actually shows the depth and thoroughness of Arabic in preserving the heritage and spirit of the Arab nation as well as its suffering and distress. Besides, the ALA discourse also understands Arabic as a 'proof' (*dalīl*) of the unique customs and spirit of the Arabs, their glorious past and their civilisational achievements, as well as their political weakness in the age of decline (ʾAbu Ḥadīd 1953). With specific reference to diglossia, linguistic unification is a proof of advancement of a nation, while linguistic fragmentation, which diglossia represents, becomes the proof of the weakness and decline of the nation (al-Jiwārī 1986).

In the ALA discourse, *fuṣḥā* is considered to be the best 'container' and proof of the heritage and spirit of the Arabs, or Arabness (*ʿurūba*). By contrast, *ʿāmmiyya* preserves many non-Arab, territorial traits of history, culture and spirit, making it a symbol of *shuʿūbiyya* and *ʾiqlīmiyya* (territorial nationalism) (ʾAbāẓa 1966: 213). Therefore, a possible impact of diglossia might be that it endows the Arabs with double personalities – one pan-Arab and one territorial. Symbolically, the *ʿāmmiyya* side of diglossia pollutes the purity of the Arab spirit, causes confusion in the national identity of the Arabs and handicaps the process of the reunification of the Arab nation in modern times.

However, some academicians also hold that *ʿāmmiyya* has preserved many traits of the Arab life that *fuṣḥā* has not. For example, when talking about colloquial proverbs, al-Baqlī (1971) argues that there are many 'ruins' (*ʾanqāḍ*) of *fuṣḥā* preserved in colloquial proverbs, which reflect aspects of Arab life that have not been recorded in *fuṣḥā*. Moreover, while it may be impure, *ʿāmmiyya* records the history and life of the ordinary people, who are also a legitimate part of the Arab nation (al-Zayyāt 1957). Therefore, *ʿāmmiyya* is an indispensable 'container' and proof of the heritage and spirit of the Arab nation.

Let us now turn to the arguments about diglossia with respect to the 'constructive' function of the Arabic language. The ALA discourse consistently and routinely views this function in two ways. First, it regards the Arabic language as a link (*rābiṭa*) that connects the elites and common people in Arab society, connects Arabs in one country with another and connects the Arab present with the past (ʾAbu Ḥadīd 1953; al-Shabībī 1957, 1962; al-Zayyāt 1957; al-Qulaybī 1978; Maḥfūẓ 1978; al-Ḥusnī 1990; Ḍayf 1997; al-Muʿallimī 2000). Arabic is seen as a bridge connecting almost all the elements (historical and contemporary, political and social, elitist and folk, and regional and communal) that are used to represent the Arab nation and inform the content and value of Arabs' national and cultural identity. Certainly only *fuṣḥā* can act as this national link for the Arabs, because it is thought to be the only language variety that is collectively shaped by Arabs coming from different regional, social and sectarian backgrounds and is, therefore, qualified to serve their common interests. *ʿĀmmiyya* is different. It is mainly a link of regional culture and interests and a symbol of territorial nationalisms. Some Orientalists and Arabs working for the interests of Western colonisers and imperialists called several times for *fuṣḥā* to be replaced with *ʿāmmiyya*, because, as is often assumed, they had an evil intention to encourage territorial nationalism and to hinder the Arabs from achieving reunification as both a political and cultural collectivity (al-Baṣīr 1978; al-Khaṭīb 1983; al-ʾAfghānī 1984). According to this perspective, diglossia is a social disease that needs to be combated and removed, for otherwise it will increase the number of cleavages of the Arab nation (Khalīfa 2001b).

The second way of perceiving the 'constructive' function of the Arabic language is based on the understanding that the linguistic 'reality' and the sociopolitical 'reality' are co-constructive – what occurred in the former will inform the latter and vice versa (ʾAbd al-Qādir 1960). This perspective calls attention to the potential threat of linguistic division to the solidarity of the Arab nation. According to some academicians, diglossia is not only linguistic but also social. They mention other types of diglossia – political diglossia, social diglossia, religious diglossia and identity diglossia in the Arabic-speaking world, although the content of some of these diglossias is not specified (Ibn al-Khūja 1978; al-Ṭayyib 1998). The academicians believe that the nature of these diglossias is the same as that of linguistic diglossia and that all diglossias are connected by a common sociopolitical reality they reflect: division, confusion and fragmentation. Therefore, eliminating Arabic diglossia and realising linguistic unification are important to the Arab nation because the unity of language will help eliminate other diglossias and build the unity of society, belief, nation and identity (al-Zayyāt 1957; al-Sāmrāʾī 1980; al-Ḥusnī 1990; al-Ṭayyib 2000). Linguistic unification and sociopolitical unification all belong to the same cause involving the Arabs today – regaining the status, strength and glory of the Arab nation and civilisation.

The role of the Arabic language in constructing the Arab nation was deeply imprinted on the minds of some ALA members, leading them to describe the Arabic language, especially *fuṣḥā*, in a passionate and emotional manner. As an example, Marqaṣ (1943: 32) uses three metaphorical phrases – wealthier sources (*ʾaghzar manbaʿ*), brighter beginnings (*ʾasṭaʿ maṭlaʿ*) and richer pastures (*ʾaṭyab martaʿ*) – to show that *fuṣḥā* is the only Arabic language variety qualified to serve pan-Arab national interests. By using the first phrase *ʾaghzar manbaʿ*, Marqaṣ likens *fuṣḥā* to a water source that is rich and abundant. *Manbaʿ* originally means 'spring' or 'well' which is often reminiscent of the well-known Zamzam Well, a heavenly miracle from which spring water suddenly rushed forth and saved Ismail and his mother Hagar from dying of thirst. In Arab culture, Ismail is believed to be the direct ancestor of all Arabs, so, if the Zamzam Well saved Ismail's life, by extension, it saved the whole Arab nation. The allusion here seems to be that, like the Zamzam Well and its spring water that saved and quenched the thirst of the Arabs, *fuṣḥā* plays the same role for the nation. The second phrase, *'asṭa' maṭla'*, enacts a metaphorical connection between *fuṣḥā* and the sun, because *maṭla'* literally means 'the place where the sun rises', and *sāṭi'* (*'asṭa'* is the comparative of *sāṭi'*) is commonly used to describe the brilliance and brightness of the sun. In the third phrase, *'aṭyab marta'*, *fuṣḥā* is imagined as a wealthy pasture where cattle, sheep and camels graze. The above three phrases present an image of *fuṣḥā* that fosters, sustains and enlightens the Arab nation. In addition, the three metaphors have a strong link to nature: water, the sun and food are necessary for the continuation of life; without any of them, life comes to an end. In that sense, *fuṣḥā* is vital for the existence of Arabs and the Arab nation; without this language, there will not be an Arab nation. These metaphors reveal Marqaṣ's deep affection and respect for *fuṣḥā*. The material I have consulted shows that he is not alone in this respect; others have likened *fuṣḥā* to light (Sam'ān 1972: 308; 'Amīn 1974: 59), 'a big star in the sky of Arabness' (Sherbatov 1984: 211) and 'the indispensable air we [the Arabs] breathe' (Būbū 1998: 571).

Based on the belief that the Arabic language and the Arab nation are co-constructive, the ALA discourse dismisses the efforts of some Orientalists and Arabs to support *'āmmiyya* and to elevate it to the status of a fully fledged language as political conspiracies against the solidarity of the Arab nation (al-Maghribī 1948; al-Nakdī 1960; al-Baṣīr 1978; al-'Afghānī 1984; al-Khaṭīb 1996; Khalīfa 2001a; Muḥjāzī 2005).[11] The proponents of *'āmmiyya* that are frequently mentioned by these academicians include (1) Wilhelm Spitta (1853–83), a German Orientalist who published *Grammatik des arabischen vulgärdialectes von Aegypten* ('The Grammar of Colloquial Arabic in Egypt') in 1880; (2) William Willcocks (1852–1932), a British engineer who published *Syria, Egypt, North Africa, and Malta speak Punic, not Arabic* in 1883 and *Why Is There no Power of Invention Among the Egyptians Now?* in 1893 to call for *fuṣḥā* to be abandoned and *'āmmiyya* to be adopted instead; (3) John Selden Willmore (1856–1931), a British judge who published *The Spoken Arabic of Egypt* in 1901; (4) Salāma Mūsā (1887–1958), an Egyptian Copt who advocated Egyptian Colloquial Arabic to be the official language of Egypt in order to seek an Egyptian political identity independent of the Arab one; and (5) 'Anīs Furayḥa (1903–92), a Lebanese linguist who proposed using

Latin script to write *ʿāmmiyya* as well as making *ʿāmmiyya* the official language(s) of Arab states.[12]

Academicians who hold this conspiracy theory strongly criticise these studies of Arabic dialects, accusing the Orientalists and their Arab fellows who undertook these studies of wanting to divide the Arab nation by making linguistic fragmentation in the Arabic-speaking world a reality that serves colonial and imperial interests. These academicians understand that these Orientalists frequently resorted to the death of Classical Latin and the rise of modern Romance languages to support their enthusiasm for *ʿāmmiyya*. Classical Latin, which had been the lingua franca in Western Europe throughout the Middle Ages, was gradually replaced by the vernaculars, which developed into autonomous Romance languages from the sixteenth century onwards. A concomitant of this linguistic division was the development of modern European nation-states, with most of these nation-states adopting their own 'national' languages. The Orientalists held that the Arabic language would go through the same process as Latin; *fuṣḥā* would eventually give way to regional colloquial varieties, collectively known as *ʿāmmiyya*. Relying on this Latin model, the Orientalists offered their suggestions on how to elevate *ʿāmmiyya* from a set of immature 'varieties' to fully fledged 'languages'. The Latin model became the source of legitimacy for their endorsement of *ʿāmmiyya*. Therefore, refuting the 'vernacular elevation' proposals requires denying this legitimacy, i.e. making invalid the application of the Latin model to forecasting the future of the Arabic language.

One of the most systematic refutations of the Latin model in the ALA discourse comes from Sāṭiʿ al-Ḥuṣrī's (d. 1968) *Ḥawla al-fuṣḥā wa-l-ʿāmmiyya* 'On *fuṣḥā* and *ʿāmmiyya*', published in the journal of the Damascus Academy in 1957. Al-Ḥuṣrī has been remembered as a leading pan-Arab nationalist thinker and as a founding father of the modern education system in Syria and Iraq, but he was also a correspondent member of both the Damascus Academy (1956–68) and the Iraqi Academy (1947–68) (MMD 31: 139; 43: 200; MMI 1: 22). His pan-Arab nationalist ideas and his insistence that *fuṣḥā* be the common language for all Arabs in the modern period were in good accordance with the agenda of the ALAs. How he dealt with Arabic diglossia could therefore be seen as representing the general tendency on this matter in the ALA discourse.

It is, then, not surprising to find out that al-Ḥuṣrī's refutation reinforces the thesis that language and nation are co-constructive. He reads the history of Latin as consisting of two processes: fragmentation (*tafarruʿ* or *tajazzuʾ*) and unification (*tawaḥḥud*) (1957: 243). The former refers to the split of Classical Latin into hundreds of vernacular languages, while the latter refers to the unification of these vernacular languages into the few Romance languages, such as French, Italian, Spanish, Portuguese and Romanian (ibid.: 243). Al-Ḥuṣrī considers the political disunity in medieval Europe – the collapse of the Roman Empire in Europe as a result of the Germanic invasion and the following consolidation of the federal states – to be a major cause of the fragmentation of Classical Latin, while the rise of the unifying modern nation-states is the cause of the unification of Romance languages (ibid.: 243–61).

Establishing this correlation between political and linguistic (dis) unity, he goes on to argue that the history of Arabic exhibits more unification than fragmentation, so *fuṣḥā* will not replicate the destiny of Classical Latin. This is because: (1) the Arabic-speaking world has never experienced political fragmentation as severe as that seen in medieval Europe (ibid.: 263); (2) unlike the huge impact of Germanic languages on Latin vernaculars, *fuṣḥā* managed to retain its social status and linguistic integrity even during the rule of non-Arabic-speaking dynasties; all foreign rulers were finally Arabised except the Ottomans, but the latter ruled outside the heartland of the Arabic-speaking world (ibid.: 262–3); (3) during the periods of political disunity, the Arabs were still connected at least by trade and pilgrimage (ibid.: 261–2); and (4) Islam only acknowledges *fuṣḥā* as the legitimate scriptural language, and so do many Arab Christian churches (ibid.: 264–5). Moreover, al-Ḥuṣrī suggests that, with the continuation of the *naḥḍa* 'revival' movement and the development of political pan-Arabism (at the time of his writing), the status and integrity of *fuṣḥā* is secure and the convergence of *ʿāmmiyya* towards *fuṣḥā* is inevitable, in a way very similar to the convergence of Latin vernaculars towards Romance languages (ibid.: 265–6).

Eliminating Arabic Diglossia

The above discussion of the organic, instrumental and symbolic perspectives on Arabic diglossia shows that there was a broad consensus within the ALAs that diglossia was a linguistic-cum-sociopolitical problem that needed to be solved. The Arab nation cannot benefit from linguistic fragmentation. Linguistic convergence was the commonly anticipated future of Arabic and a primary aim of language planning in the Arabic-speaking world. Three means of eliminating diglossia and attaining linguistic convergence were discussed in the ALA discourse, but no uniform agreement was reached.

The first means is replacing *fuṣḥā* with an *ʿāmmiyya* variety. This has been totally rejected by the ALAs. Academicians list several reasons to refute the proponents of *ʿāmmiyya*. From the perspective of 'language as an organism', some academicians ask: since any language naturally splits into sub-varieties after a period of evolution, how will the selected *ʿāmmiyya* variety prevent itself from future splits which would drag the Arabic-speaking world back to diglossia? By contrast, these academicians never apply this argument to *fuṣḥā*. This was mainly because they regard *fuṣḥā* as the variety that is already and always widely applicable in the Arabic-speaking world. From the perspective of 'language as an instrument', some academicians ask the following practical questions. Among the many *ʿāmmiyya* varieties, which one should language planners choose? How could language planners convince Arabs in one territory to abandon their mother tongue and adopt that of others? There were even more practical issues. How could writers use *ʿammiyya*, the colloquial, in writing? And, even if writing in *ʿāmmiyya* was possible, could the current Arabic orthographical system be modified to represent *ʿāmmiyya*? These academicians argue that writing in *ʿāmmiyya* is indeed very difficult and would, in fact, reduce readership. The question of orthographical representation of *ʿāmmiyya* is related to the notorious proposal of replacing Arabic letters with Latin script and is, therefore, considered unacceptable by the ALAs (see Chapter 5). From the perspective of 'language as a symbolic entity', supporting *ʿāmmiyya*, as shown in the above discussion of the colonial/imperial conspiracy and the Latin model, is seen as encouraging territorial nationalisms in the Arabic-speaking world and threatening the cause of Arab nationalism/solidarity and the common identity of the Arab people.

The second means of eliminating diglossia is replacing *ʿāmmiyya* with *fuṣḥā* or assimilating the former into the latter. This is more than welcome and has a number of followers within the ALAs. The symbolic values of *fuṣḥā* – its connection to Islam and the Arab past and heritage, and its role in shaping the Arab nation and national identity – are often mentioned as evidence of the legitimacy of *fuṣḥā* to be the lingua franca in the Arabic-speaking world. However, some academicians are not willing to see *fuṣḥā* as a diachronically unchanged and unchangeable language variety (from the organic perspective). These academicians argue that the available grammatical descriptions of *fuṣḥā* are too obscure for ordinary people to adopt this language variety in their daily communication (from the instrumental perspective); in addition, the convention of language use in the Arabic-speaking world does not favour the use of *fuṣḥā* in oral communication.

A related issue concerning the assimilation of *ʿāmmiyya* into *fuṣḥā* is whether different *ʿāmmiyya* varieties could be unified. In a panel discussion at the Cairo Academy, al-Shabībī (1962 [1957]) made a speech on Arabic diglossia. He raised the point that a chief obstacle to linguistic unification in the Arabic-speaking world is the diversity of *ʿāmmiyya* varieties, so the first step towards linguistic unification is to unify the vocabulary and pronunciation of these varieties. This radical proposal aroused wide objections from other academicians. In the discussion following the speech, the participants on the panel agreed that the unification of *ʿāmmiyya* varieties, especially on the phonetic level, was impossible. They argued that (1) language change is a natural process; it is not subject to the force of policy and regulation, nor does it comply with the will of language reformers; (2) language planners must face the reality that dialectal diversity existed in the Arabic-speaking world even before the revelation of the Qur'an; (3) although linguistic unification is a natural tendency of language change in the Arabic-speaking world, this will be achieved through a slow, gradual process of cultural and linguistic exchange between Arabs and through targeted education over several generations; (4) at the current stage, a more feasible task of the language academies is protecting the integrity of *fuṣḥā* and making it conform to modern communicative standards; and (5) the unification of dialects should therefore be excluded from the ALAs' agenda of LPLP. At the end of the discussion, al-Shabībī abandoned his proposal but insisted that language change in the Arabic-speaking world tended towards the convergence of all language varieties around *fuṣḥā*.

Al-Shabībī's proposal may sound unrealistic, but the very fact that it was made speaks of a rising confidence in the ability to engineer linguistic and social change to attain social cohesion and unity in the Arabic-speaking world during the late 1950s and the 1960s. It is not surprising to find some corresponding tenets of this proposal in Nasser's Arab socialism and the agendas of the two Baʿthist regimes in Syria and Iraq in the same period. Besides, in 1958, just one year after al-Shabībī made this proposal, the political union between Egypt and Syria was realised, which bolstered public enthusiasm for pan-Arab unity. The timing of this proposal may therefore indicate a symbolism of enforced language engineering: language unification is imagined as a part and parcel of the much-anticipated political unity. Members of the Cairo Academy were no doubt aware of the symbolic value of this proposal to the political future of the Arab nation, but competing considerations from the organic and instrumental perspectives prevented turning this symbolic gesture into a real language policy.

The third means – achieving linguistic convergence by integrating features of *fuṣḥā* and *ʿāmmiyya* into a simplified form of *fuṣḥā* – seems to be more realistic and acceptable for the ALAs. Proponents of the organic, instrumental and symbolic perspectives on Arabic diglossia all assume that integration as such was a more reasonable and feasible means to eliminate diglossia. Proponents of the organic perspective point out that *ʿāmmiyya* derived from *fuṣḥā*, retaining many distorted but originally pure Arabic words and expressions that are extinct in *fuṣḥā*. These academicians propose that language planners should identify these words and expressions from *ʿāmmiyya*, correct their structural distortions and reimport them into *fuṣḥā*. Proponents of the instrumental perspective emphasise that the merits of both *fuṣḥā* and *ʿāmmiyya* should be considered to reshape Arabic into a well-qualified instrument for modern mass communication. In their view, this entails, on the one hand, simplifying *fuṣḥā* to approach the ordinary, uneducated people and, on the other, 'elevating' *ʿāmmiyya* to reach the standard of *fuṣḥā* and to help enrich the lexicon of the latter. Linguistic convergence would be achieved through this combined process of simplification and 'elevation'.

Proponents of the symbolic perspective hold that (1) the literate elites educated in *fuṣḥā* and the *ʿāmmiyya*-speaking common people are both part of the Arab nation; and (2) since the common people should be incorporated into the nation, *ʿāmmiyya* should also be integrated into the national language rather than being abandoned, not to mention that the literate elites also speak *ʿāmmiyya* in their daily communication. This, according to these academicians, would help eliminate the identity confusion caused by diglossia.

A related issue of the above linguistic integration revolved around creating an imagined language variety called Middle Arabic. One ardent supporter of Middle Arabic was Luṭfī al-Sayyid, a reformist Egyptian thinker and the president of the Cairo Academy (1945–63). He was reported to have called for 'creating a middle language between [*fuṣḥā* and *ʿāmmiyya*] in a double trajectory of lexically enriching the standard and grammatically correcting the colloquial' (Suleiman 2003: 173). This would harness 'the living power of the colloquial to the sanctioned authority of the standard as the language of research and scientific exchange' (ibid.: 173). Shawqī Ḍayf, the president of the Cairo Academy (1996–2005), was also interested in the rapprochement between *fuṣḥā* and *ʿāmmiyya* to create a middle language between the two. In his article *Lughat al-masraḥ bayn al-ʿāmmiyya wa-l-fuṣḥā* 'The language of the theatre between *ʿāmmiyya* and *fuṣḥā*', Ḍayf (1980) approved of the Egyptian playwright Tawfīq Ḥakīm's attempt to render *ʿāmmiyya* expressions into the pattern of *fuṣḥā* to create a 'third language' that would accommodate the linguistic habits of both the upper and lower classes.

Ideas of *fuṣḥā-ʿāmmiyya* integration have informed many of the ALAs' LPLP projects. On the lexical level, the ALAs make consistent efforts to collect words relating to modern life (*ʾalfāẓ al-ḥaḍāra*), i.e.

neologisms used in daily communication. In the 1990s, they began coordinating a cross-state project *Dhakhīrat al-lugha al-ʿarabiyya* 'treasure of the Arabic language' in order to gather and unify neologisms from all over the Arabic-speaking world.[13] There are also ongoing projects of compiling dictionaries that incorporate recent coinages, including the ambitious *al-Muʿjam al-kabīr* 'the big dictionary' project of the Cairo Academy. Besides, discussions regarding simplifying pedagogical grammar and reforming Arabic script are also inspired by and believed to serve linguistic integration between *fuṣḥā* and *ʿāmmiyya*.

Arabic Diglossia, Pan-Arab Nationalism and Territorial-State Nationalisms

In this last section, I will explain why the ALA discourse consistently perceives Arabic diglossia as a problem, as shown in all three discursive habiti: organic, instrumental and symbolic. I will suggest that this perception has been conditioned by the mixing of two types of nationalism and two senses of national identity among Arab intellectuals in general throughout the twentieth century. These two types of nationalism are the romantic, pan-Arab nationalism, which has no corresponding political realisation, and the contractual, territorial-state nationalisms (explained below) which are congruent with individual Arab states. National languages are always regarded as centripetal forces in the formation and development of nations and nationalisms (Suleiman 2003: 124). In the Arabic setting, however, *fuṣḥā* and *ʿāmmiyya* are perceived to play different, sometimes contradictory roles and carry different weight in pan-Arab and territorial-state nationalisms respectively. Arabic diglossia, or the coexistence of *fuṣḥā* and *ʿāmmiyya*, naturally weakens the centripetal force of the Arabic language in both types of nationalism. Besides, national languages are also believed to be barometers that record and reflect the situation of nations and nationalisms. Languages thus become representatives of nations and nationalisms. As shown by the ALA discourse, it is routinely accepted that *fuṣḥā* is a representative of pan-Arab nationalism while *ʿāmmiyya* varieties are representatives of territorial-state nationalisms. The lack of convergence between *fuṣḥā* and *ʿāmmiyya* becomes a symbol of the lack of congruence between the two types of nationalisms in the Arabic-speaking world.

'Nationalism' is a conceptual amalgam. It can refer to the movements or processes of nation-state building, but it can also designate the ideologies and discourses in relation to both the rise of national communities and the congruence of these communities with sovereign states. Nationalist movements do not always manage to create nation-states, but they bring about and reinforce a political pattern and an international system of nation-states. Nationalist ideologies do not always have political realisations, but they ingrain nationalist feelings, attitudes and beliefs in the collective minds of potential or established national communities. In other words, nationalist movements aim to create the political reality of national communities while nationalist ideologies seek to construct the psychological-cognitive reality of such communities. Moreover, by constructing both realities, nationalism develops into a structuring force that 'structures our daily lives and the way we perceive and interpret the reality that surrounds us' (Özkirimli 2010: 2). The ALA discourse on Arabic diglossia is a product of this structuring force of nationalism in the Arabic-speaking world.

The relation between language and nationalism has long been a focus of LPLP literature. Fishman (1968a) distinguishes between nationalism and nationism as two different ideological movements of nation-building that pose different language problems. He defines nationalism as the 'process of transformation from fragmentary and tradition-bound ethnicity to unifying and ideologized nationality' (ibid.: 41) and nationality as the 'sociocultural entity that may have no corresponding politico-geographic realization' (ibid.: 39). By contrast, he creates the term 'nationism' to designate the formation of a 'political-geographic entity' called 'nation' which may not be necessarily congruent with a pre-existing nationality (ibid.: 39). The language problem posed by nationalism, according to Fishman, is 'maintenance, reinforcement, and enrichment' of the common language used in the nationality in order to 'foster the nationalistic (the vertical or ethnically single) unity, priority, or superiority of the sociocultural aggregate' (ibid.: 43); while the language problem facing nationism is quickly choosing a literary language to promote mass literacy in order to achieve 'horizontal integration' of the nation (ibid.: 43). Similarly, Wright (2012) distinguishes between ethno-linguistic and civic-contractual nationalisms. The former sees the nation (or nationality in Fishman's sense) as a mystical communion predating the state (or nation in Fishman's sense) and the national language as one, yet probably the most important, natural bond that connects members of the nation together; the nation in this sense usually has a unified 'cultural and linguistic space' but may be 'economically and politically fractured' (ibid.: 62). With respect to civic-contractual nationalism, however, the nation is formed via 'the congruence of sovereign people, inalienable territory and single national language' with or after the consolidation of the state (ibid.: 61).

The above differentiation of nationalisms and their influence on national languages is highly idealised; ethno-linguistic and civic-contractual nationalisms (or nationalism and nationism) cannot be neatly separated and most of the world's nation-states witness a mixture of both. Fishman (1968a: 44) points out that 'all nations apportion attention and resources between the claims of authenticity (sociocultural integration) on the one hand and the claims of efficiency (political integration) on the other'. Wright (2012: 64) also acknowledges that the 'desire for congruence of people, language and territory' is shared by both types of nationalism.

The mixing of ethno-linguistic and civic-contractual nationalisms is most evident in the twentieth-century Arabic-speaking world in both movements and (intellectual and popular) ideologies of nation-state building. The rise of modern sovereign states and the formation of state-based national identities in the Arabic-speaking world from the early twentieth century onwards fit the pattern of civic-contractual nationalism. For most Arab states, their sovereign powers were imposed and their territories were artificially demarcated before the formation of state-national collectivities and sentiments. These states were largely products of European colonial rules in the Middle East and North Africa (1830–1962), post-WWI settlements of the former Ottoman territory and post-WWII independence movements in European-mandated territories and colonies. Over time, these states have developed their own political institutions, formed their own citizenries and public spheres, and constructed their own national histories and myths, such as Pharaonic Egypt, Mesopotamian Iraq and Phoenician Lebanon. In general, these state-formation projects have not only brought into existence new political-cum-national communities but also shaped a multitude of state-national identities.

However, the Arab states are not immune to the influence of pan-Arab nationalism in the Arabic-speaking world. Pan-Arab nationalism fits the pattern of ethno-linguistic nationalism because it presupposes the existence of the Arab nation, which is defined first and foremost by the Arabic language, and expects a unified Arab nation-state. Although so far all projects aiming at creating a unified polity in congruence with the Arab nation have failed, pan-Arabism is still a component of the sociopolitical reality in the Arabic-speaking world (revealed in, for example, inter-state cooperation over the Palestinian cause, educational concerns, inter-state competition for Arab leadership, the flow and migration of skilled workers and intellectuals, and pan-Arab press and media) and a vital constituent of various Arab national identities. This is because nearly all Arab states and their political communities are subject to the following common factors: (1) common experience (anti-Turkification, anti-Zionism, anti-European colonialism, anti-imperialism, anti-despotism, wars, the rise and fall of secular nationalist revolutions, the rise of political Islam, economic and cultural globalisation, to name just a few); (2) common missions (state-building, industrialisation, urbanisation and modernisation); (3) common geopolitical positions in the current world-system; and (4) shared beliefs, customs, history and cultural legacy.

Ethno-linguistic and civic-contractual nationalisms in the Arabic-speaking world have been both antithetical to each other and mutually constructive. In practice, on the one hand, the maturation of Arab states and their political communities have increasingly consolidated a multi-state system in the Arabic-speaking world, making the unified Arab polity or federation an improbable dream; on the other, individual Arab states have been shaped by and continually reinforce the above-mentioned commonalities among them. In ideology, territorial civic-contractual nationalism constitutes a rejection of pan-Arab ethno-linguistic nationalism in some cases, while acting as an ally in others (Suleiman 2003: 163). Overall, 'in most Arab countries, the pull of cultural (pan-Arab) nationalism counterbalances in varying degrees the imperatives of the political nationalism of the sovereign state, and vice versa' (ibid.: 25). This is the structural context out of which the ALA discourse on diglossia has been formed, reproduced and reiterated.

However, this structural context is not diachronically fixed or unchanged. Arab nationalism, including both pan-Arab and state-patriotic variations, is itself a historical phenomenon (Choueiri 2000). Its development in the twentieth century can be roughly divided into three periods:[14] (1) the period of independence (from the collapse of the Ottoman Empire in 1918 to the mid-1950s when European colonial regimes gradually gave way to independent Arab states): Arab nationalism in this period mainly focused on constructing a system of state-polities suitable for the Arabs to achieve self-governance and independent rule; (2) the period of unity and social reform (from the mid-1950s to mid-1970s): Arab nationalism in this period attempted to acquire political unity among newly independent Arab states and promote rapid social transformation in individual Arab countries; and (3) the period of state maturation (from the mid-1970s to the end of the twentieth century): pan-Arab nationalism as a political movement and ideology witnessed a decline; the multi-state system was consolidated; state nationalisms followed a 'state-first' policy and placed more emphasis on internal socioeconomic development than before; and, finally, inter-state conflicts and enmity intensified. Although in the third period, state nationalisms became the de facto political framework, common issues in the Arabic-speaking world still affected individual Arab states, and sentiments toward the cultural solidarity of the Arabs did not die out (Humphreys 1999). It was also during this period that transnational oppositional movements against authoritarian Arab regimes gained strength, showing that the Arab states were still connected (Halliday 2005). In sum, the change of focus in Arab nationalist movements and ideologies throughout history did not change the persistence of dual nationalisms – pan-Arab and territorial-state – in the Arabic-speaking world.

With the above structural context and historical dynamism in mind, let us review the three discursive habiti of the ALA discourse on Arabic diglossia, to see how this nationalist context in its different forms has influenced the development and reiteration of this discourse.

The 'language as an organism' perspective has its counterpart in the linguistic tradition of the German Romantics. The German linguist August Schleicher (1821–68) considers linguistics to be a branch of biology. He applies the Darwinian view of evolution to language, stating that 'every language represents a branch in its evolutionary "family tree"' (Seuren 1998: 85) and 'languages are natural organisms that . . . grew according to certain laws which also determine their development, ageing and death' (Schleicher 1863: 6–7, quoted in Seuren 1998: 85). This view implies that, like organisms, languages can be grouped into families, and structurally similar languages may have the same origin. This view also implies that, like organisms, languages compete to survive, and only the 'fittest' languages remain; and, like organisms, languages around the world are in different stages of evolution, with some languages being superior to others. This organic understanding of language was accepted and developed by the German language philosopher Wilhelm von Humboldt (1767–1835). He considers languages to be living entities differing in their evolutionary statuses. He links language to culture and thought, perceiving the three as 'jointly determining as well as being determined by the degree of evolution and civilisation achieved by each language community' (Seuren 1998: 109). Here Humboldt establishes an organic connection between a language and a linguistic-national community. He further suggests that the inner destiny and spirit of a nation determines the kind of language it has (ibid.: 112). Based on this connection, Humboldt holds that Western Europe is superior to other nations and civilisations because the languages of Western Europe are evolutionarily more advanced than other languages (ibid.: 110–11). Humboldt's view on language, nation and their degree of evolution had a direct influence on German Romantic nationalism in the nineteenth and twentieth centuries, which saw the German language as a central constituent of the German nation and proof of the German spirit and superiority. It is worth mentioning that German nationalism is usually regarded as the prototype of ethno-linguistic nationalism (Wright 2012).

There is no compelling evidence to show that the ALA discourse was influenced by this German Romantic view on language and nation. However, parallel views have been found in the writings of a number of Arab nationalists, such as Sāṭiʿ al-Ḥuṣrī and Zakī al-ʾArsūzī (1900–68).[15] Besides, Arab language planners were aware of the Turkish practices of LPLP in the early decades after Turkey's independence, which adopted the German idea to demonstrate that Turks are the original people because Turkish is the original human language (see the discussion on the Sun Language Theory in Lewis (1999)).

German Romanticism links language and nation together in a way that makes language not only a defining constituent of the nation, but also an organic entity co-evolving with the nation. Language therefore becomes a living representative of the nation. The strength or weakness of a nation can be established by assessing the vitality of its national language. This logic is widely accepted in the ALA discourse, as shown in the symbolic perspective of this discourse that treats the Arabic language and the Arab nation as mutually constitutive. The Arabic language is shaped by the Arab nation and vice versa; the destiny of the Arabic language is also the destiny of the Arab nation and vice versa. This makes all perceptions, evaluations and historical narratives of Arabic potentially perceptions, evaluations and historical narratives of the Arab nation and vice versa.

This implies that how Arabic, its origin, history and future, as narrated in the organic perspective of the ALA discourse, can be well applied to the origin, history and future of the Arab nation. *Fuṣḥā*, whether a golden protolanguage established before the appearance of *ʿāmmiyya*, or a refined variety combining common features of all other varieties, is the indisputable representative of the Arab nation. The characteristics of *fuṣḥā*, such as integrity, purity, eloquence and fineness, well exemplify similar features of the Arab nation: a unified, noble collectivity who have retained incomparable courage and wisdom and to whom the divine message of Islam was revealed.[16] The characteristics of *ʿāmmiyya*, especially corruption and hybridity, represent the so-called *muwallad* communities developing from the interbreeding of the Arabs and local ethnicities following the Arab conquests. Obviously, most Arabs today are descendants of these early *muwallad* communities. In terms of national identity, they bear both an Arab ingredient and a regional, territorial ingredient. An Arab may be a Syrian, an Egyptian, an Iraqi, a Yemeni, a Moroccan and so on. The system of modern Arab states simply enhances this double identification. However, in the mind of most members of the ALAs, the Arab part of national identity should outweigh the territorial one; the latter may not be erased, but its existence should benefit rather than harm or sideline the former; and the two should be integrated with each other towards a unity of the Arab nation and a single national identity, which is always anticipated. This is well represented by the perception of the relation between *fuṣḥā* and *ʿāmmiyya*: that *ʿāmmiyya* is the descendant of *fuṣḥā*; that *ʿāmmiyya* retains many *fuṣḥā* features; that *ʿāmmiyya* should be studied to enrich *fuṣḥā*; and that the gap between *fuṣḥā* and *ʿāmmiyya* should be narrowed. Moreover, the historical narrative of Arabic about the unity of the language in the golden age, its fragmentation into multiple local *ʿāmmiyya* varieties in the age of decline and its final convergence towards *fuṣḥā* in the future is parallel to the historical narrative of the Arab nation, from unity to fragmentation and then to unity again in the future. All concern over the Arabic language is concern over the Arab nation; all aspirations for the former are aspirations for the latter.

Parallel organic perspectives can be easily found in the discourse of Arab nationalism. Like Arabic in the ALA discourse, the Arab nation was also depicted as a living being. This view was incorporated into 'a more or less standard formulation of the Arab self-view' by the end of the 1920s (Dawn 1988: 68). Darwīsh al-Miqdādī, in his textbook[17] *Tārīkh al-ʾumma al-ʿarabiyya* 'History of the Arab Nation', first published in 1931, considers the 'Arab Island' to be 'a living body' of which the 'head' is the Fertile Crescent, the 'heart' is central Arabia, and the 'extremities' are the Arabian coastlands from the Gulf of Aqaba to the Gulf of Basra (ibid.: 69; see also Choueiri 2000: 34). It is clear that, in al-Miqdādī's perception, the Arab nation is an organic whole, and the various Arab regions are its vital parts. This perception is very similar to the view in the ALA discourse that *ʿāmmiyya* varieties are descendants of *fuṣḥā* and indispensable parts of the Arabic language.

As a living being, the Arab nation had gone through efflorescence, decay, decline and awakening, like the Arabic language. This view was reflected in the discussion of *Jāhiliyya* 'the period of ignorance' in the nineteenth-century discourse on Islamic modernism and Arab *nahḍa*, which were later incorporated into Arab nationalist discourse in the early twentieth century. For example, a common view al-Miqdādī adhered to in his textbook 'implicitly divided [Semito-Arab history] into two periods of greatness, the ancient Semitic and the Islamic, each followed by two periods of decline in which the alien dominated' (ibid.: 70). According to this view, the Arabs were the best heirs of the Ancient Semitic civilisation. This great civilisation was destroyed by 'Aryan imperialism' (ibid.: 72), referring to the dominance of the Roman and Persian Sassanid Empires in the now Arabic-speaking world before the advent of Islam, leading to the first *Jāhiliyya* period in Semito-Arab history. The rise of Islam brought about the second period of greatness, but it was again challenged by Aryan imperialism, referring to the Persian and European hostilities to the Arabs throughout the Middle Ages and lasting until modern times. The Islamic civilisation gradually declined, downgraded to the second *Jāhiliyya*, of which the present Arab predicament was a part. Interestingly, although al-Miqdādī blames foreign subversion for the appearance of the two *Jāhiliyya* periods, he links this foreign subversion to the weakness of the national sentiment of the Arabs. He holds that 'the intensity of tribal solidarity (*ʿaṣabiyya*) at the expense of national sentiment' among the Arabs gave imperialists opportunities to corrupt the 'family and social life' of the Arabs and to fetter their 'minds with superstitions', causing collective weakness of the Arab people (ibid.: 72). The central argument that civilisational decline was caused by weakness of national solidarity and foreign corruption echoed the historical narrative of the appearance of linguistic errors after the Arab conquests and the deviation of *ʿāmmiyya* from *fuṣḥā* in the ALA discourse.

These parallel themes and narratives between the ALA and nationalist discourses reveal that these two discourses were co-constitutive in accordance with the organic view of Arabic and the Arab nation. The fact that al-Miqdādī's textbook represented the standard Arab self-view in the 1920s and 1930s, and that the two representatives of the organic perspective of the ALA discourse (al-Maghribī (1923) and al-Qudsī (1923) in the journal of the Damascus Academy) were produced during the same period, suggested that both discourses were guided by the sociopolitical milieu of the time. As I have mentioned before, this was the period when the majority of modern Arab states were still striving for independence and the multi-state system was yet to be consolidated. Competing ways to represent the political will of the Arabs in a unified pan-Arab polity or in multiple yet-to-be defined sovereign states co-existed. The uncertainty and openness of the Arab political future made the organic view attractive. By referring to the evolution of organisms in the natural world, the revival of Arabic and the Arab nation from the previous decay and decline could be supported by a Darwinian reading of social history. By resorting to the family (in the case of al-Maghribī on the connection between *fuṣḥā* and *ʿāmmiyya*) and the body (in the case of al-Miqdādī on the Arab nation) metaphors, the current fragmentation in the linguistic and political domains was believed not to comprise the inherent link among varieties of Arabic, on the one hand, and among Arab countries/polities, on the other; thus the future linguistic and political convergence of the Arabic-speaking world was guaranteed. By alluding to the Darwinian 'survival of the fittest' principle, both the convergence of Arabic language varieties towards *fuṣḥā* and the struggle for Arab independence and unity were justified. When independence was (largely) achieved, and the multi-state system was installed, the focus of nationalist movements and discourse turned to the issues of social reform and the pan-Arab unity of established Arab states, where the instrumental perspective of the ALA discourse found its parallels.

The period of social reform and pan-Arab unity witnessed the prevalence of Nasserism and Baʿthism as the leading political ideologies in the Arabic-speaking world. The main content of the two ideologies can be found in *al-Mīthāq al-waṭanī* 'The National Charter', promulgated as the tenets of the Egyptian president Nasser's Arab socialism in 1962 (Choueiri 2000: 194–7). *Al-Mīthāq* set the unity of the Arab nation based on language, history and hope as the ultimate aim. However, it claimed that this unity was not the responsibility of Arab governments but '"popular progressive forces" throughout the Arab world' (ibid.: 194). The Arab masses were the pillar of the 'popular progressive forces' but they had not yet led the cause of the Arab nation, because of their 'twin adversaries . . . namely "imperialism and local reactionaries"' (ibid.: 194). There should therefore be a social revolution in every Arab country to guarantee the political initiative of the Arab masses. *Al-Mīthāq* considered 'the sovereignty of the people', 'an egalitarian society, based on equal opportunity, sufficiency and production' and 'the elimination of class distinctions' to be the aims of this social revolution. Arab unity was contingent on this revolution. Only when the social transformation in individual Arab countries was completed would the pan-Arab unity be possible. Similarly, the Baʿth party, which dominated Syrian and Iraqi politics from the 1960s, persistently endorsed 'unity, freedom and socialism' as its motto and laid double emphasis on social reform and pan-Arab unity.

These seemingly socialist agendas in fact reflected the genuine need of newly independent Arab states to create responsive, coherent political communities in their own territories. The support from these communities would grant the Arab states legitimacy to survive and rule. Consolidating state-society solidarity was the immediate priority for every Arab state, while Arab unity became a long-term, if not secondary, political aim. Sticking to the ideology of Arab unity and making sporadic experiments of unity were also necessary to the consolidation of the state system in the Arabic-speaking world, because (1) in the context where state-national identities were too weak as communal identities to sustain political loyalties in individual Arab states, Arabness would be the most powerful resource to foster these loyalties; and (2) for any Arab state that wanted to claim pan-Arab leadership in a multi-state Arab world, Arabness and Arab unity were necessary to be utilised in the leadership competition. It seemed that, in the period of social reform and Arab unity, state-oriented policy was intertwined with pan-Arab unity in a sense that the former treated the latter as an indispensable ally.

Both internal social solidarity and pan-Arab unity naturally required an effective and efficient mode of communication, sustained by a standard, competent and easy-to-learn language. The instrumental perspective of the ALA discourse on Arabic diglossia could be seen as a response to this new linguistic need. The evaluations of *fuṣḥā* and *ʿāmmiyya*, blaming diglossia for illiteracy, social division in individual Arab countries and political fragmentation in the Arabic-speaking world, and the appeal for linguistic integration, were all pertinent issues to be debated and tackled. Arabic here was treated as the instrument and resource to serve extra-linguistic, socio-political agendas. The different linguistic needs recognised in Fishman's two types of nationalism were discussed in the ALA discourse, which revealed the high degree of mixture of the two nationalisms in the Arab settings.

Unlike the organic perspective on diglossia, whose parallel nationalist discourse was mainly found in the first period of Arab nationalism, and the instrumental perspective on diglossia, which was mainly a response to Arab nationalism in its second period, the symbolic perspective on diglossia found its parallels in both the first and second periods of Arab nationalism. Any view which links Arabic to Arab nationalism in a way that goes beyond the normal functions of language as an instrument of communication can be seen as symbolic.

Accordingly, claims, such as that the rise and decline of Arabic indicate the rise and fall of the Arab nation, that *fuṣḥā* sustains the survival of the Arab nation and that *ʿāmmiyya* varieties are colonial/imperial proxies that subvert Arab solidarity, established a connection between language and nation that cannot be proven empirically; rather, this connection was largely invented or imagined in a similar manner to 'the invention of tradition' (Hobsbawm 1983) and 'imagined communities' (Anderson 1983) notions of nationalist discourses. This inventiveness freed the ALA discourse from validating the role of Arabic in the formation of Arab nationalism and national identities on rigid empirical grounds. In other words, even if there was no de facto connection between Arabic and the Arab nation, this connection could still be established on the symbolic level as long as there was a need for it to serve the national cause. Hence, the symbolic perspective was persistently deployed in both periods of Arab nationalism.

Suleiman (2003) provides several examples of Arab intellectual discourse in the first two periods of Arab nationalism which highlight the symbolic role of Arabic as 'the marker and the ingredient of the greatest importance in the formation of the Arab national identity' (ibid.: 158). The Lebanese linguist and jurist al-Shaykh ʿAbd al-Lāh al-ʿAlāylī (1914–96), in his *Dustūr al-ʿarab al-qawmī* 'The Arab's National Constitution', first published in 1941, considers language to be 'a mirror of the nation's feelings and thinking' and 'a boundary-setter between its speakers and others' (ibid.: 121). He therefore calls for the Arabs to 'dedicate themselves completely to their language and [to] shun any form of allegiance to other languages' (ibid.: 121) in order to demarcate the Arab nation from other nations. Similarly, Nadīm al-Bīṭār (1948–93) in his early writings also points out the boundary-setting function of language. He regards language as a vital constituent of the nation to the extent that a nation losing its language will 'surely perish and die' (ibid.: 123). Like many members of the ALAs, al-Bīṭār treats promoting *ʿāmmiyya* to be official languages in Arab states as a form of colonial conspiracy that utilises the sentiments of territorial nationalisms to 'undermine the affiliative force of Arab nationalism' (ibid.: 123). Likewise, Sāṭiʿ al-Ḥuṣrī treats Arabic as a defining ingredient of Arabness and the Arab nation (ibid.: 132). Concerned that the linguistic division of Arabic would cause further political fragmentation in the Arabic speaking-world, he rejects 'the view which correlates the present boundaries of the Arab states with discrete linguistic boundaries of the dialectal kind' (ibid.: 142). In a similar but more radical fashion, Zakī al-ʾArsūzī argues that the genius of the Arab nation resides in the lexicon and grammar of the Arabic language, which is a 'storehouse' that contains both the wisdom of the Arabs and heavenly beauty (ibid.: 148, 154). For him, reviving Arabic is 'a precondition for reviving the Arabs as a nation' (ibid.: 157). Besides, Suleiman (2003: 124) reports that 'the view that Arabic is the principle centripetal force of Arab unity capable of countering the centrifugal power of the territorial state is embedded in the discourse of the Baʿth party and in [Nasser's] brand of Arab nationalism'. So here we see a clear continuity of the symbolic perspective on Arabic and the Arab nation in the first two periods of Arab nationalism.

The symbolic view in the ALA discourse was part of and a response to the symbolic perspective in the Arab nationalist discourse described above. This view supported the organic view to enhance the mirroring relation between Arabic and the Arab nation in terms of their synchronous effluence, corruption, decline and revival. It also conformed to the instrumental view, stressing that social reform and national unity can be achieved via changing and improving the situation of the Arabic language, and that social division and political fragmentation can be reversed via a rapprochement between *fuṣḥā* and *ʿāmmiyya*. These three discursive habiti – organic, instrumental and symbolic – intertwined with each other, producing a consistent and routinised ALA discourse on Arabic diglossia.

In the third period of Arab nationalism, Arab states became more comfortable with the multi-state system vis-à-vis the unstable pan-Arab framework and turned their attention to intra-state affairs and self-interests. The ALA discourse became an arena where various nationalist sentiments met with each other, including the debris of the pan-Arab unity dream, memories of the previous nationalist experiences, dissatisfaction with current inter-state Arab politics and long-term exceptions for the merger of Arab states and the revival of the Arab nation. In this discourse, Arabic diglossia became a mirror of contemporary Arab politics, where the growing focus on state interests was contrasted with the comparative weakness of the Arabic-speaking world as a whole. What this discourse depicted ardently and favourably, such as the integration and unity of *fuṣḥā* and *ʿāmmiyya*, became a compensation for both the linguistic and political realities of the Arabic-speaking world.

Overall, the change of focus in the history of Arab nationalism as an amalgam of movements and ideologies has not so far altered the discursive structure constituted by the mixing of pan-Arab and territorial-state nationalisms. This mixing means that, when thinking about the history and future of the Arabic language, the relation between *fuṣḥā* and *ʿāmmiyya*, and the connection between Arabic and the Arab nation, Arab intellectuals have to balance the interests and voices of two types of national communities. One is that of their fellow countrymen, and the other is that of their Arab brothers and sisters in other Arab states. In so doing, they cannot escape the dilemma of double loyalties and double self-identifications. This duality poses a continuing challenge to the whole Arab intellectual community, causing puzzles and worries that lead to the divergent problematisation of Arabic diglossia in the ALA discourse. Resolving the problem of diglossia by integrating *fuṣḥā* and *ʿāmmiyya* was a linguistic response to the duality of nationalism in the sociopolitical arena.

The interaction between the ALA discourse on diglossia and the duality of Arab nationalism reveals the often invisible link between metalinguistic discourses and their *longue durée* sociopolitical and ideological contexts in the Arabic-speaking world. By critically examining the statements made and the phrases and metaphorics used in the ALA discourse on diglossia, this chapter has established three discursive habiti that are linked together by a doxa – the dominant but taken-for-granted ideology that constructs a mirroring relationship between Arabic and the Arab nation(s). Due to this deep-rooted doxa, Arabic diglossia is persistently and routinely presented in the ALA discourse as both symptoms and causes of the duality of Arab nationalisms. Eliminating diglossia thus carries extra-linguistic underpinnings aiming at tackling the latter duality. The following chapter will continue to explore the relationship between discursive routinisation, ideology and *longue durée* contexts by looking at another issue discussed in the ALA discourse – Arabi(ci)sation.

Notes

1. A close reading of Ferguson's *Diglossia* shows that he does not, in fact, 'exclude' the mixed varieties between H and L in Arabic-speaking communities. He mentions that 'In Arabic, for example, a kind of spoken Arabic much used in certain semiformal or cross-dialectal situations has a highly classical vocabulary with few or no inflectional endings, with certain features of classical syntax, but with a fundamentally colloquial base in morphology and syntax, and a generous admixture of colloquial vocabulary' (Ferguson 1959: 332). However, Holes is right concerning the fact that Ferguson accentuates the H and L ends of the continuum of Arabic varieties/levels of usage to serve his description of Arabic diglossia at the cost of the intermediate forms of Arabic, whose structures and socio-communicative functions are not elaborated in his 1959 article.
2. China had lived with a diglossia between Classical Chinese as the H variety and Vernacular Written Chinese and Vernacular Spoken Chinese as the L varieties for more than a thousand years (Su 2014: 56–8). The situation began to change with the Vernacular Literature Movement of 1917 and the May Fourth Movement of 1919 which refined Vernacular Written Chinese and widened its use to replace Classical Chinese in many domains of writing, in order to realise the unification of the spoken and written languages around a standard national language in China. The government made various efforts to develop this standard language. In 1956, Putonghua was formally introduced as Standard Spoken Chinese to be used in education and broadcasting. Nowadays, the old diglossia has disappeared. As the written form of Modern Standard Chinese, 'Vernacular Written Chinese has become the standard style of writing for speakers of all varieties of Chinese throughout mainland China, Taiwan, Hong Kong and Macau' (ibid.: 59). As for the spoken counterpart of Modern Standard Chinese, a 2015 survey of the Ministry of Education shows that about 70 per cent of the Chinese population have competence in Putonghua. Ideologically, Modern Standard Chinese has been an indispensable symbol of Chinese national identity, yet in recent decades tensions have arisen between Putonghua and regional dialects with the resurgence of regional identities in some dialectal areas for various social and political reasons. It should be noted that the comparison I made here between the Chinese and Arabic language situations is to illustrate Ferguson's differentiation between standard-with-dialects and diglossia. I do not intend at all to suggest that the language situation in China is better than or superior to that in the Arabic-speaking world.
3. Suleiman (2008: 30) conceptualised the difference between *fuṣḥā* and *ʿāmmiyya* in Egypt as follows: 'The use of "mother tongue" to link *ʿāmmiyya* to speech community captures the nature of this form of Arabic as a spoken

variety that is informally acquired and as a site of cultural intimacy. The use of "native language" to link the *fuṣḥā* to linguistic community is intended to express the ideological meanings of "nativeness", the fact that although the *fuṣḥā* is not a mother tongue to the Egyptians (due to being acquired formally through instruction in school), it still is a site of belonging and intimacy to them in socio-psychological terms.' Here, Suleiman suggests that allocating 'mother tongue' and 'native language' to different language varieties can be a way of characterising Ferguson's H-L model. Based on Suleiman's conceptualisation, we may define 'standard-with-dialects' as the language situation where at least one language variety acts as both the 'mother tongue' and 'native language' for the community, whereas 'diglossia' is the language situation where the roles of the 'mother tongue' and 'native language' are performed by different language varieties.

4. Suleiman has pointed out the importance of including the dualism of *fuṣḥā* and *ʿāmmiyya*, which is deeply ingrained in the nativist perception of Arabic, in the study of Arabic in the social world as follows (2011: 30): 'The ability of this nativist dualism to serve as a crossroad for a set of important sociopolitical debates about tradition versus modernisation, change versus authenticity, pan-Arab national identity versus territorial and nation-state identities argues for the intellectual efficacy of this nativist, folk-linguistics view of the Arabic-language situation.'
5. This effort of the Jordanian Academy ended in vain. A new bill for defending the Arabic language was passed by the Committee of Education in the Jordanian House of Representatives (*Majlis al-Nuwāb*) on 8 April 2014 (*al-Madīna al-ʾIkhbāriyya* 2014).
6. Al-Maghribī's attitude reflects a language ideology deeply rooted in the Arabic grammatical tradition, which holds that 'contact leads to loss of purity or contamination in language behavior through borrowing, and that this in turn induces incorrectness in linguistic usage' (Suleiman 2011b: 7; see also Versteegh 1997: 59).
7. I am aware that there are two speculations, in both nativist and Arabist linguistic traditions, about the origin of Arabic dialects: one understands these dialects as products of language contact between Classical Arabic (known as *fuṣḥā*, which was yet to be formally codified during the Arab conquests) and languages of the conquered peoples during the Arab conquests (the seventh and eighth centuries); the other suggests that there were already old Arabic koines contemporary to Classical Arabic before the conquests and that modern Arabic dialects may have directly derived from these old Arabic varieties. Thinking in organic terms, we may call the former speculation 'outbreeding' and the latter 'inbreeding' (Classical Arabic and old Arabic koines are all descendants of a common Arabic protolanguage). See Owens (2013) for a summary of the historiography of Arabic, which considers both speculations. Al-Maghribī apparently leaned towards the 'outbreeding' view for ideological considerations explained later in this chapter.
8. This can be regarded as an example of the 'inbreeding' view of a native Arabic speaker concerning the family relationship between *fuṣḥā* and *ʿāmmiyya*. The paper of Taymūr (1961) discussed in the section '*Fuṣḥā* and *ʿĀmmiyya* as Instruments and Resources' is another.

9. There is a tendency in the Arabic grammatical tradition privileging what sounds rare over what is common.
10. That the fossilised Arabic grammar becomes an obstacle to progress and renewal in Arab society and its pedagogy should be tailored to meet changing social needs is in fact a perennial thesis reiterated in modern situations. It is reported that al-Jāḥiẓ (d. 868/9) had already warned against over-teaching of grammar in schools beyond the purpose of preventing solecisms and ignorance (Suleiman 2013a: 131–2).
11. This position found echoes in the wider intellectual community of the Arabs beyond the ALAs. For example, similar views are found in a survey of eight televised debates aired on Al-Jazeera between 1998 and 2010 which focused on the Arabic language, such as that 'the push for *'amiyyat* to be considered separate languages is part of a long standing colonial and Orientalist agenda to abandon fifteen centuries of Arab heritage and weaken the East' (Nasr al-Din al-Bahra), that 'the push from *fusha* to *'amiyya* was an Orientalist and western plot to weaken the Arabs and the Arabic language' ('Isam Nur al-Din), that 'Arabic has been "conspired against from Cromer [Evelyn Baring] to [Paul] Bremer"' ('Ali 'Uqla 'Ursan) and that 'the process of colonialism was an attack on the Arabic language' (Yusuf al-Qaradawi) (Suleiman and Lucas 2012: 195–8).
12. For detailed critiques of these pro-*ʿāmmiyya* views and corresponding polemics, please refer to Suleiman (2003, 2004, 2013a).
13. Hasan al-Shāfiʿī, President of the Cairo Academy, mentioned in a recent press interview that Arabic language academies are currently coordinating with each other on an ambitious project called *al-mudawwana* 'the Corpus', which is intended to record 'all said by the Arab mouth' (al-Kharīj al-Jadīd 2017).
14. My periodisation echoes Tibi in his classic assessment of Arab nationalism. He understands the rise of Arab nationalism as a consequence of 'the shrinking of the globe' (1997: 16) of our modern world, which was marked by 'the globalisation of the European international system of sovereign states' (ibid.: 15). In his narrative, Arab nationalism began in a cultural form and was politicised 'within the context of the disintegration of the Ottoman Empire as well as in the framework of the structurally supported spread of the idea of nationalism in the Arab part of the Empire' (ibid.: 20). He depicts 'the history of Arab nationalism in the period 1920 to 1952' as 'a royal history of kings struggling for larger entities to sustain their power', in the period 1952 to 1967 as 'pan-Arab populism' characteristic of not only a 'shift from "kings to people" as a focus of legitimacy' but also 'a model of development' (ibid.: 22) and that after 1967 as the end of pan-Arabism featuring the demise of the aspiration for 'a great comprehensive Arab state stretching from the Atlantic to the Gulf', the rise of Islamism as an alternative, less feasible utopia and the survival of 'the pan-Arab link . . . in various forms of regional and sub-regional cooperation' among the participating states, all of which maintain their own sovereignty' (ibid.: 24–5). However, our focuses differ as Tibi attends to the diachronically changing articulations of Arab nationalism, while I am concerned with the varying and continuing reification of the duality of pan-Arab and territorial-state nationalisms beneath these articulations.

15. Tibi notes that 'the fundamental change of direction within Arab nationalism between the two World Wars was from francophilia to germanophilia' (1997: xii), that 'this changeover from liberal anglophone and francophone nationalism to a form of nationalism modelled on that of the nineteenth-century German Romantics is one of the characteristic features of the voluminous works of Sati' al-Husri' (ibid.: 21) and that 'the significance of the transition from francophilia to germanophilia lies in the fact that it was not peculiar to al-Husri, but also took place in the minds of other Arab nationalists' (ibid.: xiii). Yet it should be noted that, concerning language and nation, al-Ḥusrī differs from the views of the German Romantics in several regards. He never ascribes to Arabic and Arabs 'the status of "original" language and "original" people', nor does he combine language and race 'to launch claims of racial superiority towards other nations and their languages' (Suleiman 2003: 131). By contrast, al-ʾArsūzī seems to accept both views and applies them to demonstrating the uniqueness and superiority of Arabic and the Arab nation (ibid.: 148, 151–2, 154, 156–7).
16. This view echoes Ibn Sinān al-Khafājī's (d. 466/1073) essentialist rendering of the link between Arabic and the Arabs in his book *Sirr al-faṣāḥa* as follows (quoted in Suleiman 2013a: 52): 'The superiority of the Arabic language over other languages is an integral part of the superiority of its Arab speakers as a nation/people (*ʾumma*) unsurpassed by other nations in quality of character. It is, therefore, not unreasonable to assume that if the Arabic language is indeed the creation of the Arabs by convention, it is bound to reflect their character. In claiming this, I am not driven by blind allegiance to either the language or its speakers.'
17. Al-Miqdādī's book was 'selected as the text for the teaching of Arab history in the secondary schools of Palestine, Syria, and Iraq, where it continued to be the standard text of Arab youth for several student generations' (Faris 1954: 156–7, quoted in Choueiri 2000: 222).

4

Arabi(ci)sation and Counter-peripheralisation

This chapter moves from intra-language issues (e.g. diglossia) to inter-language ones, by exploring the ALA discourse on Arabi(ci)sation (*taʿrīb*). Arabi(ci)sation was formulated as a language-policy response to the spread of foreign languages in Arab society – a language situation that was thought to weaken the national and international status of Arabic and bring foreignness into the corpus of the language. Yet this linguistic 'predicament' was part of the overall peripheralisation of the Arabs in the modern world-system. In this context, what were considered to be foreign threats to Arabic became refractions of the 'sufferings' of the Arabs under the dominant Other in the world-system. Accordingly, the ALA discourse on Arabi(ci)sation needed to confront the peripherality of both the language and the people.

Introduction: Arabi(ci)sation and Peripherality

The term *taʿrīb* conveys multiple meanings. Linguistically, it refers to (1) assimilating foreign loanwords in line with Arabic phono-morphological conventions; (2) translating foreign texts into Arabic; and (3) reviving and strengthening Arabic as a vibrant, national language to be used in all walks of Arab life (ʾAḥmad 1999: 198). These dimensions of *taʿrīb* can be named 'Arabicisation' (from 'Arabic'); in addition, following the division between corpus and status language planning (see Chapter 2), dimensions (1) and (2) belong to corpus Arabicisation, while dimension (3) belongs to status Arabicisation. In this context, corpus Arabicisation aims to pre-empt or ward off foreignness in the structure and use of Arabic, while status Arabicisation aims to curb the spread and domination of (former) colonial or international languages such as English and French in public communication.

Taʿrīb also has extra-linguistic dimensions, including, at least, as al-Ṣayyādī et al. (1982: 13–14) summarise, (1) recovering 'Arabness' (*ʿurūba*) in Arab society after it was sabotaged under colonial rule; (2) striving for the revival (*nahḍa*) and solidarity (*waḥda*) of the Arab nation – two causes interrupted and undermined by colonialism and imperialism; and (3) ridding Arab society of its overall backwardness (*takhalluf*) and dependence (*tabaʿiyya*) on developed countries in economic matters, science and technology. Since the above extra-linguistic dimensions of *taʿrīb* target the Arabs/Arab nation/Arab society/Arab countries rather than the Arabic language, they should be called 'Arabisation' (from 'Arab'). Due to its conceptual plurality, as discussed above, *taʿrīb* cannot be rendered into English properly unless we compound 'Arabicisation' and 'Arabisation' into 'Arabi(ci)sation',[1] hence the use of this term in this book.

Using the one term *taʿrīb* to refer to both Arabicisation and Arabisation indicates their symbiosis in the Arab setting. For example, talking about Arabicisation in Egyptian universities and schools, Maḥmūd Ḥāfiẓ[2] stresses that Arabicising science and education is 'a national/patriotic (*waṭanī*) cause that has scientific, social and cultural dimensions that are firmly linked to our national language, our Arab being (*kiyān*) and the future of the rising generations in Egypt' (1999: 73). It is clear that, in Ḥāfiẓ's mind, restoring Arabic as the language of instruction in Egypt goes beyond language planning to become a measure of preserving and cultivating Arab identity.

This symbiosis of Arabicisation and Arabisation invites explanation. What binds the two together? A preliminary answer to this question, from the multiple meanings of *taʿrīb* I mentioned above, would be: both Arabicisation and Arabisation are bound by an aspiration to revive or reinstate 'Arabness' in the Arab social life, be it linguistic, educational, economic, or political, to counter, resist, or eliminate what are perceived to be non-Arab (foreign) and anti-Arab (colonialism and imperialism) elements in Arab society. The non- and anti-Arab elements have to be resisted because they are believed to either sabotage the linguistic and sociopolitical authenticity of the Arabs or to dominate Arab social life, thereby getting the Arabs into a state of backwardness and dependency. It follows that it is this sabotage and dominance by the non- and anti-Arab elements that prompts a counteraction combining Arabicisation and Arabisation in one.

On a deeper level, as I will explain below, the above-mentioned sabotage and dominance are corollaries and indexes of the peripheralisation of the Arabs in the modern world-system. To begin with, the 'world-system' is a unit of socio-historical analysis developed by Immanuel Wallerstein

(1974) to refer to 'all the people of the earth and all their cultural, economic, and political institutions and the interactions and connections among them' (Chase-Dunn 2007: 1060). In the pre-modern world, there might be several world-systems functioning in parallel in different parts of the globe. In modern times, however, the world increasingly converges into a single world-system. From the perspective of political economy, Wallerstein (1974, 2000) himself suggests that the capitalist world economy has been the overarching world-system since the seventeenth century, and all other social, political and cultural units are secondary sub-systems depending on it. Others, such as Ramón Grosfoguel (2007), argue that the modern world is governed by a more fundamental world-system, not of political economy, but of knowledge and epistemology.

The debate about the nature of the modern world-system is marginal to the concerns of this chapter. What matters here is a core-periphery hierarchy emerging out of the convergence of the globe into the overarching world-system. In terms of political economy, the core areas control worldwide allocation of economic resources, international division of labour and appropriation of the surplus of world economy (Wallerstein 1974: 401). In terms of knowledge and epistemology, the world-views, value systems and epistemic patterns developed in the core areas challenge and replace those in the periphery. Establishing and maintaining this core-periphery hierarchy naturally involves the core's exploitation of and domination over the periphery via hegemony and/or colonisation. Over time, the core-periphery hierarchy develops into a *longue durée* power structure or matrix, where exploitation and domination become routine, banal and unfelt. Globalisation is one such example, a de facto universalisation, via hegemony, of a 'provincial' (i.e. American or Western) rather than a truly global culture.

In the modern world-system (regardless of its exact nature), the West (Western Europe from the seventeenth century and the United States from the nineteenth century) continuously occupies the core, bringing others, notably what was known as the Global South, within its purview and making them peripheral. The Arabic-speaking world is part of the periphery. Western economic exploitation, military occupation, colonisation, missionary activities, and the unilateral flow of values, ideas, technology and models of governance and economy from the West in the nineteenth and twentieth centuries have significantly challenged or weakened indigenous economic, political, social and epistemic systems in the Arabic-speaking world. As a result, this peripheral world is vulnerable to strategic manipulations of the core and is also dependent on it. Following from this view, it is clear that what the Arabs perceive to be sabotage and domination from the West are signs and consequences of their de facto peripherality vis-à-vis the West in the modern world-system.[3]

It follows that Arabi(ci)sation is ultimately a response of Arab intellectuals and policy-makers to the peripheralisation of their societies. It is a response preoccupied with language but aiming at altering the overall Arab peripherality. Apparently language is used here as a proxy for counter-peripheralisation as a broad sociopolitical cause. This proxification is possible because inter-language relations (between Arabic and Turkish until World War I on the one hand, and French and/or English on the other) in the Arabic-speaking world refracted the core-periphery hierarchy described above, as will be shown in the following discussion of the changing relations among languages and the currents of Arabi(ci)sation in the Arabic-speaking world over the past two centuries.

Inter-language Relations and Arabi(ci)sation

At the turn of the nineteenth century, the majority of the Arabic-speaking world had been incorporated into the Ottoman Empire for around three centuries. Although this incorporation was not devoid of stresses and conflicts, the power balance among the Ottoman ruling elites, the Arabic-speaking notables and *ʿulamāʾ* and the local populations was stabilised and normalised. This balance was also reflected in the language situation in the Arab provinces, where Arabic and Ottoman Turkish lived side by side, with the former used in daily communication (*ʿāmmiyya*s), as well as Islamic liturgies and schooling (*fuṣḥā*), and the latter in the administration and military (Versteegh 1997: 175; Holes 2004: 42; Sayahi 2011: 3). Generally speaking, under Ottoman rule, the Arabs did not feel that their language was peripheralised until the second half of the nineteenth century (see below).

In the nineteenth and early twentieth centuries, the Arabic-speaking world suffered from a double peripheralisation that altered the old power balance therein: first by European imperialism, which subsumed the Middle East and North Africa into the global economic, social, intellectual and political networks it created and dominated via indirect influence and, when needed, colonisation (the last of which ended in Algeria in 1962); and, second, by segments of the Ottoman ruling elites, who from the mid-nineteenth century onwards until the defeat of the Ottomans in World War I, sought to assimilate non-Turk ethnic groups in the Empire in line with a uniform Ottoman or Turkish identity, to prevent the disintegration of the Empire at the hands of European imperial powers and their local collaborators.

These two developments challenged the status of Arabic in the Arabic-speaking world. On the one hand, modern European languages, especially French and English, spread among professional circles and secular, European-style schools; worse still, French and English began to dominate administration, business and education as a result of colonial language policies,[4] although these policies varied in degree in different countries.[5] By contrast, Arabic was marginalised in the above sectors because it was thought to be outdated for modern use. On the other hand, Turkish was valued higher than other local languages as a unifying force in the Ottoman Empire. In the early twentieth century, as part of the Turkification policy,[6] Turkish was promoted as the sole official language and 'the language of instruction in all state schools' (Suleiman 2003: 85) in the Empire. In the Arab provinces controlled by the Ottoman authorities, especially Greater Syria, Arabic was denied equal status with Turkish. It was reported that government schools even taught Arabic grammar in Turkish (ibid.: 85; al-Mubārak 2007: 56).

It is clear that the declining status of Arabic described above refracted the waning fortune of the Arabs in both the Ottoman Empire and the international system. It follows that Arabi(ci)sation was promulgated to play a role in resisting the peripheralisation not only of Arabic but also of the Arabs. The precedents of Arabi(ci)sation included: (1) Muḥammad ʿAlī's (d. 1849) modernisation of Egypt in the first half of the nineteenth century, during which Arabic replaced Turkish in the administration and the School of Languages was established to teach European languages and translate European treatises into Arabic; and (2) the *nahḍa* 'revival' movement in Lebanon in the second half of the nineteenth century, when Arabic was used in new literary genres and the teaching in missionary schools (Suleiman 2006: 175). In both cases, Arabic was deployed as a tool to nurture an autonomous Arabic-based identity independent from the Ottoman Turks and to modernise Arab societies in the European fashion.

Calls for Arabi(ci)sation intensified around the turn of the twentieth century. In Egypt, British colonial authorities' imposition of English in schools deepened the anxiety of many Egyptian intellectuals over the destiny of Arabic,[7] leading to the convening of proto-ALAs that discussed plans for Arabicising science and education (see Chapter 2); Arabi(ci)sation thus acquired anti-colonial meanings. In Greater Syria, Syrian/Arab nationalists fought for their linguistic rights dismissed in Turkification (Suleiman 2003: 79–96), preparing the way for the 'Arab awakening' to strive for independence and 'liberation' from the Ottoman Empire. Arabi(ci)sation first emerged as an official policy in Syria in the reign of Prince Fayṣal (1918–20), when Arabic began to replace Turkish in the administration and education. To support Arabi(ci)sation, the government established a department of lexical coinage and translation which later developed into the Damascus Academy (see Chapter 2). The drive for Arabi(ci)sation continued in Syria during the French mandate. When the Syrian University (now Damascus University) was opened in 1923, all courses, including science and medicine, were taught in Arabic. The Syrian practice of Arabi(ci)sation influenced other parts of the Arabic-speaking world. It was echoed in Iraq when Fayṣal and some of his Syrian cabinet moved there. It also prompted King Fu'ād I of Egypt to found the Cairo Academy in 1932 to vie with the Hashimites (who then ruled both Iraq and Transjordan) for authority over Arabic and Arabi(ci)sation in the Arabic-speaking world (see Chapter 2).

Arabi(ci)sation as an official policy witnessed a second stimulus in the 1950s and 1960s with the independence of Tunisia (1956), Morocco (1956) and Algeria (1962) from France. Regimes in these countries adopted Arabi(ci)sation as a decolonisation measure to boost their legitimacy. Implementation of this policy was uneven among the three countries, and none of them was willing or able to get rid of French. However, in rhetoric, their political leaders declared Arabi(ci)sation as a matter of principle for the independence and survival of their national communities. North Africa's strong stance on Arabi(ci)sation received wide acclaim and support from other Arab countries. A pan-Arab cooperative framework on Arabi(ci)sation took shape with the convening of the First Arabi(ci)sation Conference and the foundation of the Bureau for Arabisation in Morocco in 1961 (see Chapter 2).

In spite of the official commitment to it, Arabi(ci)sation did not achieve its stated outcomes.[8] However, discussions of Arabi(ci)sation remained active at the official and intellectual levels in the Arabic-speaking world (e.g. pan-Arab Arabi(ci)sation conferences, Arabi(ci)sation seminars held by ALAs and so on), mainly responding to the conditions of 'peripherality' in the post-colonial period. The Arab states relied on the capital and technology of the developed core, mainly the West, for their survival and modernisation. Moreover, for security reasons (e.g. oil and energy, counter-communism during the Cold War, etc.), the West (led by the United States) retained influence over the Arab states via strategic alliances, aid, investment and military intervention or invasion. This continuing peripherality was also revealed in language use. Science subjects were taught in English or French in Arab universities; probably the only exception was Syria, where Arabic was used throughout the education system. With economic liberalisation from the late 1970s onwards, European languages, notably English and French (in North Africa), increased their popularity in business and tourism sectors, and the linguistic landscape in many Arab cities became replete with foreign neologisms in either their original forms or unchecked Arabic transliterations.

It has become clear from the above review that (1) the declining status of Arabic vis-à-vis Turkish (until World War I) and Western languages was a refraction of the peripheralisation of the Arabs in the modern world-system; and (2) the continuing peripheralisation of both Arabic and the Arabs perpetuated Arabi(ci)sation throughout the twentieth century as a response. With these understandings in mind, I will explore, in the following sections, how Arabi(ci)sation was conceptualised in the ALA discourse.

Conceptualising Arabi(ci)sation in the Discourse of Arabic Language Academies

The ALA discourse displayed two tendencies when conceptualising Arabi(ci)sation that aimed to counter the peripherality of Arabic (and ultimately the Arabs). One tendency is to construct an inalienable link between Arabic and the Arab people to demonstrate that Arabic is indispensable to modern Arab life and central to cultivating and strengthening Arab national identity. The other tendency calls for equilibrium in language contact and exchange to alter the asymmetrical relations between Arabic and foreign languages. These tendencies were so consistent diachronically, making them discursive habiti that characterised the routinisation of the ALA discourse on Arabi(ci)sation around the ideological doxa that melded the destinies of Arabic and the Arab people in one.

Inalienability between Arabic and the Arab People

I call the language-people link in the ALA discourse 'inalienable' for the following reasons. To begin with, this link is not constructed on instrumental grounds, i.e. the Arabs are associated with Arabic because they use the language as an instrument of communication. If the link is instrumental, it cannot be called 'inalienable' because it is severable; in theory, with effort of learning Arabs can communicate in any languages.

The 'inalienability' here is, by contrast, largely ideological. It is based on two perennial notions in the Arab-Islamic tradition. One is the 'wisdom of the Arabs' (*ḥikmat al-ʿarab*) principle[9] which claims that the inner patterns of Arabic embody the genetic wisdom of the Arab people (Suleiman 2003: 47). The other is represented by the saying of the Prophet Muḥammad 'Whoever speaks Arabic is an Arab', which defines an individual's Arab identity according to his competence in Arabic instead of his tribal, ethnic and racial affiliations.[10] These two notions play complementary roles in constructing the inalienable link between Arabic and the Arab people.

The first notion attends to the fixity of this link. It treats the speech of a closed segment of the Arab people known as 'the Arabs',[11] whose natural disposition and linguistic intuition were believed to be uncorrupted, as the most trusted source to establish the inner patterns of Arabic and, by extension, the atemporal 'Arabness' of the Arab people embodied therein. The second notion emphasises the openness of the above language-people link. It sees competence in Arabic as proof of 'Arabness'; following from this, mastering Arabic becomes a way for those (e.g. the *muwalladūn* (see Chapter 3), post-classic and modern Arabic speakers and so on.) living outside or beyond the closed segment of 'the Arabs' to acquire 'Arabness' and become proper Arabs.

The above stances on the fixity and openness of the language-people link were echoed in the ALA discourse on Arabi(ci)sation, but were subject to ideological manipulation in line with the changing conditions of 'peripherality' and 'counter-peripherality' in the Arabic-speaking world. This section explores this manipulation in three 'sites' of the discourse: (1) the 1920s and 1930s, decades that witnessed the emergence of national consciousness in colonial or semi-colonial Arab states; (2) the 1950s and 1960s, characterised by a massive movement of state-building and experiments of pan-Arab integration in the Arabic-speaking world; and (3) the period following the Arab defeat in the 1967 war with Israel, whose traumatic repercussions left the Arab nation and Arab identity in jeopardy (see below). It should be noted that these 'sites' are not used to periodise the ALA discourse because, diachronically, this discourse exhibited more continuity than change, and the themes and tendencies of the discourse in the above 'sites' were mutually overlapping rather than separate.

In the first 'site', a tension could be seen within the ALAs between those who wanted to constrain the language-people link to the speech of 'the Arabs' (in the above sense) and those who wanted to develop this link to include modern Arabic speakers and their use of Arabic. This tension took place in the context of the spread of foreign neologisms and styles in Arabic, which, in the minds of some conservative ALA members, was going to change the nature of Arabic. For example, ʾIdwār Marqaṣ, a member of the Damascus Academy, fears that, if the Arabs do not properly render foreign neologisms into Arabic, the foreignness of these words would 'dispose of' (*dhahaba bi*) most of the 'splendour' (*rawnaq*) and 'beauty' (*bahāʾ*) of Arabic (1936: 26). Similarly, ʾAḥmad al-ʾIskandarī, a member of the Cairo Academy, is worried that the 'supremacy' (*ghalaba*) of foreign languages over Arabic would distance the latter from its original 'patterns' (*ʾawḍāʿ*) and turn it into a different language (1936: 5).

Amidst these fears and worries, the Cairo Academy set out to discuss how to accept and assimilate foreign linguistic elements in Arabic in 1934. The discussion was centred on two linguistic phenomena: (1) *muwallad*, i.e. innovative use of Arabic (new words, phrases, structures, etc.) under foreign influences by Arabic speakers living beyond the first centuries of Islam,[12] which cannot be found in the speech of 'the Arabs', the Qur'an, or the pre- and early Islamic poetry (e.g. *taʿrīfat al-rusūm* 'the list of (import or export) taxes' and *zaʿbūṭ* 'woollen garment') and (2) *muʿarrab*, i.e. foreign loanwords (e.g. *nūfambar* 'November' and *mūnūlūj* 'monologue'). *Muwallad* and *muʿarrab* were the two facets of Arabic where foreignness was thought to have hit the hardest. Assimilating them into Arabic was therefore considered necessary to curb the spread of this foreignness.

In the 1934 discussion, conservative members of the Academy (for example, ʾAḥmad al-ʾIskandarī and Muḥammad al-Khaḍir Ḥusayn) adopted the 'fixity' stance concerning the language-people link and used the speech of 'the Arabs' as the only yardstick to decide the propriety of *muwallad* and *muʿarrab*. They accepted words like *taʿrīfat* as being part of Arabic but not those such as *zaʿbūṭ*, because the former conformed to the morphological patterns established from the speech of 'the Arabs' (MJMJ 1: 324–5) while the latter came from non-Arab origins and were never used by 'the Arabs' (ibid.: 329). Similarly, the conservatives accepted loanwords like *nūfambar* but not *mūnūlūj*, because the former was introduced into Arabic by 'the Arabs'[13] while the latter was introduced by modern Arabic speakers (ibid.: 306–7, 326).

Modernists in the Academy (e.g. ʿAbd al-Qādir al-Maghribī and Mansūr Fahmī) disagreed with this 'fixity' stance. They called for a clear definition of 'the Arabs' whose linguistic intuitions can be trusted. When al-ʾIskandarī responded to their request by defining 'the Arabs' as the native Arabic speakers living in sedentary areas until the second century of Islam and in desert areas until the fourth century of Islam, the modernists challenged this rigid definition by asking why an Arabic speaker who was competent in Arabic but lived beyond the above time-space framework could not be treated as a member of 'the Arabs' (ibid.: 303–5, 318, 331).

With no agreement achieved on the definition of 'the Arabs,'[14] 'taste' (*dhawq*) was proposed as an alternative yardstick to decide whether a *muwallad* or *muʿarrab* element is acceptable in Arabic. This proposal held that any Arabic speaker who had a sound 'taste' could make this decision with his or her intuitive knowledge of Arabic. Yet 'taste' is a vague concept that is subject to manipulation. Its meaning moves between an inborn linguistic 'intuition' (*salīqa* or *fiṭra*) and an acquired linguistic 'skill' (*ṣināʿa*). The conservatives considered 'taste' in Arabic to be an intuition of 'the Arabs', which was lost after the fourth century of Islam and which from then on could only be acquired by Arabic speakers as a 'skill' through learning and practising the language of the former (ibid.: 331–3). This view perceived the 'taste' of modern Arabic speakers as a continuation of that of 'the Arabs' – a perception reflecting the 'openness' stance on the language-people link mentioned at the beginning of this section. The modernists, however, wanted to push the 'openness' further. They argued that every age had its own 'taste' and, in modern times, whenever there was a conflict between the taste of 'the Arabs' and that of competent modern Arabic speakers (e.g. ALA members), the latter 'taste' should be observed (ibid.: 332–3).

When these arguments about 'the Arabs' and 'taste' dominated the seemingly linguistic discussion of *muwallad* and *muʿarrab*, curbing foreignness in the use of Arabic began to assume the significance of asserting and defending Arab identity. For the conservatives, linguistic foreignness challenged the traditional link between good Arabic and the 'purest' Arab people in the early Islamic periods – a link they insisted on maintaining in modern times. In doing so, they went for a 'primordial' understanding of Arab identity by linking it to time-honoured 'Arabness'. By contrast, the modernists, albeit also adhering to the language-people link, wanted to tailor this link to the interests of modern Arabs. The modernists therefore adopted a 'constructivist'[15] position by treating modern Arabs as the backbone of Arab identity. It was these identity considerations that made the language-people link an underlying theme in the 1934 discussion of the Cairo Academy.

The reason that 'identity' underlay the first 'site' of the ALA discourse on Arabi(ci)sation had its roots in the sociopolitical contexts of the 1920s and 1930s. On the one hand, the creation of sovereign Arab states after World War I provided the Arabs with opportunities of self-definition and self-assertion to get rid of the legacy of double peripheralisation under Ottoman rule. On the other hand, the continuing presence of European colonialism after World War I (in various forms ranging from mandate states to protectorates and colonies) reinforced the feeling of peripherality and the need for resistance in Arab society. These conditions of 'peripherality' led to the emergence of Arab identity as a central concern among Arab intellectuals, which influenced the ALA discourse.

However, in the first 'site' of this discourse, the connection between language and identity existed in covert forms. Direct statements about this connection were rare. Al-ʾIskandarī, who praised the participants in the Tenth Arab Medical Conference[16] for 'making the Arab cry (*naʿra*) and protecting the national pride' (1948 [1938]: 50) when rendering chemical terminologies into Arabic, did not elaborate on the relationship between lexical coinage and Arabism. Al-Maghribī, who suggested that Arab states could rely on their own ALAs to coordinate individual linguistic 'tastes' in their communities, did not expound the role of linguistic coordination in the formation of state identities (1935a: 348). This discursive covertness was probably related to the uncertainty of political identities in the Arabic-speaking world in the 1920s and 1930s, when regimes in most Arab states were not fully able to articulate their political visions and when the notion of pan-Arabism (frustrated by the post-World War I arrangement in the Middle East) was gathering momentum to offer an alternative to state-oriented Arab identities.

In comparison, the ALA discourse on Arabi(ci)sation in the second 'site' (the 1950s and 1960s) began to politicise the language-people link by relating this link to immediate concerns over the formation of Arab identity at both intra- and cross-state levels.

An example of this is the 'taste' discussion in this 'site', which, unlike the discussion in the first 'site', was preoccupied with 'modern Arabic speakers'. In his speech to the Congress of the Academy in 1952, Manṣūr Fahmī, secretary of the Cairo Academy (1933–59), developed the concept of 'taste' to embody the state-building agenda of newly independent Arab states. Developing from al-Maghribī (1935a) (see above), Fahmī suggests that individual 'tastes' in language may diverge, but a 'collective taste' (*dhawq mushtarak*) always connects members of a community (1955 [1951]: 413). He describes this 'taste' in terms of 'uncorrupted intuition' (*al-fiṭra al-salīma*), 'natural straightness' (*al-ṭabʿ al-mustaqīm*), and goodness and beauty (*al-khayr wa-l-ḥusn*) (ibid.: 413). The mission of the ALAs, he argues, is to promote this collective 'taste' among both the elites and the common people with the support of their hosting Arab states; he approves of the calls in Egypt and Iraq for governmental and administrative enforcement of the ALAs' decisions concerning taste promotion and purification (ibid. 413–15). Similarly, ʾAḥmad ʿAmmār (1955 [1951]: 419), a member of the Cairo Academy, talks about the role of what he called 'the common taste' (*al-dhawq al-ʿāmm*) in deciding whether a foreign neologism is acceptable in Arabic. This common 'taste', in his view, is voluntarily developed in Arabic-speaking communities through their actual use of the language. It is clear that both Fahmī and ʿAmmār believe in a unified, communal 'taste' in Arabic. Considering the thick air of state-building and pan-Arabism in the Arabic-speaking world in the 1950s and 1960s, this understanding of 'taste' indicates that ALA members at that time might have thought of Arabi(ci)sation as a path to sociopolitical integration.

This view was overtly articulated in the resolution of the First Arabi(ci) sation Conference convened by the Arab League in Morocco in 1961.[17] According to ʾAḥmad (1999: 207), the aim of the First Arabi(ci)sation Conference was 'to achieve Arabi(ci)sation in every (*kull*) compartment (*mirfaq*) of the Arab nation and in every (*kull*) Arab country (*balad*)'. The Conference called for 'making Arabic the language of instruction in all (*jamīʿ*) subjects and all (*jamīʿ*) stages and types of [formal] education' and 'unifying (*tawḥīḍ*) the public media' to 'promote *fuṣḥā* Arabic among different strata of the [Arab] people' (ibid.: 207). All measures of Arabi(ci) sation, the Conference declared, were directed towards

> bringing into being an Arab generation who are conscious and enlightened, who believe in Allah and the greatest [pan-Arab] homeland (*al-waṭan al-ʾakbar*), who pursue the highest standards (*al-muthul al-ʿulyā*) of individual and social conduct, who uphold the principles of truth and virtue, who dedicate themselves to the common struggle, self-empowerment and productive work, and who arm themselves with knowledge and morality to consolidate the position of the glorious Arab nation and safeguard their rights of freedom, security and dignity. (Ibid.: 207)

Two features of the above resolution show how the link between Arabi(ci) sation and pan-Arab integration was constructed therein. First, the resolution specified the target group of Arabi(ci)sation – the new Arab generation. This generation would have to possess all the necessary qualities to revive, sustain and strengthen the Arab nation. In order to help this new generation acquire these qualities, a total Arabi(ci)sation involving all states, social classes and domains of communication in the Arabic-speaking world was demanded, especially in the media and education. Here Arabi(ci)sation was related to the recovery and consolidation of Arabness for the Arab nation as a whole. Second, the resolution underscored its message (i.e. total Arabi(ci)sation) by using intensifiers such as *kull* and *jamīʿ* as well as superlative and comparative forms of these adjectives, such as *al-ʾakbar* and *al-ʿulyā*.

The 1961 resolution represented a voice in the second 'site' of the ALA discourse that was assertive, confident and enthusiastic about the role of Arabi(ci)sation in political integration. This voice turned the language-people link from a seemingly perennial existence to a form of causality – where linguistic homogeneity leads to sociopolitical solidarity.

The emergence of this assertive voice needs to be considered in conjunction with the sociopolitical context of the Arabic-speaking world in the 1950s and 1960s, which can be depicted as the Arabs' attempt at self-empowerment alongside their continuing peripheralisation in the post-colonial world-system. On the one hand, newly independent Arab states were eager to get rid of their colonial past and gain control over their own affairs. On the other hand, these states were unable to achieve full independence because of their overall underdevelopment. They therefore depended on the developed core for financial and technical support. The end of colonisation did not mean the end of coloniality. The continuation of dependency and coloniality impeded the Arabs' effort to empower themselves but also reinforced and, sometimes, radicalised their aspirations for doing so.[18] In the ALA discourse, this radicalism was revealed as the assertive voice concerning the link between Arabic and the Arabs and a firm determination to reify this link in concrete forms.

Such assertion and determination gave way to self-defence and self-authentication against external threats in the ALA discourse on Arabi(ci)sation following the Arab defeat in the 1967 war with Israel. As I have mentioned in the introduction, this defeat led to trauma in Arab society. Ṭarābīshī (2005) explains why this defeat was traumatic as follows (quoted in Suleiman 2011a: 131). First, it was unexpected given the Arabs' feeling of self-confidence and invincibility before the war (as also shown in the ALA discourse in the 1950s and 1960s, discussed above). Second, the humiliation created by the fact that a massive coalition of Arab armies lost the war at the hands of the Israeli army, which was numerically small and belittled by the Arabs before the war, made many Arabs believe that Arab society was backward at all levels. Third, the wounds of the 1967 defeat were not healed by any meaningful Arab victory over the Israelis in the following confrontations between the two (e.g. the 1973 Arab-Israeli war, the 1982 Lebanon War, the two Palestinian Intifadas, etc.), leaving an impression that defeats were repetitive and the Arab backwardness was endemic. Fourth, these repetitive defeats implanted a sense of victimhood into the Arab psyche, revealed as both envying and resisting the powerful, dominant Other in international and intercultural relations. The following example shows how these traumatic feelings described above affected the conception of Arabi(ci)sation in the ALA discourse.

The resolution passed by the Second Arabi(ci)sation Conference (1973) stated that:

> The language [of a nation] is the formative element (*muqawwim*) that determines the existence and continuation of that nation. What threatens (*yuhaddid*) the language also threatens the distinctive character (*shakhṣiyya*) of the nation, its continuation and the link between its generations. The deficits that have afflicted the Arabic language in recent times do not come from the language itself but from the linguistic

> invasion (*al-ghazw al-lughawī*) launched against it in various forms, from distancing it from its users, to arousing suspicion about its capability, to isolating it from life and society. (ʾAḥmad 1999: 208)

In the above example, the destiny of the Arab nation as a whole was perceived to be most intimately connected with the Arabic language, which was a reproduction of the language-people link discussed before. *Muqawwim* is the active participle of the verb *qawwama* 'to create, to shape', so Arabic was understood as an element that shapes the Arab nation. *Shakhṣiyya* is the relative noun of *shakhṣ* 'person, individual', meaning 'personality'. Here the Arab nation was perceived as a person, an abstract super-person embodying the collective qualities of the Arabs; Arabic is an indispensable emblem and constituent of this super-person.

However, this language-people link acquired a defensive sense in the post-1967 context. The keywords in the resolution were 'threats' and 'invasions'. Arabic was thought to be threatened and attacked by external forces. The consequences were understood as 'distancing' and 'isolation' in this resolution – severing the link between Arabic, on the one hand, and the Arabs and the Arab nation, on the other. It was for the purpose of defending the Arab self against the perceived 'threats' and 'invasions' that the link between Arabic, native Arabic speakers and the Arab nation was reiterated here.

This defensive sense was further elaborated in the ALA discourse from the 1980s onwards to include self-authentication. Economic liberalisation in nationalist, socialist Arab states, the oil boom in the Gulf, and the global diffusion of capitalist market economy and liberal democracy following the collapse of the Soviet Union in 1991 changed the political economy of the Arabic-speaking world. The seemingly inevitable Westernisation or globalisation of Arab society raised concerns over the stability of Arab identity. Searching for authentic Arabic values that could help stabilise the sense of being an Arab without contradicting the aim of being incorporated into the globalised world, became an important theme of intellectual debate. Arabi(ci)sation, in both its linguistic and extra-linguistic meanings, was considered an indispensable means of this self-authentication.

A set of metaphors was employed in the ALA discourse describing Arabic as a key constituent of Arab identity. For example, ʿAbd al-Hādī Hāshim (1988: 338), a member of the Damascus Academy, stated that 'Our Arabic is the storehouse of our heritage, the mirror of our civilisation, the foundation of our individuality, the representation of our thought and feeling, and the means of expressing our mind, sentiments and hope.'

In the above example, Arabic was ascribed different roles that made it a formative constituent of a number of social 'constructs', including heritage, civilisation and personality. It is useful to see how Hāshim perceived these roles through the words and metaphors he chose. A 'storehouse' is a place where goods and treasures are stored, accumulated and preserved. In the storehouse, an item can be stored safely as long as it has sufficient value in the eyes of the storehouse's owner. Besides, items that become outdated or lose their original value are usually removed from the storehouse and are replaced by new items. The statement 'the Arabic language is the storehouse of the Arabic heritage' means that Arabic contains the most important elements which shape this heritage both synchronically and diachronically. In other words, the use of 'storehouse' here indicates that Arabic preserves the most valuable part of the Arabic heritage.

A 'mirror' usually has a polished glass surface that clearly and objectively reflects entities and movements within its range of reflection. Moreover, if the reflected entities or movements change, the mirror will always instantly provide an updated image. Perceiving Arabic as a mirror of the Arab civilisation implies that Arabic always reflects the up-to-date state of this civilisation.

As for the relation between Arabic and the Arab individual, Hāshim stated that Arabic is the foundation of being an Arab, because both the rational and emotional parts of the Arab mind are expressed in this language. Here Hāshim established a close connection between language and the human mind, as if language were an inseparable part of the human being, without which the mind cannot be expressed and reflected. There is no doubt that, based on this perception, Arabic is essential for the existence and expression of the Arab individual.[19]

The social 'constructs' mentioned by Hāshim are often considered by many as constituents of Arab identity. Obviously, identity in this sense does not come from a singular source. People may identify themselves against a broad range of conceptualisations of how they are connected to and influenced by various aspects of their bodies, minds and the outside world. Historical heritage, civilisational legacy, one's way of thinking and expression, and the expected future of the self and the community belong to what Blommaert (2006: 245) calls a 'repertoire of identities'. Every component of this repertoire has its own range and function, and together they form an identity complex that informs the sense of being and belonging for an individual. In terms of the composition of Arab identity, Arabic plays an unmatchable role because it is perceived to be a formative constituent not only of identity but also of many other constituents of identity (heritage, civilisation and individuality in the case of Hāshim (1988)). It is no wonder it has often been stated in the ALA discourse that Arabic is the root (*ʾaṣl*) of the Arab nation and is emblematic of Arab identity. Below are some examples taken from this discourse.

Al-Yāfī claims that Arabic[20] is the 'spiritual motherland' (1988: 205) of the Arab nation and its people; like the physical motherland that sustained generations of Arabs, the Arabic language has supported their glorious intellectual achievements and thus has become one of the most fundamental constituents of Arab identity. Al-Khūrī (1991: 70) argues that the native language is an indispensable sign (*ʿunwān*) of the self; it is naturally inherited: people cannot choose their mother tongue just as they cannot choose their birthplace, the colour of their skin and their nation. Al-Khūrī stresses that the existence and destiny of Arabs are fundamentally related to the Arabic language. Similarly, al-Tāzī (1996: 50) states that there is an intellectual agreement that Arabic is the first element that has shaped Arab-Muslim identity. He reports that Arabic has occasionally been depicted as the 'weapon' (*silāḥ*) used to defend the Arab and Muslim community. A final example is al-Khūrī (1998: 805), who suggests that Arabic is part of the psychological 'existence' (*kiyān*) of an Arab; it is also the 'pillar' (*rakīza*) of the Arab's cultural 'self' (*dhātiyya*) and the 'sign' (*sima*) of the solidarity of the Arab nation.

Following the understanding that Arabic is the root of Arab identity, Arabi(ci)sation was interpreted in the ALA discourse to be a process of root seeking and root solidification, aimed at protecting and promoting a common Arab identity. Writing from this perspective, some ALA members reiterated the mission of Arabi(ci)sation as follows: to solidify the root of Arab identity by recovering Arabness in Arab society, especially in the linguistic and cultural spheres (ʿIzz al-Dīn 1994; Bishr 1996).

In this section, I have traced the continuation of the link between Arabic and Arab people in three 'sites' of the ALA discourse on Arabi(ci)sation. In this discourse, Arabi(ci)sation was associated with (1) the emergence of national consciousness; (2) state-building and nation-formation; and (3) national defence and identity authentication in line with the sociopolitical changes in the Arabic-speaking world. However, none of these discursive and contextual changes challenged the language-people link in the ALA discourse, which was consistently and routinely conceptualised as inalienable. This discursive consistency and routinisation was most probably a reflection of and response to the continuing peripheralisation of the Arabs in the modern world-system. This peripherality impeded the independence and empowerment of the Arabs in real terms, causing a prolonged sociopolitical malaise that may have been, to some extent, relieved by the emphasis on the uniqueness of Arabic and its link to Arab identity in the ALA discourse.

Domination, Subordination and Equilibrium in Inter-Language Relations

Differing from the first tendency of the ALA discourse on Arabi(ci)sation discussed above (demonstrating the centrality of Arabic to Arab social life by constructing the inalienable link between Arabic and the Arab people), the second tendency attends more to (1) denouncing the domination of foreign languages over Arabic in the Arabic-speaking world and (2) calling for symmetrical and mutually beneficial relationships between Arabic and foreign languages. This tendency was less evident (but did exist, as will be shown below) in the first two historical 'sites' of the ALA discourse, probably due to (1) the silence of ALA members during the colonial period regarding the political role of Arabic in general and colonial language policies in particular, and (2) self-confidence in the period of rapid state-building until 1967, which confined the attention of this discourse to self-assertion as a main way of reversing the periphery status of Arabic (and the Arabs). In the third 'site' of the ALA discourse, when rhetoric about self-assertion was toned down and gave way to self-defence and authentication (see the preceding section), appealing for equilibrium in inter-language relations was developed as a second strategy to resist the peripheralisation of Arabic.

This second strategy began with criticising what was thought to be the enforced weakening of and deliberate attacks on Arabic. Early in 1926, ʿAbd al-Qādir al-Maghribī published *al-Lugha al-ʿarabiyya fī dawlat al-turk al-ʿuthmāniyya* 'The Arabic language in the Ottoman Turkish state' in the journal of the Damascus Academy. In it, he explained the purpose for the Academy of editing a linguistic treatise called *Tanbīh* 'Warning', written by Ibn Kamāl Bāshā (d. 1536), a famous Ottoman historian who was also appointed as Sheikh of Islam under the reign of Suleiman the Magnificent (d. 1566). *Tanbīh* was written, according to al-Maghribī, to correct the common mistakes in the use of Arabic among the Turks, both elites and common people, in Anatolia, the heartland of the Ottoman Empire. Al-Maghribī considered this treatise a strong proof of the popularity of Arabic among Turkish-speaking peoples and the care of Turkish scholars (Ibn Kamāl Bāshā was a Turk) for this language in the early centuries of the Ottoman Empire. He then contrasted this historical finding with the deliberate promotion of Turkish that 'jostled against' (*zāḥama*) Arabic in the Empire from the *Tanzīmāt* 'reorganisations' in the mid-nineteenth century, leading to the Turks' loss of their competence in Arabic (al-Maghribī 1926: 217). Obviously, al-Maghribī's article and the Academy's decision to edit the above treatise played a symbolic role in decrying enforced Turkification in the last decades of the Ottoman Empire and also, very possibly, the ongoing Turkish language reform in Turkey in the 1920s. Considering the damage Turkification had caused to Arabic, ALA members like al-Maghribī had every reason to perceive this Turkish language reform as a betrayal of Islam and a continuing attack on Arabic, as it involved replacing the Arabic script with Latin letters, purging Arabic and Persian loanwords, as well as translating the Qur'an into Turkish and using Turkish as a liturgical language of Islam (including the call to prayer).

In spite of al-Maghribī's open criticism of Turkification, the ALA discourse before the 1967 defeat tended to be quiet about the 'suffering' of Arabic during European colonial rule. It was not until the 1970s that criticism of colonial language policies became common in the ALA discourse. Yet such criticism was not, in fact, targeted at the imposition of foreign languages in the colonial period but the spread and, in some spheres, dominance of English or French in the post-colonial Arabic-speaking world. Below are some examples of this from the ALA discourse.

I mentioned in the previous section the metaphor of 'linguistic invasion' in the resolution of the Second Arabi(ci)sation Conference (1973), as if Arabic had actually been attacked by some foreign languages in a similar way as European colonisers had attacked the Arabs during their colonisation of Arab countries. Al-Khūrī (1991: 73) was more straightforward in this regard when he argued that colonialism meant not only military and economic occupation, but also cultural and linguistic occupation. Similarly, ʿAmr (1999: 145) stated that Arabic was currently facing an unprecedented storm of 'modern colonialism', whose main purpose, in his view, was 'beating' (*ḍarb*), 'erasing' (*iḍmiḥlāl*) and 'defaming' (*ṭaʿn*) this language.

This so-called linguistic invasion, occupation and colonisation had, in the writing of some ALA members given below, a negative impact on both Arabic and the Arabs. Here the language-people link was activated to denounce the asymmetrical relations between Arabic and foreign languages, mainly English and French. For example, Bishr (1987) and al-Qulaybī (1998) argued that what they perceived as 'linguistic invasion' established the superiority of English and French over Arabic in Arab society. In their view, many Arabs associated competence in these two languages with better career opportunities and a higher social status than what speaking in Arabic could offer. For Bishr and al-Qulaybī, this linguistic superiority was, in fact, a symptom of the overall Western dominance over the Arabs, beginning from the French invasion of Egypt (1798–1801) and lasting until the present day, at the hands of different (neo-)colonial and (neo-)imperial powers in the West. They suggested that this long-term domination decapacitated the Arabs, making them submissive to the global order and cultural patterns created and dominated by the West. They continued to argue that Western domination created a false causality for some Arabs – economic and social progress was largely determined by the choice of language; for these people, learning English or French became a short cut to getting rid of their sociocultural backwardness and a way to join the club of the dominators. Other ALA members, such as al-Jawārī (1985), ʿIzz al-Dīn (1994) and al-Ḍābīb (2002), expressed similar concerns and warned the Arabs of a kind of identity metamorphosis (*maskh*) that might occur, due to the belief in the superiority of Western languages and culture that took hold in Arab society.

It is clear from the above examples that there was a tendency in the ALA discourse to view the spread of English and French in the post-colonial period, especially under the auspices of liberalisation and globalisation in the Arabic-speaking world in the 1980s and 1990s, as a continuation of the colonial-style language policy of the West, or as part of a long-term process of Western domination in the modern world-system. Colonial language policy, or colonialism in general, was used by some ALA members to justify their criticism of and dissatisfaction with the present status of Arabic in Arab society and some Arabs' negative attitudes towards their own language.

Criticism alone cannot change the perceived inferiority of Arabic vis-à-vis English and French. Some ALA members went further, deconstructing the whole power matrix of languages and providing a more equal and equilibrial alternative. This is revealed in some of the terms these members chose to describe this alternative: *muʿāyasha* 'co-existence' (al-Faḥḥām 1984), *tabādul* 'exchange' (al-Dasūqī 1995), *tanāfudh* 'osmosis' (ʿIzz al-Dīn 1994; 2002), *talāḥum* 'clinging together' (Ḥāfiẓ 1996), *tafāʿul* 'interaction' (al-Ṣayyid 1997) and *tawāṣul* 'connecting' (al-Dajānī 1999). It is noticeable that all these words are verbal nouns of either Form III (in the case of *muʿāyasha*) or Form VI (all the others) verbs, which usually involve two or more doers in one action. In addition, Form VI implies that the doers of the action are also its recipients; in other words, all parties involved in the action not only work with each other, but also influence and benefit from each other. The covert message behind these two common patterns is that language contact and exchange should be built on joint contribution, rather than on the domination of some languages over others. The existence of this covert message is further supported by the following analysis of the meanings of these words.

Muʿāyasha derives from *ʿāsha* 'to live', meaning 'living together'. This term reveals a common aspect of the organic world – different species of plants and animals co-exist in one space and depend on each other. It also shows an idealised image of human society – people of different ethnic and social backgrounds live and support each other in one community. Here, languages are conceptualised as organic beings. In a multilingual speech community, the survival of a healthy, balanced ecosystem depends on the survival of all its species (i.e. languages or language varieties). As for the term *tabādul*, its original stem *badala* means 'to replace', so *tabādul* gains the meaning 'replacing things and features of oneself with those of the Other and vice versa' – thus the English translation 'exchange'. In terms of language contact, *tabādul* requires the affected languages to exchange vocabularies, grammatical features and stylistic merits with each other. So *tabādul* is, in fact, a process of mutual enrichment. The term *tanāfudh*, through the meaning of its stem form *nafadha* 'to penetrate', depicts a situation of different objects penetrating each other's body, gradually reshaping each other and thus being well-connected with each other. Conceptualising language contact as *tanāfudh* implies that, in a multilingual environment, languages affect each other and are affected by each other to the extent that all these languages will go through a constant and gradual change caused by this mutual effect. The next term, *talāḥum*, has a similar implication as *tanāfudh*. Its original stem *laḥama* means 'to mend, patch, weld and solder together', so *talāḥum* literally refers to the process of one object clinging to another in order to fix the holes in both bodies. In other words, *talāḥum* describes a complementary relationship between different entities. As for the last two terms, *tafāʿul* emphasises the process of mutual influence while *tawāṣul* highlights the status of connectedness. The above analysis tells us that the ideal pattern of inter-language relations, as is endorsed in the ALA discourse on Arabi(ci)sation, should include the following features: peaceful co-existence, active participation, mutual dependence, complementarity and mutual benefits.

The ideal pattern of inter-language relations conveyed by the above terms echoes the 'new' ecology of language, recently developed as a branch of linguistics. Ecological views of language are not new, with Edwards (2009: 230) claiming that 'nuanced investigations of the social life of language have always been ecologically minded'. This can be seen, for example, in perceiving languages as belonging to 'families' in nineteenth-century historical linguistics (see also the organic view of Arabic in Chapter 3). However, the 'new' ecology of language is different. It sets its main agenda as 'building on linguistic diversity worldwide, promoting multilingualism and foreign language learning, and granting linguistic human rights to speakers of all languages' (Phillipson and Skutnabb-Kangas 1996: 429). In doing so, this ecolinguistic paradigm endorses only one side of ecology, namely diversity and co-existence, and leaves the other side unheeded, namely the 'struggle of life and survival of the fittest' (Mühlhäusler 2000: 308). This conceptual selectivity reveals that, according to Edwards (2009: 243), 'the "new" ecology of language is not so much a refinement of scientific methodology in the face of new understandings and new challenges as it is a sociopolitical ideology'. This ideology belongs to a contemporary ecological morality that condemns the damage to the environment and human society caused by 'unrestrained free-market capitalism, unfettered industrialisation, galloping globalisation' (ibid.: 241) and hegemonic nationalism. In terms of language, this damage is understood as the global spread of English and the dominance of 'national languages' in 'national' communities – two processes that deny the linguistic rights of the (global and national) minorities and cause the loss of their languages. A similar ideological agenda could also be found in the call for equality and equilibrium in language contact in the ALA discourse, which was directed at the asymmetrical relationship between Arabic and the dominant foreign languages in Arab society.

This ideological agenda became clear in ʾAḥmad Ṣidqī al-Dajānī's article *Qaḍīyyat al-taʿrīb fī ḍawʾ sunan al-tafāʿul al-ḥaḍārī* 'The issue of Arabi(ci)sation in the light of the principles of civilisational interaction', published in the journal of the Cairo Academy in 1999. In this article, al-Dajānī (1999: 224–5) singles out what he calls peaceful contact among languages in three episodes of human history that involved what is now understood as the Arab world. The first was the heyday of ancient Egyptian and Mesopotamian civilisations, where a number of ancient languages were used side by side without conflict between them. The second was the golden age of Islam, when Arabic became the lingua franca in West Asia and North Africa by absorbing terms from other local languages such as Greek, Hebrew and Syriac in a relatively peaceful environment of cultural exchange. The third episode, according to al-Dajānī, was the Renaissance in Europe, during which the Europeans rediscovered the Greek legacy of science, philosophy and literature through Arabic translations.

Al-Dajānī's reading of history is obviously teleological and contestable, yet it highlights what he means by peaceful exchange among languages. The three historical episodes are chosen in the Arabs' favour. Concerning the first episode, Egypt and Mesopotamia were conquered by the Arabs in the seventh and eighth centuries and became part of the Arab world from then on. The ancient civilisations therein were thought to be inherited by the Arabs, becoming part of their cultural legacy (which was revived in modern times to justify the existence of primordial Egyptian and Iraqi nationalisms). In the next two episodes, Arabic played a central role in the transmission of Greek learning and the European Renaissance, which are often seen as two backbones of modern civilisation. The seemingly peaceful language exchange al-Dajānī establishes from history is used, in fact, to reaffirm the historical importance of Arabic in contrast to its unfortunate peripheralisation in modern times.

The example of al-Dajānī shows that the call for equilibrium in inter-language relations in the ALA discourse might not differ much from the first strategy of counter-peripheralisation – restoring the centrality of Arabic in Arab society. It follows that, by calling for equilibrium, the ALA discourse does not aim to deconstruct the present core-periphery power matrix among languages, but uses equilibrium as a cover for the old, unfulfilled dream of empowering Arabic within the same power matrix. This cover was used when the first strategy was discredited, due to its failure in empowering Arabic in real terms. Arabi(ci)sation policies in North African states, for example, have turned from uncompromising, monolingual ones in the early decades after independence, to more tolerant, plural ones, because the early policies have alienated Francophone and Berber-speaking citizens and contributed to the rise of conservative, radical Islamism (especially in Algeria), which impeded social cohesion and threatened the political legitimacy of the ruling regimes (see note 8). Under such circumstances, a change in discursive strategy is necessary to show that Arabi(ci)sation is tolerant by nature and is different from the violent and intolerant (neo-)colonial language policies. Denouncing colonialism bestows a high moral purpose to Arabi(ci)sation and diverts attention away from the de facto failure of Arabi(ci)sation and the problems it is claimed to have created.

Corpus and Status Arabicisation in the Discourse of Arabic Language Academies

The above discussion of the conception of Arabi(ci)sation in the ALA discourse shows how the aspiration for reversing Arabic/Arab peripherality was embedded in two enduring tendencies of this discourse (asserting the centrality of Arabic to Arab society through the inalienable link between Arabic and the Arabs, on the one hand, and calling for equilibrium in inter-language relations, on the other). These two tendencies also penetrated into more concrete, policy-oriented discussions of corpus and status Arabicisation. This penetration, as will be explored in the following two sections, demonstrates that even the concrete level of the ALA discourse on Arabi(ci)sation could refract the state and the feeling of 'peripherality' as the conceptual level did.

Corpus Arabicisation: Compounding

The purpose of corpus Arabicisation is to assimilate foreign neologisms into Arabic without compromising what is thought to be the 'Arabness' (i.e. the characteristic features) of Arabic. In order to preserve this linguistic 'Arabness', the ALA discourse often emphasised that, when borrowing Western terminologies, translation (using the Arabic lexical stock for new terms) was preferable to Arabicisation (using the borrowed term but submitting it to Arabic phonological and phonetic rules, i.e. transliteration); the latter could only be used as a last resort, for its overuse was thought to increase 'foreignness' in Arabic (Lian 2010: 64–72). This tug of war between 'Arabness' and 'foreignness' in the ALA discourse, however, did not only concern the choice between translation and transliteration but also involved legitimating compounding as a method of translation in Arabic.

Compounding is a method of word formation: two or more words or lexemes (lexical morphemes) combine together to form a new word. Compounding is familiar to speakers of Indo-European languages, because it fits into the so-called 'concatenative morphology' (Larcher 2006: 573) commonly attested in these languages. In concatenative morphology, inflexions and derivations are realised by adding affixes (grammatical or lexical morphemes) 'either before, after, inside of, or around a root or another affix' (Fasold and Connor-Linton 2006: 66). An example of this morphology is the English word *antidisestablishmentarianism*, which is composed of the morphemes (*anti-*, *dis-*, *establish*, *-ment*, *-ari*, *-an* and *-ism*) 'strung together like beads on a string' (Sproat 1992: 44). This morphology makes compounding a commonly pursued means of coining new scientific terminologies in modern European languages. This was most evident in the 'Neoclassical word formation' movement in these languages during the seventeenth and eighteenth centuries: elements of Greek and Latin origins were borrowed and combined with native morphemes concatenatively to form modern scientific and technological terminologies (Lüdeling 2006: 580). This method of coinage is very productive.

Since a large number of European scientific terminologies are compounds, it is straightforward to translate them into Arabic without changing their compounding structures. To be more precise, Arab scholars, when rendering terminology in European languages, can choose to translate all its constituent morphemes into Arabic and then compound the translated morphemes together in line with the original composition of the word. This method of 'translation via compounding' has two advantages (see Table 4.1 for an experiment using this method). First, it helps create

Table 4.1 Examples of translating English medical terms into Arabic via compounding

-ectomy	nephrectomy	→	*ṣalkala* (*isti’ṣāl* ‘removal’ + *kulya* ‘kidney’)
↓	tonsillectomy	→	*ṣalwaza* (*isti’ṣāl* ‘removal’ + *lawzatān* ‘tonsils’)
ṣal-	lobectomy	→	*ṣalfaṣa* (*isti’ṣāl* ‘removal’ + *faṣṣ* ‘lobe’)
	gastrectomy	→	*ṣalʿada* (*isti’ṣāl* ‘removal’ + *maʿida* ‘stomach’)
	enterectomy	→	*ṣalmaʿa* (*isti’ṣāl* ‘removal’ + *’amʿā’* ‘entrails’)
	splenectomy	→	*ṣalḥala* (*isti’ṣāl* ‘removal’ + *ṭiḥāl* ‘spleen’)
-algia	gastralgia	→	*wajʿada* (*wajaʿ* ‘pain’ + *maʿida* ‘stomach’)
↓	enteralgia	→	*wajmaʿa* (*wajaʿ* ‘pain’ + *’amʿā’* ‘entrails’)
waj-	hepatalgia	→	*wajbada* (*wajaʿ* ‘pain’ + *kabid* ‘liver’)
	cystalgia	→	*wajthana* (*wajaʿ* ‘pain’ + *mathāna* ‘bladder’)
-stomy	nephrostomy	→	*fatkala* (*fatḥ* ‘opening’ + *kulwa* ‘kidney’)
↓	gastrostomy	→	*fatʿada* (*fatḥ* ‘opening’ + *maʿida* ‘stomach’)
fat-	enterostomy	→	*fatmaʿa* (*fatḥ* ‘opening’ + *’amʿā’* ‘entrails’)
-tomy	arteriotomy	→	*qaṭshara* (*qaṭʿ* ‘cutting’ + *shiryān* ‘artery’)
↓	craniotomy	→	*qaṭrasa* (*qaṭʿ* ‘cutting’ + *ra’s* ‘head’)
qaṭ-	laryngotomy	→	*qaṭjara* (*qaṭʿ* ‘cutting’ + *ḥanjara* ‘larynx’)
	enterectomy	→	*qaṭmaʿa* (*qaṭʿ* ‘cutting’ + *’amʿā’* ‘entrails’)

Source: Jirjis (1961: 66)

concise Arabic terminologies, which are preferred by ALA members. Second, it confines the translation of terminologies to that of morphemes, which reduces the effort devoted to terminological translation and helps standardise translated terminologies across Arabic-speaking communities (because it is easier to agree on the translations of a limited list of morphemes than the vast and growing number of terminologies). Accordingly, this method, if legitimated and adopted, is believed to benefit modern users of Arabic.

However, the legitimacy of compounding in Arabic is weak, since this method is less known in the Arabic linguistic tradition. This is due to the fact that Arabic morphology is largely ‘non-concatenative’ (Larcher 2006: 573), as Arabic words are usually formed via internal morphological inflexion of triliteral roots.[21] The closest phenomenon to compounding in Arabic is what is known as *naḥṭ* in the Arabic linguistic tradition. Literally meaning hewing or chiselling a piece of stone or wood, *naḥṭ* is used terminologically to refer to the type of word formation that combines elements of two or more words to form a single word. Yet *naḥṭ* differs from compounding in Indo-European languages in that *naḥṭ* is abbreviative in nature rather than achieved through a lineal combination of affixes and morphemes, as the two major types of *naḥt* attested from the speech of ‘the Arabs’ show (see Table 4.2 below). Besides, even if *naḥṭ*

Table 4.2 Two types of *naḥt* in Arabic

Naḥt of construct phrases	*Naḥt* of sentences
ʿAbd Shams → ʿAbshamī	*Al-Ḥamd li-l-lāh. → ḥamdala*
Raʾs ʿAyn → Rasʿanī	*Subḥān al-lāh. → sabḥala*
ʿAbd al-Dār → ʿAbdarī	*Lā ḥawl wa-lā qūwa ʾillā bi-l-lāh. → ḥawqala*
Dār al-Biṭṭīkh → Darbakhī	*Bi-ism al-lāh al-raḥmān al-raḥīm. → basmala*

Source: al-Shahābī (1959: 545–6)

is counted as a form of compounding, compounding cannot be seen as a major feature of Arabic morphology because attested examples of *naḥt* are rare. Generally speaking, compounding is foreign to the Arabic linguistic system, so instituting compounding as a method of lexical coinage in Arabic is tantamount to, at least potentially, bringing a foreign linguistic element into Arabic, which, in the long run, is thought to contaminate the 'Arabness' of the language.

Discussions have been ongoing within the ALAs to justify the use of compounding in Arabic for almost a century. It suffices here to give the following examples of discourse to illustrate the two stances ALA members used in this regard. The first stance was to demonstrate that compounding is part of Arabic morphology, which is less recognised in the Arabic linguistic tradition but can be rediscovered to legitimate its use in corpus Arabicisation.

In 1946, the Cairo Academy formed an internal committee studying *naḥt* in Arabic. The committee considered a radical view on *naḥt* in the Arabic linguistic tradition promulgated by Ibn Fāris (d. 1004), who viewed Arabic words having more than three root letters as instances of *naḥt*. This view significantly expanded how *naḥt* was usually understood by Arab grammarians as shown in Table 4.2 and brought *naḥt* closer to compounding in Indo-European languages. Using the above view of Ibn Fāris as the source of legitimation, the committee suggested accepting the use of *naḥt* (in the sense of compounding) in lexical coinage. However, the committee was cautious not to over-rely on Ibn Fāris's view, which is a minority view in the Arabic grammatical tradition. In its report submitted to the Academy, the committee described Ibn Fāris's view as an 'aberration' (*taʿassuf*). This was possibly a rhetorical stance to pre-empt criticism. Behind this rhetoric lay the committee members' deep fear of being accused of compromising the 'Arabness' of Arabic. Regardless of this fear, the Academy approved the committee's report and passed a resolution 'permitting the use of *naḥt* [in the sense of compounding] to meet the urgent need (*al-ḥāja al-mulihḥa*) for expressing scientific and technological concepts in concise Arabic words' (MMQ 7: 203).

Not all ALA members were convinced by the above resolution, so discussions on compounding continued in the ALA discourse. One view of the resolution concerned whether *naḥt* could be permitted as an analogical (*qiyāsī*) principle of word formation or should be treated as attested linguistic usage (*samāʿī*) in the speech of 'the Arabs', the Qur'an, and pre- and early Islamic poetry. Conventionally, only linguistic phenomena frequently attested in the above linguistic sources can be seen as analogical creations or the basis of such creations. Attested examples of *naḥt*, even in a sense as broad as Ibn Fārīs's, do not exceed 400 (Ṣāliḥ, quoted in al-Sammān 1982a: 98), making them too rare and marginal to be the basis for *naḥt* in the modern period. To tackle this problem, some ALA members made further efforts to expand the range of *naḥt*. Al-Tawwāb (1973), for example, suggests that some triliteral words are also compounds, such as *ʾasmar* 'brown' (from *ʾas* in *ʾaswad* 'black' and *mar* in *ʾaḥmar* 'red'). Al-Sammān (1982a: 96) points out that many particles in Arabic are compounds as well, such as *hallā* 'would not . . . or why not . . .?' (from *hal* 'an interrogative particle' and *lā* 'not'), *lawlā* 'if not' (from *law* 'if' and *lā*), *ʾillā* 'if not, unless' (from *ʾin* 'if' and *lā*), etc. The purpose behind these efforts was clear: demonstrating that compounding is an authentic and common feature of Arabic morphology.

The second stance towards justifying the use of compounding in Arabic was to declare that compounding is a universal feature of human languages; it is therefore legitimate for Arabic users to use compounding in Arabic in the way that this method is used in Indo-European languages. Early in 1935, a debate about the nature of compounding took place between Mārūn Ghuṣn and Salīm al-Jundī – both members of the Damascus Academy – which was published in the Academy's journal (Ghuṣn 1935). Al-Jundī insists that introducing compounding into Arabic is a linguistic innovation contradictory to the principle of the Arabic linguistic tradition, which stipulates that linguistic innovations are not accepted beyond the time-space framework of the speech of 'the Arabs' (see the previous section for an explanation of this framework). Ghuṣn, by contrast, argues that accepting compounding is a common feature of language development. To support this, he points out that languages in both the West and East, such as French, Turkish and Japanese, have already used compounding to coin neologisms. It is, in his view, unjustifiable to reject compounding in Arabic because this rejection is tantamount to denying that Arabic is a modern and developing language.

In a similar manner, Ramsīs Jirjis (1961: 61), a member of the Cairo

Academy, claims in a report he submitted to the Academy that languages including Arabic have gone through a process of development starting from words with one root consonant to words with two root consonants and then to three or more. As for Semitic languages, he suggests that all lexical roots, be they biliteral, triliteral, quadraliteral, or more, are compounds of one root consonant; each consonant has its own original meaning. In that sense, compounding becomes a primary method of word formation shared among all languages, including Indo-European and Semitic languages, although the latter does not conventionally belong to the family of 'compounding' languages. Compounding was thus interpreted as universal across language families and therefore indigenous to Arabic.

The Academy asked another member, ʾIbrāhīm ʾAnīs, to review Jirjis's report. In support of Jirjis, ʾAnīs expressed the following view, in which he understood compounding as belonging to a wider universal tendency of human languages towards concision (quoted in al-Sammān 1982a: 108):

> Morphological development attested in ancient languages and most modern European languages exhibits a common tendency towards reduction (*taqṣīr*) and abridgement (*ikhtiṣār*). This common tendency has dominated speech in the modern age, which is characterised as the age of speed . . . The phenomenon of compounding discussed by early Arab scholars is, in fact, an aspect of this common tendency. There is no doubt that many examples of this phenomenon have been recorded [in the treatises of] these scholars.

Based on ʾAnīs's opinion above, the Academy passed a second resolution on permitting the use of compounding in Arabic in 1965. Unlike its first resolution, which legitimated compounding as part of Arabic morphology, this resolution accepted compounding as 'a linguistic phenomenon attested in both classical and modern languages' (ibid.: 109).

However, legitimating compounding on the ground of its universality did not mean it could be used in Arabic without limitations. Muṣṭafā al-Shahābī, president of the Damascus Academy (1959–68), had already warned that using compounding without attending to the linguistic taste of the Arabs would lead to the emergence of a new Nabatean (*nabaṭī*) language, a term he used to designate a form of Arabic mixed with foreign elements (al-Shahābī 1959: 551).[22] ʾIbrāhīm ʾAnīs specified the concept of 'taste' in his report to the Academy (see above) in the following set of phono-morphological patterns (quoted in al-Sammān 1982a: 108–9):

> If the compound is a transitive verb, it should follow *faʿlala* [e.g. *ḥalmaha* 'hydrolyse' from *ḥalla* 'to dissolve' and *miyāh* 'water'] and

its verbal noun *faʿlalah* [e.g. *halmahah* 'hydrolysis']; if the compound is an intransitive verb, it should follow *tafaʿlala* [e.g. *taḥamḍana* 'to be acidotic' from *ḥamḍ* 'acid' and *-n* 'a suffix referring to a process'] and its verbal noun *tafaʿlul* [e.g. *taḥamḍun* 'acidosis']; the adjective form should follow *faʿlalī* [e.g. *ʿabshamī* from ʿAbd Shams].

The purpose of proposing the above patterns was, in ʾAnīs's words, to make sure that Arabicised compounds did not violate the 'sound harmony' (*ḥusn al-jars*) of Arabic, which, we assume, was thought to represent the 'Arabness' of the Arabic language. The Cairo Academy approved ʾAnīs's proposal by including the above patterns in its second resolution on compounding. The stipulation of these patterns reflects that neither ʾAnīs nor the Academy truly believed in the universality of compounding but only used this thesis to justify the use of compounding in Arabic.

In practice, confining compounds to the above phono-morphological patterns cannot satisfy the demands for compounding in lexical coinage, because these patterns are all quadraliteral in form, which means that Arabic compounds are not allowed to contain more than four root consonants. In order to break this limit, some ALA members proposed more general rules of 'sound harmony', stipulating not patterns but principles of consonantal combination. Below are some of these principles (al-Sammān 1982b: 348–9):

(1) *Al-Jīm* cannot be combined with *al-qāf*, *al-ṣād*, or *al-ṭāʾ*.
(2) *Al-Sīn* cannot be combined with *al-dhāl*.
(3) *Al-Dāl* cannot be followed by *al-zāy*.
(4) *Al-Nūn* cannot be followed by *al-rāʾ*.
(5) Combining consonants whose pronunciations are similar should be avoided, such as *saṣṣ*, *ẓass*, *ẓathth*, *thaẓẓ*, *ḍashsh*, *shaḍḍ*, *qajj*, *jaqq*, *kaqq*, *qakk*, *kajj* and *jakk*.

According to al-Sammān, the consonantal combinations mentioned above have been treated as 'foreign' (*ʿajamī*) in the Arabic linguistic tradition and, accordingly, should not be accepted in modern Arabic compounds (ibid.: 348–9).

Apart from the above criterion of 'sound harmony', the use of compounding in corpus Arabicisation was also conditioned by the so-called 'urgent need' in the ALA discourse. This was expressed in the first resolution of the Cairo Academy on compounding (see above). Yet this resolution did not mention where this 'urgent need' lay. Al-Shahābī (1959: 548) reports that this vagueness led to two different interpretations of the resolution: the first read it as an authoritative encouragement of expanding compounding, while the second saw it as an attempt to restrain the use of compounding to the minimum.

Al-Sammān (1982a) offers three opinions on what 'urgent need' meant. First, according to ʾAnastās al-Karmalī, compounding is not needed at all in coining scientific terminologies. Al-Karmalī bases this view on his observation that Arab scientists in the Abbasid period, faced with huge demands of coinage, had never coined a single scientific terminology via compounding (ibid.: 102). Second, according to Muṣṭafā Jawād, compounding is a lesser-known phenomenon in Arabic and this method should only be used as a last resort to meet the 'urgent need' for terminological coinage, in order not to radically change the nature of Arabic (ibid.: 102). Third, according to Sāṭiʿ al-Ḥuṣrī, compounds, due to their concision, are vastly needed in modern science. Unlike al-Karmalī, al-Ḥuṣrī argues that compounding had helped Abbasid scientists greatly in lexical coinage. Al-Ḥuṣrī understands the Abbasid period as the first intellectual renaissance of the Arab nation and the twentieth century as the second. In his view, the need for scientific terminologies in the second renaissance was bigger than that of the first, so compounding should be more intensively applied. However, al-Ḥuṣrī also maintains that only compounds not contradictory to the phono-morphological properties of Arabic could be accepted (ibid.: 103–5).

Many of the above attempts of the ALA members to justify or limit the use of compounding in Arabic sought the legitimacy of their arguments from the past. In doing so, these members in fact reinterpreted the linguistic past of Arabic in a manner similar to what Hobsbawm (1983) calls 'the invention of tradition'. Özkirimli (2010: 94) understands this invention as consisting of two processes, namely 'the adaptation of old traditions and institutions to new situations and the deliberate invention of "new" traditions for quite novel purposes'. In the discussion of compounding, reinterpreting Ibn Fāris's view as proof of the authenticity of compounding belongs to 'adaptation', while claiming all lexical roots (consisting of more than two consonants) of Semitic languages to be compounds could be understood as a 'deliberate invention'. Both 'adaptation' and 'invention' illustrate that the past of Arabic is subject to manipulation. This is most evident in the contradictory views of al-Karmalī and al-Ḥuṣrī about terminological coinage in the Abbasid period. In this case, history became a site of discursive duelling to serve competing language ideologies. In spite of these ideological differences, the conscious association of the present with the past can be read as an underlying intellectual consensus about the existence of an atemporal 'Arabness' and the importance of its continuation in modern times.

To summarise: the above two stances for legitimating compounding in Arabic were in accord with the two tendencies of the ALA discourse on Arabi(ci)sation discussed in the previous section. The first stance, which sought support from the Arabic grammatical tradition to justify the use of compounding in modern Arabic, revealed a conscious effort of ALA members to maintain the inherited 'Arabness' of the language. This is reminiscent of how this linguistic 'Arabness' was correlated with the linguistic intuition of 'the Arabs' and how this correlation reflected an inalienable language-people link in the *muwallad* and *muʿarrab* discussion I dealt with before in this chapter. The second stance tried to legitimate compounding in Arabic by viewing it as a universal feature of human languages. This is equivalent to saying that compounding is acceptable in Arabic not because Arabic is subject to the influence of the powerful Indo-European languages such as English and French but because compounding is a common 'asset' equally shared among languages. It is clear that this stance reproduces the thesis of 'equilibrium in inter-language relations'. In addition, similar to the adoption of 'equilibrium' as a cover for de facto Arabic/Arab centralism, discussed in the previous section, here the ALA members stipulated a set of phono-morphological patterns to condition the use of the 'universal' compounding in Arabic and constrained this use to serving the 'urgent need' for coining scientific terminologies only.

Status Arabicisation: Language-in-Education

Discussions of status Arabicisation in the ALAs often focused on the language of instruction in the educational sector, due to (1) the importance of this sector in the cultivation of 'Arabness' among younger generations and (2) the use of English or French in, notably, university science programmes, which, in the minds of many ALA members, reflected the persistent inferiority and peripherality of Arabic vis-à-vis these two languages. A full summary of these discussions is beyond the scope of this chapter. In what follows, I will examine two recurrent issues in these discussions to illustrate how the two tendencies of conceptualising Arabi(ci)sation were also embedded in discussions of status Arabicisation.

The first issue is about the influence of the spread of foreign languages on Arab identity. Commenting on the popularity of private foreign schools in Egypt, Kamāl Muḥammad Bishr (1987), a member of the Cairo and Damascus Academies, points out that, in Egyptian public opinion, a sense of 'superiority' (*fawqiyya*) and 'privilege' (*imtiyāz*) has been attached to those Egyptians who have received education in Western languages.

Because of this, Bishr says, Egyptian parents who can afford private education prefer to send their children to foreign schools. These parents consider these schools to be 'special invitation cards', which can bring their children to the *khawājāt* – Western expatriates and Westernised Egyptian elites who have privilege and enjoy a high social status in Egypt. It should be mentioned that *khawāja* is an honorific of Persian origin, meaning 'sir, lord, or master'; in Egypt, *khawāja* is used to mean a wealthy foreigner who resides among Egyptians. By using this word, Bishr implies that, in the minds of some Egyptian parents, Western-style education can grant their children a Western identity that is more privileged than their Arab identity. However, in his view, this never happens. He depicts receiving education in Western languages in the Arab lands as planting artificial flowers that have no root, no natural fragrance and no hope for future growth (ibid.: 190), implying that these Egyptian children can only be Westernised superficially.[23] Worse still, warns Bishr, they will lose their competence in Arabic and the connection to their Arab-Islamic cultural legacy and, by extension, their Arab identity. Based on the above arguments, Bishr declares that Arabicising language-in-education is not merely a linguistic mission but also one of recovering and enhancing the Arabs' national and cultural identity. This view is reiterated in the writings of other ALA members (e.g. al-Khūrī 1991; ʿIzz al-Dīn 1994; al-Khūrī 1998). In Bishr (1987) above, status Arabicisation is clearly linked with recovering 'Arabness' or Arab identity to counter the superiority of Western languages. This is in accord with the first tendency of the ALA discourse on Arabi(ci)sation – the inalienability of Arabic and the Arab people.

The second issue concerning status Arabicisation in education is about the different roles played by Arabic and Western languages. The Second Arabi(ci)sation Conference (1973) has made it clear that Arabicising education does not mean 'disallowing the teaching of foreign languages' (ʾAḥmad 1999: 208), since these languages are useful in acquiring new knowledge from external sources. ʿAbd al-Ḥāfiẓ Ḥilmī Muḥammd (1996: 33), a member of the Cairo Academy, considers using Arabic a *farḍ ʿayn* 'individual duty' incumbent on every science teacher and student while, by contrast, using one or more foreign languages is a *farḍ kifāya* 'collective duty' on the scientific community. These – *farḍ ʿayn* and *farḍ kifāya* – are terminologies of Islamic law; the former refers to obligatory duties every Muslim needs to fulfil, such as prayer, fasting, etc., and the latter refers to those duties 'the fulfilment of which by a sufficient number of individuals excuses the other individuals from fulfilling it, such as funeral prayer, holy war, etc.' (Juynboll 1991: 790).

Muḥammd's use of these legal terminologies is noteworthy in two respects. On the one hand, he perceives the competence in Arabic and in foreign languages as mutually complementary in a way similar to the relationship between the two types of duties understood in the Islamic legal tradition. Like those duties whose fulfilment is vital for the sustenance of the Islamic *ʾumma*, both Arabic and foreign languages are considered to be indispensable to the scientific community in the Arabic-speaking world. On the other hand, Arabic and foreign languages are not thought to have the same degree of indispensability. While every member of the community is required to master Arabic, only a 'sufficient' number of the members need to know foreign languages. In other words, Arabic is central to scientific learning in the Arabic-speaking world while foreign languages are supplementary. Muḥammd's argument above conforms to the 'equilibrium in inter-language relations' thesis discussed before, which endorses a mutually beneficial relationship between Arabic and foreign languages but nonetheless posits Arabic in a more central and advantageous position therein.

Conclusion: Arabi(ci)sation as Symbolic Resistance and Symbolic Compensation

In this chapter, I have traced two tendencies in the ALA discourse on Arabi(ci)sation over time (the three 'sites') and across domains (conceptual and policy discussions), aiming at improving the state of Arabic vis-à-vis other languages by resorting to different strategies. My analysis of the content, metaphorics and other morpho-semantic elements of this discourse in this chapter shows that these tendencies were stable and persistent to the extent that they could be treated as 'discursive habiti' in the sense I defined in the Introduction.

By critically examining the interconnectedness between this discourse and its sociopolitical context, I argue that the reason for the above tendencies to become habiti lay in the conditions of 'peripherality' the Arabs experienced within the twentieth century: the reorganisation of the Ottoman Empire around Ottoman/Turkish identity (until the end of World War I), European colonialism (until the mid-twentieth century) and 'the continuing, often covert, operation of an imperialist system of economic, political and cultural domination' (Young 2001: 58) in the postcolonial period. The same peripherality also applied to the state of Arabic in modern Arab society, where the language was thought to be threatened by English and/or French in both public and professional domains of communication. To reverse this language situation, Arabi(ci)sation was formulated as a language-policy response.

However, Arabic peripherality was in fact a refraction of Arab peripherality; the former would exist whenever the latter existed, and would disappear whenever it disappeared. This symbiosis between Arabic and Arab peripherality had two impacts on Arabi(ci)sation. First, when 'diagnosing' Arabic peripherality, policy-makers cannot avoid going beyond the language to address the extra-linguistic causes behind this language situation. Accordingly, when making 'prescriptions', they conceived Arabi(ci)sation as a fix to the problems not just of Arabic but of the Arabs as well, for they regarded the return of Arabic to its central status in Arab society as correlating with the empowerment of the Arabs in the modern world-system. In doing so, they employed Arabicisation (linguistic) as a proxy for Arabisation (extra-linguistic). Proxification as such relied on exploiting the symbolism of Arabic through its (often constructed) links with the extra-linguistic world. In the case given here, the destiny of Arabic was perceived to be bound together with that of the Arab people and vice versa, and this perception was so deep-rooted and pervasive that it assumed the position of a doxa. This doxa nurtured the many symbolic meanings of Arabic that made Arabi(ci)sation symbolic. Second, as long as Arab peripherality continued, Arabi(ci)sation could not improve the status of Arabic in real terms. This mismatch between policy and reality led to the instrumental impotence of Arabi(ci)sation, which heightened the symbolic value of this policy.

In this context, the ALA discourse on Arabi(ci)sation exerted two symbolic effects. On the one hand, it offered a way for the symbolic resistance to the peripheralisation of both Arabic and the Arabs. On the other, it kept alive, in the context of continuing peripheralisation, the Arabs' aspiration for self-empowerment and their vision of a more equilibrial and balanced international order than the order found at present, to counterbalance the powerful Other in the modern world-system. This second effect, which constructed an attractive alternative to an unsatisfying reality, through symbolic mediums such as narrative and discourse, fits what Larson (2000: 49) describes as 'symbolic compensation'. We therefore witness a tendency of the ALA discourse to emphasise the uniqueness of Arabic and its alienable link with the Arabs in order to reverse the core-periphery hierarchy imposed on both Arabic and the Arabs, and another tendency attempting to replace this hierarchy with a more balanced alternative where Arabic and the Arabs can be equal with the powerful Other. Such symbolic resistance and compensation became routine and habitual when the conditions of 'peripherality' lasted for too long, as in the case of the twentieth-century Arabic-speaking world. This long-lasting peripherality also nurtured, among ALA members, a dyadic view of the relationship between Self (the Arabs) and the Other (the West), which will be discussed in the next chapter, on the modernisation of Arabic. The combined analysis of content, semantics, metaphorics and sociopolitical contexts of the ALA discourse together with the notion of discursive habitus, symbolism and doxa, as has been carried out in this and the previous chapters to explain the routinisation and reiteration of certain statements in this discourse, will be developed further in the next chapter.

Notes

1. Although Shaaban (2007) states that 'Arabisation' and 'Arabicisation' are used 'interchangeably in the literature on language planning in the Arab world', I am arguing that it is necessary to distinguish between the two to reveal the conceptual plurality of the Arabic term *taʿrīb*. See also Suleiman (1999b) for a similar view.
2. Maḥmūd Ḥāfiẓ was elected the vice president of the Cairo Academy in 1995 and became its president from 2005 until his death in 2011.
3. Scholars working on the Arab world and the Middle East, regardless of their different focuses, perspectives and agendas, seem to describe the position of the Arabs in the modern world in ways that confirm the perception of Arab peripherality in this book. For example, in *What Went Wrong? Western Impact and Middle Eastern Response* (2002), Bernard Lewis perceives the ascendancy of the West over the Middle East from the seventeenth century onwards as an alternation of superiority-inferiority power relations between Christendom and the Muslim world in the former's favour. In *The Modern Middle East: A History* (2011), James L. Gelvin applies the world-system(s) analysis to the Middle East and states that 'the Middle East was integrated into the world economy in the status of periphery' (38) and this 'affected not only economic relations in the region, but social relations as well' (44). Leila Ahmad, in *Women and Gender in Islam* (1992), argues that calling for women's liberation in the writing of Qāsim ʾAmīn [d. 1908, an Egyptian lawyer who published his controversial book *Tahrīr al-marʾa* 'The Emancipation of Women' in Egypt in 1899] 'was in fact calling for the transformation of Muslim society along the lines of the Western model and for the substitution of the garb of Islamic-style male dominance by that of Western-style male dominance', which 'in its fundamentals reproduced the colonizer's attack on native culture and society' (161). In *Desiring Arabs* (2007), Joseph A. Massad describes how a 'hegemonic understanding of Arab culture and its past achievements' was produced in modern Arab intellectual discourse within the epistemic framework created by Orientalism in the West (48). Finally, in *Formations of the Secular: Christianity, Islam, Modernity* (2003), Talal Asad considers the global diffusion of modernity as a hegemonic project carrying with it a political goal. In his view, this project 'aims at institutionalizing a number of (sometimes conflicting, often evolving) principles: constitutionalism, moral autonomy, democracy, human rights, civil equality, industry, consumerism, freedom of the market – and secularism. It employs proliferating technologies (of production, warfare,

travel, entertainment, medicine) that generate new experiences of space and time, of cruelty and health, of consumption and knowledge [sic]' (13). In his book, Asad examines the secularisation process in colonial Egypt, pointing out that the changing concept of secularism in Arabic, the focus on rationality in Islamic reformist thinking, and the transformation of family and economic relations in Egypt were not the results of civilisation, progress, modernisation, or globalisation but those of the hegemonic political project described above (205–56). The above analyses signal the peripherality of the Arabs in the modern economic, political, social and epistemic world-system and the global power matrix that accompanies it.

4. The French ruled Algeria between 1830 and 1962, Tunisia between 1881 and 1956, parts of Morocco between 1912 and 1956, and Lebanon and Syria between 1920 and 1946. The British ruled Egypt between 1882 and 1922, Iraq between 1920 and 1932, and Transjordan between 1922 and 1946.
5. See Bassiouney (2009: 210–54) for a description of the various colonial language policies and their legacy in Algeria, Morocco, Tunisia, Syria, Lebanon, Egypt, Sudan, Israel and Palestine.
6. Turkification refers to reconstructing a collective self in the Ottoman Empire in line with a revived Turkic national identity and the Turkish language. It was initially a cultural movement associated with the Young Turks, responding to the political weakness and fragmentation of the Empire, which in the mid-nineteenth century was caught between secessionist national movements within and European imperialist threats without. It became an Empire-wide policy when the Young Turks took power in 1909 (Suleiman 2003: 79).
7. Tignor (1966) reports that 'the British-controlled Department of Public Instruction made concerted efforts to relegate Arabic to a lesser position – in Egypt's public schools – behind English . . . A definite push came about near the turn of the [twentieth] century to teach all secondary school subjects in English, except for Arabic and some mathematics classes. However, nationalist attacks and protests were directed against the repression of Arabic in the schools. Early in the twentieth century, the British administrator Lord Cromer reversed the stance of the education bureaucracy somewhat as a conciliatory gesture' (quoted in Schaub 2003: 227).
8. It was difficult to challenge the dominance of English and French (in North Africa) in university science teaching, business and some professional domains because these were the areas in which Arab dependence on the core countries was far-reaching. Without changing the asymmetrical power relations between the Arabs and the West in the Arabic-speaking world, Arabi(ci)sation was doomed to fail, sometimes leading to the disillusionment of the younger generations. Commenting on Arabi(ci)sation in Algeria, Mostari (2004: 34) says, 'Carried out in an authoritarian way, Arabi[ci]sation has seriously affected the capacity of the education system to acquire the scientific and technical knowledge needed for any improvement.' Similarly, according to Daoud (2011: 18), some Tunisians consider that 'the switch to Arabic had an impoverishing impact on the course content and teaching approach, particularly in the humanities and social sciences which could no longer rely on "enlightening" Western/French references, thus nurturing new generations of school graduates with a conservative, traditionalist, less Westernized

mindset'. Accessing educational Arabicisation in Morocco, Ennaji and Sadiqi (2008: 51) argue that 'the present education system has double standards in the sense that it discriminates against the poor and benefits the well-off both pedagogically and socio-economically', because students educated in Arabic have dimmer job prospects than their French-educated counterparts. Poor quality of education, unemployment and conservative mentality caused by improper Arabicisation of education led to the disillusionment of some North African youth, which might account for the rise of Islamic fundamentalism in North African countries in recent decades (Grandguillaume 1991: 50–1; Ennaji 1999: 390; Ennaji and Sadiqi 2008: 50–1).

9. The 'wisdom of the Arabs' principle serves as a guiding language ideology in the formation of grammatical theories, especially the theory of *taʿlīl* 'causation', in the Arabic grammatical tradition. See Suleiman (1999a; 2003: 47–9) for the reiteration of this principle in the grammar works of Ibn al-Sarrāj (d. 928), ʾAbu al-Qāsim Zajjājī (d. 948), and Ibn Jinnī (d. 1002). This principle was ideological in nature and cannot be read without the political context of its construction, which was 'the interethnic strife in the first centuries of Islam (and beyond) between the Arabs and non-Arabs in the Muslim Empire, especially the Persians' (Suleiman 2011b: 19).
10. Ibn ʿAsākir (d. 1176) reported the incident of this saying as follows (1995: 224): 'Qays ibn Maṭṭāṭiyya came to a circle where Salmān the Persian, Ṣuhayb the Byzantine, and Bilāl the Abyssinian were present. He was heard saying that "This is [a circle of] al-ʾAws and al-Khazraj [two Arab tribes constituted the *ʾAnṣār* 'helpers' of Muḥammad], but what is the situation like this?" [Hearing this], Muʿādh ibn Jabal rose up to him, seized him by the collar, brought him to the Prophet, and informed the latter of what he had said. The Prophet stood up, trailing his garment until he entered the mosque where a gathering to pray was called. He said: "O people! The Lord is one, and the Father [Adam] is one. The Arabness (*ʿarabiyya*) that embraces you is not from your fathers nor your mothers. It is a tongue (*lisān*) [i.e. a spoken language]. So whoever speaks Arabic is an Arab." Muʿādh ibn Jabal stood up, still holding Qays's collar, and asked: "What do you order us to do with this hypocrite (*munāfiq*), O Messenger of Allah?" The Prophet replied: "Leave him to the Fire!" Qays was among those who [later] renounced their faith in Islam and was killed during the Wars of Apostasy (*al-ridda*).' This particular saying is considered weak (*ḍaʿīf*) or forged (*mawḍūʿ*) not only because its chain of transmission is weak (al-ʾAlbānī 1992: 325) but also because the Arab superiority associated with this saying is thought to be contradictory to the universalism of Islam (Haddad [1999]). However, it can be argued that, by defining Arabness on linguistic terms, this saying denies pedigree as a defining element of Arab-Muslim identity. This denial was needed in the time of the Prophet (or the early Islamic periods in general) to strengthen the solidarity of the newly formed Muslim community against pre-existing affiliations, e.g. tribes, ethnicities and races. In spite of the doubts cast upon its authenticity, how this saying used Arabic to define Arabness was echoed in the Arab-Islamic tradition and was revived in the discourse of Arabic and Arab nationalism in the nineteenth and twentieth centuries (see Suleiman 2003 and Chapter 3 of this book).

11. They were, according to Suleiman (2003: 47), 'the Arabic-speakers of Central Arabia (Najd and the immediately surrounding areas) up to (approximately) the middle of the ninth century'. 'The Arabs' was not clearly defined in the Arabic grammatical tradition, which subjected this concept to ideological manipulation in the ALA discourse, as will be shown in this section.
12. *Muwallad* is considered to be the language innovation of the Arabs who are not pure-born (*muwalldūn*) (see also Chapter 2). It is a linguistic-cum-ethnic concept. Arguably all native Arabic speakers living after the fourth century of Islam belonged to the *muwalldūn*, not only because their Arab pedigree might be compromised by inter-marriage with non-Arabs but also because their intuitions about Arabic were believed to be corrupted by contact with foreign languages.
13. Al-ʾIskandarī considered *nūfambar* to be introduced by 'the Arabs' before the end of the second century of Islam during their conquest of North Africa (MJMJ 1: 307).
14. The Cairo Academy passed its resolution on Arabicisation in 1934 as 'When necessary, the Academy permits Arabicising some foreign words in the Arabs' way' (MJMJ 1: 422) to keep the concept of 'the Arabs' vague.
15. It should be noted that the 'primordial' position is also constructivist. However, its acceptance and long history made it look like a 'natural' category of the social world rather than a construction of the past.
16. This conference was held in Bagdad in 1938, and al-ʾIskandarī's speech at this conference was published in the journal of the Cairo Academy in 1948.
17. The resolution is considered as an example of the ALA discourse here because this Conference gave birth to the Bureau for Arabicisation, which is treated as an ALA in this book (see Chapter 2), and set the tone for the agenda of the Bureau and the following Arabi(ci)sation Conferences the Bureau convened.
18. A typical event illustrating the sociopolitical circumstances described above was the Suez Crisis in 1956. The British retained control of the Suez Canal after granting Egypt formal independence in 1922 because of the importance of the canal as 'an imperial lifeline facilitating the flow of oil, trade, and troops' (Little 2010: 306). This was at odds with Nasser's ambition to establish a new political order in Egypt and the Arab world after he led the Young Officer Revolution that overthrew the Egyptian monarchy in 1952. While pressing the British to leave the canal, Nasser had no economic and military leverage to secure the interests of Egypt in line with his political ambition. He needed to negotiate with the US-led capitalist block and the Soviet-led communist block to proceed with the Aswan Dam project and defend Egypt from Israeli aggressions. Notwithstanding this economic and military dependence, Nasser and his cabinet boycotted, together with some other Arab states, the British-backed Baghdad Pact – a defence alliance imposed on the Middle East – on the grounds of anti-imperialism and non-alliance principles. This diplomatic move worried the West and caused the US to withdraw its financial aid to the Dam project. In response, Nasser requested help from the Soviets and nationalised the Suez Canal, confiscating the income from the canal to compensate for the withdrawn aid. In retaliation, Britain and French collaborated with Israel and invaded the Suez region in 1956. The Suez Crisis ended with US and Soviet intervention. Nasser's military setback during

the crisis was paid back by Egypt's boosted position in the Arab world as a pan-Arab leader against so-called Western imperialism.

19. Here Hāshim's reading of Arabic and the Arab mind falls into a line of linguistic determinism or relativism in both Arab and non-Arab writings about Arabic. This line sees lexical, structural and stylistic features of Arabic form, condition, or influence the Arabs' way of perceiving and understanding the exterior world. Such linguistic determinism and relativism, as Suleiman (2013a) points out, is often proposed without sufficient empirical support and is driven by ideological and political purposes. For example, Suleiman compares al-Arsuzi's positive and al-Qsimī and Sharabi's negative assessments of the influence of Arabic on the Arab mind and attributes their difference to the changing political atmosphere after the 1967 defeat: while al-Arsuzi's view reflected pre-1967 optimism in the Arab world concerning the realisation of pan-Arabism as a political order, the latter assessments were driven by the post-1967 social malaise, making al-Qsimī and Sharabi express their dismay about the political impotence of the Arab states through criticising the negative influence of Arabic on the Arabs (ibid.: 270–1). Worse still, some other writings similar to the above, such as Shouby and Patai, who 'consider Arabic to be responsible for influencing Arab thought and behaviour in ways in which exaggeration, overstatement, repetition and empty talk play a major part' (ibid.: 272), may contain or 'be exploited for blatant cultural racism or even worse' (ibid.: 273). In Hāshim's case here, his emphasis on the constitutive role of Arabic in the formation of the Arab mind and Arab individuality was also ideological in nature, as he intended to demonstrate the essential centrality of Arabic to Arab life to resist the encroachment of Westernisation on Arabic and Arab identity.
20. Al-Yāfī is literally talking about any national language, but it is clear from his writing that his central concern is Arabic.
21. In the French Arabist tradition, this morphology is called 'crossing', as if a root were crossed with a morphological pattern (Cantineau 1950, quoted in Larcher 2006: 573).
22. The Nabateans refer to the Aramaic-speaking peoples inhabiting northern Arabia and Mesopotamia before the Islamic conquests. In Arabic historical and folkloristic accounts, the Nabateans were sedentary peoples specialising in 'the levying of taxes and exploitation of the land', who were put into sharp contrast with the Bedouin Arabs (Graf and Fahd 1993: 836). The Nabatean language was considered to be a mixture of Aramaic and Arabic. One view regarded this language to be 'the direct descendant of Classical Arabic but termed [*n*]*abaṭī* to indicate that it does not conform strictly to the rules of literary Arabic' (Emery 1993: 838). In a slightly different manner, al-Jāḥiẓ used *nabaṭī* to mean a group of people who lived in Iraq and whose Arabic speech was defective. It is clear that, in both ethnic and linguistic senses, 'Nabatean' is the opposite of the purity of the Arabs and the Arabic language. Here al-Shahābī may have used this concept to show that the unchecked use of compounding would corrupt the Arabic language and Arab identity.
23. To give this superficial learning some concrete proof, ʾAḥmad Shafīq al-Khaṭīb (2000), a member of the Cairo Academy, describes a 'dual weakness' in the language competence of lectures and students in Arab universi-

ties. He reveals that, although Western languages such as English and French are widely used in university-based physical and social science courses, most lecturers and students are, in fact, not good at these languages. According to al-Khaṭīb, they do not use Standard English or French but mix the two languages with idioms and expressions of Colloquial Arabic; nor do they use *fuṣḥā* Arabic; their competence in English or French on the one hand and *fuṣḥā* Arabic on the other are equally poor (*rakīk*).

5

Language Modernisation between Self and the Other

This chapter examines how the modernisation of Arabic was conceptualised in the ALA discourse in line with a persistent dyad of both an exogenous and endogenous understanding of modernisation. From an instrumental perspective, Arabic was perceived to be challenged by the incompatibility between an inherited linguistic tradition and an imported linguistic modernity, making the status of Arabic perilous in the modern Arabic-speaking world. From the symbolic perspective, as a marker of the Arab nation, Arabic was believed to exemplify the modern predicaments of the Arab nation, which was thought to be caught between continuing stagnation from within, and unremitting colonial and imperial threats from without. Modernising Arabic therefore became a language planning project always directed at a national cause. The reconciliation of tradition and modernity for Arabic was, in fact, part of the search of the Arab national self in new sociopolitical circumstances, emerging and evolving from the late eighteenth century, to counterbalance the hegemony of the powerful Other, mainly the West.

Modernity and Modernisation between Self and the Other

Broadly speaking, modernity means different things or has different meanings to Westerners and Arabs. For Westerners, modernity refers to the overall social features that distinguish 'a traditional, agrarian past from the modern, industrial present' (Bhambra 2007: 1). This modernity is a product of interrelated, deep processes unfolding from the sixteenth century onwards in the West, including: (1) secularisation – 'a process by which the overarching and transcendent religious system of old is reduced in modern functionally differentiated societies to a subsystem alongside other subsystems' (Dobbelaere 2007: 4148); (2) differentiation – a process by which the life world (the ontological physical and social world) and knowledge (epistemology) are divided into relatively independent functional subsystems and are managed on matching bases; and (3) rationalisation – the rise of instrumental rationality which transfers social authority from traditional, often religious, forms, to objective, rational calculations managed by human beings based on their social needs and common welfare.

Linguistic modernity in the West was also a phenomenon correlating with these three processes. Secularisation involved liberating knowledge and education from ecclesiastical authority – a process facilitated by replacing Latin with various national languages based on which mass literacy and public education could be promoted. These national languages were standardised and simplified to ensure they were equally accessible to both literary elites and the common people. Development in mass communication, notably printed books, journals, newspapers, and, later, radio and television, contributed to the standardisation, spread and consolidation of national languages. Differentiation was accompanied by the rise of new domains of social communication, diversifying the function and style and expanding the vocabulary of modern languages. Rationalisation was revealed in the development of 'the plain style', which preferred expressiveness, precision and clarity to elaboration of form and rhetoric as the norm of prose writing (Barber et al. 2009: 228).

For the Arabs, by contrast, modernity is an imported product deprived of any reference to the processes of its making. When the Arabs encountered Western modernity during the Napoleonic invasion of Egypt (1798–1801), they viewed it with awe and panic. Beginning from Muḥammad ʿAlī's (d. 1849) modernisation reform in Egypt in the early nineteenth century, reformers in the Arabic-speaking world were eager to reformulate their society in accordance with Western modernity. They received this modernity as a pre-packaged 'item', regardless of its four-century-long formation. New military, political, social and educational institutions, as well as new ideas and values, were introduced into Arab society in a comparatively short period. This abrupt and sudden introduction of modernity created a rupture in Arab society, making reconciliation between Arab-Islamic tradition and Western modernity a contested issue persisting over generations of Arabs until today.

Moreover, for the Arabs, the introduction of modernity was always tinted with European colonialism and Western imperialism. Modernity represented a new sociopolitical reality imposed upon Arab society by Western industrial powers during their colonial rule in the Arabic-speaking world. In the mid-twentieth century, when Arab states gained independence and military colonialism retreated, Arabs felt that the West still maintained its hegemony over the Arabs in the political, economic and cultural spheres in a variety of overt and covert ways (see the discussion of Arab peripherality in Chapter 4). This thesis of colonial modernity was abetted directly or indirectly by Oriental scholarship, which treated the fixity and stagnation of the Arab-Islamic tradition to be responsible for the backwardness of the Arabs in modern times (see the discussion of Oriental despotism in Chapter 3). This scholarship further claimed that Western modernity was universal and should be observed and emulated if the Arabic-speaking world was to be modernised.[1] By associating modernisation with Western hegemony, the colonial and imperial tint of modernity impeded its easy reconciliation with Arab-Islamic tradition.

The observation that modernity is both an imported package and a colonial imposition for Arabs also applies to the introduction of Western linguistic modernity to the Arabic-speaking world. The transformation of Arab society in accordance with Western modernity from the end of the eighteenth century onwards placed new requirements on the Arabic language: the Arabic-speaking world now needed a standard language that combined spoken and written functions, a common language that was easily accessible for both elites and the common people, a multifunctional language with a rich vocabulary that could be used in differentiated domains of communication, and a plain language that met the stylistic standard of journalistic and scientific prose writing. Arab reformers and modernists made every effort to reshape Arabic in line with these requirements. They brought in printing and the press,[2] established schools teaching modern languages and sciences, sent student delegations to Europe, coined new vocabularies for both specialist and general purposes, encouraged translation from European languages, compiled modern dictionaries and encyclopedias, and proposed plans for simplifying or reforming the Arabic language. In Europe, these new requirements were cumulative features of a long process of language modernisation. Emulating these new features without going through the deep processes leading to their formation caused worries among Arab intellectuals over the integrity of the Arabic language system in the modern age, on the one hand, and its adaptability to modern communicative needs, on the other. Modernising Arabic became a protracted process where the tension between the 'abruptly' imported linguistic modernity and the linguistic tradition of Arabic was inevitable.

Worse still, the colonial and semi-colonial incursions in the Arabic-speaking world between the mid-nineteenth and mid-twentieth centuries

– Algeria (1830–1962), Tunisia (1881–1956), Egypt (1882–1922 and beyond until 1952), Morocco (1912–56), Iraq (1920–32), Syria (1920–46), and Syria and Lebanon (1920–46) – soon transformed the introduction of linguistic modernity from voluntary emulation to enforced imposition. As I mentioned in Chapter 4, colonial language policies, albeit in varying degrees of coercion, all tended to promote modern European languages, mainly French and English, in many walks of life (notably administration and education) at the cost of Arabic. The colonial powers imposed their languages as markers of power and instruments of control, but these languages were promoted and also received by some Arabs as languages of modernity that were superior to Arabic. The tendency of favouring French and English over Arabic continued in some professional sectors of Arab society in the postcolonial era, becoming intensified in the last two decades of the twentieth century due to economic liberalisation and globalisation (see Chapter 4). Colonial language policies and their postcolonial repercussions helped consolidate the view among conservative Arab intellectuals that linguistic modernity was inherently alien to the Arabic linguistic tradition and dangerous to the integrity of the Arabic language. Consequently, reshaping Arabic in line with linguistic modernity became contentious in the Arabic-speaking world. An alternative method of language modernisation arose: reviving Arabic based on the Arabic linguistic tradition to obtain equal status with English and French in the modern world.

The different understanding of modernity between the West and the Arabic-speaking world poses two critical questions regarding modernity and modernisation. Is there only one modernity or are there many modernities? And is there one type of modernisation or are there many? As for the first question, Western modernity appeared to be universal when it was introduced into the Arabic-speaking world, but this universalism was severely weakened with local reformers' precipitate adoption of this modernity and European colonisers' enthusiastic promotion of it (to vie for global hegemony under the pretence of civilising the 'barbarian'). Recent scholarship in the West favours the 'multiple modernities' theory which suggests that modernity first appeared in the West and then spread to the rest of the world; during the spread of modernity, the modern institutions and values developed in Western societies were interpreted and appropriated by local cultures and traditions in different ways (Eisenstadt 2003). For the Arabs in the previous two centuries, modernity seemed to be both universal and multiple. On the one hand, modernity instituted a global order in the modern world; if the Arabs wanted to be part of the global world, they had no choice but to succumb to this universal order. On the other hand, the representation of modernity diffused with European colonialism and Western imperialism was foreign and inimical to the Arabs, and they believed that they could develop their own forms of modernity in Arab society based on their own traditions, to counterbalance the hegemony of Western modernity. In sum, modernity as a universal order seemed to be incontestable, but various local forms of modernity should also be acknowledged. Modernity seemed to be universal, but the means to acquire and interpret modernity were not all the same. This leads to the second question, the one concerning modernisation.

Modernisation is also both universal and multiple. As an ongoing, and possibly never ending, progression towards the furthest end of modernity, modernisation could be seen as a universal phenomenon involving humanity as a whole. As a way of interpreting, appropriating and representing modernity in local and contingent situations, modernisation varies across time and locality. For the Arabs in the nineteenth and twentieth centuries, the universal meaning of modernisation was expressed in various braided concepts such as renaissance (*nahḍa*), progress (*taqaddum*), reform (*ʾiṣlāḥ*) and revolution (*thawra*), all pointing to the progress of the Arabs as a political, national and civilisational collectivity towards a better end. However, since modernisation in the Arabic-speaking world was not endogenously generated but triggered by the importation and imposition of Western forms of modernity, for the Arabs modernisation also involved rediscovering and revaluating their cultural heritage (*turāth*) to develop their own forms of modernity to counterbalance the West. As Massad (2007: 29) puts it, ‘what remains constant [in the Arab cultural debates on modernity] is a commitment to an evolutionary temporal schema that recognizes change only within the dyad of *turāth* and [Western] modernity’. This dyad divides modernisation in the Arab context into two: an endogenous modernisation that looks for Arab forms of universal modernity from within and an exogenous modernisation that seeks to reproduce or copy Western forms of modernity from without. As I will discuss in detail in the following sections, this dyad of modernisation has been a constant feature of the ALA discourse on the modernisation of Arabic.

‘Catching up with Modern Requirements’ versus ‘Revival and Reform’

In the ALA discourse, exogenous modernisation is usually associated with the conceptual cluster of ‘catching up with modern requirements’ and endogenous modernisation is often characterised by the conceptual cluster of ‘revival and reform’. From the CDA point of view adopted throughout this book, these two conceptual associations signpost the functioning of the exogenous-endogenous dyad as a discursive habitus that links the routinisation of the ALA discourse on language modernisation with the diachronically puzzling relationship between the peripheralised Arab self and the powerful, dominant Other.

A number of terms or terminological phrases belong to the 'catching up with modern requirements' cluster. This first is *musāyara*, literally meaning 'walking alongside someone'. In discussions of the ALAs, we often encounter phrases like *sayruhā maʿ madaniyyat al-ʿaṣr al-ḥāḍir* '[Arabic] proceeding with the civilisation of the current age' (al-Jundī 1925: 399), *musāyarat ḥājāt al-ʿaṣr* 'moving with the needs of the age' (Rifāʿiyya 1969: 35) and *musāyarat al-taṭawwur al-taknulūjī* 'keeping up with technological development' (al-Jalīl 1974: 323). The second term, whose meaning is similar to the first one, is *mujārā*, literally meaning 'flowing together'. An example is *tujārī al-taqaddum* '[Arabic] keeps pace with progress' (Qunṣul 1973: 83). The third term is *wafā*, meaning 'to meet or fulfil (needs or obligations)'. For example, there is *wafat al-ʿarabiyya bi-gharaḍihā* 'Arabic has fulfilled its purpose' (Kurd ʿAlī 1944). The fourth term is *talbiya*, meaning 'following and obeying'. For instance, when discussing modern Arabic dictionaries, ʿAbd al-Raḥmān (1988: 21) emphasises that these dictionaries appeared 'to comply with the requirements of learning' (*talbiya li-l-mutaṭallabāt al-dirāsiyya*). The fifth term is *taṭwīʿ*, meaning 'rendering obedient'. In a report on the work of ALECSO, *taṭwīʿ al-ḥarf al-ʿarabī li-l-ḥāsūb al-ʾilkturūnī* 'making the Arabic script suitable for the computer' (LS 15 (1): 8) is used to introduce the task of script reform along with the development of digital technology. Similarly, Shawqī ʾAmīn uses *taṭwīʿuhā li-l-taṭawwur al-lughawī wa-l-taʿbīr al-ʿaṣrī* 'making [Arabic grammar] suitable for language development and contemporary expressions' to show the necessity of grammatical reform (MJMT 43: 315). More terms and phrases can be listed within this conceptual cluster, but they are omitted here because the above five terms have adequately illustrated the meaning of 'catching up with modern requirements'.

A common feature of the meanings these terms designate is that they all point to existing conditions which are independent of the Arabic language system and to which this language needs to be adapted. Nearly all these existing conditions, such as 'the current age', 'technological development' and 'progress', are exclusively 'modern'. Whether these modern conditions were introduced into the Arabic-speaking world as foreign borrowings or as representations of universal modernity, they act as the normative criteria that demand that the Arabic language respond. It is this 'demanding' imperative that brings the 'catching up with modern requirements' cluster close to the 'exogenous modernisation' vis-à-vis the Arabic language.

Now let us turn to the 'revival and reform' cluster, which includes two sets of terms and phrases. The first set contains *nahḍa* 'revival to reach efflorescence', *ʾiḥyāʾ* 'reviving', *ʾinʿāsh* 'revitalising' and *ʿawda* 'return or restoring'.[3] These terms all refer to the process of revitalising the previously vibrant but currently stagnant Arabic language. Examples of these are *ʾaṣbaḥat wasāʾil al-ʾiṣlāḥ wa-muqawwimāt al-nuhūḍ bi-l-ʿarabiyya wāḍiḥa maʿrūfa* 'the means of reforming and reviving Arabic have become clear and well-known' (al-Shabībī 1955: 20), *ʾinʿāsh al-ʿarabiyya* 'revitalising Arabic' (al-Jundī 1925: 397), *fī sabīl ʾiḥyāʾ al-ʿarabiyya wa-ʾinʿāshihā* 'for the sake of reviving and revitalising Arabic' (al-Jamālī 1969: 23) and *khidmat al-lugha al-ʿarabiyya wa-l-ʿawda bihā ʾilā ʾaṣālatihā wa-ʾamjādihā* 'serving Arabic and restoring it to its authenticity and glory' (al-Sayyid 1972: 457). The second set of terms contains *taṭwīr* 'developing', *tanmiya* 'developing', *ʾighnāʾ* 'enriching', *nashr* 'spreading', *tajdīd* 'renewing', *taysīr* 'simplifying' and *ʾiṣlāḥ* 'reforming'. These terms refer to the process of modifying and improving the structure and state of the Arabic language. The following are examples: *taṭwīr al-lugha al-ʿarabiyya li-musāyarat al-taṭawwur al-ʿilmī al-taqnī* 'developing the Arabic language to make it compatible with technological development' (al-Jalīl 1974: 323), *yakūn ʿamalunā mustamirran fī taʾṣīlihā ʾawwalan thumma fī tanmiyatihā* 'our ongoing effort aims to authenticate and develop [Arabic]' (Fayṣal 1975: 7), *al-muṣṭalaḥ al-ʿilmī bayna al-tharāʾ wa-l-ʾighnāʾ* '[Arabic] scientific terminology between richness and enrichment' (Shawqī 1992: 11), *nashruhā fī bīʾāt lā ʿahda lahā bihā* 'spreading [Arabic] in domains where Arabic is not known' (Madkūr 1969: 14), *mustaʿidda li-l-tajaddud ghayr jāmida wa-lā rākida* '[Arabic] is ready for renewal [owing to the fact that] it is neither fossilised nor stagnant' (Kurd ʿAlī 1944: 259), *taysīr qawāʿid al-naḥw wa-l-ṣarf min dūn mass ʾaṣl al-lugha* 'simplifying [Arabic] syntax and morphology without touching the root of the language' (al-Shahābī 1966: 357) and *al-ʾiṣlāḥ al-lughawī ʾaw al-tarmīm al-lughawī* 'language reform or language repair' (al-Maghribī 1923: 238).

The 'revival and reform' cluster reveals an important aspect of the understanding of language modernisation in the ALA discourse: language modernisation does not mean exclusive obedience to imported, albeit universal, models; it also includes exploiting the potential of Arabic for adaptation and renewal to regain in modern times its historical position as a vibrant world language. The latter sense is closer to endogenous modernisation: it emphasises the internal – rather than the imposed – will and means of acquiring modernity.

By making the above exogenous-endogenous distinction, I do not claim that there were always neatly differentiated positions vis-à-vis the modernisation of Arabic in the ALA discourse. Rather, what I want to highlight here is the existence of a dyadic understanding of modernisation in this discourse, marked by the symbiosis between exogenous and endogenous modes of modernisation. This modernisation dyad will be my central concern in the following analyses of the ALA discourse on the modernisation of Arabic.

Modernising the Arabic Language: A History of Conceptual Formation

In what follows, I will trace how the modernisation of Arabic as a concept was shaped and changed by examining six historical 'sites' of the ALA discourse. As in Chapter 4, by singling out these 'sites', I do not aim to periodise this discourse but to reveal how sociopolitical changes in the Arabic-speaking world both affected and perpetuated the dyad of exogenous and endogenous modernisation described above. As will be shown below, no matter how the understanding of modernising Arabic moved between exogenous and endogenous modernisation and how the meanings of the two shifted between narrowing and expansion in the ALA discourse, the modernisation dyad was always present. It served as a discursive habitus guiding this discourse throughout its development and routinisation in the twentieth century. The habitual presence of the modernisation dyad in the ALA discourse revealed, first, how the modernisation of Arabic embodied the ongoing search for an Arab form of modernity (and, ultimately, a solid Arab national self) under external pressure and threat, and, second, how Arabic was treated as a proxy for articulating hope and frustration during this search. Both were sustained by the perceived inalienable and destined connection between Arabic and the Arab people/nation – the enduring ideological 'doxa' functioning underneath the seemingly routinised and banal production of the ALA discourse.

Modernisation between Catch-up and Renaissance

The speech entitled *ʾinʿāsh al-ʿarabiyya* 'Revitalising Arabic', which al-Sayyid Salīm al-Jundī addressed to the Damascus Academy in 1925, represented one of the earliest examples of the ALA discourse where the modernisation dyad was present. This speech was published twice in the journal of the Damascus Academy in 1925 and 1928 respectively, indicating its salience for the official agenda of the Academy.

To begin with, the modernisation dyad was revealed in al-Jundī's understanding of modernity and its connection with language. Al-Jundī reads modernity through the lens of the rise and fall of nations (*ʾumam*); modernity is merely the status of civilisation (*madaniyya*) achieved by the most advanced nations in the modern age. In his view, the Arabs were the most advanced nation in the past, but their decline in more recent times has allowed their status of civilisation to be surpassed by other nations, most notably those in the West. Language is both a barometer of and a causal factor behind this change in civilisational status. Al-Jundī asserts that 'the [national] language is an epitome (*namūdhaj* and *ʿunwān*) of the nation, showing its time-honoured esteem (*ḥasabuhā al-tālid*), its unique eminence (*sharafuhā al-ṭārif*) [vis-à-vis other nations] and its level of civilisation, progress and history' (1925: 397); and that language always plays an important role in the composition and evolution of social institutions. One common feature of all advanced nations across time, claims al-Jundī, is their assiduous attention to the cultivation and spread of their national languages: Western nations, in the recent past and at present, use their national languages to facilitate their colonial conquests; they spare no effort to promote their languages globally to ensure their scientific, literary, cultural and intellectual hegemony over other nations (ibid.: 397–8). This linguistic means of colonisation, according to al-Jundī, has managed to deprive many weak nations of their nationhood and assimilate them into the powerful nations (ibid.: 397–8). The Arabs took great care of their national language, *fuṣḥā* Arabic, in their golden age of civilisational strength and hegemony (roughly between the seventh and tenth centuries; see also a similar motif in Chapter 2); accordingly, Arabic achieved wide circulation in Asia and Africa as the carrier of the Arab-Islamic civilisation, and it became the most favourable medium of intellectual production (ibid.: 398). When this golden age was over, the Arab nation went into protracted decay and gradually lost its previous civilisational status. Al-Jundī considers the neglect of *fuṣḥā* Arabic to be both a symptom of and a major cause for this decay; when the national language was corrupted, ignorance dominated the nation and diminished its chance of continuous progress (ibid.: 398–9). In sum, the strength/weakness of the nation and the strength/weakness of the national language are two sides of the same coin. Based on this understanding, al-Jundī states that the revitalisation of Arabic will be vital for the revival of the Arab nation and vice versa.

How does the above conception of the relation between modernity, nation and language exhibit the modernisation dyad in al-Jundī's mind? Modernisation is exogenous because al-Jundī sees modernity as a new stage of human civilisation that is marked by the ascendancy of the West and Western languages among other nations and languages. For him, modernisation involves the West's imposition of modernity on non-Western peoples through hegemony and colonisation. Yet modernisation is also endogenous because al-Jundī does not understand it as a fully committed embracement of Western modernity. On the contrary, he invites his audience and readers to reason about the Arabs' loss of civilisational ascendancy at present, which, for him, lies, on the one hand, in the Arabs' neglect of their national language for centuries, and, on the other, in Western linguistic and cultural colonialism. This reasoning suggests that al-Jundī understands modernisation in the Arab context as also involving reviving the self and resisting the colonial agenda of the West.

The modernisation dyad is further revealed in al-Jundī's explanation of the aim and means of the modernisation of Arabic. On the one hand, he admits that it is inevitable to adapt the Arabic language in line with modern civilisation (*madaniyyat al-ʿaṣr al-ḥāḍir*) (ibid.: 399). For him, this entails, first, enriching the Arabic lexicon to make the language fit for the different domains of modern life, such as medicine, commerce, industry and literature; and, second, elevating Arabic through this and other means to the same status as other 'living' (*ḥayya*) languages (ibid.: 401). In al-Jundī's mind, there are emerging communicative needs for Arabic to fulfil, and there are examples of modern 'living' languages for it to be modelled on. On the other hand, al-Jundī insists that any modernisation of Arabic, especially in the field of lexical coinage, should conform to the linguistic principles (*sharṭ*) of *balāgha* 'rhetoric' and *faṣāḥa* 'eloquence' in the Arabic grammatical and literary tradition (ibid.: 400). This is to ensure that the 'essence' (*jawhar*) of Arabic will be preserved in the process of accommodating the language to modernity (ibid.: 399). Al-Jundī therefore rejects the over-reliance on lexical borrowings (*dakhīl*), as this will corrupt (*ʾifsād*) Arabic and bring it foreignness (*ʿujma*), feebleness (*rakāka*) and chaos (*fawḍā*) (ibid.: 399).

Finally, the modernisation dyad is manifest in al-Jundī's inconsistent evaluations of the procedural time concerning the social and linguistic processes in relation to modernity and modernisation, as shown in the examples below. On the ascendancy and decline of a nation's civilisational status, he sees the transfer of civilisational leadership from the Arabs to the West as a centuries-long process of rise and fall, but, in contrast, he depicts the spread of the Arabic language and civilisation in early Islamic periods as 'quicker than the glance of the eye' (*ʾasraʿ min lamḥ al-baṣar*) (ibid.: 398). On the difference between political and linguistic modernisation, al-Jundī regards the former to be a mission of 'politicians and war heroes' restrained by imminent sociopolitical conditions, while he considers the latter to be an everlasting intellectual endeavour of 'men of knowledge' transcending temporal, historical contingencies (ibid.: 397). However, he also contends that Arabic can be revitalised to become a member of the 'living' languages within 'a short term' (*waqt qaṣīr*) if sufficient efforts can be made to cultivate the use and spread of Arabic in different sectors of Arab society (ibid.: 401). On the acceptance of archaic Arabic neologisms instead of foreign borrowings, al-Jundī considers that 'a long period' (*radḥ min al-zaman*) is required to allow Arabic speakers to become familiar with these neologisms (ibid.: 400); however, elsewhere, he says that 'a short period' (*mudda yasīra*) is enough (ibid.: 400).

How do we make sense of these varying evaluations of procedural time? A convincing explanation may be that al-Jundī has two different perceptions of language modernisation in mind: exogenous modernisation that gives Arabic a modern feel, modelling it on other 'living', especially Western, languages, and endogenous modernisation that guards and enhances the fundamental features of Arabic to make them *always* sound, stable and persistent, thus guaranteeing the linguistic consistency and integrity of Arabic over time. All his references to the short time in which the above-mentioned processes can unfold and have an impact are associated with the first perception of modernisation to emphasise the contingent necessity for the Arabs to catch up with Western languages and civilisation, on the one hand, and the ability of the Arabs to do so in a limited period, on the other. By contrast, all his references to the long period of time in which the same processes unfold are related to the second perception of modernisation, to underscore the view that the modernisation of Arabic should be rooted in the Arabic linguistic tradition, and should contribute to the continuation and revival of the glorious past of Arab civilisation. Clearly, exogenous and endogenous modernisation are understood as processes unfolding on different historical time-scales but are 'synchronised'[4] to justify the varying evaluations of procedural time in al-Jundī's speech. Deep in his mind, this synchronisation reflects a tendency of 'telescoping' (Das Gupta 1968: 18) the long-term, gradual process of modernisation and national revival into a significantly shortened period.

Al-Jundī's conception of language modernisation should be read in a wider sociopolitical context. For Syria and the Arab world as a whole, the 1920s was a time of both opportunity and threat. After the British forces and their allies in the Arab Revolt (1916–18) drove the Ottomans out of Syria in 1918, the Arabs 'were electrified by a vision of a renascent Arab world emerging into the community of nations as an independent, unified state' (Rogan 2009: 150). For many Arab intellectuals at the time, this was an opportunity to resume the renaissance of the Arab nation and civilisation interrupted by the so-called 'five-century despotic rule' of the Ottomans. However, the ephemeral Syrian Kingdom (1918–20) and the following British and French mandate jeopardised this aspirational vision and aroused collective concern among Arab intellectuals over the growing colonial and imperialist threat to their national communities and the progress of their national renaissance. In that case, only a quick elevation of the Arab nation to equal status with the West could dispel this threat. Accordingly, serious consideration of a long-term national renaissance had to be combined with a quick, 'catch-up' style of development. Such an accommodation was fully revealed in the blending of the two senses of language modernisation in al-Jundī's speech.

Modernisation between Holistic Revival/Reform and Cosmetic Change

The dyad of exogenous and endogenous modernisation continued to inform the ALA discourse in later decades and appeared in the 1940s to be associated with positions differing on the target and scale of the modernisation of Arabic. Three of these positions were represented respectively by the three reports discussed at the Annual Assembly of Cairo Academy in 1944: Muḥammad Kurd ʿAlī's *Hal wafat al-ʿarabiyya bi-gharaḍihā?* 'Has Arabic fulfilled its purpose?', ʾAḥmad ʾAmīn's *Iqtirāḥ bi-baʿḍ al-ʾiṣlāḥ fī matn al-lugha* 'Some suggestions on reforming the corpus of the language' and ʿAbd al-ʿAzīz Fahmī's *Iqtirāḥ ittikhādh al-ḥurūf al-lātīniyya li-rasm al-kitāba al-ʿarabiyya* 'A suggestion on using Latin letters to write Arabic script'.

Kurd ʿAlī's report aims to justify the adaptability of Arabic in modern society by enlisting historical proof showing that, throughout history, the language was always able to fulfil the communicative needs of various sectors in the Arabic-speaking world and beyond. Behind this aim, however, Kurd ʿAlī tends to advance the thesis that modernising Arabic cannot deviate from the 'substance', which I will explain below, of the language. When describing how, in the early centuries of Islam, Arabic developed out of the Bedouin environment and embraced knowledge and civilisation, he highlights that this language successfully met new communicative challenges by developing a large number of neologisms while keeping its original structural patterns intact (Kurd ʿAlī 1944: 259). Elsewhere, he blames the deviation from classical Arabic styles and structural patterns on the decline of the language competence of Arabic speakers from the end of the Arab-Islamic golden age to the present (ibid.: 259–60). In this respect, he criticises the modern *bidʿa* 'heretical novelties' in the use of Arabic, which are claimed to be modern (*ʿāṣrī*) but are, in fact, linguistic errors due to ignorance and lack of care for the language (ibid.: 260).

In the discussion following the report, Kurd ʿAlī calls for linguistically rehabilitating the present and future generations of Arabic speakers by familiarising them with the most refined and authentic examples of Arabic prose and poetry, following the ways set by al-Jāḥiẓ.

We need to elaborate a little on Kurd ʿAlī's concept of the 'substance of Arabic'. A number of terms relating to this concept are found in his report. The first are *ṭabīʿa* 'nature' and *ṭabʿ* 'natural disposition'. Kurd ʿAlī uses these terms when he narrates how Arabic began with a style of graceful concision (*rashāqa*) in the seventh century, became dominated by an extravagant use of rhyme (*sajʿ*) from the thirteenth century onwards and then regained its concision at the end of the nineteenth century. For Kurd ʿAlī, abandoning *rashāqa* meant corruption in linguistic *malaka* 'habit and aptitude'[5] and deviation from the *ṭabīʿa* of Arabic, while regaining *rashāqa* meant the return to its *ṭabʿ* (ibid.: 259). The second term is *niẓām* 'order or system'. Kurd ʿAlī claims that Arabic has followed, since its known beginning, a single *niẓām*, revealed in the unchanging structural paradigms and patterns of a language. The third term is *maṣādir* 'sources'. Kurd ʿAlī explains that the reason for the development of a shared literary tradition in the eastern and western parts of the Arabic-speaking world is due to the unified linguistic *maṣādir* for Arabic writers. According to him, the Qur'an, mostly due to its linguistic rather than religious unmatched excellence, is the foremost source of the Arabic language (ibid.: 261). The fourth term is *ʾasrār* 'secrets'. Kurd ʿAlī mentions in a metaphorical turn of phrase that whenever Arabic suffered from 'sickness', a group of 'eloquent Arabic speakers' (*bulaghāʾ*) would come forth to unveil and spread the *ʾasrār* of Arabic and guide its use along correct paths (ibid.: 261). The fifth term is *khaṣāʾiṣ* 'characteristics'. Kurd ʿAlī emphasises at the end of his report that Arabic is one of the most widely used languages in the world and that its unique *khaṣāʾiṣ* distinguish it from other languages. By adopting the above terms, Kurd ʿAlī vaguely specifies the content of what he perceives as the substance of Arabic and hints that the modernisation of Arabic should concentrate on identifying, recovering and consolidating this substance and should not encourage any linguistic innovation outside its purview. He also establishes, in line with the 'language-people inalienability' thesis I discussed in Chapter 4, a close link between the substance of Arabic and the linguistic aptitude of native Arabic speakers.

It is clear that Kurd ʿAlī's conceptualisation of the substance of Arabic covers several aspects of Arabic from the structural and stylistic features of the language, to its classic sources, to more vague concepts such as 'nature' and 'aptitude' which treat Arabic as a unique ontological system and link it to its social and cultural environment. The multiple terms used by Kurd ʿAlī indicate that, in his mind, the substance that makes Arabic unique over time and across regions does not exist in only one aspect of Arabic but in the language as a whole. In other words, Kurd ʿAlī understands Arabic holistically as a comprehensive system, and every component of this system exhibits a certain degree of uniqueness due to an underlying substance. Any language modernisation efforts, insists Kurd ʿAlī, should be made in line with this holistically perceived substance to avoid inflicting damage on the integrity of the language.

In contrast to Kurd ʿAlī's position on the substance of Arabic in language modernisation, ʾAḥmad ʾAmīn calls for a comprehensive reform of the corpus (*matn*) of the Arabic language. In the proposal he submitted to the Cairo Academy, ʾAmīn diagnoses the 'predicaments' of Arabic in the modern age by providing the following two explanations. Firstly, the Arabic language was not properly described by the first generations of Arabic grammarians and lexicographers. They collected their data samples from the Bedouin Arab tribes only and wrongly perceived that these skewed samples represented the whole corpus of the Arabic language. Secondly, the standard corpus and grammatical principles established by these first generations of grammarians became fixed and unchallengeable, because the door of *ijtihād* 'independent reasoning' vis-à-vis the Arabic language was closed for the following generations of scholars. Therefore, the Arabic language today keeps too rich a lexicon about the medieval Bedouin life to be fit for modern urban life. Based on these two observations, ʾAmīn proposes to reform the corpus of Arabic by eliminating unnecessary lexical richness as exhibited in the large number of synonyms and polysemy, and by regulating irregularities in some morphological categories such as the triliteral verb, gender and the verbal noun (*maṣdar*).

ʾAmīn's reformist proposal, although different from Kurd ʿAlī's conservative tendency, is constructed around similar holistic thinking in the following two aspects. Firstly, he compares Arabic with Islamic law, whose function has been limited to a minimum in modern society and whose place, to some extent, has been given to European-inspired law. For him, this seems to be a complete replacement of one indigenous legal system with another. He blames the closed door of *ijtihād* and poor legislative reform in modern times for the current peripheralisation of Islamic law. He hints that if necessary reforms are not implemented, Arabic will face a similar destiny as Islamic law and be replaced by foreign languages.[6] Secondly, unlike other Arabic language reformers, who usually focus on one aspect of the language, such as grammar or orthography, ʾAmīn directs his reform agenda towards the whole 'corpus' (*matn*) of the language. The term *matn* has two meanings. As a noun, it means 'the main part of something'; as an adjective, it means 'strong or solid'. The 'main part' *matn*, therefore, should be strong and solid enough to sustain the whole entity or system to which it belongs. In that sense, *matn* can hardly be a particular component, but is rather an aggregation of several components which can represent the whole entity or system. This is the sense ʾAmīn wants to express when he chooses the term *matn*. His criticism covers a number of components of the Arabic language, including the lexicon, semantics and morphology. As long as these components exhibit the same symptoms of excessiveness and irregularity, they all need to be regulated and 'reformed'.

These two aspects of ʾAmīn's holism provoked varying reactions from other members of the Cairo Academy. In the discussion of his language reform proposal, many academicians were worried that this proposal went too far in simplifying and reforming the Arabic language. Some went even further to claim that ʾAmīn's proposal involved modifications to the deep structure of Arabic, which would be very difficult to carry out (ʿAbd al-ʿAzīz Fahmī) and should be avoided to prevent hurting the substance of Arabic (Fāris al-Namir). Others, such as ʿAlī al-Jārim, considered this deep reform necessary to facilitate other partial, cosmetic reforms such as the script reform. Although ʾAmīn himself made it clear that his proposal did not touch upon the 'defining' elements (*muqawwimāt*) of Arabic, such as its basic syntactic and morphological structures, this clarification was merely a defensive argument aiming to enlist maximum support from the academicians for his proposal. The holism of his reformist agenda in terms of its depth and breadth was very obvious. It was ʿAbd al-ʿAzīz Fahmī's who proposed a different, partial reform of the Arabic language.

Fahmī proposed replacing part of the Arabic script with Latin letters to make Arabic suitable for modern communication.[7] The main reason for him choosing the Arabic script as the target of his reformist agenda is his belief that this script is responsible for the many barriers existing between the Arabic language and its modern speakers. For him, Arabic is sick not because some parts of its substance are incompatible with the criteria of modern languages but because this substance has not been properly represented by the surface layer of this language, especially the script. Here is his diagnosis:

> The real and primary causal factor, which sickens this beautiful language and isolates (*inziwāʾ*) it [from common language activities], is that the speakers of this language force it to appear in an unfit garment (*thawb*) and an obscure (*mubhima mushikila*) image (*ṣūra*) not reflecting its beauty at all: I mean the [Arabic] script. (MLAQ 1946: 8)

I will not discuss the technical details of Fahmī's proposal here but merely want to highlight his use of the metaphors of 'garment' and 'image', which support his argument that the script is only a surface element of the Arabic language, and it is this surface element that has dragged the language into various 'predicaments'. Therefore, reforming Arabic, or simplifying its acquisition, can be done only by modifying the surface without touching the deeper layer, the substance of this language. In other words, in order to survive in the modern age, the Arabic language needs only a partial, cosmetic modification rather than a thorough, systematic reform. Representing Arabic in Latin letters will not damage the language, because its substance will be kept intact in this reform. Fahmī thus distinguished his proposal from Kurd ʿAlī and ʾAmīn's holist reforms.

The above three pieces of discourse in 1944 revealed the modernisation dyad in the ALA discourse in three respects. Firstly, there seems to be a disagreement about whether Arabic should go through a thorough revival and reform or some partial adjustments only. This disagreement reflects two understandings of the nature of Arabic and its modern 'predicaments'. The holistic understanding views the language as a coherent system, wherein all components are closely connected, displaying a common trend of rise and decline and a common need of revival and reform. The other, partial understanding does not perceive the language as such; it holds that the 'disease' of Arabic is not systemic but localised and can be treated by fixing the dysfunctional 'organ' or replacing it with a healthy one. On a deeper level, the partial understanding represents a selective type of language modernisation, which targets certain aspects of the language and leaves the rest unchanged. Like the telescoping modernisation I discussed before, selective modernisation aims to rid Arabic of its modern 'predicaments' as soon as possible. The holistic understanding favours endogenous over exogenous modernisation; it demands the maintenance of the systemic coherence of Arabic during language revival and reform and warns against complete language replacement and loss. The partial understanding tends to endorse exogenous modernisation because, as shown in Fahmī's proposal, the partial reform of Arabic usually involves borrowing or absorbing certain linguistic features from other languages.

Secondly, exemplified by Kurd ʿAlī's conceptualisation of language modernisation, thorough language reform often attends to the substance of the Arabic language system. By contrast, partial language reform tends to focus on the surface and avoids touching the substance, for the latter will inevitably trigger a systemic effect in the language system beyond the control of language planners and policy-makers. In this respect, thorough reform is used to justify endogenous language modernisation and delegitimise its exogenous counterpart, because any language reform involving the substance of Arabic can only be endogenous rather than exogenous, otherwise Arabic will lose its unique nature. By contrast, partial reform is used to legitimise exogenous modernisation; no matter how the surface of Arabic is changed, the substance of Arabic remains intact, so exogenous language modernisation, such as Latinising the Arabic script and the direct borrowing of foreign neologisms, will not change the nature of Arabic. In this regard, all three pieces of discourse coalesce around one central tenet: keeping the substance of Arabic intact from internal corruption and external intrusion.

Lastly, all three pieces of discourse exhibited a combination of the two modes of modernisation by proposing to revive or reform Arabic in line with the linguistic criteria of concision, clarity and regularity: Kurd ʿAlī's call for regaining *rashāqa* 'graceful concision' for Arabic, ʾAmīn's dislike for extravagance and irregularity across several domains in Arabic, and Fahmī's proposal for regulating language use by adopting a new script. These criteria tend to be pursued in modern prose writing, especially in science and journalism, introduced from Europe. It is worth mentioning that Kurd ʿAlī's conception of concision as an innate feature of Arabic reads similarly to Jamāl al-Dīn al-ʾAfghānī's defence of the Islamic reason in the nineteenth century; both were attempts to accommodate European norms by seeking their counterparts in the Arab-Islamic tradition.

Why did the above three reports, submitted to the Cairo Academy in the same year, exhibit different understandings regarding the target and scale of the modernisation of Arabic and varying attitudes towards exogenous and endogenous modernisation? To answer this question, we should relate these reports to the sociopolitical context of the time of their production.

Generally speaking, the Arabic-speaking world in the 1930s and 1940s was faced with two challenges. One was the then yet-to-be defined political reality represented by (1) the collapse of the traditional political order with the detachment of the Arab provinces from the Ottoman Empire after World War I, which was confirmed by the Turks' symbolic abolishment of the Caliphate in 1924; (2) the emergence of Arab nation-states whose boundaries were artificially set based on colonial design and mandate arrangements; and (3) the competing representation of the Arabic-speaking world among state, territorial and pan-Arab nationalisms. The other challenge was the intensifying, often violent, monopoly of Britain and France over the Arabic-speaking world and their persistent intervention into Arab politics, due to the strategic importance of this region to their military and other interests during World War II.

Three responses emerged to meet the above challenges. The first was *Salafism* calling for a return to the political and social order of the early Islamic periods. The Muslim Brotherhood movement in Egypt and 'the political revival of *Wahhabism*' (Cleveland and Bunton 2009: 231) leading to the establishment of Saudi Arabia in 1932 were two examples of this response. The second was progressive social reforms aiming at reshaping Arab society in line with modern, secular social institutions. In this regard, constitutional systems, secular legislature and public education were introduced into most of the newly created Arab states; the Atatürk revolution in Turkey seemed to encourage a similar agenda of progressive, secular social reforms in the Arabic-speaking world (ibid.: 235–6). The third was the so-called 'honourable cooperation' (ibid.: 223) with the colonial, mandate authorities, represented by the 'politics of the notables' adopted by the ruling elites in Egypt, Great Syria, Iraq and Transjordan, to pursue a balance between colonial hegemony and local Arabs' aspirations for national independence.

There seemed to be parallels between the three responses to sociopolitical challenges and the three positions vis-à-vis the modernisation of Arabic. Kurd ʿAlī's emphasis on protecting the substance of Arabic and recovering the classic linguistic patterns and literary styles resonated with the *Salafist* tenet of a return to the origins of Islam and the early Islamic social order. ʾAmīn's appeal for a comprehensive reform of the corpus and grammatical description of Arabic in line with modern linguistic criteria was similar to the agenda of progressive social reforms. Fahmī's proposal of selective, cosmetic language reform, which attempted to Westernise the script of Arabic while preserving the other aspects of this language, seemed to resemble the collaborationism of Arab ruling elites in World War II.

By identifying the above parallels, I do not intend to argue that Arabic language planning and policy in the 1930s and 1940s was merely a branch of Arab politics in general. In other words, these parallels are not offered here as historical, material correlates between Arabic language policy and Arab politics. I will instead propose that this parallelism suggested that, in the ALA discourse, debates about Arabic probably emerged as a refraction of Arab politics, to the extent that the challenges facing the latter and the responses thereto were projected onto the discussion of language modernisation. This parallelism further suggested the extent to which the ALA discourse on language modernisation was affected by the uncertainty surrounding Arab political identity, against the background of colonial and imperial presence in the Arabic-speaking world during this period.

Leaning towards Endogenous Modernisation

In the 1940s, we find varying positions on the dyad of exogenous and endogenous directions in the ALA discourse on language modernisation. In the 1950s, by contrast, this discourse received a more pronounced endogenous direction with an increasing emphasis on the internal developmental potential of Arabic and a general distaste for language reform via the direct, uncritical borrowing of exogenous linguistic features. The consolidation of independent Arab states and the rise of anti-colonial, anti-imperialist pan-Arabism in the Arabic-speaking world were probably responsible for this discursive phenomenon.

I will analyse three pieces of discourse to explain this change. The first two are Muḥammad Riḍā al-Shabībī's *Baʿth al-ʿarabiyya* 'Renaissance of Arabic' (1955) and *Sunnat al-taṭawwur fī al-lugha* 'The path to development in language' (1959), and the third is Manṣūr Fahmī's *Majmaʿ Miṣr wa-l-lugha al-ʿarabiyya* 'The Egyptian [Cairo] Academy and the Arabic language' (1957 [1956]).

Al-Shabībī's first speech calls for a coordinated pan-Arab action under the leadership of the Cairo Academy, to 'revive Arabic and free it from its current deficiencies (*ʿathra*)' (1955: 19). He articulates these 'deficiencies' in two ways. On the one hand, he admits that currently Arabic is extremely poor in 'means of its life subsistence' (*muqawwimāt hayātihā*) to make it compatible with the 'richest' modern languages in the world (ibid.: 20). In order to catch up with these languages, he calls for drawing on the successful 'European experience' (*minwāl al-farnaja*) of language cultivation and devoting sufficient effort to modernise Arabic (ibid.: 20). On the other hand, he perceives the life of Arabic as that of a rise and fall alongside the changing political situation in the Arabic-speaking world.[8] The reason for the current stagnation of Arabic, according to him, is the decline caused by the despotic rule of the Mongols, Mamluks and Ottomans in the last five centuries. He blames this long-term decline for the weakness and deficiency of Arabic in confronting modern European civilisation. He anticipates that, with a growing hope for Arab solidarity between newly independent Arab states and the possibility for coordinated action of language reform and renewal, Arabic will witness a revival in the near future.

Clearly, in this speech, we can still see a blend of exogenous and endogenous positions vis-à-vis language modernisation. Although Arabic follows a historical logic of rise and fall, its modern revival should be modelled on the developmental path of the advanced modern European languages. Besides, there is also a fusion of both holistic and partial modernisation in this speech. When evaluating the methodology of the Cairo Academy, al-Shabībī says: '[these methods] have enriched our cultural and linguistic resources, bestowed on the Arabic language a new dress (*ḥulla*) and rid it of the defects (*shāʾiba*) of decline and degradation (1955: 19)'.

The metaphor of 'bestowing a new dress'[9] is reminiscent of ʿAbd al-ʿAzīz Fahmī's 'replacing the unfit garment', which is used to denote the modification of the surface layer of Arabic. 'Enriching cultural and linguistic resources', by contrast, seems to refer to a more systemic 'root and branch' kind of development in the Arabic language.

Yet al-Shabībī puts more weight on the endogenous side when he includes language defence in language modernisation. He mentions that there are many foreign schools in the Arabic-speaking world; some of these teach and research Arabic while the majority do not, guided by various hidden political agendas. He points out that these schools bring different cultural and philosophical ideas and world-views to the younger generations of Arabs. In line with these ideas and world-views, attitudes towards the Arabic language and culture diversify in Arab society, ranging from ultra-conservative to radical-reformist. According to al-Shabībī, there has been and still is, albeit to a lesser extent, 'a battlefield of principles and ideas' (*muʿtarakat al-mabādiʾ wa-l-ʾārāʾ*) between those who side with and against[10] the Arabic language and culture (ibid.: 19). In this battle, Egypt has always been 'the spearhead (*al-muqaddima min al-jaysh*) or the front line (*al-khaṭṭ al-ʾawwal*) that defends the bastions (*maʿāqil*) of Arabic culture' (ibid.: 19). The way of winning this 'battle', states al-Shahābī, is to sift (*gharbala*) and fuse (*ṣahr*) the various ideas, world-views and attitudes to distinguish between what is beneficial to the Arabs and what is not (ibid.: 19). To support this view, al-Shahābī reiterates a verse from the Qur'an: 'As for that which benefits the people, it remains on the earth; but as for the foam, it vanishes, [being] cast off' (*fa-ʾammā mā yanfaʿ al-nās fa-yamkuth fī al-ʾarḍ, wa-ʾammā al-zabad fa-yadhhab jufāʾ*) (ibid.: 19).

The metaphors of 'battle', 'spearhead', 'front line', 'bastions', 'sift', 'fuse' and 'foam' deserve a close reading to reveal al-Shabībī's true stance concerning the modernisation of Arabic: a defensive eclecticism with a preference for endogenous modernisation. First of all, modernising Arabic is perceived as an ideological 'battle'. The 'battle' here appears to be an intellectual 'civil war' due to internal conflicts within the Arab intelligentsia; however, these conflicts are caused by the infiltration of foreign ideas and world-views along with hidden political agendas. Secondly, the first and foremost aim for those who side with Arabic in this 'battle' is not the revival and reform of Arabic per se, but guaranteeing the progress of this revival and reform in a coherent and independent intellectual environment, deprived of the chaos of ideas and foreign influence. Arabic is perceived as being defended by the righteous and courageous leaders of the Arabic-speaking world, such as the Egyptian state and the Cairo Academy. Thirdly, the use of 'sift' and 'fuse' may be understood as referring to an eclectic mixture of both domestic and imported ideas and world-views. However, the fact that the sentence 'as for that which benefits the people, it remains on the earth; but as for the foam, it vanishes, [being] cast off' was a direct quotation of the Qur'an (13: 17) with only a slight modification of the sentential order[11] suggests an inclination towards endogenous direction in this eclecticism. The original verse refers to the authority of Allah over the determination of truth and falsehood; this quotation reaffirms this authority in modern circumstances and hints that the Qur'an and the linguistic, cultural and value system it promulgated in the past should still be the pillar of Arabs' linguistic and cultural life in modern times.

The above slant towards endogenous modernisation became more evident in al-Shabībī's second paper four years later (1959). In this paper, he discusses the relationship between language and development and confirms that Arabic has the ability of self-renewal. He rejects the idea of radical language reform and instead calls for a gradual and balanced development of Arabic. This endogenous turn is revealed in the following aspects of this speech.

To begin with, al-Shabībī argues that pride in the national language should be the starting point for every nation who seeks revival. This pride is the key to independence and the gateway leading to national freedom. He also emphasises that respecting and using *fuṣḥā* Arabic is part of the Arab national life; neglecting this national language will cause disruption of the life of the Arab nation.

Moreover, al-Shabībī claims that Arabic is the richest language in terms of the high, noble meanings of humanism (*al-maʿānī al-ʾinsāniyya*) it preserves. He argues that humanism, rather than the ability to produce neologisms and scientific terminologies, should be the utmost criterion of the richness of a language; according to this criterion, Arabic is not poor at all. This point most clearly marks his inclination to the endogenous mode of language modernisation. While, in the first speech, he admits Arabic is poor because it does not possess as many 'means of subsistence' as the 'richest' languages, he now rescinds this statement by claiming that Arabic is one of the finest and 'richest' human languages.

At the end of the speech, al-Shabībī reformulates his position vis-à-vis the modernisation of Arabic. He makes it clear that he opposes language stagnation and supports the reform and reconstruction (*bināʾ*) of Arabic; however, he perceives many radical reforms as disguises for linguistic destruction and erasure. These radical reforms include Latinising the Arabic script, cancelling *ʾiʿrāb* 'declensional endings' in Arabic grammar, and borrowing neologisms and scientific terminologies directly from Western languages. For al-Shabībī, people who advocate these reforms aim to subjugate Arabs to Western civilisation and sever the link between the Arabs and the Orient, 'the origin of light and the beginning of life' (1959: 60). Contrary to what these people claim, that radical language reforms can connect Arabic to the progress of the modern civilisation, al-Shabībī considers these reforms as 'stepping backwards and developing inversely (*taṭawwur maʿkūs*)' (ibid.: 60). In his view, what leads to these reformist agendas is a kind of cultural 'indigestion' (*tukhma*), caused by focusing on the 'outer shells' (*qushūr*) of modern civilisation and imitating some of its 'hollow appearances' (*maẓāhiruhā al-fārigha*) (ibid.: 60). Such reforms are destructive and unnecessary, because Arabic can renew itself from within, capturing new social phenomena and meanings while retaining *fuṣḥā* and the Arabic script. The real 'secret', or guideline, of language modernisation, al-Shabībī summarises, is a gradual, balanced mode of language renewal, in line with the substance of the language and the needs of its speakers.

In al-Shabībī's first speech we can still see eclecticism between exogenous and endogenous modernisation; the second speech seems to support the latter uncompromisingly. This discursive shift is constructed upon a schematic understanding of both exogenous and endogenous modernisation. The former is perceived as no more than an uncritical, superficial borrowing of Western linguistic elements into Arabic, and the latter becomes a mixture of an apology of Arabic and a laissez-faire approach regarding intervention in language practice. Denouncing the legitimacy of 'radical' language reform proposals, language modernisation develops into a symbolic disguise for de facto linguistic protectionism.

It is striking to witness this swift turn from modernist eclecticism to uncompromising protectionism vis-à-vis the modernisation of Arabic in one intellectual's discourse within only a four-year period. However, al-Shabībī is not alone in this regard, as we can see a similar tendency in Manṣūr Fahmī's speech in 1956.

Fahmī made this speech at the First Conference of ALAs held in Damascus between 29 September and 5 October 1956. This speech was supposed to be a general introduction to the history and work of the Cairo Academy. However, Fahmī took this opportunity to elaborate on his understanding of the duty of ALAs in order to reach a pan-Arab agreement on the principles of language planning and policy. Like al-Shahābī's speeches above, Fahmī's speech placed an exclusive emphasis on the endogenous mode of language modernisation. The fact that this conference was convened amidst the Suez Crisis that led to the tripartite (Israel, France and Britain) invasion of Egypt between 29 October and 7 November 1956 might have contributed to Fahmī's inclination towards endogenous modernisation.

1. Like al-Shabībī, Fahmī shows similar enmity towards the superficial borrowing of Western linguistic features. On the origin of ALAs, he says that in the early twentieth century there were a large number of foreign neologisms penetrating various domains of language use in the Arabic-speaking world. Fahmī perceives this penetration as a 'frightening, overflowing influx' (*al-tadaffuq al-ghāmir al-mukhīf*) or a 'flood' (*sayl*) (1957 [1956]: 59). This seemingly irreversible 'flood' made colonialists, superficialists (*saṭḥiyyūn*) and 'those who were sick in their hearts' collaborate with each other to weaken and fragment 'the language of *al-ḍād*' by calling for the replacement of *fuṣḥā* with local dialects. Fearing (*khawf*) for this 'flood' and 'concerted' attack on Arabic, and inspired by Arab nationalism, some Arab intellectuals started to consider elevating Arabic to the status it deserved, by consolidating its link with Arabness (ibid.: 59). This consideration was then concretised in the form of ALAs in Damascus and Cairo. Fahmī calls for collective confidence (*thiqa*) in Arabic as a duty of the ALA members. With this confidence, these members can deploy 'weapons' from the core resources of Arabic and win 'victory' in 'making Arabic compatible with (*mujārā*) the progress of the age' (ibid.: 63). The purpose of this battle is preventing the dominance of foreign languages, or foreign terminologies, in the Arabic-speaking world. If these foreign languages dominate, he warns, the supremacy of Arabic, the national language of the Arabs, will become an illusion (*wahm*) or myth (*ʾusṭūra*), while, in reality, there will only be 'hateful occupation' (*al-iḥtilāl wa-l-istīlāʾ al-baghīḍ*) of Arab minds (ibid.: 65).

Three concepts, 'flood', 'battle' and 'fear', need to be highlighted here. Fahmī deploys a series of terms, including 'flood', 'overflowing' and 'influx', to highlight what he considers to be the large-scale and severe spread of foreign neologisms – a phenomenon of linguistic modernity in the Arabic-speaking world. For Arabs, there is no choice but to make Arabic conform to this linguistic modernity. However, there is a fundamental difference between subordinating Arabic to this linguistic modernity and reviving Arabic to make it compatible with this modernity. For Fahmī, between these two approaches to language modernisation, there can only be a 'battle', because the former will lead to mental 'occupation', while the latter is intended to guarantee 'the supremacy of Arabic' in the Arabic-speaking world. Besides, according to Fahmī, the 'weapon' used to win 'victory' in this 'battle' comes from the Arabic language itself, rather than from any foreign language. Fahmī also indicates that, psychologically, both notions of subordinating and reviving Arabic are triggered by 'fear'; however, the former cannot dispel 'fear', because the 'frightening influx' of linguistic modernity is 'overflowing', while the latter can conquer 'fear' by means of bolstering 'confidence' in Arabic and unlocking the developmental potential of this language. The above concepts of 'flood', 'battle' and 'fear' show a sharp antithesis between the exogenous and endogenous modes of language modernisation.

2. Like al-Shabībī, Fahmī also takes an apologetic position on the Arabic language and its adaptability to modern conditions. When doing so, he confirms that Arabic is not weak in terms of precision, eloquence and richness, but he also points out that Arabic has its own unique nature, and, for this reason, the development of Arabic must follow a unique path that is different from that of other languages. In other words, Fahmī does not believe that Arabic needs to follow the developmental path of other, especially modern European, languages. For him, this unique, endogenous path of language development is the convergence of various Arabic varieties into the revived, corrected *fuṣḥā* Arabic, whose standard has been set by the Qur'an. The language of the Qur'an, he insists, has always been the reference and guidance for language planning and reform in the Arabic-speaking world.

Fahmī depicts the language of the Qur'an in two ways. First, the Qur'an is a 'glittering lighthouse' (*manāra mutalaʾliʾa*) which guides linguists to understand Arabic grammar and to maintain the integrity and health of this language; any language simplification or reform deviating from this 'lighthouse' is invalid (ibid.: 67). In a more metaphorical way, Fahmī describes that, under the guidance of this 'lighthouse', linguists can easily 'hover and encircle' (*yaḥūm wa-yaḥūṭ*)[12] without going astray (ibid.: 68).

Second, the language of the Qur'an is the 'foremost resource' (*al-manbaʿ al-ʾumm*) and the '*qibla* for the prayer leaders' (*al-qibla al-ʾimāmiyya*) that Arab linguists need to 'turn to' (*yaʾtamm*) (ibid.: 68). To be more precise, Fahmī understands the Qur'an to be the 'source' (*ūmm*) of 'eloquence' (*balāgha*) and the resource Arabs rely on to protect the integrity of Arabic; the *fuṣḥā* represented in the Qur'an is the *qibla* for Arab linguists and language planners: as long as this *qibla* is followed, they will do no harm to Arabic when simplifying or reforming the style and pedagogy of this language (ibid.: 68). Notice here the play of the root *ʾ-m-m* between *ʾumm* ‘mother, resource’, *ʾimām* ‘prayer leader’ and *yaʾtamm* ‘obey, follow’. In that sense, the Qur’an is the resource, authority and direction for modernising the Arabic language.

3. Based on the rejection of superficial borrowing as a means of acquiring linguistic modernity, and the confirmation of the developmental potential of Arabic, Fahmī specifies the following aims of modernising Arabic: (1) increasing the lexical richness of Arabic by exploiting the morphological potential of the language; (2) simplifying Arabic pedagogy and acquisition without deviating from the fundamentals of the language; (3) cultivating and strengthening the linguistic intuitions of modern Arabic speakers; and (4) seeking coordinated, pan-Arab actions on this matter. The ultimate purpose of these missions, according to Fahmī, is to impart ‘power’ (*quwwa*), ‘vitality’ (*ḥayawiyya*), and, most importantly, ‘eternity’ (*khulūd*) to the Arabic language (ibid.: 68, 71). The theme of ‘eternity’ is reminiscent of al-Jundī’s (1925) ‘long-term modernisation’ I have discussed above. Eternity here can be roughly equated to a historical continuity that links the modern revival of Arabic to the codified high standard form of the Arabic language in the early Islamic period. In that case, the only correct norms for the Arabic language in modern times are those perceived to be endogenously developed and accepted.

The leaning towards endogenous modernisation in the ALA discourse during the 1950s, which highlighted the inherent developmental potential of Arabic and the necessity of pan-Arab action to defend Arabic from foreign intrusions, seemed to be in line with two dominant features of Arab politics of the time. One was the competition among newly independent Arab states for pan-Arab leadership; the other was the consolidation of Arab independence and the pursuit of unity of Arab states to counter imperialist influence across the Arabic-speaking world. These two features were often interrelated. The independence of key Arab states such as Egypt, Syria, Iraq and Jordan in the late 1940s and early 1950s marked a new stage of independent state-building in the Arabic-speaking world. However, political independence did not lead to economic independence from the erstwhile colonial powers in such fields as energy and trade. To protect these interests, which were then under the threat of the perceived spread of communism, these powers tried to fashion pacts and alliances regionally, such as the Baghdad Pact, among Middle Eastern countries. For many Arabs, such pacts and alliances might be covers for the continuation of the colonial and imperial presence of the West in the Arabic-speaking world. This shared colonial legacy and anti-colonial, anti-imperialist sentiment made national independence a pan-Arab issue in post-independence Arab politics. National independence thus became a central issue for pan-Arab leadership competition. President Gamal Abdel Nasser of Egypt (1956–70) led the diplomatic campaign against the Baghdad Pact (1955), achieved political success in the Suez Crisis (1956) and experimented with the idea of political pan-Arabism in the union with Syria (1958–60). He was quick to proclaim himself as a champion of Arabism for adhering to the principle of independence. Similarly, the Baʿthists in Syria also advocated national freedom from Western imperialism to promote their pan-Arab agenda over other states and communities in the Arabic-speaking world.

Arabic, believed to be the best representation of the common link among Arab states, naturally became political capital to be exploited in the campaign against imperialism and the competition for pan-Arab leadership. For this purpose, no Arab state would be willing to reform Arabic, for any unilateral change to this language would increase linguistic differences among Arab states and decrease the political value of the language. This explains why, in the ALA discourse in the 1950s, exogenous modernisation of Arabic had to be rejected, and radical reforms to the structure and script of Arabic were also avoided; only defending the social status, structural integrity and developmental potential of Arabic could help retain the political value of this language. This also explains why the Cairo Academy was depicted as the spearhead to protect rather than reform the Arabic language; in this regard, the competition among Arab states for political leadership was projected to the competition among ALAs for language authority in the modern Arabic-speaking world.

Dilemma, Dignity and Universalism of Arabic

After the defeat of 1967, intellectual life in the Arabic-speaking world, including that of the ALAs, could be characterised by the two terms 'trauma' (see Suleiman 2011a and also the previous chapter) and 'dilemma' (see below). In the preceding two decades, members of these academies tended to promote an endogenous mode of language modernisation within the framework of pan-Arab coordination. However, after 1967, the legitimacy of this endogenous mode, along with pan-Arab nationalism in the political sphere, was challenged. This did not entail resorting to large-scale borrowing from foreign languages, because of the growing enmity towards what were perceived to be Israeli neo-colonialism and Western imperialism. To resolve this dilemma, a discursive tendency emerged calling for bridging the gap between exogenous and endogenous modernisation in line with an Arab-Islamic version of universal humanism.

This intellectual dilemma is well reflected in the concept of 'crossroads' (*muftariq al-ṭuruq*) Muḥammad Yaḥyā al-Hāshimī uses in his article *Naḥnu ʿalā muftariq al-ṭuruq* 'we are at the crossroads' published in *al-Lisān al-ʿarabī* in 1969. Although a crossroads usually leads in four directions, al-Hāshimī uses this concept to denote binary choices that Arab intellectuals are faced with. The 'crossroads' in Arab intellectual life has changed, he claims. According to him, for the first generation of Arab intellectuals who studied abroad in Europe, the 'crossroads' was between preserving tradition and advocating the spirit of the West (1969: 81). For the generation who witnessed the 1967 defeat, however, the 'crossroads' is between life and death (ibid.: 86): Arabs can either develop their own innovative power by initially imitating other civilisations while at the same time taking 'benevolence' (*raḥma*) and 'humanism' (*ʾinsāniyya*, referring to an European idea) into consideration, or they can live on the periphery of modern life and lose their pride (*ʿizza*) and dignity (*karāma*) (ibid.: 85).

The above conceptualisation of 'crossroads' contains several layers of meaning. First, whether a nation or civilisation is properly alive depends on whether it has innovative power or not. Second, a nation or civilisation without innovative power has to fully depend on others, which leads to the loss of self-pride and dignity. Third, a nation or civilisation losing its pride or dignity is doomed to fail. Fourth, to survive, a nation or civilisation has to acquire its own innovative power. Fifth, acquiring innovative power should start with imitating other, advanced nations or civilisations. Sixth, during imitation, the precepts and values of 'benevolence and humanism' should also be observed.

These layers of meaning reveal a paradox between 'dignity' and 'imitation' which characterised the intellectual dilemma of the post-1967 Arabic-speaking world. Rejecting imitation and adhering to endogenous modernisation may pre-empt the so-called 'cultural invasion', but it may also cause cultural seclusion and stagnation, thus failing to empower the Arab nation and allowing Arabs to retain dignity and pride. Resorting to imitation seemed to exacerbate the Arab dependence on the West, which harmed dignity; however, as long as the Arabs managed to develop their own capacity for innovation out of imitation, they would, in the long run, regain their national and cultural dignity. It is clear that, for al-Hāshimī, 'dignity' becomes a key word in his perception of the 'crossroads' or intellectual dilemma after 1967.

Nonetheless, al-Hāshimī also hints at a way out of this dilemma. He combines *raḥma* 'benevolence' and 'humanism' (*ʾinsāniyya*) (see above) to show that both should be observed during modernisation, even if this modernisation has to begin with imitating the other. *Raḥma* is a Qur'anic term denoting the benevolence and mercy of Allah, while humanism is the very idea of Renaissance and Enlightenment that formed the basis of modern Western civilisation. Al-Hāshimī uses the two terms interchangeably more than once in this article. For him, they refer to the same principle of morality and social order, which could help liberate the Arabs and inspire them to empower themselves and serve the Arab nation. The core values of Islam and modern Western civilisation meet here, to show that, on the one hand, both exogenous and endogenous values should be respected during the process of modernisation, while on the other hand, these values can be universal. This is an example of how exogenous and endogenous modernisation were fused around the precept of universalism in the post-1967 ALA discourse.

These themes of 'dignity', 'dilemma' and 'universalism' were also well presented in Fāḍil al-Jamālī's article *al-ʿArabiyya bayn ḥumātihā wa-ghuzātihā* 'Arabic between its defenders and attackers' published in *al-Lisān al-ʿarabī* in 1969. Regarding 'dignity', al-Jamālī makes it clear at the beginning of his article that 'the [national] language is the epitome of the nation's characteristics, the manifestation of its dignity and the yardstick of its civilisational status' (1969: 24). According to him, on the individual level, he who is proud of his own language is also proud of himself and his personality, while he who debases his own language also debases himself and his personality; on the national level, the vibrancy of the national language demonstrates the prosperity of the nation, while any neglect of the national language indicates the decline of the nation. Based on this understanding, he goes on to appeal for (1) self-respect and self-esteem for the Arabic language and (2) cultural exchange based on mutual respect between languages and cultures. For him, these two attitudes are necessary for modernising the Arabic language. The former ensures that the development of Arabic is compatible with the revival of the Arab nation, and the latter guarantees that learning from Western civilisations via Western languages is not distorted by the 'hidden cultural war' whose aim is Western hegemony over other nations and cultures. The emphasis on the connection between the Arabic language and the personal and national dignity of the Arabs reiterates the dilemma between dignity and imitation I have discussed before.

Establishing this premise of 'dignity', al-Jamālī continues to discuss different stances, both defensive and antagonistic, towards Arabic. These stances exemplify the then intellectual dilemma vis-à-vis the modernisation of Arabic. According to him, there are three groups of people who defend or support the Arabic language. The first are the ultra-conservative (*mutazammitūn*) Arab linguists who stick to the traditional structural and stylistic patterns of Arabic and do not permit any deviation (*zaḥzaḥa*) from or development of this language; they are 'the aristocracy' (*al-ʾaristuqrāṭiyya*) in the field of language (ibid.: 28). The second group are the simplifiers, those scholars who call for Arabic to be simplified in terms of grammar (for the written language) and speech (constructing a middle language between *fuṣḥā* and *ʿāmmiyya*); they consider such simplification necessary because they believe Arabic to be too complicated and too difficult to meet the communicative needs of the modern age; they are 'the bourgeoisie' (*al-būrjuwāziyya*) in the field of language (ibid.: 28–9). The third group are those who actually use Arabic in their daily lives; not linguists, but rather language practitioners who enrich this language via compilation and translation; they are 'the working class' (*al-ṭabaqa al-ʿāmila*) in the field of language (ibid.: 29).

Al-Jamālī also specifies four groups of people who distrust or even attack the Arabic language. He speculates that these people, most of whom come from the Arabic-speaking world itself, either want to strike at the root of Arabic or claim that Arabic is not suitable for modern life, and thence a symbol of backwardness. The first group are those who support Arabic dialects and the Latin script (ibid.: 29–30). The second are those who have some knowledge about foreign languages and regard Arabic as comparatively backward (ibid.: 30). The third are those who used to serve colonial governments in the Arab world and are accustomed to using foreign languages, mainly English or French. They believe that Arabic is only used among the lower classes and attempt to create the sense of a 'new aristocracy' (*ʾaristuqrāṭiyya jadīda*) based on competence in foreign languages in Arab society (ibid.: 30). The last group are the educated Arab youth who prefer to use foreign languages or insert foreign terms into their use of Arabic (code-switching) as if Arabic cannot fully express their ideas. Al-Jamālī contends that this code-switching shows that these young Arabs are suffering from the 'dissolution of the national being' (*inḥilāl fī al-kiyān al-qawmī*) and 'moral limpness' (*tarākhin khuluqī*) (ibid.: 30). He equates this moral limpness to intoxication and quotes al-Mutanabbī's (d. 965) poem 'those who are contemptible are more prone to contempt' (*man yahun yashul al-hawān ʿalayhī*) to warn that moral weakness could become habitual (ibid.: 31).

Al-Jamālī perceives the dilemma of modernising Arabic in both endogenous and exogenous ways. The endogenous dilemma is revealed in the ideological struggle regarding the Arabic language among the different social classes in Arab society. 'Aristocracies', 'neo-aristocracies', 'bourgeoisie' and 'the working class' are all ideology-laden terminologies. By transplanting these terminologies into the discourse on language, al-Jamālī implies that the field of Arabic language planning and policy exhibits a similar tendency of internal fray and fragmentation as found in Arab society. The exogenous dilemma is reflected in the uncritical advocacy and adoption of foreign languages and their lexicon and structural features on the one hand, and distrust of and disrespect for Arabic on the other. Both dilemmas are detrimental to the minds of the Arab youth. Their confidence and competence in Arabic is weak, because social and ideological fragmentation has impeded the process of modernising Arabic and simplifying its acquisition. This lack of confidence and competence, along with continuous attacks on Arabic in terms of its modern adaptability, make the Arab youth prone to trusting and relying on foreign languages while neglecting Arabic, their national language. What makes this situation worse is that they have been accustomed to the neglect of Arabic. In al-Jamālī's eyes, these dilemmas are both causes and symptoms of a loss of 'dignity'.

One way to resolve these dilemmas is by re-evaluating the Arabic language and the cultural and spiritual values embedded therein. In this regard, al-Jamālī argues that Arabic is not only the language of the Arabs but also the language of Islam; since Islam bears the true spirit of humanism, which both 'world communism' and 'Zionist capitalism' fail to deliver, Arabic is and needs to be a language of 'world humanism' (ibid.: 32). He mentions that many newly independent African and Asian countries, especially those whose citizens are mainly Muslims, welcome the revival and spread of Arabic in their communities and around the world (ibid.: 33). The mission of modernising Arabic therefore goes beyond the framework of Arab nationalism to that of universal humanism. Al-Jamālī ends his article with the Qur'anic verse 'Verily, we have sent it down as an Arabic Qur'an in order that you may understand' (Qur'an 12: 2) to accentuate this eternal mission of the Arabic language.

The theme of Arabic as a world language became more prominent in ʾIbrahīm Madkūr's two speeches published in 1969 and 1973 respectively, both titled *al-ʿArabiyya bayna al-lughāt al-ʿālamiyya al-kubrā* 'Arabic vis-à-vis the biggest world languages'. In these two speeches, Madkūr tries to demonstrate that Arabic is a world language in terms of its easy acquisition and its eternal humanistic mission against ethnic, racial, sectarian and political segregation among human beings. The purpose of modernising Arabic therefore also includes facilitating the spread of Arabic around the world, especially in those Asian and African communities that are part of or close to the Arab-Islamic civilisation.

According to Madkūr, Arabic is one of the most important world languages because it complies with the linguistic criteria of an ideal universal language in terms of clarity, concision, regularity and easiness-to-learn.

These criteria were adopted in movements aiming to create an artificial universal language. Madkūr traces the history of these universal language movements as follows. In the seventeenth century, worrying about the 'linguistic chaos' in Europe following the rise of nation-states and national languages, some European scholars planned to construct a universal language. A proponent of this was Gottfried Wilhelm Leibniz (d. 1716), who considered collecting all concepts within the human mind and then allocating every concept a unique symbol; a universal language could be constructed out of these symbols. Leibniz's idea was not put into practice. In the nineteenth century, Ludovic Lazar Zamenhof (d. 1917) invented an artificial world language called Esperanto, which according to Madkūr achieved certain success in some scientific institutions, but did not succeed to the extent of being a universal language. Since then, a number of proposals had been made to revise or improve Esperanto in conformity with the principles of an ideal universal language. Madkūr reports that these principles include an alphabet having minimal letters, a limited vocabulary sufficient to meet communicative needs without repetitions or synonyms, a regular, easy-to-learn grammar and a simple, clear orthography. He then argues that Arabic has the potential to become a universal world language in line with the above principles. As for the alphabet, Arabic has a limited number of letters that is nonetheless enough to represent the various consonants and vowels of human languages. As for vocabulary, although Arabic has an extremely large lexicon, only a small portion is actually used; this usage-based lexicon is limited in scale and can be easily collected and standardised.

As for grammar, although traditional Arabic grammar is full of both linguistic and philosophical speculation, a number of regular, easy-to-learn grammatical principles can be selected to facilitate Arabic learning. Better still, according to Madkūr, Arabic is a natural universal language surpassing the artificiality of Esperanto.

Madkūr argues that Arabic is one of the most important world languages because it has already been used widely in Asia and Africa across ethnic and national boundaries. He states that the idea of creating a universal language would face severe opposition, mainly because it is very difficult to put an artificially constructed language such as Esperanto into actual language use.[13] There are languages spoken in several nations and among several peoples which are qualified to become universal world languages as alternatives to Esperanto. According to Madkūr, French used to be the world language of politics and diplomacy, English is now the world language of business and finance, and between the eighth and sixteenth centuries, Arabic was one of the two world languages (the other was Latin) of science and philosophy, used by different Asian, African and European peoples. The status of Arabic as a world language was challenged from the seventeenth century onwards, due partly to the inner decline of this language and partly to the colonial conspiracy against it in the nineteenth and twentieth centuries, especially in North Africa. However, Arabic has survived this colonial violence (*baṭsh*) and tyranny (*jabarūt*) and is now recovering its old status and glory in the world.

It should be mentioned that Madkūr perceives the relation between Arabic and the other two world languages as competitive and conflictual. On the one hand, Arabic seems to be a more 'eternal' world language than French and English because 'science and philosophy' bear a more transcendent mission than 'politics and diplomacy' and 'business and finance' do. On the other hand, French and English were the two main languages promoted in the Arabic-speaking world during the colonial period. The spread and, in some cases, dominance of the two languages was certainly facilitated by the 'violence' and 'tyranny' against Arabic.

With the revival of Arabic following the independence of the Arab states in the mid-twentieth century, a new round of competition between Arabic and French/English began in the Arabic-speaking world, in other Asian and African communities, and in the international arena. Within the Arabic-speaking world, Madkūr describes Arabic as undergoing continuous refinement and renewal to fulfil modern social, scientific and literary needs. A concomitant development, according to him, was the elevation of modern Arabic literature to world status, with more and more translations from Arabic into other languages. In the area of education, Madkūr considers that Arabic was replacing English and French to be used in university science courses. Moreover, he tells us that more and more foreigners came to Arab universities to study Arabic. Beyond the Arabic-speaking world in Asia and Africa, claims Madkūr, newly independent states resorted or would like to resort to Arabic to solve their language problems. Madkūr understands that there was a traditional link between Arabic and many Asian and African languages written in the Arabic script or possessing large numbers of Arabic borrowings. This made Arabic influential in the language policy of these Asian and African states. Pakistan, for example, had considered adopting Arabic as one of its national languages following its independence. Indonesia, in Madkūr's opinion, would certainly welcome the promotion of Arabic in its territory. In Africa, reports Madkūr, even UNESCO had approved the role of Arabic in resolving the chaotic linguistic situation, trapped in quarrels between Anglophonism and Francophonism over the selection of official languages.

In the international arena, Arabic was accepted as one of the official languages of the UN General Assembly in 1973 and of UNESCO in 1974 and has, since then, been widely used at the international level.[14]

In this 'world language' competition, Madkūr suggests that Arabic is in an advanced position because of its embedded universal, humanistic character. First of all, Arabic serves a cultural mission that both English and French have failed to accomplish so far. Madkūr praises Arabic for its growing role in promoting international cultural exchange. 'The cultural world', he comments, 'is more broad-minded (*'awsa' ṣadran*) than the political and economic worlds, and this is fortunate for humanism' (1973: 19). Apparently, in Madkūr's eyes, a language bearing a cultural mission carries more humanism than those mainly serving politics (French, the language of 'politics and diplomacy') and economics (English, the language of 'business and finance').

Arabic also serves a unification mission, while English and French are often associated with conflict and fragmentation. According to Madkūr, English and French belong to those modern European languages that replaced Latin in line with the rise of nationalism in Europe. For him, these languages were symptoms of language fragmentation in the era of modern nation-states. It was this language fragmentation that worried scholars such as Leibniz and Zamenhof, prompting them to argue for a so-called 'universal language'. Moreover, English and French embodied the linguistic image of European colonialism, aiming at division rather than unification in the Arab world and other Asian and African communities. Madkūr understands that this colonial legacy still influences language policy in Africa, as shown in the Anglophone-Francophone debate mentioned above. Arabic, however, does not cause conflict and fragmentation. In its medieval heyday, Arabic speakers came from different ethnic, racial, religious and sectarian backgrounds. In modern times, Arabic not only fosters solidarity within the Arabic-speaking world, but also helps with resolving language issues in newly independent Asian and African nation-states.

Finally, Madkūr asserts that Arabic carries the humanistic message of Islam, calling for peace and solidarity. At the beginning of his 1969 speech, Madkūr points out that Arabic has two attributes, divine and social; it is both a language of worship conveying Islamic revelation and a language of society retaining the collective dignity of the Arab nation. He goes on to link the spread of Arabic to Islam, to the extent that every Muslim was obliged to use Arabic in prayers, no matter what his or her national language was. It was owing to this religious obligation that Arabic developed into a world language, widely used in a large number of nations and ethnicities in Asia and Africa. In his 1973 speech, Madkūr does not talk about Islam directly but hints at it. In the beginning, he calls for 'the language of the pen' to be substituted for 'the language of the sword and cannon' in order to resolve the conflicts in and beyond the Arab world. When praising the Lebanese publishers for their contribution to the spread of Arabic around the world, he metaphorically describes Lebanon as a big lighthouse that shines (*ʾishʿāʿ*) the light (*ʾaḍwāʾ*) of Arabic to East and West, as if Arabic were bearing a mission to the whole world. The indication is clear that, like Islam, Arabic is a universal language that human beings would be prepared to commit themselves to.

These references to Islam indicate that the attribute of Arabic that Madkūr wants to highlight is not its religiosity, but its embedded values of universal humanism. He links Arabic to Islam, or to religion in general, in order to demonstrate that Arabic has the potential to be as transcendent and universal as religion. According to him, the fact that, within the Muslim world, Arabic is the lingua franca connecting different tribal, ethnic and sectarian communities and helping maintain order and peace among them, confirms its potential to be a universal language. In that sense, Arabic is able to contribute to development and progress, not only for Arabs but for other human communities as well.

Madkūr's argument concerning promoting Arabic as a universal/ world language is replete with obvious faults, making it more like wishful thinking than a statement of facts. For example, Madkūr suggests that Arabic can serve as a universal language like Esperanto. However, demonstrating that Arabic is structurally close to the ideal form of Esperanto is one thing, while tailoring Arabic to the norm of Esperanto to proclaim this closeness is another. What Madkūr does is in fact the latter. Using his logic, we can claim that many languages other than Arabic are also potentially universal. A second example is Madkūr's distinction among French, English and Arabic as the languages of diplomacy, business and science respectively. Apparently no language is restricted to limited domains, and instrumentally no language is more suitable than another for a specific purpose of communication.

The fact that Madkūr's faulty arguments were not challenged by his fellow academicians and that, instead, he continued to publish similar ideas in the journal of the Cairo Academy invites explanation. Probably it was the convention of politeness observed by the academicians that prevented them from criticising Madkūr, who was elected president of the Academy in 1974. Yet more probably, Madkūr's reading of Arabic as a universal/ world language relieved the common concern of the academicians over the inferior and weak status of Arabic – a concern that was amplified after the 1967 defeat. Considering this, the notion of Arabic being empowered and privileged vis-à-vis other world languages, even in wishful ways, was naturally welcome to the academicians.

Reading the papers of al-Hāshimī, al-Jamālī and Madkūr together, we see renewed efforts to reconcile exogenous and endogenous language modernisation in the ALA discourse. The reconciliation was not easy because, in the two decades prior to 1967 (see the previous section), exogenous modernisation was generally understood as linguistic foreignisation, referring to the uncritical borrowing from and dependence on English or French, and endogenous modernisation was often reduced to apologetic defences of Arabic. As discussed in Chapter 4, linguistic foreignisation as such was often associated with the imposition of English or French in Arab countries during the colonial period. After 1967, Arab intellectuals were more sensitive to this type of exogenous modernisation, which was connected in the public imaginary with Zionism and imperialism and was, therefore, opposed. However, exclusive reliance on endogenous modernisation also lost its legitimacy, because no real development and progress was achieved in the two decades before 1967. This social and cultural (including linguistic) stagnation became a refraction of the defeat in 1967. The Arabs experienced both a deep trauma, as their dignity was destroyed, and a dilemma, as neither exogenous nor endogenous modernisation could actually bring them the level of modernity expected.

Nonetheless, endogenous and exogenous modernisation share a persistent aim: making Arabic compatible with modern communicative needs and recovering its historical status in the world. It was on the basis of this aim that the two modes of modernisation were reconciled anew, for otherwise there was no way to rid Arabic of stagnation. However, this reconciliation needed to dispel the distrust of both modes of modernisation. Universal humanism was deployed to serve this purpose. On the one hand, understanding exogenous modernisation in the framework of universal humanism rather than linguistic foreignisation could remove enmity towards the borrowing of foreign linguistic elements and standards. On the other hand, associating Arabic with universal humanism could (1) increase collective confidence in this language by highlighting its importance globally, and (2) legitimise the modernisation of this language in line with other modern world languages such as English and French, without falling into accusations of blind imitation of and dependence on the West. Universal humanism was used to ensure sufficient equilibrium between these two modes of modernisation so that Arabic could achieve real development and modernisation.

Qunṣul (1971: 211) provides a further example of the reconciliation of exogenous and endogenous modernisation around universal humanism in the ALA discourse:

> For Arabs, [the wish] to proceed with modern civilisation cannot be fulfilled unless equilibrium between our Arab self and our civilisational humanism is achieved. The core component of this self is the Arabic language which has always been an unadulterated tool transmitting ingenious thoughts around the world and a central constituent of peace in the future between nations and peoples.

The post-1967 ALA discourse on language modernisation showed that Arabic consistently served as an index of sociopolitical change in the Arabic-speaking world. The 1967 defeat traumatised Arab society for it discredited the political and military institutions developed in the so-called 'progressive' Arab countries in the preceding two decades, and shook the Arabs' confidence in the developmental capability of the Arab nation as a whole. This social trauma was projected into the dilemma between exogenous and endogenous language modernisations in the ALA discourse. Consequently, the search for a way out of this dilemma was an attempt not merely to reorient the path of modernising Arabic, but also to alleviate the social trauma and to regain confidence in the future of the Arab nation. The adoption of Arabic as a working language in UN organisations in 1973 brought great comfort to post-1967 Arab society, as if the power of the Arab nation had once again been recognised by the international community. Hence we saw the discussion of Arabic as a universal humanistic language appearing in the ALA discourse. By consolidating the international status of Arabic, members of the ALAs believed that they found the solution to the post-1967 dilemma vis-à-vis language modernisation and wanted to project this new status back into the ongoing sociopolitical readjustments in the Arabic-speaking world. This tendency continued in the ALA discourse on modernisation in the next two decades.

Critical Reflections on Modernity and Authenticity

The post-1967 trauma, dilemma and the reconciliation of exogenous and endogenous modernisation around universal humanism soon gave way to a critical reflection on the two modes of modernisation in the ALA discourse in the 1970s and 1980s. The schematic understanding of both modes of modernisation in the 1950s and 1960s was expanded. Exogenous modernisation became more than blind imitation and cosmetic change, and endogenous modernisation became more than apologetic defence of and adherence to the fixed traditions of Arabic. This tendency could be seen in the intensified discussion about the relation between authenticity and modernity vis-à-vis the modernisation of Arabic in the ALAs.

In 1971, ALECSO held a conference entitled *al-ʾAṣāla wa-l-tajdīd fī al-thāqāfa al-ʿarabiyya al-muʿāṣira* 'Authenticity and renewal in contemporary Arab culture' in Cairo.[15] As one of the earliest pan-Arab conferences on authenticity and modernity, how the relation between the two concepts was understood in this conference set the tone for later discussions on the issue, including those in the ALAs.

According to Nāṣir al-Dīn al-ʾAsad's report on this conference, published in *al-Lisān al-ʿarabī* in 1972, authenticity was understood as both fixed and flexible among participants of the conference. They agreed that authenticity meant dealing with cultural and linguistic affairs by relying on the linguistic, intellectual and civilisational fundamentals (*ʾuṣūl*) of the nation. They believed that every nation had its specific spirit and nature embedded in its cultural products no matter how the form and content of these products changed over time. They thus suggested that the nation could always find, from its heritage, the root or fundamental principles on the basis of which its modernity could develop; seeking authenticity required identifying this fixed, specific spirit and root (al-ʾAsad 1972: 195). However, the participants of the conference also acknowledged that seeking authenticity did not entail sticking to the whole heritage, just like modernisation does not mean embracing everything new without discrimination (ibid.: 195). In the encounter between authentication and modernisation, both should be examined against the modern needs of Arab society (ibid.: 196). Authenticity and modernity were not conflictual but complementary and were in need of reconciliation (*tawfīq*) in the social and cultural revival of the Arab nation (ibid.: 196).

The co-existence of fixity and flexibility constituted a paradox, which showed that cultural certainty and social development were both demanded in the Arabic-speaking world. This was confirmed by another, more detailed report on this conference. According to Kassab (2010: 118–19), Shukrī ʿAyyād, one participant at the conference, stated that 'whether the focus of the present age is on tradition and innovation or on authenticity and renewal, all are seeking a certain sense of self in the current conditions, marked by the influence of Western cultural trends'. Another participant, Muḥammad Mazālī, challenged the view that the dominating theme of this age was development, not nationalism, by arguing that this view did not apply to societies that had experienced 'economic, political, military and cultural aggression through colonialism' (ibid.: 119). Clearly, participants in this conference were aware of the importance and necessity of development and modernisation in Arab society, but they also prioritised cultural certainty to make sure Arabness would not be diluted by modernity. Besides, ʿAyyād's and Mazālī's arguments showed how difficult the critical reflection on authenticity and modernity could be when the colonial experience still dominated the collective imagination of the Arab public.

In line with the above understanding of authenticity and modernity, the ALA discourse in the 1970s and 1980s reassessed the situation of Arabic. A leading opinion considered the underdevelopment of Arabic as a deficit of modernity in the Arabic-speaking world partially caused by cultural protectionism in the 1950s and 1960s. ALA members who held this opinion then called for a new way of language modernisation to be devised, one that could combine authenticity and modernity. This discursive development was reflected firstly by the two papers submitted to the Third Arabi(ci)sation Conference convened in Libya in 1977, both addressing the relation between Arabic and social development, and secondly by a series of discussions held within the ALAs on the role of Arabic heritage (*turāth*) in the modernisation of Arabic.

The paper *Madā tafāʿul al-lugha maʿ qaḍāyā al-numuww al-ijtimāʿī* 'The extent of interaction between language and social development', submitted by the General Culture Administration of Libya, distinguishes between material and spiritual development and identifies a 'chasm' (*huwwa*) (IATWDL 1977: 56) between the two in Libyan society. According to this paper, Libya had witnessed 'a grand civilisational transformation' (*naqla ḥaḍāriyya ḍakhma*) (ibid.: 55) on the material side since the 1969 Libyan Revolution (*thawra*); however, the spiritual side did not follow this transformation at an equal pace. The Arabic language, as a component of the Libyan collectivity and as a tool of social communication, needed 'a prod' (*ʾithāra*) (ibid.: 56) to catch up with the fast-changing social life of Libya. The shared lexical root *th-w-r* related *ʾithāra* to *thawra*, indicating that what the Arabic language needed in Libya was a 'revolution' and an equally 'grand transformation'. At the end, the paper points out that the pace of social and linguistic development was uneven among different Arab countries; accordingly, the material-spiritual 'chasm' in these countries varied. The paper then appealed to the Bureau for the Coordination of Arabisation to coordinate the development of Arabic in the Arabic-speaking world.

The paper *al-Taṭawwur al-ʾijtimāʿī wa-l-taṭawwur al-lughawī* 'social development and language development', written by Shukrī Fayṣal, the Syrian representative to the Third Arabi(ci)sation Conference, also addresses the imbalance between social and linguistic development in the Arabic-speaking world. The overall context for this imbalance, he believes, was the explosive (*mutafajjir*) progress of human civilisation; what human beings had achieved in the previous fifty years surpassed all their preceding achievements in history (Fayṣal 1977: 33). This explosive progress, according to Fayṣal, had affected all nations and their sub-units (*muqawwimāt*); the Arab nation was one of them and the Arabic language was a sub-unit of the Arab nation (ibid.: 33). Full attention should therefore be paid to social and linguistic development in the Arab nation to catch up with civilisational progress. For Fayṣal, development (*numuww*) means both quantitative and qualitative change, which should be distinguished from expansion (*ittisāʿ*), referring to merely quantitative growth (*tazāyud*); quantitative growth is often unsteady (*takhalkhul*), while qualitative change tends to be gradual, organised and cohesive (ibid.: 33). In Fayṣal's view, language plays an important role in promoting qualitative change, because it links thinking and practice to create a new social reality in an organised manner; making linguistic development compatible with social development, therefore, could guarantee the genuine development and empowerment of a nation (ibid.: 34). Fayṣal points out that the efficacy of the connection between linguistic and social development has been demonstrated by China, Vietnam[16] and Israel, who combined these two areas of development and have now achieved significant social progress (ibid.: 37). By contrast, argues Fayṣal, the situation in the Arabic-speaking world was different; although there seemed to be an ongoing socioeconomic development towards a consumer economy, there was no compatible linguistic development (ibid.: 37). In other words, linguistic life ranked 'below' (*dūna*) social life (ibid.: 37).

Fayṣal then warns the Arabs of the dangers of an imbalance between social and linguistic development in the Arabic-speaking world. If this imbalance continued, Arabs would not be able to benefit from modern civilisational achievements when meeting their social needs; on the contrary, they would be enslaved by modernity and become its 'prisoners of war' (*ʾasrā*) (ibid.: 37). Modernity, or modern civilisation, is Janus-like for Arabs. The question is whether the Arabs could take the initiative and accommodate modernity in their society, or lose this initiative and, consequently, subordinate themselves to modernity. For Fayṣal, underdevelopment and cultural uncertainty are two aspects of the same problem; the only way to solve this problem is the innovative transplantation of modern civilisation into the Arab soil. In other words, exogenous modernisation can be transformed into endogenous modernisation as long as the former process is under the control of the Arabs.

Whilst reflection on the underdevelopment of Arabic mainly focused on the relationship between Arabic and (exogenous) modernity, reflection on cultural uncertainty in relation to Arabic usually turned inwards to assess the role of Arabic heritage (*turāth*) in the modernisation of Arabic. Although reviving Arabic heritage, revealed in the collection, editing and publication of Arabic manuscripts, had been part of the duty of the ALAs since their inception, it was during the 1970s and 1980s that heritage became a frequent theme in the discourse of these academies. The Cairo Academy, for example, 'restarted the work of its heritage committee in the mid-1970s, and established an annual award from 1979 to encourage public participation in reviving this heritage' (Lian 2010: 47). In 1982, the Academy even set 'Arabic heritage and the Arabic language' as the theme of its Annual Assembly, which showed a growing intellectual interest in this issue.

The standpoint of the majority of the participants in this discussion about Arabic heritage was still uncritically apologetic, affirming the incomparable richness of this heritage and its continuing contribution to the modern revival of Arabic language and culture. What was hidden behind this apology, however, was deep concern for the status of this heritage in modern Arab society. A quick review of the titles of some papers devoted to the heritage discussion confirms the existence of this concern, such as *Li-mādhā nuʿnā bi-turāthinā?* 'Why do we care about our heritage?' (al-Ḥawfī 1980), *Mā zāl turāthunā al-ʿarabī manārat al-fikr* 'Our Arabic heritage is still our intellectual lighthouse' (al-Baṣīr 1986), *al-Turāth al-lughawī wa-l-taqaddum al-ijtimāʿī* 'Linguistic heritage and social progress' (al-Jawārī 1986) and *al-Turāth al-ʿarabī wa-l-muʿāṣara* 'Arabic heritage and contemporaneity' (ʿIzz al-Dīn 1986). The last two titles suggested that there was a tension between this heritage and modernity, so that the relationship between the two needed to be clarified. The phrase *mā zāl* 'still' in the second title indicated an apologetic attitude towards Arabic heritage, and the first title showed that the value of this heritage in the modern age was in need of justification.

On defending Arabic heritage, the metaphor of 'water' is commonly deployed in these papers. Al-Ḥawfī describes this heritage as 'the overflowing (*zākhir*) river that provides us with nutrition and water and brings us development and efflorescence' (1980: 20). Al-Baṣīr compares this heritage to 'the overflowing (*zākhir*) ocean consisting of rivers with which scholars, writers, theologians and linguists quench their thirst (*yartawī*)' (1986: 204). In the same article, he depicts this heritage as 'a spring abundant [with water] (*ghazīr*)' (ibid.: 207). In a slightly different way, al-Jawārī conceptualises Arabic linguistic heritage as 'a shady, fruitful and deep-rooted tree that knows how to absorb nutrition from the soil and air and draw water (*tartawī*) from rivers, springs, rain and dew' (1986: 94–5).

ʿIzz al-Dīn also resorts to this metaphor when he discusses the revival of the early Islamic style in modern Arabic poetry and prose; he characterises this revival as 'bringing fresh liquid (*rawāʾ*) and pure water' to the Arabic literary style (1986: 190). The metaphor of 'water' indicates that Arabic heritage is perceived to be always feeding, sustaining and inspiring Arabic culture and literature.

Defending Arabic heritage helped to dissolve feelings of cultural uncertainty and to consolidate confidence in Arabic culture and language. However, this did not necessarily mean invariably adhering to or exclusively relying on this heritage, which might lead to self-closure. In this regard, participants in the heritage discussions agreed that Arabic heritage should be open for re-discovery, criticism and renewal. First of all, Arabs today should be able to identify the beneficial components of their heritage (Ḥawfī 1980: 19) and to get rid of those components not suitable for modern civilisation (ʿIzz al-Dīn 1986: 191). Secondly, Arabs today should realise that Arabic heritage is a plural concept, consisting of many different schools of thought and exhibited in different media, ranging from manuscripts to popular custom. This plurality requires an open attitude towards the heritage (al-Baṣīr 1986: 206; ʿIzz al-Dīn 1986: 189). Lastly, Arabic heritage needs evaluation (*taqyīm*) and correction (*taqwīm*) according to the modern needs of Arab society until the modern, collective Arab taste (*dhawq*) is solidly shaped. This evaluation and correction process demands abandoning the stance of self-closure and opening the gate of intellectual speculation (ʿIzz al-Dīn 1986: 192–3).

The critical assessment of language underdevelopment and the role of Arabic heritage in language modernisation led to bitter criticism of the schematic understanding of both exogenous and endogenous modernisation in the previous two decades. ʾIbrahīm Madkūr (1981: 15) considers 'concord' (*muwāʾama*) between the old and new, and between Arab principles and Western civilisation, to be a characteristic feature of Arab intellectual life in the first half of the twentieth century, which brought progress and stability to Arabic culture. However, according to him, Arab intellectual life suffered from a 'relapse' (*naksa*) in the 1950s and 1960s, when the previously established 'concord' between exogenous and endogenous modernisation was denied (ibid.: 15). Alternatively, the concept of 'European [cultural] invasion' was promulgated, and attempts were made to close 'the open window towards the West'; Islam and the Arab-Islamic tradition were perceived in a dark, static (*qātim*) way contradictory to the laws of development and progress (*sunan al-taṭawwur wa-l-irtiqāʾ*) (ibid.: 15). In Madkūr's view, this relapse was destructive. He was therefore pleased to see the recent return of the early principle of 'concord', and confirmed its importance to the development of Arabic language and culture.

Muḥammad ʿAzīz al-Ḥabābī (1982) made a similar criticism. He identifies a type of dualism called *ʾimmiyya*, an abstracted noun created by attaching *-iyya* to *ʾimmā* 'either', in the Arab intellectual discourse on modernisation: Arab society can either (*ʾimmā*) choose to be Westernised to acquire modernity or (*ʾimmā*) stick to the Arab-Islamic tradition with self-closure. This *ʾimmiyya* treats Western civilisation and Arab-Islamic tradition, or modernity and authenticity, as two mutually exclusive entities and denies the possibility of co-existence and any fusion of the two. For al-Ḥabābī, this *ʾimmiyya* is, in fact, *ʾummiyya* 'illiteracy', because in the modern era, knowing only one language or sticking to only one culture equals ignorance and illiteracy. Here al-Ḥabābī uses a paronomasia, associating *ʾimmiyya* with *ʾummiyya* to denounce the prevailing dualism vis-à-vis modernisation. In line with al-Ḥabābī's criticism, the correct attitude tends to be that modernisation is not Westernisation, and authentication is not exclusive reliance on cultural heritage; modernity should be authenticated, while authenticity should be modernised. In his view, only by adopting this attitude can Arabs get rid of cultural and linguistic retardation.

Criticism of previous understandings of modernisation marked a new era of critical assessment of both exogenous and endogenous modes of modernisation, in order to seek balance and convergence between the two. The ultimate purpose of this critical assessment was making the Arabic language and culture both modern and authentic. From this came the following questions: how can Arabs achieve this purpose? Regarding the Arabic language, what are the criteria of being modern and authentic at the same time?

Kamāl Muḥammad Bishr's article *al-Lugha bayna al-taṭawwur wa-fikrat al-ṣawāb wa-l-khaṭaʾ* 'Language between development and the idea of right and wrong' published in 1988 provides good answers to the above questions. In this article, Bishr relates the realisation of linguistic modernity and authenticity to the establishment of certain principles when judging 'right' and 'wrong' in language use. This is because, as long as new language phenomena pass the agreed yardstick of 'right' and 'wrong', they can be incorporated into the inherited language system and become authentic. There are, however, different positions regarding the relationship between language development and the criteria of 'right' and 'wrong'. Bishr identifies four: (1) the newer, the more right, because the newer always represents the progress of language; (2) the newer, the more wrong, because language development means deviation from established language norms; (3) it is hard to decide, because deviation from established norms does not equal wrong usage; and (4) it is unnecessary to decide, because language development means language change, which has nothing to do with 'right' and 'wrong' (in the linguistic-cum-moral sense). Position (1) accepts new usage uncritically; position (2) rejects new usage uncritically; position (3) aims to correct new usage in line with established norms; and position (4) records language change objectively and scientifically. Bishr regards the first three positions fallacious, which indicates that, in his mind, neither exogenous nor endogenous language norms can be the yardstick of 'right' and 'wrong'. He prefers the fourth position because its objectivity makes it indifferent to other, extra-linguistic considerations. For him, this position is the first step towards establishing objective, scientific norms of 'right' and 'wrong'.

How are these norms established? Bishr suggests a descriptive-cum-prescriptive method: observing and describing new language phenomena, establishing regular patterns out of these phenomena within the broad limits of extant and inherited linguistic patterns, and applying these patterns as norms to regulate new development in the language. Regarding the sources of linguistic patterns or norms, he proposes three complementary principles (1988: 145):

(1) Refer to commonly-used language textbooks or references for extant and inherited linguistic laws and patterns;
(2) When these references cannot help understand new language phenomena, language experts can make their own reasoning (*ijtihād*);
(3) It is also possible to adopt popular, regular language patterns out of new language phenomena even if these phenomena deviate from the extant and inherited laws and patterns.

Bishr calls this method 'examining the new in the light of the old' (*al-naẓar fī al-jadīd fī ḍawʾ al-qadīm*) (ibid.: 145), a method that may authenticate and regulate new developments in the Arabic language and achieve equilibrium between language authenticity and modernity in the Arabic-speaking world at the same time. Clearly, by proposing this method of language development, Bishr is attempting to reinstate the eclectic principle to avoid the dualism between exogenous and endogenous modernisation.

The above-discussed features (the awareness of the underdevelopment of Arabic, the relatively flexible but defensive attitude towards Arab-Islamic heritage, the criticism against the schematic understanding of both exogenous and endogenous modernisation, and the search for a middle ground between the two) together characterised the ALA discourse on language modernisation in the 1970s and 1980s. These features were in accordance with the two dominant sociopolitical tendencies in the Arabic-speaking world in these two decades, illustrating how Arabic consistently served as an index and as a proxy of extra-linguistic causes in the ALA discourse.

The first sociopolitical tendency was the increasing focus on economic and social development in most Arab states, sustained by economic liberalisation policies and rapidly increasing oil revenues. Sadat initiated a 'corrective revolution' in Egypt in the early 1970s, reversing the radical, socialist mode of development under Nasser and opening the Egyptian economy to the global capitalist market and foreign investors. Ḥāfiẓ al-ʾAsad adopted a limited economic liberalisation policy in Syria by lifting restrictions on the private sector. Saddam Hussein, although holding the Baʿthist anti-imperialist and pro-Arab unity ideology, relied on Iraq's oil revenue to attract foreign expertise and led a vast transformation of infrastructure and education in Iraq. The Gulf states, benefiting from the sudden boom of oil revenues after a coordinated oil embargo during the 1973 Arab-Israeli war, managed to promote rapid material development projects and establish social welfare systems in their societies. Development became a common pursuit for these Arab states from the early 1970s onwards. This development was made possible by the Arabs' independent control and management of their own natural resources, but it also largely relied on the importation of technology, expertise and labour from outside, and on increasing integration into the global market. This inevitable entanglement of independence and dependence accompanied the 'turn to development' in the Arabic-speaking world in the 1970s and 1980s.

The second sociopolitical tendency in these two decades was the rising exploitation of Islamic symbols by both the ruling regimes and oppositional forces in the Arabic-speaking world. The public disillusionment with the leading Arab states after the 1967 defeat, the discrepancy between material and social developments in wealthy Arab countries and between rising expectations of material improvement and economic stagnation in others, as well as the corruption and pro-West tendency of some Arab leaders were factors in the rise of oppositional movements, linked to claims of a return to Islamic morality and modes of governance. The ruling regimes, from Egypt to Saudi Arabia, frequently resorted to Islam and Islamic symbols to boost their political legitimacy. This focus on Islam reflected a genuine sentiment in Arab society, yearning for a more authentic future for their communities in relation to the realisation of development and progress, on the one hand, and resistance to the intrusion of foreign values and life styles, on the other.

Both tendencies were reflected in the ALA discourse on language modernisation. The development tendency was projected onto the diagnoses of the underdevelopment of Arabic and the reaffirmed role of language modernisation in the realisation of social development. The rising attention to Islamic values was reflected in the growing interest of the ALAs in the valuation and validation of Arab-Islamic heritage and its connection to the modernisation of Arabic. The turn from the ideological battles of the 1950s and 1960s to developmental issues in the 1970s and 1980s brought an open and moderate attitude towards the material and cultural products of Western industrial powers and a relatively less rigid stance towards the maintenance of national pride and self-sustainability. This attitudinal change was revealed in the ALA discourse as the abandonment of the bifurcated, schematic understanding of exogenous and endogenous modernisation and the rapprochement between the two.

Cultural Invasion and Comprehensive Development

At the end of the twentieth century, the ALA discourse on language modernisation exhibited a mixture of warnings against so-called 'cultural invasion' and calls for a comprehensive development of the Arabic language. The former showed continuous suspicion and enmity towards the perceived 'Western cultural hegemony' in modern Arab society, while the latter indicated the Arab yearning to participate in an increasingly globalising world. I will analyse three articles to illustrate the above tendency: Fawāz Muḥammad al-Rāshid ʿAbd al-Ḥaqq's *Marʾiyyāt al-takhṭīṭ al-lughawī: ʿarḍ wa-naqd* 'Ideas on language planning: presentation and critique' (1996), Marwān al-Maḥāsinī's *al-Lugha wa-l-ʾaṣāla* 'Language and authenticity' (1996) and Maḥmūd Fahmī Ḥijāzī's *al-Lugha al-ʿarabiyya fī al-qarn al-ḥādī wa-l-ʿishrīn* 'The Arabic language in the twenty-first century' (1998).

In his review and critique of language planning theories in Western academia, ʿAbd al-Ḥaqq reveals the hidden imperialist agenda and capitalist ideology behind the development of these theories. He argues that language planning was proposed by Western scholars after World War II to solve language problems in newly independent nation-states around the world. In his view, these scholars wrongly assumed that language development in these nation-states would follow the path of modern European languages, so they equated development and modernisation with Westernisation; moreover, they applied economic models to language planning and regarded native or national languages of economically underdeveloped countries as underdeveloped. According to al-Ḥaqq, the purpose and consequence of this kind of language planning were enhancing Western hegemony and Arab subordination in the cultural and linguistic fields, which may be perceived as 'cultural invasion'. He insists that the Arabs, especially Arab language policy-makers, should be aware of this imperialist and capitalist underpinning of Western language planning theories, and avoid uncritically copying Western models to develop the Arabic language. For ʿAbd al-Ḥaqq, acquiescence to these language planning models and theories is wrong. He emphasises that every society and language have their specificities, which should entail crafting their own methods of development and modernisation.

Al-Maḥāsinī repeats the theme of 'cultural invasion' but does not treat it as the main feature of modernisation. He holds that modernisation means benefiting from the West, apart from recognising the superior position of Western civilisation. He points out that, for Arabs, modernisation is necessary to reverse the historical conditions which caused the loss of their leading position in the world, although this does not entail subordination (*tabaʿiyya*) to the West at the cost of their national and cultural identity; this understanding of modernisation requires the Arabs to seek innovative and authentic ways of accommodating modernity in the Arab world. According to al-Maḥāsinī, however, authenticity vis-à-vis the Arabic language does not mean sanctifying (*taqdīs*) and glorifying (*tamjīd*) the language to freeze its character and particularities against change and renewal. In the eyes of al-Maḥāsinī, such sanctification and glorification, in fact, 'slowly covers the sun (i.e. the Arab nation) and keeps the development [of this nation] to a snail's pace' (1996: 155). It is the Orientalists, al-Maḥāsinī argues, who promulgate the precept that the features and dispositions of a culture are fixed, and it is on the basis of this precept that they perceive the East and the West to be essentially different. For al-Maḥāsinī, the proper attitude towards language authenticity is treating Arabic as a linguistic repository rather than a singular entity that is different from other languages. In his view, this linguistic repository constantly absorbs new elements from different languages, cultures and civilisations to meet communicative needs throughout history, which demonstrates that Arabic is always a living language, participating in the development of human civilisation; this linguistic repository also constructs a historical continuity that links the Arab past and present in an authentic way. Understanding Arabic as the linguistic repository, al-Maḥāsinī says, could help the Arabs acquire modernity without causing civilisational 'ruptures' (*sharkh*) (ibid.: 156).

The concept of 'linguistic repository' acknowledges that the Arabic language is a polyphyletic system, where different cultures and civilisations are fused throughout history; therefore, modernising this language will benefit not only the Arabs but also humanity as a whole. This idea is echoed in Ḥijāzī's concept of the 'comprehensive development' (*al-tanmiyya al-shāmila*) of the Arabic language.

According to Ḥijāzī, this comprehensive development has at least three dimensions. First, developing Arabic should cover every component and domain of the language, rather than focusing on coining scientific terminologies. Second, developing Arabic to meet modern communicative needs should not sever the link between this language and Arabic heritage. Ḥijāzī emphasises that Arabic has a long literary tradition, the planning of which is different from the planning of languages with little or no history of writing. Lastly, developing Arabic should consider the needs of local, national, international, native and non-native speakers of the language. Regarding developing Arabic at the international level, Ḥijāzī discusses the use of Arabic in international organisations, the adoption of the Arabic script in non-Arabic-speaking communities, teaching Arabic to non-native speakers, especially Muslims, and Arabic studies in Western universities. He regards facilitating the acquisition, use and spread of Arabic internationally as an important mission of Arabic language planning in the twenty-first century. He insists that Arabic is a world language and needs to be engaged in all levels of international communication.

The above pieces of the ALA discourse on language modernisation exhibited two tendencies: (1) a wish to accommodate Arabic to global modernity along with a resentment of the Western hegemony in the linguistic and cultural spheres of Arab society and (2) recognising that Arabic, albeit having a codified, time-honoured linguistic tradition in need of preservation, is plural (both synchronically and diachronically) and vibrant by nature. These tendencies should be read together with the following two major sociopolitical developments affecting the Arabic-speaking world in the 1990s.

The first was the end of the Cold War following the collapse of the Soviet Bloc, which changed the international power balance, making the United States the only superpower in the world. This power change led to or accelerated the convergence of former communist/socialist and Third World countries into capitalist market economies, as well as neo-liberalism. This convergence, cheered by some as globalisation, in fact consolidated the hegemony of the core (mainly the West) over the periphery (including the Arabs). Western hegemony in the Arabic-speaking world already had its mundane ramifications in multiple aspects of Arab social life, including economic relations, education and language use. Yet this mundane hegemony became overt during and after the Iraqi invasion of Kuwait in 1990 that escalated into the Gulf War (1990–1); a massive coalition army led by the United States was deployed to Saudi Arabia to help defend the Gulf states against Iraqi aggression.

Opening Saudi territory (where two of the holy sites of Islam are to be found) for foreign troops was symbolically devastating in the Arabic-speaking world. One form or another of West-phobia or America-phobia began to spread in Arab public discourse, labelling Western influence or intervention in various domains of Arab social life as neo-colonialism or neo-imperialism. In the above circumstances, it was natural to witness, in the ALA discourse, parallel reactions to globalisation and Western hegemony in both positive (al-Maḥāsinī and Ḥijāzī's call for modernising Arabic and promoting it internationally) and negative (ʿAbd al-Ḥaqq's concept of 'cultural invasion' concerning Western LPLP theories) ways.

The second sociopolitical development was the consolidation of the political reality in the Arabic-speaking world where state interests predominated over pan-Arab ones. This development was most evident in the political divide among Arab states over military action against the Iraqi invasion of Kuwait and the isolation of Saddam Hussein's Iraqi regime after the Gulf War – a regime that was acclaimed in the Arab street and self-promoted to be the last remaining champion of pan-Arab causes in the twentieth century, especially with respect to the political rights of the Palestinians (Cleveland and Bunton 2009: 478). This political development was also refracted in the ALA discourse on language modernisation concerning the plurality of Arabic, although this refraction was not directly immediately visible.

Acknowledging the inherent plurality of Arabic, as in the writings of al-Maḥāsinī and Ḥijāzī above, was certainly a strategy to deconstruct the staid and static understanding of Arabic that prioritised the time-honoured purity and integrity of *fuṣḥā*, which blocked or delegitimised the necessary changes in the structure and use of Arabic to meet modern communicative needs. Yet this acknowledgement started to appear in the ALA discourse only when the grand unitary ideology of pan-Arabism, which was in symbiosis with an equally grand unitary understanding of linguistic integrity as a form and basis of Arab unity, lost its last strong base (with the isolation of Iraq) at the official level of Arab politics. In other words, the plurality thesis concerning Arabic tended to be more attractive because this thesis accorded with the fragmented political reality (therefore appearing to be more plural than that in the heyday of political pan-Arabism) in the Arabic-speaking world where (1) the Arab states looked more inwardly to their own economic and security interests than outwardly to pan-Arab causes as some of these states used to do and (2) political movements at sub-state, ethnic and sectarian levels challenged, more intensively than ever in the post-colonial period, the authority of the Arab states.

The above analyses suggest that, in our final 'site' of the ALA discourse on language modernisation, the relationship between endogenous and exogenous modernisation tended to be more complicated in terms of the compromise and conflict between the two than before, in that they were linked to the search for a modern, solid Arab self under the double threat of political fragmentation from within, and 'neo-colonialist/imperialist' hegemony from without.

Conclusion: Reviving the Arab Nation and Counterbalancing the West

By tracing the formation, development and routinisation of the ALA discourse on language modernisation via content, semantic and metaphorical analyses together with examining the changing sociopolitical circumstances in the above six 'sites', this chapter has shown that the discourses in these 'sites' had three features in common. Firstly, all 'sites' exhibited a conceptual dyad between exogenous and endogenous modes of modernisation, which appeared to be consistent enough to be treated as a discursive habitus in spite of sociopolitical changes in the Arabic-speaking world in the twentieth century. Secondly, the meanings of exogenous and endogenous modernisation and the relationship between the two were affected by the sociopolitical changes in all 'sites'. Lastly, the modernisation of Arabic conceptualised in these 'sites' aimed not only at improving the language as an instrument of communication, but also at constructing a linguistic representation of the transformation of the Arabs towards modernity. Here Arabic was regarded as both an index illustrating the modernisation status of the Arabs and a proxy deployed to contribute to this modernisation project.

Together these three features presented a paradox involving the persistence of the modernisation dyad and the inevitable discursive change in a turbulent social environment. The third feature above showed that the linguistic cause and the national cause were closely connected and mutually constitutive in the ALA discourse. The link between the two causes was fed by the 'doxa' in Arabic society that emphasised the inalienable interconnectedness between Arabic and the Arabs, as we have also and already seen in the previous two chapters. Consequently, this discourse naturally reflected and articulated sociopolitical contingencies in the Arabic-speaking world. The second feature above confirmed this, as the meanings of and the relationship between exogenous and endogenous modernisation changed in tandem with sociopolitical development.

However, these changes of meaning and relationship did not challenge the modernisation dyad, as revealed by the first feature above. This indicated that there was a deep sociopolitical reality yet to be challenged in the twentieth-century Arabic-speaking world, which helped perpetuate this conceptual dyad. Uncovering this deep reality requires us to seek similarities among the sociopolitical milieus of the six 'sites' of the ALA discourse.

These similarities can be summarised as follows. On the one hand, throughout the twentieth century, the Arabs were struggling with creating their own representation of modernity. The search for Arab modernity involved reorienting Arabs' political, economic, social and cultural lives in line with a new sense of collectivity, the Arab nation. This was indeed a new collectivity: although it retained a certain congruence with old collectives in the Arab-Islamic tradition, such as the Islamic *ʾumma* and the Arab ethnicity, it was mainly inspired by the model of European nation-states, which accentuated the central role of political unity in the formation of a nation. As I discussed in Chapter 3, the Arabs in the twentieth century were always caught between the aspiration for a politically unified Arab nation and the reality of the maturation of individual Arab states. Whether the modern Arab collectivity should be revealed as one nation-state or many was never certain. The lack of national certainty impeded the search for an Arab national self that was stable enough to be the base of the Arab form of modernity. In the sociopolitical milieus of the six 'sites' discussed above, we have seen (1) the tension between the aspiration for a unified Arab polity and the colonial legacy of states and borders; (2) the symbiosis between appeals for Arab unity and competitions for Arab leadership; and (3) concurrence of the maturation of Arab states and the common Arab frustration caused by military defeats, stagnating industrialisation and Western hegemony. All pointed to an unstable national framework and an unfinished mission of self-definition and national renaissance.

On the other hand, in pursuing these aims, the Arabs felt themselves to be in constant confrontation with the West, whose hegemony in the Arabic-speaking world has persisted from the colonial period until now. The sociopolitical milieus of the six 'sites' revealed various forms of this hegemony throughout the twentieth century, ranging from direct colonial rule, to military presence, to seeking strategic alliances with the Arab states, to integrating Arab economies into global capitalism and, finally, to cultural 'invasion'. Western hegemony brought pressure, compelling the Arabs to accelerate the process of modernisation in order to match the modernisation status of the West in an unreasonably short period. Western hegemony also aroused collective resentments towards the West, leading

Western modernity to be perceived as alien and antithetical to the Arab-Islamic tradition.

In sum, the ongoing search for the Arab national self and Arab modernity, under the pressure and threat from the hegemonic West, formed the sociopolitical reality that made the dyad of exogenous and endogenous modernisation a discursive habitus, guiding the articulation and reiteration of certain patterned understanding of language modernisation in the ALA discourse. The presence of this discursive habitus showed that, for members of the ALAs, modernising Arabic went beyond the realm of LPLP to become part of the national cause of reviving the self and counterbalancing the powerful Other.

Notes

1. An example of this view is the modernisation theory developed in the US from the early 1950s into the 1970s. Commenting on this theory, Lockman (2010: 137) says: 'Whatever the differences among them, adherents of modernization theory tended to see traditional societies as essentially static. Unlike the early modern West, they were said to lack the institutions and internal dynamics which might lead to fundamental social transformation from within. As a result, change had to come from outside, which meant largely from the political, cultural and economic influence of the West.' For a discussion on the connection between Orientalism and the modernisation theory, see Lockman (2010: 134–41).
2. Commenting on how printing changed the mode of communication in Muslim societies in modern times, Ayalon (2010: 572) says: 'Once relying on oral means for all interpersonal activities, these societies have come to employ writing as a standard implement of social exchange and individual expression. By the mid-twentieth century, mass-produced written and printed messages had come to permeate public communication, supplementing, if not quite supplanting, the age-old oral modes. As ever, the changes evolved differentially in different parts of the Islamic world. But eventually they came to affect most people, relegating those unaffected to the margins of communal activity.'
3. The reason to include *ʿawda* 'return or restoring' in this conceptual cluster is that, in the Arabic setting, the concept of 'revival', which is one way of articulating the concept of 'modernisation' in the ALA discourse as is being argued here, combines senses of both 'return to the origin' and 'renewal in new conditions'. It follows that *ʿawda* should not be understood as irrelevant to modernisation but in fact the former is inspired by and constitutes part of the latter.
4. See Blommaert (2005: 125–57) for a discussion of 'synchronisation' as a discursive strategy.
5. The concept *malaka* was developed and elaborated by Ibn Khaldūn (d. 1406) in his *Muqaddima* 'Prolegomena'. He describes *malaka* as a habit acquired via repetitive practice and learning (Ahmad 2003: 26–7), which is in contrast to knowledge and understanding (*fahm*) (ibid.: 100). When people acquire the

malaka of a craft (including speech and writing), it is their aptitude that helps them practise this craft intuitively and spontaneously (ibid.: 145). In this regard, Ibn Khaldūn makes it clear that *malaka* is not a natural given (ibid.: 102). In terms of language, he argues that an Arab is not necessarily a good Arabic speaker by nature; similarly he denies any natural connection between the *malaka* of the Arabic language and the Arabs as an ethnicity (ibid.: 143, 146). Yet when dealing with the corruption of the linguistic *malaka* among the Arabs beyond the formative centuries of Islam, he seems to associate this *malaka* to the Arabs. For example, he suggests that non-Arabs cannot acquire the *malaka* of Arabic unless they have grown up among Arabs (ibid.: 143–4). This link between the *malaka* of Arabic and the Arabs becomes more evident in Ibn Khaldūn's understanding of the status of the former as an index of that of the latter. The corruption of this *malaka*, in his view, results from and marks the decline of the political and civilisational strength of the Arabs (ibid.: 144–7). It is based on this understanding that some modern Arab intellectuals highlight the importance of the sustenance/revival of Arabic to the sustenance/revival of the Arab nation, as can be found in many examples of the ALA discourse analysed in this book.

6. Traditionally, Arabic grammar and Islamic jurisprudence had many goals and methods in common. Both 'depended on the interpretation of a textual corpus to derive rules for human behavior' (Carter 2007: 187), and both resorted to principles such as *qiyās* 'analogy' and *istiṣḥāb al-ḥāl* 'presumption of continuity' for rule derivation (Suleiman 1999a). These two disciplines were further linked in that they were both connected, albeit in different degrees, to Islamic revelation and were both used to offer correct 'paths' (*sunan*) for Muslims to follow in their social and linguistic lives. In the modern age, both were challenged by the legal and intellectual dominance of Western modernity, and the thesis of 'opening the gate of *ijtihād*' was seen as a response to modernity in intellectual debates in both disciplines. It was therefore fairly reasonable to see the analogy between the destiny of Arabic and that of Islamic law in ʾAmīn's writing.
7. Ḍayf reports that 'this proposal provoked a big outcry in the press and the [Cairo] Academy itself because of the severance this proposal would cause between contemporary Arabs and the glorious religious, scientific, and literary heritage of their ancestors' (1984: 182–3).
8. I have discussed, early in this chapter and also in Chapter 3, a similar thesis in the ALA discourse that links the rise and fall of Arabic with that of the political strength of the Arabs. Here I want to further contextualise this thesis with Ibn Khaldūn's (d. 1406) theory of the rise and fall of urban civilisations, which was revived in both the Arab-Islamic world and the West in the nineteenth and twentieth centuries to explain the ascendancy of the West and the decline of the East in modern times.
9. The word *ḥulla* can be easily linked to *ḥall* 'solution' because they have the same triliteral root *ḥ-l-l*. This may be a paronomasia indicating that granting Arabic a new face is actually a solution to the language's problems.
10. Al-Shabībī did not clarify who were with and who were against Arabic. A clearer description of these people could be found in al-Jamālī (1969), which will be discussed in the following section.

11. The original verse is *fa-ʾammā al-zabad fa-yadhhab jufāʾ, wa-ʾammā mā yantafiʿ al-nās fa-yamkuth fī al-ʾarḍ* 'as for the foam, it vanishes, [being] cast off; but as for that which benefits the people, it remains on the earth' (Qur'an 13: 17).
12. The concept 'hover and encircle' is reminiscent of the rite of *ṭawāf* during *ḥajj* and *ʿumra* pilgrimages to Mecca, where pilgrims should circumambulate the Kaaba seven times. This centripetal movement symbolically reveals and enhances the central position of Islam in the life and belief of Muslims. In his work *Magnetism* (Porter et al. 2012: 252–3), the Saudi artist Ahmed Mater al-Ziad uses a magnet and iron filings to depict the spectacle of *ṭawāf*, which captures the very essence of the relation between Islam and Muslims. It is highly possible that Fahmī sees the relation between the Qur'an and Arabic linguists in the same manner.
13. Wells (2006: 223) reports that 'originating as an artificial language, [Esperanto] is unique in that it has enjoyed sufficient success to have acquired a speech community and even to have undergone a degree of creolization'. Nonetheless, Esperanto is still far from being a widely used lingua franca in the world, not to mention becoming a universal language.
14. In 2010, UNESCO decided that 18 December, 'the day in 1973 when the General Assembly approved Arabic as an official UN language', should be the annual UN Arabic Language Day (*UN News* 2010).
15. Kassab (2010: 117) reports that this conference was ambitiously wide in terms of its topics but 'failed to attract contributions that would have allowed the conference to do justice to [these] topics'.
16. The reason for Fayṣal to include Vietnam as an example here is not clear and needs further research to reveal the motivations and ideologies behind the (mis-)perception of each other, among peoples in the 'Orient', the Global South, or the 'periphery' in the modern world-system.

6

Conclusion: The Ideologisation of Language via Language Symbolism

The analysis of the discursive habiti of the ALA discourse in the previous chapters shows that this discourse, as a vibrant representative of the genre of linguistics sociopolitical in the Arabic-speaking world, partakes in two long-lasting struggles of the Arabs in modern times: a struggle with a dual definition of the national self and a struggle with a chequered revival and modernisation in a peripheralised position in the modern world-system. The discourse does so through the two processes of language symbolism: first, indexication that naturalises and 'factualises' the concurrence of the linguistic and the socio-political; and second, proxification that uses language as a proxy to address and alleviate sociopolitical concerns. The linguistic ideal – a strong national standard of Arabic, devoid of diglossia and foreignness and used in all domains of public communication – and the sociopolitical ideal – an empowered, unified Arab nation able to catch up with modernity and stand on a par with the West in the modern world-system – are believed to concur with each other. Deviation from the former ideal is treated as language 'problems', and deviation from the latter is seen as sociopolitical 'predicaments'. The 'problems' are seen as indexes to the 'predicaments'. Arabic LPLP, accordingly, aims not only to solve the 'problems' but also, in doing so, to tackle the 'predicaments'. In other words, language is not the only and ultimate object of LPLP as is commonly understood. The sociopolitical is. Language accordingly serves as a proxy for extra-linguistic causes.

The entanglement among language, ideology and sociopolitical concerns in the ALA discourse illustrates how language symbolism acts as an important and marked mechanism of the language-ideology interface in the Arabic-speaking world. In this concluding chapter, I give a systematic description of this mechanism in and beyond the Arabic setting. I first compare it with another, communication-based language-ideology mechanism to highlight some distinctive features of language symbolism. Next, I discuss the effects of language symbolism on the sociopolitical realm as well as the consequences of de-symbolisation. Finally, I bring up the notion of dual anxiety as a driving force behind language symbolism in 'Oriental' societies, with a comparison between the script Romanisation movements in the Arabic-speaking world and in China to demonstrate. I hope my description will be a step forward in understanding and theorising 'the ideologisation of language via language symbolism' – a widespread phenomenon in our sociolinguistic life.

Characteristics of the Ideologisation of Language via Language Symbolism

As a mechanism of language-ideology interface in the Arabic-speaking world, language symbolism operates via discourse, so I call it ideology-in-discourse. It accords with, differs from and complements language indexicality, another mechanism of language-ideology interface which functions through linguistic communication. I call this second mechanism ideology-in-communication. It should be noted that indexicality is a mode of semiotics, which is not exclusive to ideology-in-communication. As I have showed in the previous chapters, indexicality is attested in and indispensable to language symbolism. However, since currently indexicality is mostly studied in the ethnography of communication, it becomes a convenient label for the second mechanism. A comparison of the two mechanisms reveals characteristics of the ideologisation of language via language symbolism.

To begin with, both mechanisms work on the non-referential dimension and the social meaning of language. Many 'mainstream' linguistic models reduce 'linguistic meaning to denotation, or "reference," and predication' and emphasise 'the work of language in providing "words for things"' (Kroskrity 2004: 500). But language does more than merely refer to the external world and convey ideas from the mind. It is also indexical, as formal and stylistic variations in language use index social differences: settings, topics, positions, institutions and, ultimately, identities of language users. It is also symbolic, as conceptions of language make language stand for the extra-linguistic world, so the linguistic realm is manipulated to project power relations and partake in power negotiations in the sociopolitical realm. It is in this indexical and symbolic dimension of language that ideology exerts its influence and dominates, because indexical and symbolic meanings are not arbitrary but always contextual and positional. The concurrence and correlation between the linguistic and the sociopolitical is not a natural given but is constructed and reconstructed in line with the dynamism of ideology in different contexts.

Within the two mechanisms, however, ideology works in different terrains of the 'non-referential'. Within language indexicality, ideology functions on the 'orders of indexicality' of language forms and styles in speech acts or communicative events, activating, manipulating and contextually remaking extant indexical connections between formal and stylistic variation and social difference to do identity work. For example, Ghāda ʿAbbūd, a journalist based in Alexandria, deliberately wrote in the Alexandrian dialect after a church bombing in Alexandria on New Year's Eve 2011 to imply 'a shared identity that surpasses religious differences' and sectarian violence. This political message was delivered through an incremental effect of three orders of the indexicality of the dialectal form in actual language use: being an Alexandrian (*n*-th order indexicality), being a typical Alexandrian who is 'tough, helpful, and cannot be deceived easily by outsiders' (*n*+1st order indexicality) and being a typical Alexandrian who 'shares an identity with Christians' and 'does not differentiate between people according to religion' (*n*+2nd order indexicality) (Bassiouney 2014: 60–1). Within language symbolism, by contrast, ideology works on the conceptions of language in discourse to construct a naturalised, inseverable link between the linguistic and the sociopolitical. We have seen that the discursive habiti of the ALA discourse are sustained by a doxic notion in Arab society that sees the Arabic language and the Arab people as in a bond of common destiny; what happens to the former will naturally involve the latter and vice versa.

Different terrains of the 'non-referential' entail different modes of ideologisation. Language indexicality is based on verbal communication, while language symbolism is embedded in meta-linguistic discourse. The multiple orders of indexicality are not directly articulated but performed together with the referential function of language in communication. Their uptake and reception depend on contexts of individual communicative events. The ideologies that nurture language indexicality are always hidden beneath the surface layer of communication. Symbolic meanings of language, by contrast, are not performed but conveyed through words. This, however, does not mean that language symbolism is always explicitly articulated and the ideologies sustaining it can be straightforwardly inferred. Quite the contrary, as the case of the ALA discourse demonstrates: symbolic conceptions of language are often banal and unfelt and need to be established via a close analysis of the statements made and phrases and metaphors used in the discourse. The ideologies that frame these conceptions are also elusive, especially when they are in the form of doxa deeply rooted in collective unconsciousness of the language community in question.

The communicative and discursive modes of ideologisation differ in their relationship with the referential function of language. Language indexicality is concomitant with reference, and reference is the backbone of indexicality. Without reference, indexicality has no base to work on. In a speech act or a communicative event, reference and indexicality work through the same language, albeit within different meaning systems, referential-denotational meaning and social meaning respectively. Language symbolism is conveyed through but nonetheless independent from the referential function of the meta-linguistic discourse. Language symbolism and discursive reference involve two different languages. One is the language that is talked about, and the other is the language that is talked in. The term 'meta-linguistic' and the fact that the ALA discourse uses Arabic to talk about Arabic imply the convergence of the 'talked-in' and the 'talked-about'. This is misleading. The language used in the discourse to construct symbolism is not necessarily the language that is imbued with this symbolism. It is common to see *ʿammiyya* supporters write in *fuṣḥā* and *fuṣḥā* defenders speak in *ʿammiyya*. Symbolism and reference are separate processes.

Separation from reference allows language symbolism to move freely between concordance with and detachment from the linguistic reality – the actual language situation and language use. Language indexicality, conversely, is restrained. Concomitant with reference, indexicality and its underlying ideology are confined in the acceptable compass of language use in the language community. Only forms and styles actually used in communication can partake in the game of indexicality. The work of ideology is therefore as curtailed as dancing in chains. By contrast, its work on symbolism is not. Symbolic conceptions of language can go beyond the linguistic reality to be tailored to meet the need of standing for the sociopolitical, wherever the need goes. The structure, status and history of language can be conceptualised separately from (but not independently of) the reality. In language symbolism, language is subject to a more potent, less restrained ideologisation. Ideology often creates a symbolic world of language parallel to and floating above the actual one. This symbolic world can be very unrealistic. Mismatch between the symbolic and the real language situations is often not an exception but the norm. The leeway that ideology has to make, maintain, modify and manipulate this mismatch is a fundamental feature that differentiates language symbolism from language indexicality.

Effects of the Ideologisation of Language via Language Symbolism

This ideology-made, symbolic world of language exerts a variety of effects on the sociopolitical causes it engages in as a proxy. The ALA discourse showcases three of these effects. The first is symbolic compliance. This is to comply with, justify and support expected change of the status quo in the sociopolitical arena. In the early twentieth century, the narrative of the rise, decline and revival of the Arabic language was constructed in the ALA discourse to support the much-anticipated revival of the Arab nation, whose modern organisation was still vague in shape. In the 1930s and 1940s, the three language reform/revival proposals in the ALA discourse were largely in line with three orientations of social reform, ranging between a return to the pristine 'golden age' and a radical 'catching up' with modernity. The call for integrating varieties of Arabic around *fuṣḥā* in the ALA discourse in the 1950s and 1960s was to facilitate the formation of responsive citizenry in individual Arab states and the competition over regional ascendency in the name of pan-Arab unity. The above examples show that, when a sociopolitical orientation is believed to be likely to change the status quo, language symbolism can be tailored to boost public confidence in this likelihood. LPLP accordingly becomes an ally of sociopolitical agendas.

The second effect is symbolic resistance. This refers to the employment of language symbolism to battle against the displeasing status quo that is hard to change. It is most evident in the two discursive habiti of the ALA discourse on Arabi(ci)sation. As discussed in Chapter 4, the emphasis on the inalienability between Arabic and the Arab people together with a call for language equilibrium constitute a symbolic resistance to the peripheralisation of the Arabs in the modern world-system. This peripheral status is a product of the centuries-long change of the overall global power structure from the sixteenth century onwards, which is yet to be challenged. The increasing incrimination of the spread of foreign languages as linguistic invasion in the ALA discourse following the traumatising defeat in the 1967 war with Israel offers another example of symbolic resistance to an impossible reality.

The third effect is symbolic compensation. When a promised sociopolitical change fails to be delivered in reality, this promise can live on in the discursively constructed world of language to compensate for the failure. The ALA discourse on diglossia from the mid-1970s onwards is illustrative. The once heightened pan-Arabism declined and gave way to overt pre-eminence of state interests, and the prospect of building a civic, contractual, meritocratic and integrated polity was diminished by the resurgence of sectarianism and tribalism, the rise of cronyism and rent-seeking, the persisting gap between the rich and the poor, and the increasing solidification of social strata. The disparity between the anticipated revival, modernisation and development, on the one hand, and the disappointing reality, on the other, led to a widespread social malaise and a legitimacy crisis of the ruling regimes. In this context, the ALA discourse, through its praise for the beautiful *fuṣḥā*, its lament about colloquialism in classroom and media, and its persistent calls for integrating *fuṣḥā* and *ʿammiyya*, kept the unfulfilled anticipation alive. It did so by reinforcing the causality that scapegoated diglossia for political fragmentation, social division and underdevelopment, and envisioned pan-Arab solidarity, social cohesion and development through linguistic unity. This envisioned linguistic ideal compensated for the repetitive failure in delivering promised sociopolitical change, thence mitigating the above-mentioned social malaise and legitimacy crisis. In a similar manner, the rhetorical dedication to Arabi(ci)sation and language equilibrium in the ALA discourse also served to compensate for the endurance of English or French in business, technology and education, resulting from the Arab dependence on the West in the global structure of economy and knowledge.

It should be emphasised that the above compliance, resistance and compensation are symbolic. They alone cannot change the actual situation, linguistic and sociopolitical alike. Moreover, for these effects to be effective and sustainable, they have to be always built on and confined to language symbolism. This is the secret of the survival of the ALAs for the past century. Had they been purely language planners, they would not have survived, as they proved to be weak in language policy-making and implementation. They managed to survive because they acted as purveyors of the symbolism of language that was continuously needed in a world characterised by sociopolitical vulnerability and impotence.

In cases where language symbolism is enforced upon the reality it is incompatible with, which may be termed as 'de-symbolisation of language symbolism', undesirable, sometimes tragic consequences follow. The Arabi(ci)sation policy in post-independence Algeria is an example. Upon independence, Arabi(ci)sation, a combination of 'the replacement of French by Arabic in all walks of life' (Arabicisation) and the 'linguistic and cultural assimilation for national unity and the affirmation of an identity that is exclusively Arab and Muslim' (Arabisation), moved from rhetoric to policy, from symbolism to reality (Benrabah 2013: 53). Eager to boost their legitimacy resting on the promised decolonisation and building of a new Algeria in line with its 'authentic' Arab-Islamic identity, Algerian regimes in the 1960s and 1970s resorted to zealous and hasty Arabi(ci)sation in education, ignoring the then very unfavourable language situation, marked by a high rate of illiteracy in Arabic, a de facto Arabic-French bilingualism, and a severe lack of Arabic instructors and textbooks. Nonetheless, the political motivation was so high that ʾAḥmad Ṭālib al-ʾIbrāhīmī, Minister of Education (1965–70), once declared: 'This [Arabization] will not work, but we have to do it . . .' (Grandguillaume 1995: 18).

Enforced Arabi(ci)sation led to social division and conflicts in Algeria along identity lines. It alienated and radicalised both the Arabophones and the Berberphones. The youth educated in the Arabic monolingual tract were disappointed by the low quality of education and the limited access to the job market, which favoured children of French-speaking elites, after graduation. Social mobility was curtailed. The dimming prospects, together with a doctrinal understanding of Islam they acquired through the learning of Arabic, drove many of the Arabophones to fundamentalism, culminating in the showdown between the army and the Islamists in the 1990s. As for the Berbers, Arabi(ci)sation, with its uncompromising monolingualism, deprived them of the right to be educated in their mother tongues. This deprivation in the name of national unity ignited anti-Arab and extremist Berberist movements to resist the assimilation endeavour of the state. Riots and even armed resistance recurred in the Berber regions throughout the post-independence era, the most severe one being the 'Berber Spring' of 1980. These language-induced conflicts constitute the legacy of the 'de-symbolisation of language symbolism' in Algeria, which still haunts Algerian society today. Whether the recent turn to multilingualism in official rhetoric and constitutional amendments can bring language conflicts back to the symbolic realm is not yet clear. Yet it will be extremely challenging to mend the social fracture of a decades-long making. For now, language remains a cause of identity politics in Algeria and in the Maghreb in general (Benrabah 2013; Lefevre 2015).

Causes of the Ideologisation of Language via Language Symbolism

The ALA discourse and its routinisation and banalisation evident in the discursive habiti show that language has been subject to continuous ideologisation in the Arabic-speaking world. The cause behind this, as I have demonstrated in the previous chapters, lies in the two *longue dureé* sociopolitical circumstances of the twentieth-century Arabic-speaking world – duality of Arab nationalisms and Arab peripherality. Their endurance purpurates widespread anxiety or even malaise in Arab society, and the ideologised language world, with its symbolic effects to tackle the impossible reality (scapegoating language for the sociopolitical wrong and envisioning the causality from language change to sociopolitical change), serves as a psychological relief. Suleiman (2014: 59) uses the concept of 'language anxiety' to explain such anxiety-induced language symbolism:

> I use the term 'language anxiety' to refer to heightened and generalized concerns about language that straddle the linguistic and extralinguistic worlds, coming to the fore at times of stress, crisis, or conflict in society. Language anxiety is future oriented and demands vigilance to ensure that the perceived dangers it anticipates – the decline of the language both instrumentally and symbolically – do not come to pass, hence its role as a motivating factor in task-orientation in society. In this sense, language anxiety is anxiety about language (its communicative instrumentality in society) that goes beyond language (what it symbolizes sociopolitically for the society in question).

Neither language anxiety nor language symbolism is unique to the Arabic-speaking world. It is attested across human societies, including America, Britain and France (Amin 2000; Machan 2009; Suleiman 2011a) – the primary norm-setters of the now globalising modernity. However, the modern Arab anxiety differs from those of the latter societies in that it involves a dual anxiety of modernity and civilisation. The anxiety of modernity arose during the grand reorganisation and transformation of politics, economy and society, which gained unprecedented momentum and rapidity in some core areas of the Arabic-speaking world from the mid-nineteenth century onwards. The change was so overwhelming that it compelled the Arabs to accommodate a seemingly universal rationale of modernity and catch up with Europe through learning and reform. They needed to do so urgently since time did not allow them to replicate stage by stage the process that had transformed the 'West'. They had to telescope the stages towards modernity. In the Arab context, this anxiety was aggravated by an additional anxiety – the anxiety of civilisation, for the rise of the 'West' as the epitome of modernity and the core of the modern world-system posed a sharp contrast with the glorious past of the Arabs, when their ancestors, instead of the Europeans, acted as the norm-setters of order and civilisation, if not globally, then at least in the wide territory where their influence reached. This reversed civilisational status brought on a sense of frustration and humiliation, and growing colonialism and imperialism of the 'West' by the turn of the twentieth century only worsened the situation.

The Arabs, again, were not alone in experiencing this dual anxiety. It was commonly shared by those peoples who once had a thriving civilisation but had to, with the rise and global spread of Western modernity, adapt to a new world order not of their making. They were the peoples of the so-called 'Orient'. When Edward Said blames the Orientalism of the Western Orientalists for producing 'the ideological suppositions, images and fantasies about a currently important and politically urgent region of the world called the Orient' (1986: 211), he occults another Orientalism – the 'Orientalism of the Orientals'. Although this latter Orientalism is intended to search for an authentic self to counterbalance the Western hegemony, it draws on, according to Dirlik (1996), Euro-American scholarship in their self-evaluation and adopts the same logic of reductionist, essentialist demarcation of the East and the West as the former Orientalism. 'Self-essentialization may serve the cause of mobilization against "Western" domination; but in the very process it also consolidates "Western" ideological hegemony by internalizing the historical assumptions of orientalism' (ibid.: 114).

Yet what I want to highlight here is that the 'Orientalism of the Orientals' is not only featured by this paradox of resistance and complicity, but also derives from the common experience shared by the Oriental peoples of the unprecedented change of the global power structure not in their favour and the mutual identification and reference among themselves. In Egypt in the 1930s, for example, there was a marked turn towards the East to re-define the Egyptian self against the overt identification with the West and the enthusiasm for Westernisation in the 1920s. An 'Oriental link' (*rābiṭa sharqiyya*) was established to connect Egypt with the rest of the Arabic-speaking world and other Asian communities. The East was connected by a common suffering of the self-loss under the threat of Western modernity and imperialism and by a shared cause of revival, reform and progress while preserving the authenticity of the self. Among the Eastern nations, there were bad and good examples. For the Eastern-inclined Egyptian intellectuals, the Turkish model of modernisation based on a thorough emulation of the West needed to be rejected because it allowed alien materialism to overwhelm authentic spirituality. In contrast, they favoured the Japan's 'successful modernization accomplished with due regard for cultural authenticity' (Gershoni and Jankowski 1995: 43). In China in the early twentieth century, a similar attachment to the East also developed. Writings on 'the demised countries' in the East emerged to warn the Chinese of the cost of succumbing to Western monopoly. For example, the Japanese scholar Shiba Shirō's (d. 1922) *Ejiputo kindaishi* (Contemporary History of Egypt, 1889) was translated into Chinese to be used as a lesson of 'national collapses': Egypt, a once independent country with an ancient civilisation like China, lost its sovereignty when it became a protectorate of Britain in 1882 (Yu 2013: 5). The good example, in the Chinese context, was also Japan, whose path to modernisation was inspirational for those who were battling for the national revival in China. This 'Oriental link' persisted throughout the twentieth century, becoming an ideological basis of the Non-Aligned Movement and various forms of Third-Worldism.

Nowadays, with the economic rise of China bringing renewed hope of an East-led new international order, China fever is spreading across the Arabic-speaking world. Many Arab intellectuals are eager to establish what may be termed the Chinese model of development. However, the old hierarchy in the current world-system remains unchanged. China fever is becoming a new lodge of the unfulfilled dream of the 'Oriental revival'. Recurring hope and frustration over the past century perpetuate the dual anxiety of modernity and civilisation defined earlier, which is a cornerstone of the Orientalism of the Orientals.

Script Romanisation in China and the Arabic-Speaking World

The above discussion of the Orientalism of the Orientals paves the way for the final argument of the book: the ideologisation of language via language symbolism is not confined to the Arabic-speaking world but is attested in other 'Oriental' societies as well, with the above-defined dual anxiety being a common driving force. The comparison below of the script Romanisation movements in China and the Arabic-speaking world is illustrative.

Script Romanisation movements in China began in the final decades of the nineteenth century with the European and American missionaries who, puzzled by the disaccord between speaking and writing in China that they believed to be a major cause of mass illiteracy and ignorance, used Roman letters to render the Bible into local vernaculars. Some native intellectuals, humiliated by the Chinese defeat in the First Sino-Japanese War (1894–5), which led to the dissolution of the China-centred order in East Asia and the ensuing dominance of Japan, devised a total of twenty-eight schemes of phonetic alphabets to promote mass literacy and enlightenment to modern 'Western' knowledge, for they believed this was the secret behind the rise of Japan. The Ministry of Education of the Republic of China announced in 1918 the official scheme of the *Qieyin* character[1] – *Zhuyin Zimu* 'phonetic alphabet', an adapted form of Chinese characters similar to and inspired by the phonetic kana symbols of Japanese. Following the May Fourth Movement of 1919, a more radical initiative of script reform was developed, deeming the Chinese characters a major obstacle in the way of the anticipated social and cultural revolution and calling for a new phonetic scheme based on the Roman alphabet to replace the characters. This new scheme, the reformers believed, would realise the concord between speaking and writing around a unified national language (*Guoyu*). In 1928, the Ministry of Education promulgated the new scheme as the second alphabet for the national language, to be used side by side with *Zhuyin Zimu*. In the 1930s, the Chinese communists, together with the Left who were convinced of a social revolution to rebuild China, initiated the Latinised New Writing Movement to enable the toiling masses to read and write in their own languages without knowing Chinese characters. And, finally, as a serious measure of state building, the government of the People's Republic of China promulgated the Latin-based *Pinyin* in 1958, as the official phonetic script of Chinese to facilitate the acquisition of the national language, renamed from *Guoyu* to *Putonghua* 'the common tongue'. Rhetorically, the government stuck to the ultimate Latinisation of Chinese well until the turn of the twenty-first century. In practice, no further Latinisation was implemented.[2]

Similarly to China, Romanisation movements in the Arabic-speaking world began with foreign initiatives. Orientalists and colonial expatriates were puzzled by a similar disaccord between writing and speaking in Arabic, now known as diglossia. Early in 1895, the Oxford scholar Francis W. Newman deemed the Arabic script insufficient to express modern nomenclature in his *Handbook of Modern Arabic* and called for the use of the Roman alphabet (Suleiman 2004: 64–5). In 1901, William Willcocks, an agricultural engineer in Cairo, called for Egyptian Arabic to be written using the Roman alphabet in his book *The Spoken Arabic of Egypt*. In 1922, the Beirut newspaper *La Syrie* proposed adopting Latin to replace the Arabic script (Shivtiel 1998: 187). The Arab Academy (now the Arabic Language Academy in Damascus) asked its member ʾIlyās Qudsī to reply, and he refuted the proposal completely (Qudsī 1923). Internally, the Egyptian Copt Salāma Mūsa (1887–1958) advocated the replacement of the Arabic script by the Latin alphabet in 1935. Persuaded by the English Orientalist Edward Denison (d. 1940), King Fuʾād I of Egypt during his reign (1922–36) invested great effort and funds to devise a new alphabet called *ḥurūf al-ṭāj* 'the crown letters' to replace the Arabic script. This scheme was not implemented. In 1944, ʿAbd al-ʿAzīz Fahmī sparked a bitter controversy at the annual convention of the Fuʾād I Academy for the Arabic Language (now the Arabic Language Academy in Cairo) with his partial Latinisation proposal. It was rejected. Thereafter, there were only sporadic discussions of script reform at the official level, and Romanisation was never raised again.[3]

The debates on script Romanisation in China and the Arabic-speaking world shared similar lines of argument, ideologising script to make it a proxy to respond to the dual anxiety of modernity and civilisation afflicting both the Chinese and the Arabs.

A major line of argument was the causality between the Roman/Latin script and progress and that between the native script and backwardness. The missionaries in China, challenged by a very different writing system from their own and what they perceived as stagnation, despotism and an illiterate mass to be enlightened, first constructed these causalities. The missionary W. N. Brewster published two famous articles, 'China's intellectual thraldom and the way to escape' and 'The evolution of new China', in 1901, in which he argued that Romanisation was necessary to improve the spirit and intellect of the Chinese. He attacked the Chinese writing system, describing it as a fortress of despotism and a symbol of slavery that were doomed to be overthrown (Ni 1948: 15–16). In 1903, the American missionary Rev. M. Hubber claimed that the difficult square characters were the most intriguing anachronism in the twentieth century and argued that the Roman script could make the rapid spread of new ideas possible (ibid.: 17). The missionaries active in China at the turn of the twentieth century generally associated the Chinese characters and the Roman script with the backwardness of Chinese society and the progress of theirs.

These missionaries, motivated by a sincere curiosity to reason out the developmental contrast between China and their own country, suggested that the native script was the one to blame and the Roman script the remedy to offer, thus attaching different civilisational values to the two writing systems. This was also the case for the Orientalists and colonial expatriates in the Arabic-speaking world. William Willcocks claimed that the Arabic script 'belongs to a pre-scientific age and people, and is wholly unfitted to represent the living sounds of a modern Arabic language [i.e. Egyptian Arabic]. For this we must have recourse to some modifications of the Latin alphabet' (1901: vi, quoted in Suleiman 2004).

Yet it was the native intellectuals who incorporated and developed this correlation between script and progress/backwardness, linking it to the rise and fall of nations and civilisations and how to rid their own nations and civilisations of stagnation and decadence for a modern rebirth. A more systematic exposition of the above correlation was developed among the native intellectuals during the *Qieyin* Character Movement. The renowned reformer Liang Qichao (d. 1929) clearly stated in 1902:

> The writing system is the first element for the invention of ways and implements. The complexity and simplicity of a writing system often correspond to the low and high degrees of civilisation of a nation. In

> all the nations, writing began with pictographs and then developed into phonetic letters. (Liang 2017: 46)

He further distinguished between the phonetic nations where writing and speaking are in accord with each other and the pictographic nations where they are not. The latter nations like China lag behind the scientific age because the people there use ossified script which cannot express their daily needs (ibid.: 46). Here we see a dual hierarchy, which projected a perceived hierarchy of nations onto the claimed hierarchy of writing systems. This view found wide resonance among the reformers. Justified by this dual hierarchy, reformers could move on to call for script reform based on a phonetic alphabet to rescue their impoverished and enfeebled country.

The causal link between script and progress became more radical from 1919, due to the stagnation of reform and the growing threat of imperial powers. Intellectuals of the May Fourth generation attacked the Chinese characters more fiercely and insisted on Romanisation as the only viable means of script reform. Their representative Qian Xuantong (d. 1939) claimed in 1925 that the difference between pictographic and phonetic writing is the difference between barbarism and civilisation and that sticking to the Chinese characters was tantamount to a perpetual degradation of the Chinese nation into barbarism (Qian 1999b: 350).

The Latinised New Writing movement gave this causal link a Marxist interpretation. Qu Qiubai (d. 1935), an early leader of the Chinese Communist Party, was heavily influenced by the theories of Mikolai Jakovlevich Marr (d. 1934), which dominated Soviet linguistics from 1929 to 1950 (Du Feu 2006). Marr divided world languages into four stages of evolution and understood them as a reflection of the different stages of the development of the material culture. Chinese was ascribed to the first stage, while the Semitic and Indo-European languages the fourth. Qu thus claimed in 1931 that the Chinese characters are 'a backward medieval language' and 'a corpse in the history of social development'. He considered the Chinese language and the Chinese script backward due to the backwardness of economic development and the simplicity and barbarism of social relations. It was incumbent on the Chinese, he argued, to launch a thorough script revolution, abolishing the Chinese characters and adopting a phonetic alphabet. Without this revolution, neither literature nor science could develop in China to enable Chinese society to adapt to modern life (Qu 1998: 212–13).

Supporters of script Romanisation in the Arabic-speaking world exhibited similar tendencies to correlate progress and backwardness with types of script. If we follow the logic of script hierarchy delineated above and assume Chinese characters are pictographic,[4] then the Arabic script is less backward than the Chinese one because it is phonetic. However, it was still considered inferior to the Roman/Latin script because the former is only a consonantal alphabet (known as an abjad) while the latter is a full alphabet representing both consonants and vowels. In Arabic, short vowels are represented by diacritics which are often omitted in writing and print. Like the non-phonetic Chinese, the Arabic script, it was argued, also caused the disaccord between speaking and writing because, without vowel representation, most Arabs would not know how to read the written text correctly. It follows that the Arabic script, albeit belonging to the phonetic camp, is deficient and backward, and this backwardness of the script is a correlate of the backwardness of the Arab nation and the Arab-Islamic civilisation in the modern age.

One of the most outspoken voices in this regard was ʿAbd al-ʿAzīz Fahmī. In his memorandum of the Latinisation proposal distributed to the delegates of the annual convention of the Cairo Academy in 1944, he did not shy away at all from denouncing Arabic and its script. He began the memo by assuming a perspective from the Orientalists, claiming that 'the British, French, Italian, German and American Orientalists would be surprised by us the weak people who bend their backs in front of the statue of the [Arabic] language to carry a burden of the past 1500 years' (MLAQ 1946: 1). He moved on to critique the disaccord between speaking and writing, lamenting the increasing gap between *fuṣḥā* and *ʿammiyya* and the unwillingness of any Arab government to intervene. Contrasting the language situation in the Arabic-speaking world with the accordance between speaking and writing around a national language in European states, Fahmī described the Arabs as 'the most wretched creature of the God' (ibid.: 3). What caused the miserable situation was *fuṣḥā*, which was too difficult for the commoners to learn. He claimed that the Arabic language was a reason for the backwardness of the Orient (ibid.: 8). Yet for him, the remedy was not abandoning *fuṣḥā* in favour of *ʿammiyya*. In his view, the root cause was not the language per se but the incompetent script. Unable to represent vowels, the script became a barrier between the Arab people and *fuṣḥā*. The only viable way to tackle this problem was to reform the script, adopting the mechanism of the Latin script, especially its vowel representation. He linked this latter feature to the status of progress, stating that 'all the nations using vowel letters in their writing are advanced in science and industry – they are the peoples of Europe and America', and 'all the nations not using vowel letters such as China, Iran, Turkey (before now) and the Arabs are backward in science and industry' (ibid.: 9–10). Here, the script-progress link was clearly and directly articulated.

The above survey of the script-progress link in the words of those advocating Romanisation in both the Chinese and Arabic settings demonstrates that script was indeed used by Chinese and Arabs to tackle and alleviate the dual anxiety of modernity and civilisation. The Chinese script and the Arabic alphabet, regardless of the significant difference between them, were both evaluated as inferior to the Roman/Latin alphabet. This script hierarchy did not seem convincing because of the structural advancements of the Roman/Latin alphabet over the other two systems but more because of an apparent extra-linguistic reality – the most advanced and powerful nations of the time all used this script. Therefore, the idea of script hierarchy could not be objective and innocent of non-academic influence. It was indeed a projection of a new world order and a proxy to deal with the perceived rise of the 'West' and the fall of the 'Orient', which caused the dual anxiety.

It is also worthwhile looking at the counter-arguments to see how those who opposed Romanisation rejected the script-progress link. An obvious strategy was to replace hierarchy with difference. For example, Zhang Taiyan (d. 1936), an uncompromising opponent of the Romanisation of Chinese during the *Qieyin* Character Movement, pointed out that language is a social and historical being, so social and historical difference will naturally lead to variation in language and script, and this difference does not necessarily correspond to progress and backwardness (Zhao 2012: 45). ʿAlī al-Jārim (d. 1949), in his refutation of Fahmī's proposal, resorted to the medieval history of the Arabic-speaking world and Europe, when the former used a consonantal alphabet and the latter a full alphabet, but the Arabs were the most advanced in the world and the Europeans were in their dark age (MLAQ 1946: 53). Here al-Jārim deprived the pro-Romanisation judgement about progress and backwardness of its modern context, understanding this judgement as one of power relations between nations and civilisations only. Refuting the script-progress link was intended to alleviate the anxiety caused by the inferior status of the Arabs in a 'West'-dominated world-system.

The counter-arguments also adopted a second strategy to elevate and downgrade the positions of Arabic and Latin respectively within the established hierarchy. A number of opponents of Fahmī's proposal pointed to the fallacies of the English and French alphabets and their rules of spelling, demonstrating how these alphabets fail to obey the 'one letter one sound' principle that Fahmī was proud of as a merit of his Latinisation scheme. In the meantime, many of the delegates praised highly the Arabic language and script, reinterpreting the difficulties and defects Fahmī listed as unparalleled advantages over other languages and scripts. In their view, lacking vowel letters makes the Arabic script concise and flexible to accommodate the widespread dialectal variation across the Arabic-speaking world while maintaining the unity around *fuṣḥā*. The merit of flexibility also lies in the fact that many non-Arabic-speaking Muslims adopted the Arabic script to represent their own languages without much difficulty.

This strategy was also adopted in the Romanisation debates in China. Zhang Taiyan spoke highly of the non-phonetic nature of the Chinese characters. He considered it a cause for the diachronic stability of the Chinese script, which would boost linguistic unity of the Chinese nation. He warned that Romanisation at the cost of the extant characters would lead to a rupture of the future generations with the cultural tradition of the nation (Zhao 2012: 54). Qian Xuantong, before advocating the link between the Chinese characters and barbarism, had been a defender of this non-phonetic writing system. He stated in 1910:

> The writing system of our country is the earliest, its structure is the best and its utility is the most comprehensive. Truly, these are enough to crown it among the writing systems of other countries . . . The writing system of a nation is the banner of its people. To discard it is to let the nation perish. (Qian 1999a: 313)

Qian's change of tone from one pole of the argument to the other was most striking. This change needs an explanation beyond the scope of the current analysis, yet it is highly illustrative of the ideology-driven proxification of script in Romanisation movements. It shows that the evaluation of the Chinese script could indeed change with socio-political contingencies and ideological stances beyond its seemingly innocent instrumentality as a medium of writing and communication.

There was a reason for a script to be a proxy to symbolically address the dual anxiety. From the nineteenth century onwards, modernity, with both its appealing commitment to an unstoppable betterment of human society and its appalling destruction of extant social order and renegotiation of power relations among nations and civilisations, encroached nearly every corner of society and social life in China and the Arabic-speaking world. The change was so rapid and the threat to national and civilisational survival so imminent that there was little time for a thorough structural adjustment as a proper response to the pressure of modernity. Compared with any long-term structural reform, script change seemed to be much quicker and easier and less harmful to the extant social order. The script, together with the national costume, infrastructure and city landscape, were considered as the external façade of a civilisation whose change was likened to cosmetic surgery that would not damage the essence. This was indeed the case in the Chinese and Arabic script Romanisation movements, where reformers insisted that script was merely an instrument of writing and a surface layer of language. An illustration of this tendency was Fahmī's metaphors that depicted Arabic script as 'an unfit garment' enforced on the Arabic language and 'an obscure image' not reflecting the beauty of the language at all (MLAQ 1946: 8; see also Chapter 5). Therefore, in the minds of the reformers, script Romanisation was probably a good proxy to alleviate the duel anxiety, for it would quickly give the nation and civilisation in question a modern image and, at the same time, leave their very essence intact.

Opponents of Romanisation, however, considered script an indispensable part of their nation and civilisation and a constituent of their identity. They were agitated by the indifference shown towards the values embedded in the native script. For them, script Romanisation meant loss of self and submission to the external Other. They therefore fiercely defended the native script as if they were defending the nation and civilisation. Here again, script was used as a proxy, not for reform but for defence, which constituted another response to the dual anxiety.

Prevalence of the Ideologisation of Language via Language Symbolism

The comparative study above and its dialogue with the Orientalism of the Orientals imply that the ideologisation of language via language symbolism is part of our sociolinguistic life. It is prevalent and vibrant. Recent decades provide ample examples.

In the Arabic-speaking world, the Arab Spring and its challenge to the legitimacy of extant Arab regimes ignited a new tug of war among parties and segments of Arab societies to negotiate their national identities, which involved language as a proxy. In Egypt, a new wave of territorial nationalism correlating a unique, authentic and largely secular Egyptian identity with Egyptian *ʿāmmiyya*, perceived as a language unrelated to and independent of *fuṣḥā*, arose years before the Arab Spring and played a vital role in countering the Islamists, who advocated *fuṣḥā* as a key ingredient of Egyptian identity, during and after the toppling of Mohamed Morsi in 2013 (Aboelezz 2018). In the meantime, however, *ʿāmmiyya* was associated with claimed foreign conspiracy to deny the participants in the 2011 protest as fake Egyptians, driving the protests to demonstrate their competence in *fuṣḥā* as a reaction, on the one hand, and Fārūq Shūsha (d. 2016), the late secretary of the Cairo Academy, to openly legitimate, after the fall of Hosni Mubarak's regime, the cause of the 'revolutionary youth' for their self-identification with *fuṣḥā*, on the other (Bassiouney 2014: 294–340).[5] A recent move came from the Cairo Academy. In 2018, in collaboration with Sūlāf Darwīsh, a member of the Egyptian parliament, the Academy pressured the cabinet and the parliament to discuss a draft of the Law on the Endorsement of Arabic (*Qanūn al-nuhūḍ bi-l-lugha al-ʿarabiyya*) to ensure the supremacy of Arabic, referring here to *fuṣḥā*, in all walks of Egyptian life. No progress on this matter has been reported since (ʿIwaḍ al-Lāh 2018; ʿAbd al-Raḥmān 2018).

In Morocco, the Arab Spring intensified an already heated debate on linguistic pluralism. ʿAbd al-Qādir al-Fāsī al-Fihrī (2011), a veteran linguist and the president of the Moroccan Linguistic Association, spoke on 'language revolution' (*al-thawra al-lughawiyya*) in early 2011, calling for language policy in Morocco to be reformulated in line with the principles of dignity, civil rights, democracy and pluralism that were endorsed in the protests across the region. While the regime complied and resorted to linguistic pluralism to counteract the spillover of the Arab Spring into their country, it also instigated a new battle over language and identity among liberals, nationalists and Islamists, and among Arabophones, Francophones and Berberphones (Lefevre 2015). In July 2011, the regime forced the constitution to be modified to recognise Tamazight as the second official language alongside Arabic, in an obvious bid to undermine Berber support for a potentially country-wide anti-regime protest. In 2015, a national debate broke out over the introduction into primary education of the *dārija*, the Moroccan colloquial form of Arabic, with the liberals, who supported the agenda, pitting themselves against the nationalists and the Islamists, who fiercely opposed it, to defend the Arab and Islamic components of Moroccan identity. In 2019, a legislative bill reinstalling French as a language of instruction for science subjects in Moroccan schools sparked an outcry in Moroccan political and intellectual circles. The bill was considered to be a triumph of the Francophone lobby, and the Islamist Justice and Development Party (PJD) that led the ruling coalition was faced with a crisis of internal division and criticisms from the opposition. Once a party that anchored its support on the rhetorical commitment to defending the status of Arabic in Morocco, it was now accused of complicity in re-empowering the colonial language at the cost of the decades-long cause of Arabi(ci)sation and the Moroccan identity (al-Talīdī 2019a; b). Clearly, in the case of Morocco, language was saturated with ideological significance and involved in power struggles and identity politics as a proxy.

Beyond the Arabic-speaking world, Chinese scholars are contemplating the role of language in poverty reduction and in sustaining the vision of a new international order in the Belt and Road Initiative. Kazakhs are debating their government's initiative to change Kazakh script from Cyrillic to Latin, with supporters enthusiastic about freedom from Russia's political and cultural influence and opponents concerned with the severance of future generations from the national written culture (Mirovalev 2019). The mainstream media in Quebec is linking authentic Canadian-French ancestry and Quebecois identity to monolingual competence in 'correct' French (Bosworth 2019). In African countries, ongoing debates on mother tongue-based education and multilingualism are caught between what Wolff (2017: 1) calls '19th century European nation state-ideology' and '20th/21st century African Renaissance-ideology'. The former derives from the historical experience of Europe and endorses linguistic and cultural homogeneity, while the latter is 'informed by anti-colonialist struggle and anti-imperialist philosophy which, further, rest on the recognition of sociolinguistic realities in Africa that are different from "the West," i.e. being characterised by extreme ethno-linguistic plurality and diversity' (ibid.). The global prevalence and vibrancy of the ideologisation of language via language symbolism to serve sociopolitical causes mean that a long-term commitment to studying and theorising this phenomenon is in demand.

Notes

1. *Qieyin*, roughly meaning 'phonetic transcription', refers to a way of using Chinese characters to represent the pronunciation of other characters, widely adopted in classical Chinese lexicography. However, in this movement, the medium of *Qieyin* was changed from full-shape characters to simple strokes extracted from the characters. Pioneers of the movement devised twenty-eight schemes of *Qieyin* characters. They were initially aimed at replacing the Chinese characters but in the end only became additional systems of phonetic transcription.
2. For a thorough review of the Romanisation movement of Chinese script, see Ni (1948), Zhao (2012) and Wang (2015), all of which are written in Chinese. For a history of the Chinese language reform around Modern Spoken Chinese, Modern Written Chinese and the modern Chinese writing system, the most informative and accessible text in English is Chen (1999).
3. An exception to this was the Lebanese nationalist Saʿīd ʿAql (d. 2014), who considered the Lebanese dialect an independent language separate from and more ancient than Arabic and published in 1961 a collection of his dialectal poems entitled *Yaara* in the Latin script he devised (Salameh 2010: 215–58). The influence of this individual effort cannot match what Fahmī exerted from the platform of the Cairo Academy – an official institute of Egypt, then the epicentre of modernisation and reform in the Arabic-speaking world.
4. This statement has been proved wrong. Although there are photographic residues in the Chinese writing system, it is, like other writing systems, a

mixture of phonetic and logographic representation and can be more precisely described as logo-syllabic. See Robinson (2009) for an accessible review of the typology of the writing systems around the world.

5. Fārūq Shūsha's position was consistent, as he had, in a televised debate on Al-Jazeera in 2008 before the Arab Spring, blamed Egypt's 'negligence of Arabic as its national language' and 'the lack of support of Arabic at the institutional level' for the failure of Egypt in 'joining the developed world' like Japan (Suleiman and Lucas 2012: 201).

Glossary

ʾabnāʾ al-ʿallāt	children of the concubines, or children whose fathers are Arab but whose mothers are non-Arab, referring to foreign borrowings in Arabic that happen to contain the same root letters as Arabic words do
ʾadā	(language as an) instrument
ʾaḍwāʾ	the light (of Arabic)
ʾaghzar manbaʿ	wealthier in being a source, used as a quality of *fuṣḥā*
ʿajamī	foreign
ʾalfāẓ al-ḥaḍāra	words of modern life
al-ʿāmma	the common people, or the low class
ʿāmmiyya	regional colloquial variety of Arabic
ʾanqāḍ	ruins, referring to *fuṣḥā* words or expressions that keep being used in *ʿāmmiyya*
ʿarabiyya	Arabic or the Arabic language, a cover term designating Arabic in its various forms, both synchronically and diachronically, but often referring to *fuṣḥā* only in Arab/Arabic discourse due to the high status of this variety in Arab-Islamic tradition and society
ʾaristuqrāṭiyya	aristocracy (of Arab linguists)
ʾaṣāla	authenticity
ʾasrā	(Arabs as modernity's) prisoners of war
ʾasraʿ min lamḥ al-baṣar	quicker than the glance of the eye, referring to the spread of Arabic during the Arab conquests

ʾasrār	secrets (of Arabic)
ʿāṣrī	modern
ʾasṭaʿ maṭlaʿ	brighter (of a beginning), used as a quality of *fuṣḥā*
ʿathra	(linguistic) deficiencies
ʾaṭyab martaʿ	richer (of a pasture), used to refer to a quality of *fuṣḥā*
ʾawḍāʿ	(linguistic) patterns
ʿawda	returning or restoring (the old status of Arabic)
ʾawsaʿ ṣadran	more broad-minded
ʾazma muzmina	chronic crisis, referring to endemic linguistic issues in the Arabic-speaking world such as Arabic diglossia
bahāʾ	beauty (of Arabic)
balad	country
balāgha	rhetoric
baʿth	renaissance (of Arabic)
baṭsh	(colonial) violence
bidʿa	heretical novelties (in the use of Arabic)
bināʾ	reconstruction (of Arabic)
bulaghāʾ	eloquent (Arabic) speakers or rhetoricians
būrjuwāziyya	bourgeoisie (of Arab linguists)
dakhīl	lexical borrowings
dalīl	proof, referring to Arabic as 'proof' of the unique customs and spirit of the Arabs, their glorious past and their civilisational achievements, as well as their political weakness in the age of decline
ḍarb	beating (Arabic)
dārija	regional colloquial variety of Arabic
Dhakhīrat al-lugha al-ʿarabiyya	*Treasure of the Arabic Language*, a pan-Arab project aiming at gathering and unifying neologisms from all over the Arabic-speaking world
dhātiyya	self
dhawq	(linguistic) taste
dhawq al-ʿāmm	common (linguistic) taste
dhawq mushtarak	collective (linguistic) taste
dunyā	horizon
farḍ ʿayn	individual duty
farḍ kifāya	collective duty
fasād	the erroneous use of *fuṣḥā* that has been accepted as normal in *ʿāmmiyya*

faṣāḥa	eloquence
faṣīḥa	articulate and eloquent (of a speaker); refined and elegant (of a language)
fawḍā	(linguistic) chaos
fawqiyya	superiority
fitna	civil strife
fiṭra salīma	uncorrupted intuition
fuṣḥā	the standard variety of Arabic used across Arabic-speaking communities, which is regarded to be the most elegant and eloquent variety of Arabic and a symbol of both Islam and the Arab people/nation
ghalaba	supremacy (of foreign languages over Arabic)
gharbala	sifting (of ideas)
ghazīr	abundant (of the 'spring' of Arabic heritage)
ghazw lughawī	linguistic invasion
ghiyāḍ	thickets, referring to *ʿāmmiyya* which is thought to be underdeveloped and unrefined
haddada	to threat
ḥadīqa ghannāʾ	a gorgeous garden, referring to *fuṣḥā* which is described as refined and elegant
ḥāja muliḥḥa	urgent need
ḥasab tālid	time-honoured esteem (of Arabic)
hawāʾ	(Arabic as) the air (the Arabs breathe)
ḥayawiyya	(linguistic) vitality
ḥayya	living (languages)
ḥikmat al-ʿarab	the 'wisdom of the Arabs' principle in the Arabic grammatical tradition which claims that the inner patterns of Arabic embody the genetic wisdom of the Arab people
ḥulla	dress, referring to the surface features of Arabic
ḥusn al-jars	sound harmony
huwiyya	identity
huwwa	chasm (between linguistic and social development)
iḍmiḥlāl	erasure (of Arabic)
ʾifsād	corrupting (Arabic)
ʾighnāʾ	enriching (Arabic)
inḥiṭāṭ	decline
iḥtilāl wa-istīlāʾ baghīḍ	hateful occupation (of Arab minds)
ʾiḥyāʾ	reviving (Arabic)

ijtihād	independent reasoning
ikhtiṣār	(linguistic) abridgement
ikhtizāl	abridgement, referring to the simplification of *fuṣḥā* codes in *ʿāmmiyya*
ʿilm	knowledge, including both religious scholarship and applied sciences, in traditional usage and science in modern usage (both meanings can be found in the ALA discourse)
ʾimmiyya	dualism
imtiyāz	privilege
ʾinʿāsh	revitalising (Arabic)
inḥilāl fī al-kiyān al-qawmī	dissolution of the national being
ʾinsāniyya	humanism
inziwāʾ	isolating (Arabic)
ʾiqlīmiyya	territorial nationalism
ʾiʿrāb	desinential inflection or declensional endings
ʾishʿāʿ	shining (the light of Arabic)
ishtiqāq	word-making via derivation from Arabic roots
ʾiṣlāḥ	reform
istawʿaba	to embrace or enclose (social and historical traits of the Arabs)
iʾtamma	to turn to, obey or follow
ʾithāra	a prod
ittisāʿ	expansion (as a form of quantitative social change)
izdiwājiyya lughawiyya	diglossia
ʿizza	pride
jabrūt	tyranny
jāhiliyya	the period of ignorance
jahl	ignorance
jawhar	essence
kāʾin ḥāyy	(language as a) living creature
kalām	speech
karāma	dignity
al-kathra al-ʿāmma al-muntija	the common manufacturing majority
al-khālidūn	the immortals, referring to the ALA members; a term translated from the French phrase *les immortels*, which is used to refer to the forty life members of the Académie française, but

	also carrying the Islamic and Arab-nationalist connotation of 'martyrs'
khaṣāʾiṣ	characteristics of (Arabic)
al-khāṣṣa	the elite or the high class
al-khaṭṭ al-ʾawwal	the front line (of defending Arabic)
khawājāt	Western expatriates and Westernised Egyptian elites who have privilege and enjoy high social status in Egypt
khawf	fear (for the destiny of Arabic)
khalāya ḥayya	live beehives (of the Arab nation), referring to priceless lexical treasures in *ʿāmmiyya*
khulūd	eternity (of Arabic)
kiyān	(Arabic as part of the) existence (of an Arab)
laḥn	grammatical errors considered to be caused by the contact between pure Arabic and various foreign languages during and after the Arab conquests
al-lugha al-ʿarabiyya al-salīma	the sound Arabic language, referring to the use of Arabic that complies with the established grammatical principles of Arabic
lugha nabaṭiyya	a Nabatean language
luguat al-ḍād	the language of *al-ḍād*, i.e. *fuṣḥā* Arabic
maʿāqil	strongholds or bastions (of Arabic language and culture), referring to the ALAs that defend the Arabic language and the Arab nation
madaniyya	civilisation
māddat ghufl	(language as) raw material
malaka	(linguistic) habit and aptitude
manāra mutalaʾliʾa	glittering lighthouse, referring to the Qur'an
al-manbaʿ al-ʾumm	(Arabic as) the foremost resource (of national life)
maṣādir	(linguistic) sources
maskh	(identity) metamorphosis
matn	(linguistic) corpus
mawhūm	delusional
maẓāhiru fārigha	hollow appearances (of modern civilisation)
minwāl al-farnaja	European experience
mirʾā	(Arabic as) a mirror
mirfaq	compartment
muʿarrab	foreign loanword
muʿāyasha	(linguistic) co-existence
mubhima	obscure
mubtadhala	trite (of words)

mudda yasīra	a short period
muftariq al-ṭuruq	crossroads
al-Muʿjam al-kabīr	the 'big dictionary' project of the Cairo Academy
mujārā	(Arabic) flowing together with (modernity)
al-muqaddima min al-jaysh	the spearhead (of defending Arabic)
muqawwim	formative element
muqawwimāt al-ḥayā	means of subsistence (of Arabic)
musāyara	proceeding with (modernity) (of Arabic)
mushikila	problematic
mustawdaʿ	(Arabic as a) storehouse
mutafajjir	explosive, referring to the progress of human civilisation
muʿtarakat al-mabādiʾ wa-l-ʾārāʾ	a battlefield of principles and ideas
al-mutazammitūn	the narrow-minded, referring to the ultra-conservative Arab linguists
al-muthul al-ʿulyā	the highest standard
muwāʾama	concord (between the old and new and between Arab principles and Western civilisation)
muwallad	a cross-breed who, without being of Arab origin, has been born among Arabs and received an Arabic education (arguably all native Arabic speakers living after the fourth century of Islam belonged to the *muwallad* category); a word or expression that is used by those 'cross-breed' Arabic speakers and is not found in the orthodox corpus of the Arabic language
nahḍa	renaissance, revival to reach efflorescence
naḥt	compounding
najma kubrā fī samāʾ al-ʿurūba	(Arabic as a) big star in the sky of Arabness
naksa	(intellectual) relapse
namūdhaj	(Arabic as an) epitome (of the Arab nation)
naʿra	an Arab cry
nashr	spreading (Arabic)
al-naẓar fī al-jadīd fī ḍawʾ al-qadīm	examining the new in the light of the old
niẓām	(linguistic) order or system

qātim	dark, static
qibla ʾimāmiyya	*qibla* for the prayer leaders
al-qilla al-shāʿira al-mufakkira	the insightful thinking minority
qiyāsī	analogical
qushūr	outer shells (of modern civilisation)
quwwa	(linguistic) power
rābiṭa	a link, referring to Arabic that connects the elites and the common people in Arab society, connects Arabs in one country with those in another and connects the Arabs' present with their past
radḥ min al-zaman	a long period
raḥma	benevolence
rakāka	feebleness (of linguistic competence)
rakīk	poor (of linguistic competence)
rakīza	(Arabic as a) pillar
rashāqa	graceful concision
rawāʾ	(fresh) liquid (brought from the Arabic heritage)
rawnaq	splendour (of Arabic)
ṣahr	fusing (ideas)
sajʿ	rhyme
ṣalāḥiyya	(linguistic) appropriateness
salīm	structurally complete
salīqa/fiṭra	(linguistic) intuition
samāʿī	(linguistic usage) attested
sarw manẓūma	(language as an) orderly cypress
saṭḥiyyūn	superficialists
sayl	flood (of foreign neologisms)
shāʾiba	(linguistic) defect
shakhṣiyya	distinctive character
sharaf ṭārif	unique eminence (of Arabic)
sharkh	(civilisational) rupture
sharṭ	a (linguistic) principle
shudhūdh	anomaly
shuʿūbiyya	anti-Arab ethic-regionalism
silāḥ	(Arabic as a) weapon
ṣināʿa	(linguistic) skill
sitār mawhūm	imagined curtain (between *fuṣḥā* and *ʿāmmiyya*)
sunan al-taṭawwur wa-l-irtiqāʾ	the laws of development and progress
ṣūra	image, referring to the surface features of Arabic

taʿassuf	aberration
ṭabʿ	natural disposition
ṭabʿ mustaqīm	natural straightness
tabādul	(linguistic) exchange
al-ṭabaqa al-ʿāmila	the working class, referring to users of Arabic
ṭabīʿa	nature
tabaʿiyya	subordination or dependence
tadaffuq ghāmir mukhīf	frightening overflowing influx (of foreign neologisms)
tafarruʿ/tajazzuʾ	(linguistic) fragmentation
tafāʿul	(linguistic) interaction
taḥrīf/inḥirāf	(linguistic) deviation
tajdīd	renewing (Arabic)
takhalkhul	unsteadiness
takhalluf	backwardness
takhfīf	reduction
talāḥum	(languages) clinging together
talbiya	following and obeying (of Arabic) (requirements of modernity)
tamjīd	glorifying (Arabic)
ṭaʿn	defaming (Arabic)
tanāfudh	(linguistic) osmosis
tanmiya	developing (Arabic)
tanmiyya shāmila	comprehensive development (of Arabic)
taqaddum	progress
taqdīs	sanctifying (Arabic)
taqṣīr	(linguistic) reduction
taqwīm	correction
taqyīm	evaluation
tarākhin khuluqī	moral limpness
taʿrīb	(1) assimilating foreign loanwords in line with Arabic phono-morphological conventions; (2) translating foreign texts into Arabic; (3) reviving and strengthening Arabic as a vibrant, national language to be used in all walks of Arab life; (4) recovering 'Arabness' in Arab society after it was sabotaged in colonial rule; (5) striving for the revival and solidarity of the Arab nation; and (6) ridding Arab society of its overall backwardness and dependence on developed countries in economy, science and technology

taṭawwur maʿkūs	inverse development
taṭwīʿ	rendering (Arabic) obedient (to modernity)
taṭwīr	developing (Arabic)
tawaḥḥud	(linguistic) unification
tawāṣul	(linguistic) interconnection
tawfīq	reconciliation (of modernity and authenticity)
tawḥīḍ	unification
taysīr	simplifying (Arabic)
tazāyud	growth (as a form of qualitative social change)
thawb	garment, referring to the surface features of Arabic
thawra	revolution
thawra lughawiyya	language revolution
thiqa	confidence (in Arabic)
tukhma	(cultural) indigestion
turāth	(cultural) heritage
ʿujma	(linguistic) foreignness
ʾumma	nation
ʾummiyya	illiteracy
ʿunwān	(Arabic as a) sign or epitome (of the Arab nation)
ʿurūba	Arabness
ʾusṭūra	myth
ʾuṣūl	fundamentals
wafā	to meet the needs (of modernity)
waḥda	solidarity or unification
wahm	illusion
waqt qaṣīr	short term
al-waṭan al-ʾakbar	the greatest (pan-Arab) homeland
waṭan rūḥī	(Arabic as) the spiritual motherland
waṭanī	national or patriotic
wiʿāʾ	a container, referring to Arabic which preserves a large number of historical traits of the academic, religious, economic, political and social life of the Arabs
yaḥūm wa-yaḥūṭ	hover around and encircle (the Qur'an) (of Arab/Arabic linguists)
yartawī	(Arabic heritage) quenches the thirst (of Arab intellectuals)
ẓafira	to defeat (Arabic 'defeated' almost every language of the conquered peoples)

zāḥama	to jostle against (Arabic)
zaḥzaḥa	(linguistic) deviation
zākhir	(the 'river' of Arabic heritage) overflowing

Bibliography

Journals and Minutes of Arabic Language Academies up to 2000

MMQ *Majallat Majmaʿ al-Lugha al-ʿArabiyya al-Malakī* (1–3)
Majallat Majmaʿ al-Fuʾād al-ʾAwwal li-l-Lugha al-ʿArabiyya (4–6)
Majallat Majmaʿ al-Lugha al-ʿArabiyya (bi-l-Qāhira) (7–90)

MJMJ *Maḥāḍir jalasāt al-majlis (li-Majmaʿ al-Lugha al-ʿArabiyya bi-l-Qāhira)* (1–67)

MJMT *Maḥāḍir jalasāt al-muʾtamar (li-Majmaʿ al-Lugha al-ʿArabiyya bi-l-Qāhira)* (1–67)

MMD *Majallat al-Majmaʿ al-ʿIlmī al-ʿArabī* (1–35, 37–40)
Majallat Majmaʿ al-Lugha al-ʿArabiyya bi-Dimashq (36, 41–75)

MMU *Majallat Majmaʿ al-Lugha al-ʿArabiyya al-ʾUrdunnī* (1–59)

MMI *Majallat al-Majmaʿ al-ʿIlmī al-ʿIrāqī* (1–42)
Majallat al-Majmaʿ al-ʿIlmī (43–7)

LA *al-Lisān al-ʿarabī* (1–50, published by al-Maktab al-Dāʾim li-Tansīq al-Taʿrīb fī al-Waṭan al-ʿArabī bi-l-Rabāt)

Works and Interviews in Arabic Cited in the Book

ʾAbāẓa, Muḥammad ʿAzīz (1966), ʻal-Fuṣḥā wa-l-ʿāmmiyya min zāwiya jadīdaʼ. *al-Buḥūth wa-l-muḥāḍarāt* 32: 207–24.

al-ʿAbbādī, ʿAbd al-Ḥamīd (1957), ʻThalāthat ḥawādith min al-tārīkh al-ʾislāmī sāʿadat ʿalā numūw al-lugha wa-intishārihāʼ. *Majallat Majmaʿ al-Lugha al-ʿArabiyya* 9: 47–52.

ʿAbd al-ʿAzīz, Muḥammad Ḥasan (2012), Interview by Chaoqun Lian. Cairo Arabic Language Academy, 11 July 2012.

al-ʿAbd al-Ḥaqq, Fawāz Muḥammad al-Rāshid (1996), ʻMarʾiyyāt al-takhṭīṭ al-lughawī, ʿarḍ wa-naqdʼ. *Majallat Majmaʿ al-Lugha al-ʿArabiyya al-ʾUrdunnī* 20 (51): 105–42.

ʿAbd al-Laṭīf, Muḥammad Ḥamāsa (2012), Interview by Chaoqun Lian. Cairo University, 19 June 2012.

ʿAbd al-Malik, Zakī (1971), ʿal-Ṣirāʿ bayn al-fuṣḥā wa-l-ʿāmmiyya ʾaw ʾathar al-izdiwāj al-lughawī fī ʾuslūb Yūsuf al-Sibāʿī'. *al-Lisān al-ʿarabī* 8 (1): 175–80.

ʿAbd al-Mawlā, Maḥmūḍ (1979), 'al-Fuṣḥā wa-l-lahjāt, qirāʾa jadīda wa-mulāḥaẓāt'. *al-Lisān al-ʿarabī* 17: 85–91.

ʿAbd al-Qādir, Ḥāmid (1960), 'Bayn al-ʿarabiyya wa-l-fārisiyya'. *Majallat al-Majmaʿ al-ʿIlmī al-ʿArabī* 35 (3): 362–405.

ʿAbd al-Raḥīm, F (1972), '(ʾAysh) bayn al-fuṣḥā wa-l-ʿāmmiyya'. *Majallat Majmaʿ al-Lugha al-ʿArabiyya bi-Dimashq* 47 (2): 476–80.

ʿAbd al-Raḥmān, ʿAfīf (1988), 'Min qaḍāyā al-maʿjamiyya al-ʿarabiyya al-muʿāṣira'. *Majallat Majmaʿ al-Lugha al-ʿArabiyya al-ʾUrdunnī* 12 (35): 11–74.

ʿAbd al-Raḥmān, Muḥammad (2018), 'ʾAyn waṣal mashrūʿ ḥimāyat al-lugha al-ʿarabiyya al-muqaddam min al-majmaʿ li-l-barlamān?' *al-Yawm al-Sābiʿ*, 16 October 2018, https://www.youm7.com/story/2018/10/26/أين-وصل-مشروع-حماية-اللغة-العربية-المقدم-من-المجمع-للبرلمان/4006132 (accessed 13 August 2019).

ʾAbu Ḥadīd, Muḥammad Farīd (1953), 'Mawqif al-lugha al-ʿarabiyya al-ʿāmma min al-lugha al-ʿarabiyya al-fuṣḥā'. *Majallat Majmaʿ al-Lugha al-ʿArabiyya* 7: 205–29.

al-ʾAfghānī, Saʿīd (1984), 'Mazāʿim al-ṣuʿūba fī lughatinā'. *Majallat Majmaʿ al-Lugha al-ʿArabiyya* 53: 188–94.

ʾAfsaḥī, Muḥammad (1990), 'Maktab Tansīq al-Taʿrīb, munjazāt wa-ʾahdāf (1961–1991)'. *al-Lisān al-ʿarabī* 34: 189–256.

ʾAḥmad, ʾAslamū Walad Sayyidī (1999), 'al-Taʿrīb . . . min khilāl tajribat Maktab Tansīq al-Taʿrīb'. *Majallat Majmaʿ al-Lugha al-ʿArabiyya* 84: 198–219.

al-ʾAhrām (2002), 'Shawqī Ḍayf: ʾImkāniyyāt Majmaʿ al-Lugha al-ʿArabiyya al-Miṣrī ʾamām Majmaʿ Lībiyā'. *Jarīdat al-ʾAhrām*, 17 June 2002, http://ahram.org.eg/archive/2002/6/17/EGYP9.HTM (accessed 18 December 2013).

al-ʿAjlānī, Munīr (1957), 'ʾAthar al-lugha al-ʿarabiyya fī waḥdat al-ʾumma'. *Majallat al-Majmaʿ al-ʿIlmī al-ʿArabī* 32 (1): 33–43.

al-ʾAlbānī, Muḥammad Nāṣir al-Dīn (1992), *Silsilat al-ʾaḥādīth al-ḍaʿīfa wa-l-mawḍūʿa wa-ʾatharuhā al-sayyiʾ fī al-ʾumma*, vol. 2, Riyadh: Dār al-Maʿārif.

ʿAlī, Jawād (1959), 'al-Majāmiʿ al-ʿilmiyya'. *Majallat al-Majmaʿ al-ʿIlmī al-ʿIrāqī* 6: 318–54.

al-ʾĀlūsī, Sālim (1997), *al-Majmaʿ al-ʿIlmī fi khamsīn ʿām 1947–1997*, Baghdad: Maṭbaʿat al-Majmaʿ al-ʿIlmī.

ʾAmīn, ʾAḥmad (1944), 'Iqtirāḥ bi-baʿḍ al-ʿiṣlāḥ fī matn al-lugha'. *Maḥādir jalasāt al-muʾtamar* 10: 266–74.

ʾAmīn, Muḥammad Shawqī (1974), 'al-Lugha al-ʿarabiyya: Makānatuhā al-qawmiyya wa-l-ʿālamiyya fī al-qadīm wa-l-ḥadīth'. *Majallat Majmaʿ al-Lugha al-ʿArabiyya* 34: 59–64.

AMM (ʾAkādīmiyyat al-Mamlaka al-Maghribiyya) (2013), 'ʾAhdāf al-ʾAkādīmiyya wa-hayʾātuhā al-ʾidāriyya wa-tasyīruhā'. *ʾAkādīmiyyat al-Mamlaka al-Maghribiyya*. http://www.alacademia.org.ma (accessed 18 December 2013).

ʿAmmār, ʾAḥmad (1955 [1951]), 'Muṣṭalaḥāt al-ṭibbiyya wa-nahḍat al-ʿarab bi-ṣawghihā fī al-qarn al-ʿishrīn'. *Majallat Majmaʿ al-Lugha al-ʿArabiyya* 8: 416–21.

ʿAmrū, Yūnus (1999), ʻal-Taʿrīb mafhūmuh wa-tajāribuh bayn māḍī al-lugha wa-ḥāḍirihā, wa-l-tajriba al-filasiṭīniyya'. *Majallat Majmaʿ al-Lugha al-ʿArabiyya* 85: 145–95.
al-ʾAsad, Nāṣir al-Dīn (1972), ʻal-ʾAṣāla wa-l-tajdīd fī al-lugha al-ʿarabiyya'. *al-Lisān al-ʿarabī* 9 (1): 195–6.
al-ʿAwda, ʿAlī Ḥasan (1957), ʻBayn al-lugha al-ʿarabiyya al-fuṣḥā wa-l-ʿāmmiyya'. *Majallat al-Majmaʿ al-ʿIlmī al-ʿArabī* 32 (1): 204–7.
Badawī, al-Saʿid Muḥammad (1973), *Muṣtawayāt al-ʿarabiyya al-muʿāṣira fī Miṣr*. Cairo: Dār al-Maʿārif.
al-Bakrī, Ḥāzim (1976), ʻLughatunā al-ʾaṣīla'. *al-Lisān al-ʿarabī* 13: 169–74.
al-Baqlī, Muḥammad Qindīl (1971), ʻal-Mathal bayn al-fuṣḥā wa-l-ʿāmmiyya'. *Majallat Majmaʿ al-Lugha al-ʿArabiyya* 28: 221–36.
al-Baṣīr, ʿAbd al-Razzāq (1978), ʻBayn al-ʿāmmiyya wa-l-fuṣḥā'. *Majallat Majmaʿ al-Lugha al-ʿArabiyya* 41: 155–61.
al-Baṣīr, ʿAbd al-Razzāq (1986), ʻMā zāl turāthunā al-ʿarabī manārat al-fikr'. *Majallat Majmaʿ al-Lugha al-ʿArabiyya* 58: 204–9.
Bishr, Kamāl Muḥammad (1987), ʻal-Taghrīb fī al-lugha wa-l-thaqāfa'. *Majallat Majmaʿ al-Lugha al-ʿArabiyya* 60: 186–206.
Bishr, Kamāl Muḥammad (1988), ʻal-Lugha bayn al-taṭawwur wa-fikrat al-ṣawāb wa-l-khaṭa'. *Majallat Majmaʿ al-Lugha al-ʿArabiyya* 62: 132–63.
Bishr, Kamāl Muḥammad (1996), ʻal-Taʿrīb bayn al-tafkīr wa-l-taʿbīr'. *Majallat Majmaʿ al-Lugha al-ʿArabiyya* 78: 64–83.
Būbū, Masʿūd (1998), ʻMushkilat al-ʾadāʾ fī al-lugha al-ʿarabiyya: ʾAsbāb al-ḍaʿf wa-wasāʾil al-ʿilāj'. *Majallat Majmaʿ al-Lugha al-ʿArabiyya bi-Dimashq* 73 (3): 555–71.
al-Ḍabīb, ʾAḥmad ibn Muḥammad (2002), ʻWāqiʿ al-lugha al-ʾajnabiyya fī al-tabādul baynanā wa-bayn al-gharb'. *Majallat Majmaʿ al-Lugha al-ʿArabiyya* 95: 227–39.
al-Dajānī, ʾAḥmad Ṣidqī (1999), ʻQaḍīyyat al-taʿrīb fī ḍawʾ sunan al-tafāʿul al-ḥaḍārī'. *Majallat Majmaʿ al-Lugha al-ʿArabiyya* 84: 220–30.
al-Dasūqī, Kamāl (1995), ʻʾĀn ʾan yusʿif taʿrīb al-taʿlīm al-ʿālī: Qarār tadrīs muʿjam muṣṭalāḥāt muwaḥḥad fī mādat al-takhaṣṣuṣ'. *Majallat Majmaʿ al-Lugha al-ʿArabiyya* 76: 146–76.
Ḍayf, Shawqī (1978), ʻal-Fuṣḥā al-muʿāṣīra'. *Majallat Majmaʿ al-Lugha al-ʿArabiyya* 41: 19–26.
Ḍayf, Shawqī (1980), ʻLughat al-masraḥ bayn al-ʿāmmiyya wa-l-fuṣḥā'. *Majallat Majmaʿ al-Lugha al-ʿArabiyya* 45: 51–64.
Ḍayf, Shawqī (1984), *Majmaʿ al-Lugha al-ʿArabiyya fī khamsīn ʿām, 1934–1984*, Cairo: Majmaʿ al-Lugha al-ʿArabiyya.
Ḍayf, Shawqī (1990), ʻBayn al-fuṣḥā wa-l-ʿāmmiyya al-miṣriyya'. *Majallat Majmaʿ al-Lugha al-ʿArabiyya* 66: 134–44.
Ḍayf, Shawqī (1997), ʻBayn al-fuṣḥā wa-l-ʿāmmiyya al-miṣriyya'. *Majallat Majmaʿ al-Lugha al-ʿArabiyya* 81: 75–86.
Ḍayf, Shawqī (2000a), ʻKalimat al-ʿūstāẓ al-duktūr Shawqī Ḍayf raʾīs al-Majmaʿ fī iftitāḥ muʾtamar al-dawra al-khāmisa wa-l-sittīn'. *Majallat Majmaʿ al-Lugha al-ʿArabiyya* 89: 3–6.
Ḍayf, Shawqī (2000b), ʻBayn al-fuṣḥā wa-l-ʿāmmiyya'. *Majallat Majmaʿ al-Lugha al-ʿArabiyya* 89: 35–49.

Fāḍil, ʿAbd al-Ḥaqq (1966), 'al-Taṭawwur al-ḥayyī fī al-lugha al-ʿarabiyya'. *al-Lisān al-ʿarabī* 4: 35–48.

al-Faḥḥām, Shākir (1984), 'Qaḍiyyat al-muṣṭalaḥ al-ʿilmī wa-mawqiʿih fī niṭāq taʿrīb al-taʿlīm al-ʿālī'. *Majallat Majmaʿ al-Lugha al-ʿArabiyya bi-Dimashq* 59 (4): 692–708.

al-Faḥḥām, Shākir (1996), 'Kalimat al-duktūr Shākir al-Faḥḥām'. *Majallat Majmaʿ al-Lugha al-ʿArabiyya bi-Dimashiq* 71 (1): 22–32.

Fahmī, ʿAbd al-ʿAzīz (1944), 'Iqtirāḥ ittikhādh al-ḥurūf al-lātīniyya li-rasm al-kitāba al-ʿarabiyya'. *Maḥādir jalasāt al-muʾtamar* 10: 279–315.

Fahmī, Manṣūr (1934), 'Tārīkh al-majāmiʿ ' *Majallat Majmaʿ al-Lugha al-ʿArabiyya al-Malakī* 1: 170–6.

Fahmī, Manṣūr (1955 [1951]), 'Kalimat kātib sirr al-Majma fī ʾaʿmāl al-Majmaʿ khilāl al-dawra al-māḍiyya'. *Majallat Majmaʿ al-Lugha al-ʿArabiyya* 8: 411–15.

Fahmī, Manṣūr (1957 [1956]), 'Majmaʿ Miṣr wa-l-lugha al-ʿarabiyya'. *Majallat al-Majmaʿ al-ʿIlmī al-ʿArabī* 32 (1): 57–71.

Fahmī, Manṣūr (1962 [1957]), 'Majmaʿ al-Lugha al-ʿArabiyya fī ʿām'. *Majallat Majmaʿ al-Lugha al-ʿArabiyya* 14: 5–13.

Falīsh, Hazī (1967), 'al-Mustaqbal li-l-lugha al-ʿarabiyya al-fuṣḥā'. *al-Lisān al-ʿarabī* 5: 86.

al-Fāsī al-Fihrī, ʿAbd al-Qādir (2010), *ʾAzmat al-lugha al-ʿarabiyya fī al-Maghrib: Bayn ikhtilālāt al-taʿddudiyya wa-taʿaththurāt 'al-tarjama'*. Beirut: Dār al-Kitāb al-Jadīd al-Muttaḥida.

al-Fāsī al-Fihrī, ʿAbd al-Qādir (2011), 'al-Thawra al-lughwiyya al-qādima fi al-Maghrib'. *Hespress*, 27 April 2011, http://www.hespress.com/opinions/30918.html (accessed 19 June 2014).

Fāyid, Wafāʾ Kāmil (2002), 'Majāmiʿ al-Lugha al-ʿArabiyya'. *Majallat Majmaʿ al-Lugha al-ʿArabiyya* 97: 91–117.

Fāyid, Wafāʾ Kāmil (2004), *al-Majmaʿ al-ʿarabiyya wa-qaḍāyā al-lugha: Min al-nashʾa ʾilā ʾawākhir al-qarn al-ʿishrīn*. Cairo: ʿĀlam al-Kutub.

Fayṣal, Shukrī (1975), 'al-ʿArabiyya ghayr qāṣira ʿan istīʿāb al-ʿulūm'. *al-Lisān al-ʿarabī* 12 (1): 7–8.

Fayṣal, Shukrī (1977), 'al-Taṭawwur al-ʾijtimāʿī wa-l-taṭawwur al-lughawī'. *al-Lisān al-ʿarabī* 15 (3): 33–41.

Futayyiḥ, ʾAḥmad (1956), *Tārīkh al-Majmaʿ al-ʿIlmī*. Dimashq: Maṭbaʿat al-Turqī fī Dimashiq.

Ghṣn, Mārūn (1935), 'al-Naḥt wasīla li-tawsīʿ al-lugha'. *Majallat al-Majmaʿ al-ʿIlmī al-ʿArabī* 13 (11–12): 458–65.

al-Ḥabābī, Muḥammad ʿAzīz (1978), 'al-Lugha wa-l-wāqiʿ'. *Majallat Majmaʿ al-Lugha al-ʿArabiyya* 41: 49–56.

al-Ḥabābī, Muḥammad ʿAzīz (1982), 'ʾAṣāla wa-muʿāṣara battān'. *Majallat Majmaʿ al-Lugha al-ʿArabiyya* 49: 138–47.

Ḥāfiẓ, Maḥmūd (1989), 'al-Lugha al-ʿarabiyya fī muʾassasāt al-taʿlīm al-ʿāmm wa-l-taʿlīm al-ʿālī wa-wasāʾil al-nuhūḍ bihā fī Miṣr'. *Majallat Majmaʿ al-Lugha al-ʿArabiyya* 65: 23–44.

Ḥāfiẓ, Maḥmūd (1996), 'al-Tarjama bayn al-māḍī wa-l-ḥāḍir wa-ʾahammiyyatuhā fī al-ʿulūm ʾilā al-lugha al-ʿarabiyya'. *Majallat Majmaʿ al-Lugha al-ʿArabiyya* 78: 84–97.

Ḥāfiẓ, Maḥmūd (1999), 'Qaḍiyyat al-taʿrīb fī Miṣr'. *Majallat Majmaʿ al-Lugha al-ʿArabiyya* 84: 73–93.

Ḥāfiẓ, Maḥmūd (2000), 'al-Lugha al-ʿarabiyya wa-wasāʾil al-nuhūḍ bihā fī Miṣr'. *Majallat Majmaʿ al-Lugha al-ʿArabiyya* 87: 113–25.

Ḥāfiẓ, Maḥmūd and Fārūq Shūsha, eds (2010), *ʾIṭlāla tārīkhiyya ʿalā qānūn al-Majmaʿ wa-taʿdīlātih*. Cairo: Majmaʿ al-Lugha al-ʿArabiyya bi-l-Qāhira.

al-Ḥamzāwī, Muḥammad Rashād (M. Rached Hamzaoui) (1988), *ʾAʿmāl Majmaʿ al-Lugha al-ʿArabiyya bi-l-Qāhira: Manāhij tarqiyat al-lugha, taṭwīr wa-muṣṭalaḥ wa-muʿjam*. Beirut: Dār al-Gharb al-ʾIslāmī.

al-Ḥamzāwī, Muḥammad Rashād (M. Rached Hamzaoui) (2000), 'al-Fuṣḥā wa-l-ʿāmmiyya fī riḥāb Majmaʿ al-Lugha al-ʿArabiyya bi-l-Qāhira: ʾAzma muzmina (1943–1960)'. *Majallat Majmaʿ al-Lugha al-ʿArabiyya* 90: 237–52.

Ḥasan, ʿIzza (1962), 'al-Lugha al-ʿarabiyya al-ḥadītha'. *Majallat al-Majmaʿ al-ʿIlmī al-ʿArabī* 37 (1): 132–5.

Hāshim, ʿAbd al-Hādī (1988), 'Mafhūm al-taʿrīb'. *Majallat Majmaʿ al-Lugha al-ʿArabiyya bi-Dimashq* 63 (2): 337–43.

al-Hāshimī, Muḥammad Yaḥyā (1969), 'Naḥnu ʿalā muftariq al-ṭuruq'. *al-Lisān al-ʿarabī* 6: 81–6.

al-Ḥawfī, ʾAḥmad (1980), 'Li-mādhā nuʿnā bi-turāthinā'. *Majallat Majmaʿ al-Lugha al-ʿArabiyya* 46: 19–21.

Ḥijāzī, Maḥmūd Fahmī (1998), 'al-Lugha al-ʿarabiyya fī al-qarn al-ḥādī wa-l-ʿishrīn'. *Majallat Majmaʿ al-Lugha al-ʿArabiyya bi-Dimashq* 73 (3): 449–92.

Ḥusayn, ʾAḥmad Ḥāmid, ed (2011), *ʾIttiḥād al-Majāmiʿ al-Lughawiyya al-ʿIlmiyya al-ʿArabiyya fī ʿīdih al-dhahabī*. Cairo: Maṭābiʿ Dār al-Jumhūriyya.

Ḥusayn, Ṭāha (1957), 'al-Lugha al-ʿarabiyya wa-taʿlīm al-shaʿb'. *Majallat al-Majmaʿ al-ʿIlmī al-ʿArabī* 32 (1): 44–56.

al-Ḥuṣrī, Sāṭiʿ (1957), 'Ḥawl al-fuṣḥā wa-l-ʿāmmiyya'. *Majallat al-Majmaʿ al-ʿIlmī al-ʿArabī* 32 (2): 241–66.

al-Ḥusnī, Makkī (1990), 'Lughatunā al-ʿarabiyya bayn majāmiʿ al-lugha wa-wasāʾil al-ʾiʿlām'. *Majallat Majmaʿ al-Lugha al-ʿArabiyya bi-Dimashq* 65 (3): 540–43.

IATWDL (al-ʾIdāra al-ʿĀmma li-l-Thaqāfa bi-Wizārat al-Dawla al-Lībiyya) (1977), 'Madā tafāʿul al-lugha maʿ qaḍāyā al-numūw al-ijtimāʿī'. *al-Lisān al-ʿarabī* 15 (3): 55–6.

Ibn ʿAsākir, ʿAlī ibn al-Ḥasan (1995), *Tārīkh Madīnat Dimashq,* vol. 24. Beirut: Dār al-Fikr.

Ibn al-Khūja, Muḥammad al-Jabīb (1978), 'al-ʿArabiyya fī Tūnis: Bayn al-fuṣḥā wa-l-ʿāmmiyya'. *Majallat Majmaʿ al-Lugha al-ʿArabiyya* 41: 69–111.

Ibn Manẓūr, Muḥammad ibn Mukarram (1302 AH.), *Lisān al-ʿarab*, vol. 13. Cairo: al-Maṭbaʿa al-Mīriyya.

al-ʾIskandarī, ʾAḥmad (1936), 'Kalimat ḥaḍrat al-shaykh ʾAḥmad al-ʾIskandarī'. *Majallat Majmaʿ al-Lugha al-ʿArabiyya al-Malakī* 2: 5–13.

al-ʾIskandarī, ʾAḥmad (1948 [1938]), 'ʾIqtirāḥāt ʾasmāʾ ʿarabiyya li-muṣṭalaḥāt kīmiyāʾiyya'. *Majallat Majmaʿ al-Fuʾād al-ʾAwwal li-l-Lugha al-ʿArabiyya* 5: 49–57.

ʿIwaḍ al-Lah, Ḥusayn (2018), 'Raʾīs al-majmaʿ al-lughawī: Lā yūjad balad fī al-ʿālam yudarris al-ʿulūm bi-ghayr lughatih ʿillā Miṣr . . . wa-istiḥdāth imtiḥān 'al-ʿarabī' ʿalā ghirār 'al-tūiful'.' *al-Waṭan*, 18 December 2018, https://www.elwatannews.com/news/details/3875928 (accessed 13 August 2019).

ʿIzz al-Dīn, Yūsuf (1986), 'al-Turāth al-ʿarabī wa-l-muʿāṣara'. *Majallat Majmaʿ al-Lugha al-ʿArabiyya* 58: 188–203.

ʿIzz al-Dīn, Yūsuf (1994), 'Thqāfat al-ʾadīb al-muʿāṣir wa-l-taʿrīb'. *Majallat Majmaʿ al-Lugha al-ʿArabiyya* 74: 57–79.

ʿIzz al-Dīn, Yūsuf (2002), 'al-Tanāfudh al-ʾadabī bayn al-ʿarabiyya wa-l-ʾinjlīziyya'. *Majallat Majmaʿ al-Lugha al-ʿArabiyya* 95: 205–26.

Jabrī, Shafīq (1943), 'al-Muḥkam fī ʿuṣūl al-kalimāt al-ʿāmmiyya'. *Majallat al-Majmaʿ al-ʿIlmī al-ʿArabī* 18 (5–6): 260–2.

Jabrī, Shafīq (1968), 'Muhimmat rijāl al-lugha'. *Majallat Majmaʿ al-Lugha al-ʿArabiyya bi-Dimashiq* 43 (1): 14–18.

al-Jalīlī, Maḥmūd (1974), 'Mulāḥaẓāt ḥawl taṭwīr al-lugha al-ʿarabiyya'. *al-Lisān al-ʿarabī* 11 (1): 323–5.

al-Jamālī, Fāḍil (1969), 'al-ʿArabiyya bayn ḥumātihā wa-ghuzātihā'. *al-Lisān al-ʿarabī* 6: 23–33.

al-Jawārī, ʾAḥmad ʿAbd al-Sattār (1985), 'Fī taʿrīb al-taʿlīm'. *Majallat Majmaʿ al-Lugha al-ʿArabiyya* 56: 37–42.

al-Jawārī, ʾAḥmad ʿAbd al-Sattār (1986), 'al-Turāth al-lughawī wa-l-taqaddum al-ijtimāʿī'. *Majallat Majmaʿ al-Lugha al-ʿArabiyya* 58: 88–95.

Jirjis, Ramsīs (1961), 'al-Naḥt fī al-ʿarabiyya'. *Majallat Majmaʿ al-Lugha al-ʿArabiyya* 13: 61–78.

al-Jundī, Salīm (1925), 'ʾInʿāsh al-ʿarabiyya'. *Majallat al-Majmaʿ al-ʿIlmī al-ʿArabī* 5 (9): 397–401.

al-Jundī, Salīm (1928), 'ʾInʿāsh al-ʿarabiyya'. *Majallat al-Majmaʿ al-ʿIlmī al-ʿArabī* 8 (11–12): 720–4.

Khalīfa, ʿAbd al-Karīm (1987), *al-Lugha al-ʿarabiyya wa-l-tʿrīb fī al-ʿaṣr al-ḥadīth*. Amman: Manshūrāt Majmaʿ al-Lugha al-ʿArabiyya al-ʾUrdunnī.

Khalīfa, ʿAbd al-Karīm (2001a), 'al-ʿArabiyya al-fuṣḥā wa-l-ʿāmmiyya fī al-ʾidhāʿa wa-l-tilfāz'. *Majallat Majmaʿ al-Lugha al-ʿArabiyya* 91: 67–85.

Khalīfa, ʿAbd al-Karīm (2001b), 'Qaḍāyā al-ʿarabiyya ʿalā madārij al-qarn al-ḥādī wa-l-ʿishrīn'. *Majallat Majmaʿ al-Lugha al-ʿArabiyya* 93: 85–107.

al-Khaṭīb, ʿAdnān (1983), 'Lughat al-ṣaḥāfa fī bilād al-shām'. *Majallat Majmaʿ al-Lugha al-ʿArabiyya* 51: 29–44.

al-Kharīj al-Jadīd (2017), 'Majmaʿ al-Lugha al-ʿArabiyya bi-l-Shāriqa . . . rāfid jadīd yasʿā ʾilā ʾiḥyāʾ lughat al-ḍād'. *al-Kharīj al-Jadīd*, 23 January 2017, https://thenewkhalij.news/article/57384/مجمع-اللغة-العربية-بالشارقة-رافد-جديد-يسعى-إلى-إحياء-لغة-الضاد (accessed 6 October 2019).

al-Khaṭīb, ʿAdnān (1996), 'Tilk: ʾUmma tuqaddis lughatanā'. *Majallat Majmaʿ al-Lugha al-ʿArabiyya* 78: 39–49.

al-Khaṭīb, ʾAḥmad Shafīq (2000), 'Min qaḍāyā al-lugha al-ʿarabiyya wa-mashākilihā fī majāl al-musṭalaḥāt al-ʿilmiyya (munāqashat ḥāl hādhihi al-muṣṭalaḥāt bayn al-taʿrīb wa-l-waḍʿ)'. *Majallat Majmaʿ al-Lugha al-ʿArabiyya* 87: 203–26.

al-Khūrī, Shaḥāda (1989), 'al-Lugha al-ʿarabiyya wa-l-baḥth al-ʿilmī'. *Majallat Majmaʿ al-Lugha al-ʿArabiyya bi-Dimashq* 64 (1): 91–104.

al-Khūrī, Shaḥāda (1991), 'Taʿrīb taʿlīm al-ʿulūm wa-l-taknūlūjiyā'. *Majallat Majmaʿ al-Lugha al-ʿArabiyya bi-Dimashq* 66 (1): 65–76.

al-Khūrī, Shaḥāda (1998), ‘al-Taʿrīb wa-l-muṣṭalaḥ’. *Majallat Majmaʿ al-Lugha al-ʿArabiyya bi-Dimashq* 73 (4): 797–816.

Kunūn, ʿAbd al-Lāh (1978), ‘al-ʿArabiyya ʾams wa-l-yawm’. *Majallat Majmaʿ al-Lugha al-ʿArabiyya* 41: 115–20.

Kurd ʿAlī, Muḥammad (1921), ‘Nashaʾat al-Majmaʿ al-ʿIlmī al-ʿArabī’. *Majallat al-Majmaʿ al-ʿIlmī al-ʿArabī* 1 (1): 2–5.

Kurd ʿAlī, Muḥammad (1944), ‘Hal wafat al-ʿarabiyya bi-gharaḍihā’. *Maḥādir jalasāt al-muʾtamar* 10: 258–66.

Kurd ʿAlī, Muḥammad (1953), ‘Bayn al-fuṣḥā wa-l-ʿāmmiyya’. *Majallat al-Majmaʿ al-ʿIlmī al-ʿArabī* 28 (1): 154–7.

al-Madīna al-ʾAkhbāriyya (2014), ‘al-Tarbiyat al-niyābiyya taqarr mashrūʿ qānūn Majmaʿ al-Lugha al-ʿArabiyya wa-ḥimāyat al-lugha al-ʿarabiyya li-sanat 2014’. *al-Madīna al-ʾAkhbāriyya*, 8 April 2014, http://www.almadenahnews.com/article/286827--التربية-النيابية-تقر-مشروع-قانون-مجمع-اللغة-العربية-وحماية-اللغة-العربية-لسنة-2014 (accessed 13 August 2019).

Madkūr, ʿAbd al-Ḥamīd (2018), ‘Bayn muʾtamarayn: Kalimat al-ʾamīn al-ʿāmm li-l-majmaʿ’. *Majmaʿiyyāt: ʿAdad khāṣṣ bi-muʾtamar al-majmaʿ* 2018 (34–36): 9–17.

Madkūr, ʾIbrāhīm (1964), *Majmaʿ al-Lugha al-ʿArabiyya fī thalāthīn ʿām, 1933–1962: Māḍīh wa-ḥāḍiruh*. Cairo: al-Hayʾa al-ʿĀmma li-Shuʾūn al-Maṭābiʿ al-ʾAmīriyya.

Madkūr, ʾIbrāhīm (1967), ‘al-Majmaʿ fī khidmat al-lugha al-ʿarabiyya’. *Majallat Majmaʿ al-Lugha al-ʿArabiyya* 22: 15–24.

Madkūr, ʾIbrāhīm (1969), ‘al-ʿArabiyya bayn al-lughāt al-ʿālamiyya al-kubrā’. *Majallat Majmaʿ al-Lugha al-ʿArabiyya* 25: 12–15.

Madkūr, ʾIbrāhīm (1973), ‘al-ʿArabiyya bayn al-lughāt al-ʿālamiyya al-kubrā’. *Majallat Majmaʿ al-Lugha al-ʿArabiyya* 31: 16–24.

Madkūr, ʾIbrāhīm (1978), ‘Majmaʿ al-Lugha al-ʿArabiyya’. In *ʾAḥādīth majmaʿiyya (al-ḥalqa al-ʾidhāʿiyya al-khāṣṣa ʿan Majmaʿ al-Lugha al-ʿArabiyya)*, 5–8, Cairo: al-Hayʾa al-ʿĀmma li-Shuʾūn al-Maṭābiʿ al-ʾAmīriyya.

Madkūr, ʾIbrāhīm (1981), ‘Ḥayātunā al-fikriyya fī niṣf al-qarn al-ʾakhīr (2)’. *Majallat Majmaʿ al-Lugha al-ʿArabiyya* 48: 10–16.

al-Maghribī, ʿAbd al-Qādir (1923), ‘ʾAqrab al-ṭuruq ʾilā nashr al-lugha al-fuṣḥā’. *Majallat al-Majmaʿ al-ʿIlmī al-ʿArabī* 3 (7–8): 231–8.

al-Maghribī, ʿAbd al-Qādir (1926), ‘al-Lugha al-ʿarabiyya fī dawlat al-turk al-ʿuthmāniyya’. *Majallat al-Majmaʿ al-ʿIlmī al-ʿArabī* 6 (5): 217–23.

al-Maghribī, ʿAbd al-Qādir (1935a), ‘Taʿrīb al-ʾasālīb’. *Majallat Majmaʿ al-Lugha al-ʿArabiyya al-Malakī* 1: 332–49.

al-Maghribī, ʿAbd al-Qādir (1935b), ‘Kalimat ḥaḍrat al-ʾustādh al-shaykh ʿAbd al-Qādir al-Maghribī’. *Majallat Majmaʿ al-Lugha al-ʿArabiyya al-Malakī* 2: 16–20.

al-Maghribī, ʿAbd al-Qādir (1948), ‘Muʿjam al-ʾalfāẓ al-ʿāmmiyya’. *Majallat al-Majmaʿ al-ʿIlmī al-ʿArabī* 23 (1): 116–20.

al-Maghribī, ʿAbd al-Qādir (1955), ‘Fī al-lugha ʾabnāʾ ʿallāt kamā fī al-bashar’. *Majallat al-Majmaʿ al-ʿIlmī al-ʿArabī* 30 (2): 253–67.

al-Maḥāsinī, Marwān (1996), ‘al-Lugha wa-l-ʾaṣāla’. *Majallat Majmaʿ al-Lugha al-ʿArabiyya bi-Dimashq* 71 (1): 147–61.

al-Maḥāsinī, Marwān (2009), ‘Kalimat al-duktūr Marwān al-Maḥāsinī raʾīs al-Majma' fī ḥafl murūr tis'īn 'ām 'alā 'inshā' Majma' al-Lugha al-'Arabiyya bi-Dimashiq, 1919–2009'. *Majallat Majma' al-Lugha al-'Arabiyya bi-Dimashiq* 84 (4): 1152–63.

Maḥfūẓ, Ḥusayn 'Alī (1978), 'Taqrīb al-'āmmiyya min al-fuṣḥā'. *Majallat Majma' al-Lugha al-'Arabiyya* 41: 9–18.

al-Ma'lūf, 'Īsā 'Iskandar (1923), 'Kitāb tahdhīb al-'alfāẓ al-'āmmiyya'. *Majallat al-Majma' al-'Ilmī al-'Arabī* 3 (6): 188–9.

Mārdīnī, Ṣubḥī (1970), 'al-Lahjāt al-'āmmiyya wa-l-fuṣḥā'. *Majallat Majma' al-Lugha al-'Arabiyya bi-Dimashq* 45 (3): 614–21.

Marqaṣ, 'Idwār (1936), 'Lamḥa fī al-ta'rīb wa-shurūṭih'. *Majallat al-Majma' al-'Ilmī al-'Arabī* 14 (1–2): 26–32.

Marqaṣ, 'Idwār (1943), 'al-'Arabiyya al-'āmmiyya wa-'alāqatuhā bi-l-'arabiyya al-fuṣḥā (1)'. *Majallat al-Majma' al-'Ilmī al-'Arabī* 18 (1–2): 30–43.

Maṭlūb, 'Aḥmad (2008), 'Juhūd al-Majma' al-'Ilmī fī nashr al-thaqāfa'. *Majallat al-Majma' al-'Ilmī* 55 (4): 5–34.

MLAQ (Majma' al-Lugha al-'Arabiyya bi-l-Qāhira) (1946), *Taysīr al-kitāba al-'arabiyya*. al-Qāhira: Maṭba'at al-'Amīriyya bi-l-Qāhira.

MLAU (Majma' al-Lugha al-'Arabiyya al-'Urdunnī) (2008), ''Akādīmiyyat al-Mamlaka al-Maghribiyya'. *Majma' al-Lugha al-'Arabiyya al-'Urdunnī*, 22 December 2008, http://www.majma.org.jo/majma/index.php/2008–12–22–10–13–40/89–2008–12–22–09–53–00.html (accessed 18 December 2013).

al-Mu'allimī, Yaḥayā ibn 'Abd al-Lāh (2000), 'al-Lugha al-'arabiyya lughat al-'islām'. *Majallat Majma' al-Lugha al-'Arabiyya* 88: 237–40.

al-Mubārak, Māzin (2007), 'Min tārīkh al-ta'rīb, al-qism al-'awwal: al-Nahḍa al-lughawiyya fī al-Shām 'aqba jalā' al-'atrāk'. *Majallat Majma' al-Lugha al-'Arabiyya bi-Dimashq* 82 (1): 55–64.

al-Mubārak, Māzin (2009), 'Kalimat al-duktūr Māzin al-Mubārak 'uḍw al-Majma' fī al-iḥtifāl bi-murūr tis'īn 'ām 'alā ta'sīs al-Majma''. *Majallat Majma' al-Lugha al-'Arabiyya bi-Dimashiq* 84 (4): 1164–73.

Muḥammad, 'Abu al-Ḥāfiẓ Ḥilmī (1996), 'Ta'rīb al-ta'līm al-jāmi'ī: Ḍarūrāt mulzima, wa-manāfi' mu'akkada, wa-i'tirāḍāt mufannada'. *Majallat Majma' al-Lugha al-'Arabiyya* 79: 25–35.

Muḥjāzī, Fātin al-Khalīl (2005), 'al-Inḥirāf al-lughawī: 'Asbābuh wa-'ilājuh (al-qism al-'awwal)'. *Majallat Majma' al-Lugha al-'Arabiyya bi-Dimashq* 80 (1): 91–108.

al-Muqaddasī, 'Anīs (1971), 'Lughatunā fi 'aṣr al-'inḥiṭāṭ'. *Majallat Majma' al-Lugha al-'Arabiyya* 28: 29–42.

Murād, Riyāḍ (1996), 'Min tārīkh Majma' al-Lugha al-'Arabiyya bi-Dimashiq'. *Majallat Majma' al-Lugha al-'Arabiyya bi-Dimashiq* 71 (1): 49–63.

Musṭafā, Muhannad (2013), 'Majāmī' al-lugha al-'arabiyya fī al-siyāq al-'isrā'īlī: Bayn al-dawr al-baḥthī wa-l-qīma al-qawmiyya'. Unpublished paper.

al-Nakdī, 'Ārif (1957), 'al-Lugha al-'arabiyya bayn al-fuṣḥā wa-l-'āmmiyya'. *Majallat al-Majma' al-'Ilmī al-'Arabī* 32 (1): 189–203.

al-Nakdī, 'Ārif (1960), 'al-'Arabiyya bayn al-fuṣḥā wa-l-'āmmiyya wa-kitāb radd al-'āmmī 'ilā al-faṣīḥ'. *Majallat al-Majma' al-'Ilmī al-'Arabī* 35 (1): 12–9.

al-Nakdī, 'Ārif (1969), 'al-'Arabiyya bayn al-fuṣḥā wa-l-'āmmiyya'. *Majallat Majma' al-Lugha al-'Arabiyya bi-Dimashq* 44 (1–2): 45–60.

Qudsī, 'Ilyās (1923), 'Tabdīl al-ḥurūf al-'arabiyya'. *Majallat al-Majma' al-'Ilmī al-'Arabī* 3 (5–6): 177–84.

al-Qulaybī, al-Shādhilī (1978), 'Bayn al-lughāt al-'āmmiyya wa-l-lisān al-mudawwan'. *Majallat Majma' al-Lugha al-'Arabiyya* 41: 133–44.
al-Qulaybī, al-Shādhilī (1998), 'Ba'ḍ al-'ishkāliyyāt al-muta'allaqa bi-lughatinā al-'arabiyya'. *Majallat Majma' al-Lugha al-'Arabiyya* 83: 113–28.
Qunṣul, 'Ilyās (1971), 'Taṭawwur al-fikr al-'ilmī wa-lugha al-taqniyyāt bi-l-maghrib'. *al-Lisān al-'arabī* 8 (1): 196–211.
Qunṣul, 'Ilyās (1973), 'al-Lugha al-'arabiyya tumāshī al-'umma al-'arabiyya 'ilā al-'amām li-'annahā juz' min hā'. *al-Lisān al-'arabī* 10 (1): 82–4.
al-Rāwī, Nājiḥ (2002), 'Ittiḥād al-Majāmi' al-Lughawiyya al-'Ilmiyya al-'Arabiyya'. *Majallat al-Majma' al-'Ilmī* 49 (1): 5–16.
Rifā'iyya, Yāsīn (1969), 'al-'Arabiyya bayn mu'ayyidīhā wa-mu'āriḍīhā'. *al-Lisān al-'arabī* 6: 34–7.
Subḥ, Ḥusnī (1970), 'Kalimat al-duktūr Ḥusnī Subḥ ra'īs Majma' al-Lugha al-'Arabiyya bi-Dimashiq fī al-iḥtifāl bi-murūr khamsīn 'ām 'alā ta'sīsih'. *Majallat Majma' al-Lugha al-'Arabiyya bi-Dimashiq* 45 (1): 3–14.
Ṣalāḥ, Faḍl (2012), Interview by Chaoqun Lian. Cairo, 2 July 2012.
Salmān, 'Adnān Muḥammad (1988), 'Ḥaqīqat al-lugha wa-mufradātiha'. *Majallat al-Majma' al-'Ilmī al-'Irāqī* 39 (4): 293–330.
Sam'ān, Khalīl (1972), ''Asbaqiyyat al-lugha al-'arabiyya al-fuṣḥā 'alā al-'āmmiyya'. *al-Lisān al-'arabī* 9 (1): 295–308.
al-Sammān, Wajīh (1982a), 'al-Naḥt'. *Majallat Majma' al-Lugha al-'Arabiyya bi-Dimashq* 57 (1–2): 92–114.
al-Sammān, Wajīh (1982b), 'al-Naḥt'. *Majallat Majma' al-Lugha al-'Arabiyya bi-Dimashq* 57 (3): 343–64.
al-Sāmrā'ī, 'Ibrāhīm (1980), 'al-'Arabiyya al-dārija fī al-quṭr al-jazā'irī'. *Majallat Majma' al-Lugha al-'Arabiyya bi-Dimashq* 55 (4): 767–79.
al-Sāmrā'ī, 'Ibrāhīm (1990), 'al-'Āmmī al-faṣīḥ'. *Majallat Majma' al-Lugha al-'Arabiyya* 66: 80–103.
al-Sāmrā'ī, 'Ibrāhīm (1995), 'Fī al-'arabiyya al-mu'āṣira wa-mu'jamihā'. *Majallat Majma' al-Lugha al-'Arabiyya* 76: 78–96.
al-Sāmrā'ī, 'Ibrāhīm (2001), 'Min "al-'arabiyya al-mu'āṣira"'. *Majallat Majma' al-Lugha al-'Arabiyya* 91: 87–114.
Ṣawt al-'Aqṣā (2013), 'al-Mazīnī yaftataḥ Majma' al-Lugha al-'Arabiyya'. *'Idhā'at Ṣawt al-'Aqṣā*, 7 July 2013, http://www.alaqsavoice.ps/arabic/index.php?action=detail&id=116561 (accessed 18 December 2013).
al-Ṣayyādī, Muḥammad al-Munjī et al (1982), *al-Ta'rīb wa-dawruh fī tad'īm al-wujūd al-'arabī wa-l-waḥda al-'arabiyya.* Beirut: Markaz Dirāsāt al-Waḥda al-'Arabiyya.
al-Sayyid, 'Abd al-'Azīz (1972), 'al-'Arabiyya lughat al-ḥaḍāra wa-l-fikr wa-l-ma'rifa'. *al-Lisān al-'arabī* 9 (1): 457–8.
al-Sayyid, 'Amīn 'Alī (1990), 'al-'Āmmī al-faṣīḥ: Shudhūr min waḥy hādhā al-'unwān'. *Majallat Majma' al-Lugha al-'Arabiyya* 66: 168–89.
al-Sayyid, Fu'ād Bahīy (1971), 'al-Lugha al-'asāsiyya'. *Majallat Majma' al-Lugha al-'Arabiyya* 27: 129–40.
al-Sayyid, Maḥmūd 'Aḥmad (1997), ''Ishkāliyyat ta'rīb al-ta'līm al-'ālī'. *Majallat Majma' al-Lugha al-'Arabiyya* 81: 239–59.
al-Shabībī, Muḥammad Riḍā (1955), 'Ba'th al-'arabiyya'. *Majallat Majma' al-Lugha al-'Arabiyya* 8: 16–20.

al-Shabībī, Muḥammad Riḍā (1957), 'Bayn al-fuṣḥā wa-lahjātihā'. *Majallat Majma' al-Lugha al-'Arabiyya* 9: 70–5.

al-Shabībī, Muḥammad Riḍā (1959), 'Sunnat al-taṭawwur fī al-lugha'. *Majallat Majma' al-Lugha al-'Arabiyya* 11: 59–61.

al-Shabībī, Muḥammad Riḍā (1960), 'Fī tārīkh al-lahja al-miṣriyya'. *Majallat Majma' al-Lugha al-'Arabiyya* 12: 129–34.

al-Shabībī, Muḥammad Riḍā (1962 [1957]), 'al-Lahjāt al-qawmiyya wa-tawḥīduhā fī al-bilād al-'arabiyya'. *Majallat Majma' al-Lugha al-'Arabiyya* 14: 85–99.

al-Shāfi'ī, Ḥasan (2018), 'Kalimat ra'īs al-majma''. *Majma'iyyāt: 'Adad khāṣṣ bi-mu'tamar al-majma'* 2018 (34–6): 6–7.

al-Shahābī, Muṣṭafā (1959), 'Madā al-naḥt fī al-lugha al-'arabiyya'. *Majallat al-Majma' al-'Ilmī al-'Arabī* 34 (4): 545–54.

al-Shahābī, Muṣṭafā (1966), 'Mushkilāt al-'arabiyya'. *al-Lisān al-'arabī* 4: 357–9.

Shawqī, Jalāl (1992), 'al-Muṣṭalaḥ al-'ilmī bayn al-tharā' wa-l-'ighnā''. *Majallat Majma' al-Lugha al-'Arabiyya al-'Urdunnī* 16 (42–3): 11–66.

Sherbatov, G. (1984), 'Ba'ḍ khaṣā'iṣ lughat al-mukhāṭaba bayn al-lugha al-fuṣḥā wa-l-lahjāt fī al-'ālam al-'arabī'. *Majallat Majma' al-Lugha al-'Arabiyya* 53: 204–11.

al-Talīdī, Bilāl (2019a), 'Hal tawarraṭ "al-'Adāla wa-l-Tanmiyya" fī farnasat al-ta'līm al-Maghribī? (1)' *'Arabī 21*, 31 July 2019, https://arabi21.com/story/1198076/المغرب-أسرار-العودة-إلى-اللغة-الفرنسية-في-المواد-العلمية (accessed 13 August 2019).

al-Talīdī, Bilāl (2019b), 'Hal tawarraṭ 'al-'Adāla wa-l-Tanmiyya' fī farnasat al-ta'līm al-Maghribī? (2)' *'Arabī 21*, 1 August 2019, https://arabi21.com/story/1198269/هل-تقسم-فرنسة-التعليم-في-المغرب-الإسلاميين (accessed 13 August 2019).

Ṭarābīshī, George (Jūrj) (2005), *al-Maraḍ bi-l-gharb: al-Taḥlīl al-nafsī li-'uṣāb jamā'ī 'arabī*. Damascus: Dār Petra li-l-Nashr wa-l-Tawzī'.

al-Tarzī, 'Ibrāhīm (1990), 'Taṣdīr'. *Majallat Majma' al-Lugha al-'Arabiyya* 66: 7–8.

Taymūr, Maḥmūd (1961), 'al-'Āmmiyya . . . al-fuṣḥā'. *Majallat Majma' al-Lugha al-'Arabiyya* 13: 123–43.

al-Ṭayyib, 'Abd al-Lāh (1998), 'Mushkilat al-'adā' fī al-lugha al-'arabiyya: 'Asbāb al-ḍa'f wa-wasā'il al-'ilāj'. *Majallat Majma' al-Lugha al-'Arabiyya bi-Dimashq* 73 (3): 535–40.

al-Ṭayyib, 'Abd al-Lāh (2000), 'Bayn al-fuṣḥā wa-l-dārija'. *Majallat Majma' al-Lugha al-'Arabiyya* 87: 127–31.

al-Tāzī, 'Abd al-Hādī (1996), 'Ṭarīqat ta'rīb al-'ulūm 'ind al-'aqdamīn'. *Majallat Majma' al-Lugha al-'Arabiyya* 78: 50–6.

Windfuhr, Volkhard (1973), 'al-Lugha al-'arabiyya al-fuṣḥā wa-l-'āmmiyya'. *al-Lisān al-'arabī* 10 (1): 286–8.

al-Yāfī, 'Abd al-Karīm (1988), 'Mushkilat al-tarjama wa-l-ta'rīb al-latī tuwājihuhā al-thaqāfa al-'arabiyya'. *Majallat Majma' al-Lugha al-'Arabiyya bi-Dimashq* 63 (2): 195–214.

al-Zaghlūl, Muḥammad Rājī (1980), 'Izdiwājiyyat al-lugha'. *Majallat Majma' al-Lugha al-'Arabiyya al-'Urdunnī* 3 (9–10): 119–53.

al-Zayyāt, 'Aḥmad Ḥasan (1957), 'Majma' al-lugha al-'arabiyya bayn al-fuṣḥā wa-l-'āmmiyya'. *Majallat al-Majma' al-'Ilmī al-'Arabī* 32 (1): 181–8.

Works in Other Languages Cited in the Book

Aboelezz, Mariam (2018), 'Language as Proxy in Egypt's Identity Politics: Examining the New Wave of Egyptian Nationalism'. In *Language, Politics and Society in the Middle East: Essays in Honour of Yasir Suleiman*, edited by Yonatan Mendel and Abeer Alnajjar, 126–47, Edinburgh: Edinburgh University Press.

Abu-Rabiʿ, Ibrahim M. (2004), *Contemporary Arab Thought: Studies in Post-1967 Arab Intellectual History*. London and Sterling, VA: Pluto Press.

Ahmad, Zaid (2003), *The Epistemology of Ibn Khaldūn*. London: RoutledgeCurzon.

Ahmed, Leila (1992), *Women and Gender in Islam: Historical Roots of a Modern Debate*. New Haven, CT: Yale University Press.

Aitchison, Jean (2013), *Language Change: Progress or Decay?*, 4th edn, Cambridge: Cambridge University Press.

Amara, Muhammad Hasan (1995), 'Arabic Diglossia in the Classroom: Assumptions and Reality'. In *Israel Oriental Studies, vol. XV, Language and Culture in the Near East*, edited by Shlomo Izreʿel and Rina Drory, 131–42, Leiden: Brill.

Anderson, Benedict (1983), *Imagined Communities: Reflections on the Origin and Spread of Nationalism*. London: Verso.

Asad, Talal (2003), *Formations of the Secular: Christianity, Islam, Modernity*. Stanford, CA: Stanford University Press.

Ayalon, Ami (2010), 'The Press and Publishing'. In *The New Cambridge History of Islam, vol. 6: Muslims and Modernity Culture and Society since 1800*, edited by Robert W. Hefner, 572–96, Cambridge: Cambridge University Press.

Ayubi, Nazih N. M. (1995), *Over-stating the Arab State: Politics and Society in the Middle East*. London and New York: I. B. Tauris.

Barber, Charles Laurence, Joan C. Beal and Philip A. Shaw (2009), *The English Language: A Historical Introduction*, 2nd edn, Cambridge: Cambridge University Press.

Bassiouney, Reem (2009), *Arabic Sociolinguistics*. Edinburgh: Edinburgh University Press.

Bassiouney, Reem (2014), *Language and Identity in Modern Egypt*. Edinburgh: Edinburgh University Press.

Bawardi, Basilius (2016), *The Lebanese-Phoenician Nationalist Movement: Literature, Language and Identity*. London and New York: I. B. Tauris.

Benrabah, Mohamed (2013), *Language Conflict in Algeria: From Colonialism to Post-Independence*. Bristol, Buffalo, NY and Toronto: Multilingual Matters.

Bhambra, Gurminder K. (2007), *Rethinking Modernity: Postcolonialism and the Sociological Imagination*. Basingstoke: Palgrave Macmillan.

Billig, Michael (1995), *Banal Nationalism*. London and Thousand Oaks, CA: Sage Publications.

Blanc, Haim (1960), 'Style Variations in Spoken Arabic: A Sample of Inter-Dialectal Conversation'. In *Contributions to Arabic Linguistics*, edited by Charles A. Ferguson, 81–156, Cambridge, MA: Harvard University Press.

Blommaert, Jan (1999), 'The Debate Is Open'. In *Language Ideological Debates*, edited by Jan Blommaert, 1–38, Berlin and New York: Mouton de Gruyter.

Blommaert, Jan (2005), *Discourse: A Critical Introduction.* Cambridge: Cambridge University Press.

Blommaert, Jan (2006), 'Language Policy and National Identity'. In *An Introduction to Language Policy: Theory and Method*, edited by Thomas Ricento, 238–54, Malden, MA: Blackwell Publishing.

Bosworth, Yulia (2019), 'The "Bad" French of Justin Trudeau: When Language, Ideology, and Politics Collide'. *American Review of Canadian Studies* 49 (1): 5–24.

Bourdieu, Pierre (1977), *Outline of a Theory of Practice.* Cambridge and New York: Cambridge University Press.

Bourdieu, Pierre (1994), *In Other Words: Essays Towards a Reflexive Sociology.* Translated by M. Adamson. Cambridge: Polity.

Boussofara-Omar, Naima (2006), 'Diglossia'. In *Encyclopedia of Arabic Language and Linguistics,* vol. I, edited by Kees Versteegh, 629–37, Leiden: Brill.

Cantineau, Jean (1950), 'Racines et schèmes'. In *Mélanges offerts à William Marçais par l'Institut d'études islamiques de l'Université de Paris*, 119–24, Paris: G. P. Maisonneuve.

Carter, Michael G. (2007), 'Grammatical Tradition: History'. In *Encyclopedia of Arabic Language and Linguistics,* vol. II, edited by Kees Versteegh, 182–91, Leiden: Brill.

Charteris-Black, Jonathan (2004), *Corpus Approaches to Critical Metaphor Analysis.* Basingstoke and New York: Palgrave Macmillan.

Chase-Dunn, Christopher K. (2007), 'Dependency and World-Systems Theories'. In *The Blackwell Encyclopedia of Sociology,* vol. III, edited by George Ritzer, 1060–2, Malden, MA and Oxford: Blackwell Publishing.

Chejne, Anwar G. (1969), *The Arabic Language: Its Role in History.* Minneapolis, MN: University of Minnesota Press.

Chen, Ping (1999), *Modern Chinese: History and Sociolinguistics.* Cambridge: Cambridge University Press.

Choueiri, Youssef M. (2000), *Arab Nationalism, a History: Nation and State in the Arab World.* Oxford: Blackwell.

Cleveland, William L. and Martin P. Bunton (2009), *A History of the Modern Middle East*, 4th edn, Boulder, CO: Westview Press.

Cooper, Robert L. (1989), *Language Planning and Social Change.* Cambridge: Cambridge University Press.

Curtis, Michael (2009), *Orientalism and Islam: European Thinkers on Oriental Despotism in the Middle East and India.* Cambridge and New York: Cambridge University Press.

Daoud, Mohamed (2011), 'The Sociolinguistic Situation in Tunisia: Language Rivalry or Accommodation?' *International Journal of the Sociology of Language* 211: 9–33.

Das Gupta, Jyotirindra (1968), 'Language Diversity and National Development'. In *Language Problems of Developing Nations*, edited by Joshua A. Fishman, Charles A. Ferguson and Jyotirindra Das Gupta, 17–26, New York: Wiley.

Dawn, C. Ernest (1988), 'An Arab Nationalist View of World Politics and History in the Interwar Period'. In *The Great Powers in the Middle East, 1919–1939*, edited by Uriel Dann, New York: Holmes and Meier.

Dirlik, Arif (1996), 'Chinese History and the Question of Orientalism'. *History and Theory* 35 (4): 96–118.

Du Feu, V. M. (2006), 'Marr, Mikolai Jakovlevich (1864–1934)'. In *Encyclopedia of Language & Linguistics*, 2nd edn, edited by Keith Brown, 520, Oxford: Elsevier.

Dobbelaere, Karel (2007), 'Secularization'. In *The Blackwell Encyclopedia of Sociology*, vol. VIII, edited by George Ritzer, 4148–56, Malden, MA; Oxford: Blackwell Publishing.

Eckert, Penelope (2008), 'Variation and the Indexical Field'. *Journal of Sociolinguistics* 12: 453–76.

Ed., P. Chalmeta and W. F. Heinrichs (1993), 'Muwallad'. In *Encyclopaedia of Islam*, 2nd edn, vol. VII, edited by C. E. Bosworth, E. van Donzel, W. P. Heinrichs and Ch. Pellat, 807–8, Leiden: Brill.

Edwards, John (2009), *Language and Identity: An Introduction*. Cambridge: Cambridge University Press.

Eisenstadt, S. N. (2003), *Comparative Civilizations and Multiple Modernities*. 2 vols. Leiden: Brill.

Emery, P. G. (1993), 'Nabaṭī'. In *Encyclopaedia of Islam*, 2nd edn, vol. VII, edited by C. E. Bosworth, E. van Donzel, W. P. Heinrichs and Ch. Pellat, 838, Leiden: Brill.

Ennaji, Moha (1999), 'The Arab World (Maghreb and Near East)'. In *Handbook of Language and Ethnic Identity*, edited by Joshua A. Fishman, 382–95, Oxford and New York: Oxford University Press.

Ennaji, Moha and Fatima Sadiqi (2008), 'Morocco: Language, Nationalism, and Gender'. In *Language and National Identity in Africa*, edited by Andrew Simpson, 44–60, Oxford: Oxford University Press.

Fairclough, Norman (1992), *Discourse and Social Change*. Cambridge: Polity.

Fairclough, Norman (2009), 'A Dialectical-Relational Approach to Critical Discourse Analysis in Social Research'. In *Methods of Critical Discourse Analysis*, 2nd edn, edited by Ruth Wodak and Michael Meyer, 162–86, London: Sage.

Fairclough, Norman, Jane Mulderrig and Ruth Wodak (2011), 'Critical Discourse Analysis'. In *Discourse Studies: A Multidisciplinary Introduction*, edited by Teun A. van Dijk, 357–78, London and Thousand Oaks, CA: Sage Publications.

Faris, Nabih Amin (1954), 'The Arabs and Their History'. *Middle East Journal* 8: 155–62.

Fasold, Ralph W. and Jeff Connor-Linton (2006), *An Introduction to Language and Linguistics*. Cambridge: Cambridge University Press.

Fauconnier, Gilles and Mark Turner (1994), *Conceptual Projection and Middle Spaces. UCSD Cognitive Science Technical Report, no. 9401*, University of California, San Diego.

Ferguson, Charles A. (1959), 'Diglossia'. *Word* 15: 325–40.

Fishman, Joshua A. (1968a), 'Nationality-Nationalism and Nation-Nationism'. In *Language Problems of Developing Nations*, edited by Joshua A. Fishman, Charles A. Ferguson and Jyotirindra Das Gupta, 39–51, New York: Wiley.

Fishman, Joshua A. (1968b), 'Language Problems and Types of Political and Sociocultural Integration: A Conceptual Summary'. In *Language Problems of Developing Nations*, edited by Joshua A. Fishman, Charles A. Ferguson and Jyotirindra Dasgupta, 489–98, New York: Wiley.

Fishman, Joshua A., Charles A. Ferguson and Jyotirindra Dasgupta, eds (1968), *Language Problems of Developing Nations*. New York: Wiley.

Foucault, Michel (1972), *The Archaeology of Knowledge*. London: Tavistock Publications.

Fox, Anthony (2006), 'Historical and Comparative Linguistics in the 19th Century'. In *Encyclopedia of Language & Linguistics*, 2nd edn, edited by Keith Brown, 317–26, Oxford: Elsevier.

Franks, David D. (2007), 'Role'. In *The Blackwell Encyclopedia of Sociology*, vol. VIII, edited by George Ritzer, 3953–6, Malden, MA and Oxford: Blackwell Publishing.

Gelvin, James L. (2011), *The Modern Middle East*, 3rd edn, Oxford and New York: Oxford University Press.

Gershoni, Israel and James P. Jankowski (1995), *Redefining the Egyptian Nation, 1930–1945*, Cambridge: Cambridge University Press.

Grady, Joseph E. (2007), 'Metaphor'. In *The Oxford Handbook of Cognitive Linguistics*, edited by Dirk Geeraerts and Hubert Cuyckens, 188–213, Oxford and New York: Oxford University Press.

Graf, D. F. and T. Fahd (1993), 'Nabaṭ'. In *Encyclopaedia of Islam*, 2nd edn, vol. VII, edited by C. E. Bosworth, E. van Donzel, W. P. Heinrichs and Ch. Pellat, 834–8, Leiden: Brill.

Grandguillaume, Gilbert (1991), 'Arabisation et langues maternelles dans le contexte national au Maghreb'. *International Journal of the Sociology of Language* 87: 45–54.

Grandguillaume, Gilbert (1995), 'Comment a-t-on pu en arriver là?' *Esprit* 208 (1): 12–34.

Grosfoguel, Ramón (2007), 'The Epistemic Decolonial Turn: Beyond Political-Economy Paradigms'. *Cultural Studies* 21 (2–3): 211–23.

Haddad, Gibril Fouad [1999]. 'Are Arabs Superior?' In *Living Islam – Islamic Tradition*. http://www.livingislam.org/fiqhi/fiqha_e94.html#9 (accessed 3 June 2014).

Halliday, Fred (2005), *The Middle East in International Relations: Power, Politics and Ideology*. Cambridge: Cambridge University Press.

al-Ḥamzāwī, Muḥammad Rashād (M. Rached Hamzaoui) (1965), *L'Académie Arabe de Damas et le problème de la modernisation de la langue arabe*. Leiden: E. J. Brill.

Hanks, William F. (2005), 'Pierre Bourdieu and the Practices of Language'. *Annual Review of Anthropology* 34: 67–83.

Hertog, Steffen (2016), 'The Oil-Driven Nation-Building of the Gulf States after the Second World War'. In *The Emergence of the Gulf States*, edited by J. E. Peterson, 323–52, London and New York: Bloomsbury.

Hindin, Michelle J. (2007), 'Role Theory'. In *The Blackwell Encyclopedia of Sociology*, vol. VIII, edited by George Ritzer, 3959–62, Malden, MA and Oxford: Blackwell Publishing.

Hobsbawm, Eric (1983), 'Introduction: Inventing Traditions'. In *The Invention of Tradition*, edited by Eric Hobsbawm and Terence Ranger, 1–14, Cambridge: Cambridge University Press.

Holes, Clive (2004), *Modern Arabic: Structures, Functions, and Varieties*. Washington, DC: Georgetown University Press.

Humphreys, R. Stephen (1999), *Between Memory and Desire: the Middle East in a Troubled Age*. Berkeley, CA: University of California Press.

Jenkins, Richard (1992), *Pierre Bourdieu*. London: Routledge.

Jernudd, Björn and Jiří Nekvapil (2012), 'History of the Field: A Sketch'. In *The Cambridge Handbook of Language Policy*, edited by Bernard Spolsky, 16–36, Cambridge: Cambridge University Press.

Johnstone, Barbara (2010), 'Locating Language in Identity'. In *Language and Identities*, edited by Carmen Llamas and Dominic Watt, 29–36, Edinburgh: Edinburgh University Press.

Juynboll, Th. W. (1991), 'Farḍ'. In *Encyclopaedia of Islam*, 2nd edn, vol. II, edited by C. E. Bosworth, E. van Donzel, W. P. Heinrichs and Ch. Pellat, 790, Leiden: Brill.

al-Kahtany, Abdallah Hadi (1997), 'The "Problem" of Diglossia in the Arab World: An Attitudinal Study of Modern Standard Arabic and the Arabic Dialects'. *al-ʿArabiyya* 30: 1–30.

Kassab, Elizabeth Suzanne (2010), *Contemporary Arab Thought: Cultural Critique in Comparative Perspective*. New York: Columbia University Press.

Kloss, Heinz (1968), 'Notes Concerning a Language-Nation Typology'. In *Language Problems of Developing Nations*, edited by Joshua A. Fishman, Charles A. Ferguson and Jyotirindra Dasgupta, 69–85, New York: Wiley.

Kroskrity, Paul V. (2004), 'Language Ideologies'. In *A Companion to Linguistic Anthropology*, edited by Alessandro Duranti, 496–517, Malden, MA and Oxford: Blackwell.

Lakoff, George and Mark Johnson (1980), *Metaphors We Live by*. Chicago, IL: University of Chicago Press.

Larcher, Pierre (2006), 'Derivation'. In *Encyclopedia of Arabic Language and Linguistics*, vol. I, edited by Kees Versteegh, 573–9, Leiden: Brill.

Larsen, Neil (2000), 'Imperialism, Colonialism, Postcolonialism'. In *A Companion to Postcolonial Studies*, edited by Henry Schwarz and Sangeeta Ray, 23–52, Malden, MA and Oxford: Blackwell Publishing.

Lefevre, Raphael (2015), 'The Coming of North Africa's "Language Wars"'. *The Journal of North African Studies* 20 (4): 499–502.

Lewis, Bernard (2002), *What Went Wrong? Western Impact and Middle Eastern Response*. London: Phoenix.

Lewis, Geoffrey (1999), *The Turkish Language Reform: A Catastrophic Success*. Oxford: Oxford University Press.

Lian, Chaoqun (2010), 'The Cairo Language Academy and Arabic Language Management in Egypt', unpublished MPhil dissertation. University of Cambridge.

Liang, Qichao (2017), *Xinmin Shuo (The New People Theory)*. Beijing: Blossom Press.

Little, Douglas (2010), 'The Cold War in the Middle East: Suez Crisis'. In *The Cambridge History of the Cold War, vol. II: Crises and Détente*, edited by Melvyn P. Leffler and Odd Arne Westad, 305–26, Cambridge: Cambridge University Press.

Lockman, Zachary (2010), *Contending Visions of the Middle East: The History and Politics of Orientalism*, 2nd edn, Cambridge: Cambridge University Press.

Lüdeling, Anke (2006), 'Neoclassical Compounding'. In *Encyclopedia of Language & Linguistics*, 2nd edn, edited by Keith Brown, 580–2, Oxford: Elsevier.

Maalouf, Amin (2000), *On Identity*. Translated by Barbara Bray. London: Harvill.

Machan, Tim William (2009), *Language Anxiety: Conflict and Change in the History of English*. Oxford: Oxford University Press.

Mahmoud, Youssef (1986), 'Arabic after Diglossia'. In *The Fergusonian Impact, vol. 1, From Phonology to Society*, edited by Joshua A. Fishman, 239–51, Berlin: Mouton de Gruyter.

Marsot, Afaf Lutfi Al-Sayyid (2007), *A History of Egypt: From the Arab Conquest to the Present*, 2nd edn, Cambridge and New York: Cambridge University Press.

Martinet, André (1955), *Économie des changements phonétiques: traité de phonologie diachronique*. Bern: A. Francke.

Massad, Joseph Andoni (2007), *Desiring Arabs*. Chicago, IL: University of Chicago Press.

Maton, Karl (2008), 'Habitus'. In *Pierre Bourdieu: Key Concepts*, edited by Michael Grenfell, 49–66, Stocksfield: Acumen.

Meiseles, Gustav (1980), 'Educated Spoken Arabic and the Arabic Language Continuum'. *Archivum Linguisticum* 11 (2): 117–48.

Mirovalev, Mansur (2019), 'Kazakhstan's troubles switching from the Cyrillic to the Latin alphabet'. *TRT World*, 7 February 2019, https://www.trtworld.com/magazine/kazakhstan-s-troubles-switching-from-the-cyrillic-to-the-latin-alphabet-23960 (accessed 13 August 2019).

Mostari, Hind A. (2004), 'A Sociolinguistic Perspective on Arabization and Language Use in Algeria'. *Language Problems and Language Planning* 28 (1): 25–43.

Mühlhäusler, Peter (2000), 'Language Planning and Language Ecology'. *Current Issues in Language Planning* 1: 306–67.

Neustupný, Jiří V. (1965), 'First Steps toward the Conception of 'Oriental Languages'. *Archiv Orientální* 33: 83–92.

Neustupný, Jiří V. (1968), 'Some General Aspects of "Language" Problems and "Language" Policy in Developing Societies'. In *Language Problems of Developing Nations*, edited by Joshua A. Fishman, Charles A. Ferguson and Jyotirindra Das Gupta, 285–94, New York: Wiley.

Neustupný, Jiří V. and Jiří Nekvapil (2003), 'Language Management in the Czech Republic'. *Current Issues in Language Planning* 4 (3–4): 181–366.

Ni, Haishu (1948), *Zhongguo Pinyin Wenzi Yundong Shi Jianbian (A Brief History of Script Phoneticisation Movement in China)*. Shanghai: Times Publishing House.

Owens, Jonathan (2013), 'History'. In *The Oxford Handbook of Arabic Linguistics*, edited by Jonathan Owens, 451–71, Oxford and New York: Oxford University Press.

Özkirimli, Umut (2010), *Theories of Nationalism: A Critical Introduction*, 2nd edn, Basingstoke: Palgrave Macmillan.

Parkinson, Dilworth B. (2003), 'Verbal Features in Oral *fuṣḥā* in Cairo'. *International Journal of the Sociology of Language* 163: 27–41.

Phillipson, Robert and Tove Skutnabb-Kangas (1996), 'English Only Worldwide, or Language Ecology'. *TESOL Quarterly* 30: 429–52.

Porter, Venetia, M. A. S. Abdel Haleem, Karen Armstrong, Robert Irwin, Hugh Kennedy and Ziauddin Sardar, eds (2012), *Hajj: Journey to the Heart of Islam*. London: British Museum Press.

Qian, Xuantong (1999a), *Qian Xuantong Wenji (Collected Works of Qian Xuantong)*, vol. 2. Beijing: Renmin University Press.

Qian, Xuantong (1999b), *Qian Xuantong Wenji (Collected Works of Qian Xuantong)*, vol. 3. Beijing: Renmin University Press.

Qu, Qiubai (1998), *Qu Qiubai Wenji: Wenxue Bian (Collected Works of Qu Qiubai: Literary Writings)*, vol. 3. Beijing: The People's Literature Publishing House.

Reisigl, Martin and Ruth Wodak (2009), 'The Discourse-Historical Approach (DHA)'. In *Methods of Critical Discourse Analysis*, 2nd edn, edited by Ruth Wodak and Michael Meyer, 87–121, London: Sage.

Robinson, Andrew (2009), *Writing and Script: A Very Short Introduction*. Oxford and New York: Oxford University Press.

Rogan, Eugene L. (2009), *The Arabs: A History*. London: Allen Lane.

Said, Edward W. (1986), 'Orientalism Reconsidered'. In *Literature, Politics and Theory: Papers from the Essex Conference, 1976–84*, edited by Francis Barker, Peter Hulme, Margaret Iversen and Diana Loxley, 210–29, London and New York: Methuen.

Salameh, Franck (2010), *Language, Memory, and Identity in the Middle East: The Case for Lebanon*. Lanham, MD: Lexington Books.

Sawaie, Mohammed (2007), 'Language Academies'. In *Encyclopedia of Arabic Language and Linguistics*, vol. II, edited by Kees Versteegh, 634–42, Leiden: Brill.

Sayahi, Lotfi (2011), 'Introduction: Current Perspectives on Tunisian Sociolinguistics'. *International Journal of the Sociology of Language* 211: 1–8.

Schaub, Mark (2000), 'English in the Arab Republic of Egypt'. *World Englishes* 19 (2): 225–38.

Schleicher, August (1863), *Die Darwinsche theorie und die sprachwissenschaft: offenes sendschreiben an herrn Ernst Häckel*. Weimar: Böhlau.

Seuren, Pieter A. M. (1998), *Western Linguistics: An Historical Introduction*. Oxford: Blackwell.

Shaaban, Kassim (2007), 'Language Policies and Language Planning'. In *Encyclopedia of Arabic Language and Linguistics*, vol. II, edited by Kees Versteegh, 694–707, Leiden: Brill.

Sharma, Aradhana and Akhil Gupta (2006), *The Anthropology of the State: A Reader*. Malden, MA and Oxford: Blackwell Publishing.

Shivtiel, Shlomit Shraybom (1998), 'The Question of Romanisation of the Script and the Emergence of Nationalism in the Middle East'. *Mediterranean Language Review* 10: 179–96.

Silverstein, Michael (2003), 'Indexical Order and the Dialectics of Sociolinguistic Life'. *Language and Communication* 23: 193–229.

Spolsky, Bernard (2004), *Language Policy*. Cambridge: Cambridge University Press.

Spolsky, Bernard (2009), *Language Management*. Cambridge: Cambridge University Press.

Spolsky, Bernard (2012), 'What Is Language Policy?' In *The Cambridge Handbook of Language Policy*, edited by Bernard Spolsky, 3–15, Cambridge: Cambridge University Press.

Sproat, Richard (1992), *Morphology and Computation*. Cambridge, MA: MIT Press.

Su, Jinzhi (2014), 'Diglossia in China: Past and Present'. In *Divided Languages?: Diglossia, Translation and the Rise of Modernity in Japan, China, and the Slavic World*, edited by Judit Árokay, Jadranka Gvozdanović and Darja Miyajima, 55–64, Cham: Springer.

Suleiman, Camelia and Russell E. Lucas (2012), 'Debating Arabic on Al-Jazeera: Endangerment and Identity in Divergent Discourses'. *Middle East Journal of Culture and Communication* 5: 190–210.

Suleiman, Salah (1986), *Jordanian Arabic between Diglossia and Bilingualism: Linguistic Analysis*. Amsterdam: John Benjamins.

Suleiman, Yasir (1999a), *The Arabic Grammatical Tradition: A Study in Taʻlīl*. Edinburgh: Edinburgh University Press.

Suleiman, Yasir (1999b), 'Language Education Policy – Arabic Speaking Countries'. In *Concise Encyclopedia of Educational Linguistics*, edited by Bernard Spolsky, 106–16, Amsterdam: Elsevier.

Suleiman, Yasir (2003), *The Arabic Language and National Identity: A Study in Ideology*. Edinburgh: Edinburgh University Press.

Suleiman, Yasir (2004), *A War of Words: Language and Conflict in the Middle East*. Cambridge: Cambridge University Press.

Suleiman, Yasir (2006), 'ʻArabiyya'. In *Encyclopedia of Arabic Language and Linguistics*, vol. I, edited by Kees Versteegh, 173–8, Leiden: Brill.

Suleiman, Yasir (2008), 'Egypt: From Egyptian to Pan-Arab Nationalism'. In *Language and National Identity in Africa*, edited by Andrew Simpson, 26–43, Oxford: Oxford University Press.

Suleiman, Yasir (2011a), *Arabic, Self and Identity: A Study in Conflict and Displacement*. Oxford and New York: Oxford University Press.

Suleiman, Yasir (2011b), 'Ideology, Grammar-Making and the Standardization of Arabic'. In *In the Shadow of Arabic: The Centrality of Language to Arabic Culture; Studies Presented to Ramzi Baalbaki on the Occasion of His Sixtieth Birthday*, edited by Bilal Orfali, 3–30, Leiden: Brill.

Suleiman, Yasir (2013a), *Arabic in the Fray: Language Ideology and Cultural Politics*. Edinburgh: Edinburgh University Press.

Suleiman, Yasir (2013b), 'Arabic Folk Linguistics: Between Mother-Tongue and Native Language'. In *The Oxford Handbook of Arabic Linguistics*, edited by Jonathan Owens, 264–80, Oxford and New York: Oxford University Press.

Suleiman, Yasir (2014), 'Arab(ic) Language Anxiety'. *al-ʻArabiyya* 47: 57–81.

Tibi, Bassam (1997), *Arab Nationalism: Between Islam and the Nation-State*, 3rd edn, Houndmills and London: Palgrave Macmillan.

Tignor, Robert L. (1966), *Modernization and British Colonial Rule in Egypt, 1882–1914*, Princeton, NJ: Princeton University Press.

Tollefson, James W. (2011), 'Language Planning and Language Policy'. In *The Cambridge Handbook of Sociolinguistics*, edited by Rajend Mesthrie, 357–76, Cambridge: Cambridge University Press.

UN News (2010), 'UN Marks English Day as Part of Celebration of Its Six Official Languages'. *UN News Centre*, 12 April 2010, http://www.un.org/apps/news/story.asp?NewsID=34469 (accessed 14 August 2019).

Van Dijk, Teun A. (2009), 'Critical Discourse Studies: A Sociocognitive Approach'. In *Methods of Critical Discourse Analysis*, 2nd edn, edited by Ruth Wodak and Michael Meyer, 62–86, London: Sage.

Versteegh, C. H. M. (1997), *The Arabic Language*. Edinburgh: Edinburgh University Press.

Vicentini, Alessandra (2003), 'The Economy Principle in Language: Notes and Observations from Early Modern English Grammars'. *Mots Palabras Words* 3: 37–57.

Wallerstein, Immanuel Maurice (1974), *The Modern World-System, vol. I: Capitalist Agriculture and the Origins of the European World-Economy in the Sixteenth Century*. New York and London: Academic Press.

Wallerstein, Immanuel Maurice (2000), *The Essential Wallerstein*. New York: New Press.

Wang, Aiyun (2015), *Zhongguo Gongchandang Lingdao de Wenzi Gaige* (*The Writing System Reform Led by the Chinese Communist Party*). Beijing: The People's Daily Press.

Wells, John (2006), 'Esperanto'. In *Encyclopedia of Language & Linguistics*, 2nd edn, edited by Keith Brown, 223–5, Oxford: Elsevier.

Wodak, Ruth (2006), 'Linguistic Analyses in Language Policies'. In *An Introduction to Language Policy: Theory and Method*, edited by Thomas Ricento, 170–93, Malden, MA: Blackwell Publishing.

Wodak, Ruth and Michael Meyer (2009), 'Critical Discourse Analysis: History, Agenda, Theory and Methodology'. In *Methods of Critical Discourse Analysis*, 2nd edn, edited by Ruth Wodak and Michael Meyer, 1–33, London: Sage.

Wolff, H. Ekkehard (2017), 'Language Ideologies and the Politics of Language in Post-Colonial Africa'. *Stellenbosch Papers in Linguistics Plus* 51: 1–22.

Wright, Sue (2004), *Language Policy and Language Planning: From Nationalism to Globalization*. Basingstoke: Palgrave Macmillan.

Wright, Sue (2012), 'Language Policy, the Nation and Nationalism'. In *The Cambridge Handbook of Language Policy*, edited by Bernard Spolsky, 59–78, Cambridge: Cambridge University Press.

Young, Robert J. C. (2001), *Postcolonialism: An Historical Introduction*. Oxford: Blackwell.

Yu, Pei (2013), 'Wei Zhongguo Shijieshi Xueke Xiushi Chuyi' ('My Humble Opinions on the Histography of the Discipline of World History in China'). *Shijie Lishi (World History)* 2013 (3): 4–5.

Zhao, Chunyan (2012), 'Yuyan Yishixingtai yu Zhongguo Hanyu Pinyin Yundong' ('Language Ideology and Script Romanization Movements in China'), Unpublished PhD dissertation. National University of Singapore.

Zipf, George Kingsley (1949), *Human Behavior and the Principle of Least Effort:*

An Introduction to Human Ecology. Cambridge, MA: Addison-Wesley Press.
Zughoul, Muhammad R. (1980), 'Diglossia in Arabic: Investigating Solutions'. *Anthropological Linguistics* 22 (5): 201–17.

Index

ʾAbāẓa, Muḥammad ʿAzīz, 70–4
ʿAbd al-Ḥaqq, Muḥammad al-Rāshid, 188–9, 191
Abridgement, 56, 58–60, 64–6, 131
Académie française, 4, 18, 31–3, 35, 47n
ʿĀdiliyya Madrasa, 33
ʿAlī, Muḥammad, 35, 109, 145
ʾAmīn, ʾAḥmad, 155, 157–61, 195n
ʿāmmiyya/dārija/lahja (Colloquial Arabic)
  and Arabic, 7, 18
  and colonial conspiracy, 98–9, 103n
  and diglossia *see* diglossia
  and foreign languages, 143n, 169
  and *fuṣḥā see fuṣḥā* and *ʿāmmiyya*
  and identity, 213–14
  and indexication, 7
  definition of, 18, 46n
  development of, 56, 59, 61–3, 79
  evaluations of, 49, 57, 64, 66, 68–74, 81–2, 86, 94, 98
  features of, 48, 50–1, 54, 58, 60, 68–74, 76, 80, 108
  in Morocco, 214
  integration, convergence or unification of, 77, 85–7
  nomenclature of, 46n
  prevalence of, 2, 65, 75
  promotion (and elevation) of, 2, 53, 83–4, 88, 99
anxiety
  dual anxiety of modernity and civilization, 198, 204, 206, 208, 211–13
  language anxiety, 204
Arab (or Islamic) conquests, 56–7, 61, 79, 94, 96, 102n, 142n
Arab League, 20, 25, 116
Arab nationalism(s), 14, 173
  discourse of, 11, 95, 140n
  duality of pan-Arab and territorial-state nationalisms, 9–11, 15, 22, 24, 26, 33, 37, 72, 77, 81 89, 93, 100–1, 102n, 160, 167, 203
  history and periodisation of, 12, 66, 92, 98, 100, 103n, 104n
  pan-Arab, 23, 46n, 49, 76, 84–7, 89, 91–2, 96–9, 112, 115–16, 142n, 162, 166, 169, 191, 201–2
  territorial-state, 22, 40, 46n, 89, 91–2, 125–6
Arab Spring, 213–14, 216n
Arabic
  and Arab mind, 119, 142n
  and backwardness, 210
  and discourse, 200
  and equilibrium in inter-language relations, 8, 121, 124, 126, 134, 202
  and foreign languages, 111, 121–2, 125, 136, 172

Arabic (*cont.*)
and humanism, 164, 173
and identity, 119–20, 135, 142n
and inalienability with the Arab people, 8, 111–14, 117, 120–2, 126, 134–5, 137, 156, 195n, 199, 201
and the Arab nation (and Arab nationalisms), 8, 16n, 19, 33, 38, 47n, 48–9, 66, 73–4, 76–7, 80–1, 94–6, 98–100, 104n, 117, 118–20, 140n, 144, 151–2, 171, 173, 182, 195n, 201
as a Bedouin language, 2, 41, 157
as a language of science, 2, 29–30
as a world language, 15, 150, 173–7, 190
as an instrument, 8, 66–77
as an official language of the UN, 175–6, 179, 196n
as organism, 8, 48, 56, 65–6, 87–9, 96, 99, 124
as symbolic entity, 66, 77–85
as the national language, 42, 152, 166, 173, 197, 216n
decline of, 65–6, 111, 201
development of, 181–2, 189–90
foreignness in, 113, 127, 132, 153, 197
history and historical narrative of, 61–2, 77–80, 102n, 195n
integration of, 7, 31, 43, 49, 98, 100, 201
mission of, 173, 176–7
modernisation of, 7, 9, 15, 17, 19, 29–30, 43, 75, 138, 144, 146–51, 153–7, 159–66, 168–9, 171–3, 178–81, 183–4, 187–8, 190–2, 194
peripherality of, 105, 109, 111, 126, 136–7, 203
predicaments of, 157, 159
reform of, 15, 29, 67, 146, 157–62, 164–5, 167, 169, 201
(re-)unification of, 48, 65–6, 74, 82, 87
revival (and revitalisation) of, 7, 66, 96, 147, 150, 153–4, 159–60, 162, 164, 167, 173, 175, 183, 201
split of, 48, 66
status of, 1–2, 105, 108–9, 111, 123, 166–7, 177–8, 181, 214
substance of, 156–61, 165
teaching and learning of, 163, 168, 174
typology, 52–3
underdevelopment of, 181–2, 186, 188
varieties of, 52–3, 96
Arabic grammar, 29, 32, 89, 103n, 109, 149, 157, 161, 165, 167, 172, 174, 195n
Arabic grammatical (or linguistic) tradition, 16n, 29, 32, 40, 60, 102n, 103n, 128–30, 132, 134, 140n, 141n, 144, 146–7, 154, 190
Arabic Language Academy (ALA)
and Académie française *see* Académie française
and knowledge and sciences, 29–30
and language authority, 2, 9, 18, 22, 27, 41, 169
and language planning and language policy *see* language planning and language policy
and language symbolism, 15, 17, 42
and the state, 4, 13, 15, 22–3, 25–9, 33, 42, 46n, 47n
as a broker of language ideologies, 27–8, 34, 40, 44, 45n
as a phenomenon, 17, 22, 36–9, 41–2, 44, 45n
as a purveyor of language symbolism, 15, 17, 40, 44, 202
as an institution, 2, 9–10, 18–20, 23, 28, 33–4, 45n, 103n
discourse of, 4–5, 7–16, 27, 42–4, 48–9, 52–5, 57, 59–60, 64, 66–8, 70, 72, 74–8, 80–1, 83–5, 89–90, 92–101, 105, 111–12, 114–27, 130, 132–8, 141n, 144, 148–51, 155, 159, 161–2, 168–9, 171, 178–80, 181, 186–8, 190–4, 195n, 197, 199–203
in Algeria, 2, 20, 26
in Cairo, 1–2, 18, 20, 22–5, 29–30, 32, 36, 39, 45n, 47n, 53–5, 86–9, 110, 112–15, 125, 129–32, 134–5, 141n, 155, 157–8, 160, 162–6, 169, 177, 183, 207, 210, 213–14, 215n
in Damascus, 2, 18, 23–5, 32–3, 35, 45n, 55, 63–4, 84, 110, 117–18, 121, 130–1, 134, 151, 165–6, 207
in Iraq *see* Iraqi Academy

in Israel, 2, 20–1, 26
in Jordan, 2, 4, 18, 20, 23, 26, 46n, 55, 102n
in Khartoum, 2, 20, 26
in Lebanon, 23
in Libya, 2, 18, 20–1, 26
in Morocco, 2, 20–1; *see also* Bureau for the Coordination of Arabisation
in Palestine, 2, 20–1, 26, 36, 46n
in Sharjah, 20–1
in the Gulf, 21, 45n
in Tunisia *see* Tunisian Academy
al-khālidūn of, 1, 41, 47n
members (academicians) of, 1, 4, 9, 13, 18, 21–4, 27–34, 41, 44, 46n, 47n, 54, 60–1, 63, 70, 74, 78–88, 94, 99, 112–15, 120–3, 128–30, 132–7, 158, 166, 169, 177–9, 181, 194
mission (orientation, agenda, duty) of, 2–3, 13, 17, 19, 29, 32, 34, 44, 46n, 53–4, 70, 84, 87, 115, 120, 141n, 151, 165–6, 183
narrative of the origin and history of, 27, 31–3, 166
nomenclature of, 29
precursors, 18, 22–3, 45n
role of, 9, 15, 17–19, 27–8, 33–4, 38, 44
union of ALAs, 21, 25–6
Arabic morphology, 29–30, 60, 63, 68–9, 73, 101n, 105, 113, 128–34, 142n, 150, 157–8, 168
Arabic orthography, 39, 86, 157
Arabic script
and Arabic, 158–9, 212–13
and non-Arabic languages, 175, 190, 212
evaluations of, 208–10, 212
print in, 2
reform of, 39, 89, 149, 158, 169, 210, 220
Romanisation (Latinisation) of, 15, 84, 86, 122, 155, 158–61, 165, 172, 198, 206–7, 209–11, 213, 215n
Arabi(ci)sation (*ta'rīb*), 12, 15, 19, 23, 25, 30–1, 43, 56–7, 85, 101, 105–6, 108–12, 114–18, 120–1, 124–7, 129, 132, 134–7, 138n, 139n, 140n, 141n, 201–3, 214
Arabi(ci)sation Conference, 23, 46, 110, 115–17, 122, 135, 141n, 181
Arabic-speaking world, 1–5, 7, 9–15, 16n, 17–19, 21–8, 30, 32–3, 36, 41–4, 47n, 48, 53–5, 59, 61, 63–5, 67–70, 72, 74, 76–80, 82, 84–7, 89–93, 96–8, 100, 101n, 107–8, 110, 112, 115–16, 118, 120–1, 123, 136, 139n, 145–9, 151, 155–6, 160–4, 166–9, 172, 175–6, 179–82, 187, 190–3, 197–8, 203–14, 215n
Arabness, 54, 72–3, 81, 83, 97, 99, 106, 112, 114, 116, 120, 127, 129, 132, 134–5, 140, 166, 181
authenticity, 35–6, 45, 72, 91, 102, 106, 133, 150, 180–1, 185–6, 188–9, 205
al-'Azhar, 29, 47n

Banal nationalism, 26, 41–2
Ba'thism, 87, 97, 169, 187
Bishr, Kamāl Muḥammad, 122, 134–5, 185–6
Bureau for the Coordination of Arabisation, 4, 20, 25, 110, 141n, 181

Caliphate, 24, 160
Chinese, 39, 50–1, 101n, 215n
Chinese characters
evaluations of, 208–10, 212
reform and revolution of, 209, 215n
Romanisation (Latinisation) of, 15, 198, 206–9, 211–13, 215n
code-switching and code-mixing, 6, 41, 50, 172
Cold War, 110, 190
colonialism and imperialism, 7, 15, 32–3, 45n, 77, 84, 91–2, 106, 108, 117, 122, 136, 142n, 144–6, 152, 155, 160, 166, 168–9, 175–6, 180, 188–9, 191–2, 204–5
coloniality, 22, 31, 117, 181
compounding, 127–34, 142n
construction and construct, 6–7, 9, 14, 19, 23, 26, 31, 38, 41, 74, 77–8, 80–4, 90, 114, 119, 141n, 165, 189, 199, 201
corruption, 59–66, 94, 96, 99, 156, 160, 195n

critical discourse analysis (CDA), 10–15, 148
cultural invasion, 170, 188–9, 191, 193

al-Dajānī, ʾAḥmad Ṣidqī, 125–6
Ḍayf, Shawqī, 1, 55, 88, 195n
decolonisation, 13, 17, 27, 33, 46n, 110, 202
dependence and dependency, 106, 117, 139n, 141n, 170, 178, 187, 202
derivation (*ishtiqāq*), 30, 57, 68, 127
development, 2, 32, 35, 51–2, 77, 92, 103n, 149–50, 178–85, 187–9, 202, 206, 208–9
deviation, 5, 59, 60–1, 63–6, 155–6, 171, 185–6
dialectology, 53–4
dictionaries of Arabic, 2, 29, 39, 47n, 57, 68, 89, 146, 149
  historical, 21, 22, 39
differentiation, 145
diglossia
  and standard-with-dialects, 50
  as a problem, 49, 51–2, 55, 65, 89
  definition of, 48, 101-2n
  elimination of, 82, 85–8, 101
  H-L model of, 49, 101n, 102n
  in Arabic, 7, 15, 19, 36–8, 40–1, 43, 48–9, 52, 55, 62–3, 65–7, 70, 74–9, 81–2, 84, 87, 89–90, 98, 100, 101n, 105, 197, 201–2, 207
  in Chinese, 50, 101n
  non-linguistic, 82
discourse
  and *longue dureé* sociopolitical circumstances *see* sociopolitical circumstances
  and short-term, epochal sociopolitical circumstances *see* sociopolitical circumstances
  and synchronisation, 154, 194n
  definition of, 42
  formations of, 44, 47n
  habitus of, 8–9, 13, 15, 43–4, 47n, 48, 55, 59, 66, 70, 77, 89, 93, 99–100, 111, 136, 138, 149, 151, 192, 194, 197, 199, 201, 203
  routinisation of, 8–10, 12–13, 43–4, 59, 70, 100–1, 111, 120, 138, 149, 151, 192, 203
doxa, 13, 100, 111, 137–8, 151, 192, 199–200

ecology of language, 52, 56–8, 64, 124–5
English, 2, 7, 19, 105, 108–10, 122–3, 125, 128, 134, 136, 139n, 143n, 147, 172, 174–8, 202, 211
Esperanto, 174, 177, 196n

Fahmī, ʿAbd al-ʿAzīz, 155, 158–61, 163, 207, 210–13, 215n
Fahmī, Mansūr, 54, 113, 115, 162, 165–8, 196n
Fayṣal, Shukrī, 181–2, 196n
Ferguson, Charles, 48–52, 101n, 102n
fragmentation
  linguistic, 48, 66, 81, 84–5, 95–6, 176
  political, 3, 7, 48–9, 54, 61–2, 79, 82, 85, 96, 98–9, 139n, 173, 176, 192, 202
French, 2, 7, 19, 47n, 85, 105, 108–10, 122–3, 130, 134, 136, 139n, 143n, 147, 172, 174–8, 202–3, 211, 214–15
Fuʾād, King of Egypt, 24, 36, 110, 207
Furayḥa, ʾAnīs, 83
fuṣḥā (Standar Arabic)
  and *ʿāmmiyya*, 41, 48–50, 53–9, 63–7, 70, 72–4, 76–7, 80, 84–5, 87–9, 94–6, 98–100, 101n, 102n, 172, 200, 202, 210
  and Arabic, 18–19, 65, 79, 96, 152, 201
  and diglossia *see* diglossia
  and identity, 213
  and indexication, 7
  archaic complexity of, 19, 36–8, 43
  competence in, 143n
  evaluations of, 68–74, 81–3, 86, 94, 98, 191, 202
  features of, 48, 50–1, 54, 58, 68–76, 85
  functional domains of, 2, 108
  maintenance of, 165, 212
  promotion (and revival) of, 116, 167
  standard of, 56
  status (and situation) of, 19, 39, 85, 164, 210

German Romantics, 66, 93–4, 104n
globalisation, 1, 92, 103n, 107, 118, 123, 125, 139n, 147, 188, 190–1, 204

al-Ḥabābī, Muḥammad ʿAzīz, 67, 185
habitus, 8–9, 43–4, 47n
Hāshim, ʿAbd al-Hādī, 118–19, 142n
al-Hāshimī, Muḥammad Yaḥyā, 169–71, 178
hegemony, 7, 36, 107, 144, 146–8, 152–3, 161, 171, 188–93, 205
heritage, 46n, 54, 80–1, 86, 103n, 118–19, 148, 180–1, 183–6, 188, 190, 195n
Ḥijāzī, Maḥmūd Fahmī, 188, 190–1
Humboldt, Wilhelm von, 93
Ḥusayn, Muḥammad al-Khaḍir, 113
Ḥusayn, Ṭāhā, 1, 22, 29
al-Ḥuṣrī, Sāṭiʿ, 84–5, 94, 99, 104n, 133

Ibn Fāris, 129–30, 133
Ibn Ḥusayn, Fayṣal, 23, 35, 109–10
ideologisation of language
  effects of, 201
  in the Arabic-speaking world, 3, 10, 15, 40, 42
  in the globe, 15, 206, 215
  mechanism of, 5, 9, 15, 197–200, 213
  see also language ideology
indexicality
  and gender, 16n
  and ideology-in-communication, 198–9
  and reference, 200
  indexical field, 5–6
  orders of indexicality, 5–6, 199
Institut d'Égypte, 31
ʾiʿrab (declensional endings), 63, 68, 165
Iraqi Academy, 2, 4, 18, 20, 23–5, 84
al-ʾIskandarī, ʾAḥmad, 112–14, 141n
Islam, 47n, 54, 80, 85–6, 94–5, 122, 155, 161, 171, 173, 176–7, 184, 187, 191, 196n, 203

Jāhiliyya, 57, 95–6
al-Jamālī, Fāḍil, 171–3, 178
Japanese, 130
al-Jārim, ʿAlī, 158, 211
al-Jundī, al-Sayyid Salīm, 130, 151–5, 168

al-khāṣṣa and *al-ʿāmma*, 75–6
Kurd ʿAlī, Muḥammad, 155–7, 159–61

laḥn (solecisms), 60–3, 79, 103n
language attitude, 27–8
language change, 59–60, 63, 65–6, 87, 186, 204
language contact, 15, 43, 62–4, 102n, 111, 123–5
language engineering, 87
language ideology, 5, 10–11, 13, 15, 27–8, 34, 44, 47n, 60, 102n, 133, 140n
language instrumentalism, 15, 37–9, 67, 70, 74, 76–7, 85–9, 97–9, 111, 144, 204, 212
language planning and language policy
  and nation-building and state-formation, 35–7, 51, 77, 90, 120
  banal, 41
  classical, 13, 35–6
  colonial, 121–3, 126, 147
  corpus planning, 38–9, 105, 126, 129
  definition of, 34, 46n
  extra-linguistic goals (and concerns), 37, 41, 106
  in Asia and Africa, 175–6
  in the Arabic-speaking world, 65, 85, 139, 144, 161, 166–7, 172–3, 190, 194, 197
  language maintenance, 15
  language reform, 15, 39, 162
  of Arabic language academies, 5, 15, 17, 34–8, 40, 44, 45n, 87–8, 136
  of Turkey, 94
  routinised, 36, 41
  sociopolitical agendas of, 201
  status planning, 39, 105, 126, 134
  theories of, 188–90
language problem, 5, 35–41, 43, 48–9, 51–2, 55, 65, 85, 89–90, 100, 137, 175, 188, 195n, 197, 210
language revolution, 181, 209, 214
language symbolism, 5, 15, 40, 42, 67, 77, 87–9, 99, 138, 144, 197–8, 206, 213, 215
  and anxiety, 204
  and ideology-in-discourse, 198–9

language symbolism (*cont.*)
and indexication, 5–7, 9–10, 38, 40, 187, 192, 197
and proxification, 7–10, 17, 30–1, 38, 40–1, 48, 74, 108, 137, 151, 187, 192, 197, 208, 211–14
and reference, 200
de-symbolisation of, 198, 202–3
symbolic compensation, 8, 15, 40, 136–7, 201–2
symbolic compliance, 201–2
symbolic resistance, 15, 136–7, 201–2
Latin, 79, 84–6, 127, 145, 174, 176
Liang, Qichao, 208–9
linguistic invasion, 117–18, 122, 201
linguistic landscape, 110
linguistic rights, 52, 109, 125
Luṭfī al-Sayyid, ʾAḥmad, 1, 22, 29, 88

Madkūr, ʾIbrāhīm, 1, 32, 173–8, 184
al-Maghribī, ʿAbd al-Qādir, 14, 16n, 32, 56–9, 65, 96, 102n, 113, 115, 121–2
al-Maḥāsinī, Marwān, 188–9, 191
malaka, 62, 156, 194–5n
matn (corpus), 155, 157–8
meta-linguistic discourse
linguistics proper, 3
linguistics sociopolitical, 3–5, 9–10, 42, 100, 199–200
metaphor, 12, 14, 16, 56–9, 82, 96, 100, 118–19, 122, 136, 138, 156, 159, 163, 167, 177, 183–4, 192, 199, 213
Middle Arabic (intermediate varieties of Arabic), 49, 53, 88, 101n
al-Miqdādī, Darwīsh, 95–6, 104n
al-Mīthāq al-waṭanī, 97
modernisation, 92, 148, 180, 185, 188–9, 192–3, 202, 205
and catching-up, 7, 148–9, 154–5, 162, 204
and return, 194n
and revival, 7, 148, 162, 194n, 197
dyad of the endogenous and exogenous modes of, 8, 15, 43, 144, 148–53, 155, 159–60, 162, 165, 167, 169, 171–2, 178–9, 184–6, 188, 192–4
endogenous mode of, 168, 170, 178–9, 182
exogenous mode of, 169, 178–9, 182
of Arabic *see* Arabic
of Chinese, 39
technology-based, 35
modernisation theory, 194n
modernity, 2, 7, 19, 27, 30, 38, 43, 52, 138n, 144–9, 151–3, 166–8, 178–83, 185–6, 189–90, 192–4, 195n, 197, 201, 204–6, 208, 211–12
muʿarrab, 113–14, 134
multilingualism, 41, 124, 203, 215
Mūsā, Salāma, 83, 207
muwallad, 56–7, 94, 113–14, 134, 141n

Nabatean, 79, 131, 142n
nahḍa, 69, 85, 95, 106, 109, 148, 150
naḥt, 128–30
Nasser, Gamal Abdel, 24, 87, 97, 99, 141n, 169, 187
Nasserism, 87, 97
nationalism, 41–2, 89–93, 98, 104n, 125, 176, 180
Neoclassical word formation, 127
neologism and terminology, 2–3, 29, 30, 39, 68, 73, 89, 111–12, 114, 115, 127–8, 130, 133–4, 150, 154–5, 160, 164–6, 190

Orientalism, 15, 138n, 194n, 205
and Oriental despotism, 52
of the Orientals, 205–6, 213
Ottoman Empire (Ottomans), 2, 19, 23, 46n, 61–2, 79, 85, 91–2, 103n, 108–9, 114, 121, 136, 139n, 154–5, 160, 162

peripherality of the Arabs, 9, 11, 15, 22, 31, 33, 37, 41, 45n, 105–12, 114, 116, 120, 126, 136–7, 138–9n, 149, 197, 201, 203
Pinyin, 207
political Islam (Islamism), 91, 103n, 126, 203, 213–14
principle of least effort, 59–60
progress, 8, 30, 32, 38, 64–6, 74–5, 103n, 123, 139n, 148–9, 152, 155, 165–6, 177–8, 182–185, 187, 205, 208–11
Putonghua, 50, 101n, 207

Qian, Xuantong, 209, 212
Qu, Qiubai, 209
Qudsī, ʾIlyās, 57–9, 96, 207
Qur'an, 18, 52, 56–8, 68–9, 72, 80, 87, 113, 122, 130, 156, 163–4, 167–8, 170, 173, 196n

rationalisation, 66, 145
Romance languages, 84–5

Schleicher, August, 93
secularisation, 139n, 144–5
al-Shabībī, Muḥammad Riḍā, 63–4, 86–7, 162–7
al-Shāfiʿī, Ḥasan, 1–2, 47n, 103n
Shūsha, Fārūq, 213, 216n
shuʿūbiyya, 81
sociopolitical circumstances
  longue dureé and enduring, 9–10, 13, 22, 33, 37, 42, 44, 100–1, 107, 203
  short-term and epochal, 10, 19, 22, 37, 42
Spitta, Wilhelm, 83
spread of foreign languages
  in the Arabic-speaking world, 7–8, 15, 19, 36–8, 43, 105, 121–2, 134, 157, 166, 173, 201
Suez Crisis, 141n, 166, 169

taste, 113–15, 131, 184
telescoping, 154, 159, 204
Taymūr, Maḥmūd, 72–4, 102n
The 1967 Arab–Israeli War, 6, 14, 103, 112, 117–18, 121–2, 142n, 169–71, 177–9, 187, 201
Tunisian Academy, 2, 20, 26
Turkification, 91, 109, 121–2, 139n
Turkish, 2, 7, 19, 23, 39, 94, 108–9, 111, 121–2, 130, 139n

ʿulamāʾ, 28, 108
unification of Egypt and Syria, 25
universal language, 173–4, 176–7, 196n

Willcocks, William, 83, 207–8
Willmore, John Selden, 83
wisdom of the Arabs, 16n, 99, 111, 140n
world-system, 7, 9, 15, 22, 31, 33, 37–8, 45n, 92, 105–8, 111, 117, 120, 123, 137, 138–9n, 196n, 197, 201, 204, 206, 211
  and core-periphery hierarchy, 107, 126, 137

Zhang, Taiyan, 211–12

EU representative:
Easy Access System Europe
Mustamäe tee 50, 10621 Tallinn, Estonia
Gpsr.requests@easproject.com

www.ingramcontent.com/pod-product-compliance
Lightning Source LLC
Chambersburg PA
CBHW051806230426
43672CB00012B/2654
9781474449953